Terms of Inquiry

Terms of Inquiry

On the Theory and Practice of Political Science

James W. Davis

The Johns Hopkins University Press
Baltimore and London

© 2005 The Johns Hopkins University Press
All rights reserved. Published 2005
Printed in the United States of America on acid-free paper
9 8 7 6 5 4 3 2 1

The Johns Hopkins University Press
2715 North Charles Street
Baltimore, Maryland 21218-4363
www.press.jhu.edu

Library of Congress Cataloging-in-Publication Data

Davis, James W., 1963–
    Terms of inquiry : on the theory and practice of political
science / James W. Davis.
        p. cm.
    Includes bibliographical references and index.
    ISBN 0-8018-8084-X (hardcover : alk. paper)—
    ISBN 0-8018-8085-8 (pbk. : alk. paper)
    1. Political science.   I. Title.
    JA71.D35 2005
    320′.01—dc22   2004019607

A catalog record for this book is available from the British
Library.

Contents

Preface

In 1988, when I began graduate studies in the Department of Political Science at Columbia University, International Relations (IR) theory was thriving. Provoked and inspired by the debates that were taking place within the discipline as a whole, but more particularly in the William T. R. Fox seminar room on the thirteenth floor of the International Affairs Building in Morningside Heights, my fellow graduate students and I were committed to discovering knowledge about a subject that was of immediate importance to mankind.

In the "real world" of international politics, the cold war between the United States and the Soviet Union was the defining feature of the international system. Understanding the origins of that epochal conflict and devising strategies to avoid a nuclear catastrophe dominated the efforts of theorists and practitioners alike. At Columbia we debated endlessly the purported stability of the bipolar world and whether the cold war was the inevitable result of anarchy and the distribution of capabilities in the international system or a function of the ideologies that dominated in Washington and Moscow. The role of deterrence and arms control in promoting stability, their relationship to one another, as well as the preconditions for success in each endeavor provided subject matter for term papers and dissertations, many of which became standard works in the field.

Looking back on what was a period of extreme intellectual vitality, I recall a shared conviction that deductive theorizing linked to empirical analysis held out the prospect for generating something approximating the truth. Although the origins of our collective optimism were many, our thinking on these matters was perhaps most strongly influenced by the first chapter of Kenneth Waltz's *Theory of International Politics* and Jack Snyder's graduate seminar on social science methods.

In what remains one of the clearest rejections of the behaviorist revolution that dominated efforts at political science theory-building well into the 1970s, Waltz suggested that parsimonious deductive theory could cut through the

complexity of social systems and provide surprisingly simple, if often quite surprising, explanations for a number of otherwise puzzling outcomes.

What in American IR circles came to be known as the "Columbia Dissertation" was in no small measure a product of Jack Snyder's methodology seminar, or "6802" as it was known to graduate students (owing to the course identification number in the university catalogue). The course was constructed
around a strong thesis: with a clearly stated theory and deductively derived hypotheses comprised of well-defined and operationalized variables, "hard" or
"critical" tests can be identified to guide empirical inquiry in the field of IR.
Because Waltz had already convinced us that in the first instance theories are
created and not discovered, the emerging debate between proponents of quantitative versus qualitative methods was for us a secondary issue. At Columbia
we were interested in testing the implications of theory. Whether we should
do so using statistics or case studies was a problem to be settled on pragmatic
rather than dogmatic grounds.

By the end of the 1980s, however, a growing skepticism regarding the prospects for significant progress in the generation of warranted knowledge about
IR began to take hold of our discussions. Two developments in particular—one
empirical, the other theoretical—contributed to the reappraisal.

In the realm of theory, critiques of Waltz's neorealism by authors such as
Robert Cox highlighted the importance of ideas in constituting the structure
of the international system, a notion that was further developed in the writings of Friedrich Kratochwil, Nicolas Onuf, John Ruggie, and, of course, Alexander Wendt. The emergence of "constructivism" in IR suggested that a number of widely held methodological assumptions (for example that the object
of analysis—politics—was given and distinct from the subjects conducting political science) were problematic and would have to be justified before we could
get on with the business of developing and testing theory.

Celebrated by millions across the globe, the peaceful end of the cold war
and the transformation of the bipolar system (into something for which a satisfactory concept remains illusive) was a sobering event for the discipline of IR.
Although prominent voices argued that the events of 1989–90 were mere
"data points" from which we could infer very little, many of us were struck by
the apparent inability of the discipline to anticipate an event of such magni-
tude and importance for the future.

In the early 1990s, few of us knew how influential constructivism would become and how the end of the cold war would eventually affect our general un-

derstanding of international relations. But by 1996, when I accepted an offer from Friedrich Kratochwil to join him in rebuilding the international relations program at the Ludwig-Maximilians-Universität in Munich, it was clear that a new "great debate" had taken hold of IR. What better way to try and make sense of what had transpired—both in the discipline and in the world—than to teach a course on research design and methods?

With my old syllabus from Snyder's 6802 as a model, I began my own reappraisal of the "science" part of "political science" by teaching (what I came to recognize as American) research methods to a group of eager and refreshingly critical (mostly German) students. And in keeping with the ideals of Alexander von Humboldt, many of the issues analyzed here first emerged as questions from my students; questions for which I had no satisfactory answer. Increasingly convinced that much of what I had come to believe about the scientific method stood up to neither close philosophical nor empirical analysis and frustrated by the efforts of well-known colleagues to come to terms with many of the same questions, I began to put my thoughts into words, and eventually decided to write a book.

My thinking on the questions addressed here has benefited from numerous conversations with students and colleagues on both sides of the Atlantic. Many of the ideas I develop in chapter 2 emerged from a graduate seminar devoted to questions of epistemology that I taught together with my colleague Armin Adam. During a sabbatical spent at Columbia University's Institute of War and Peace Studies, I benefited immensely from discussions with David Baldwin, Page Fortna, Robert Jervis, and Ken Waltz. Others who have influenced my thinking in various conversations include Ned Lebow, Wilhelm Vossenkuhl, Lars-Erik Cedermann, and Renate Strassner. Individual chapters benefited from the critical comments of Jack Snyder and Geoffrey Herrera. Henning Ottmann, Ulrich Beck, Friedrich Kratochwil, and an anonymous reviewer read the entire manuscript and provided detailed comments. The final product is much improved for their efforts.

I would be remiss, however, if I did not single out Fritz Kratochwil for special mention. This book would have never appeared had he not challenged me to write it and provided me with the sort of collegial environment within which such an unusual project was possible. Owing to the countless hours we spent together discussing questions of epistemology and method, as well as the pathologies that from time to time seem to dominate the practice of our discipline, he has influenced my thinking more than any other.

Although I have benefited from the wisdom of many, most of what I have written is nonetheless unorthodox and often idiosyncratic. The critique of mainstream political science practice developed here is based primarily on an evaluation of developments in IR and Comparative Politics, the two subfields I know best. Whether in the end it is persuasive, or perhaps found to apply more widely, is a judgment I leave to the reader.

Terms of Inquiry

CHAPTER ONE

Introduction

Research designed to help us understand social reality can only succeed if it follows the logic of scientific inference.
— GARY KING, ROBERT O. KEOHANE, AND SIDNEY VERBA,
DESIGNING SOCIAL INQUIRY

The notions that the goal of social science is to make explanatory inferences on the basis of empirical observations and that the validity of such inferences is a function of the strict application of accepted rules are widely held.[1] In my own field of international politics, the move toward a "scientific approach" began in earnest with the end of World War II and has since progressed through a series of "revolutions," "movements," or "great debates." By the 1990s the scientific approach was arguably dominant, with the vast majority of publications in peer-reviewed periodicals or university presses proudly proclaiming adherence to the "scientific rules of inference."[2]

The dominance of "science" in the systematic study of politics has given purpose and focus—that is, *discipline*—to a field that had traditionally comprised scholars representing a diverse range of intellectual traditions and approaches to study, including history, philosophy, theology, and law.[3] The consensus on the appropriate approach and methods has allowed for the emergence of large research programs, which at first glance appear to be both fruitful in terms of their scholarly product and cumulative, in that successive generations of scholars base their research on that which came before them.

Yet despite a half-century of science, many remain dissatisfied with the pace and scope of progress in the field. Although the number of scientifically conducted studies has exploded and individual studies increasingly begin from conclusions or anomalies uncovered in previous research—a defining characteristic of "normal science"—there is a curious lack of a corresponding cumulation of general knowledge, often regarded as the measure of "progressive" research programs.[4]

Moreover, with the acquisition of the external trappings of science, the field has become increasingly detached and irrelevant to political practice. Whereas the distinction between basic and applied research, or theory and application, makes sense in many of the natural sciences or can be justified on the grounds that the basic laws governing the universe are not amenable to change, the postwar proponents of the application of scientific methods to the study of political phenomena were motivated by a strong desire to improve the world around them. Armed with the tools of science, these scholars set out to uncover the root causes of such social ills as war, civil unrest, poverty, and racism, in the hopes that they could be thereby eradicated.

But the incidence of such outcomes has not significantly abated. Despite increased theoretical and methodological sophistication, the social sciences have not proven capable of anticipating major empirical developments or of providing unambiguous answers regarding appropriate responses. Consider, for example, the end of the cold war. Whether realist, liberal, institutionalist, or from the peace research movement, international relations theorists uniformly failed to anticipate both the reorientation of Soviet foreign policy initiated by Mikhail Gorbachev and the subsequent end of the cold war. Moreover, they have proven incapable of providing clear and persuasive guidance for effective action in the international system left in its wake.[5]

The apparent inability of political scientists to produce either robust theories capable of both explaining and predicting political events or generic knowledge relevant to the needs and questions confronting policymakers has, in recent years, given rise to three general reactions. The first, common among decision makers and other members of the political elite, is simply to ignore the academic study of politics.[6] Very few policymakers consult the leading academic journals or bother to seek the advice of recognized experts in the field. For their part, academics have tended to return the favor. Most no longer even pretend to write for the commonweal.[7]

The second tendency, perhaps best illustrated by the publication of *Design-*

ing Social Inquiry, has been to argue that the field is still *not scientific enough.* The problem, from this perspective, is that some practitioners simply have not gotten the message. Many, especially qualitatively oriented researchers, need "to take scientific inference seriously and to incorporate it into their work."[8]

The third reaction has been to question the general claims made on behalf of the scientific method, with emphasis on whether politics is amenable to scientific explanation. The most fundamental critique of the scientific revolution in the social sciences has been offered by postmodernists, who challenge both the privileged status of science as a ground for knowledge claims as well as assertions that science is objective or value-neutral.[9] Less radical but still skeptical of the strong claims made on behalf of the scientific method are scholars representing interpretive or hermeneutic traditions as well as those lingering "traditionalists" who restrict their analysis to historical events and make no claims with regard to grand theory.[10]

This study, largely in keeping with the third response, is an outgrowth of a growing skepticism vis-à-vis the strong claims made by proponents of the scientific method. An empirically oriented social scientist with training in both the methods of large-N statistical analysis and small-N comparative research, I have become increasingly persuaded that many of the general claims made on behalf of the scientific method cannot be sustained. Moreover, owing to its particular ontological base, the subject matter of interest to most political scientists is poorly suited to explanation in terms of generally valid covering laws. The problem, I am convinced, lies not with the practitioners but with the subject itself.[11]

What follows is a series of essays, each of which is devoted to the analysis of the central claims or assumptions of the scientific method in general or to the specific problems confronting the scientific analysis of social outcomes. Although the "case studies" and examples used to make general points are drawn predominantly from the field of political science, the implications of my arguments extend to most, if not all, of the social sciences. Owing both to my training as a political scientist as well as my interest in the practical problems of political life, my aim is not so much a comprehensive critique of the governing philosophy of social science but rather the discovery of a "middle way" between, on the one hand, the claim that scientific progress is merely a matter of a stricter adherence to the proper "rules of inference" and, on the other, the assertions of radical postmodernists that "anything goes."

The study proceeds from the bottom up, from the parts to the whole. It begins with an analysis of concepts and processes of conceptualization—the essential building blocks of science—and then moves to larger questions of theory development and hypothesis testing. While interested in fundamental questions of scientific inquiry, I am nonetheless concerned by the increasing irrelevance of the field of political science to the actual practice of politics. Thus, the final chapter is devoted to the question of producing useful knowledge, including a plea for a basic reorienting of both the scope and method of the discipline.

Concepts

Proponents of a nomothetical approach to the study of politics place great emphasis on the attributes of what they consider to be good, or useful, social scientific concepts. Of the multitude of problems plaguing the field, advocates of the scientific method hold the failure to define and operationalize basic concepts adequately to be central. They also lament the tendency of social scientists to use terms that are vague, ambiguous, and/or used in a variety of contexts in which their meanings may differ. Take, for example, the concept of the "balance of power." It has been variously used to describe: a political system in which power is equally balanced, the actual distribution of power in any political system, a principle held to guide the foreign policy goals of nation states, and a mechanism that operates independent of the intentions of individual states when they compete for security under anarchy.[12]

Whereas a certain degree of vagueness or ambiguity is acknowledged to be consistent with the needs of everyday communication, the proponents of a scientific approach to the study of social phenomena regard these qualities as incompatible with the goals of explanation and theory development. Science, they argue, requires precision. Scientific communication requires a special language comprised of concepts that are devoid of ambiguity and can be used to construct meaningful statements about the real world.[13] Since the goal of science is to uncover and explain regularities in the universe, good scientific concepts are those that reflect essential natural properties of the universe. From this perspective, the formation of concepts must proceed from the identification of essential properties that can be apprehended by means of our sensory apparatus. Scientific concepts are those that are defined in terms of empirical referents whose presence or absence can be established by resort to observation.[14]

The utility of an empirical concept thus becomes a function of its operational specification. Operationalization is the process of defining a concept in terms of properties or conditions that can be analyzed for the purpose of determining the existence of a phenomenon. For a phenomenon that is not directly observable, as is the case with many theoretical concepts, operational definitions will require reference to the consequences that result from its presence or absence, consequences that may themselves be directly observable or may require the scientist to make use of special instruments.[15]

In the 1950s it was widely believed that if the political science community could only stipulate the definitions of concepts and their operationalization, an important barrier to progress would be breached. Lasswell and Kaplan were characteristic of the times. Arguing that the "degree of vagueness and ambiguity of the terms usually employed in the field required a considerable exercise in definition," they set out to construct a general framework for future empirical analysis and produced an entire volume—a recognized classic in the field of political science—comprised almost exclusively of definitions.[16]

But the optimism of the early postwar years was misplaced. Efforts to stipulate the definitions and operational measures of concepts in the field tended to produce as many debates as applications. For example, the considerable effort with which Almond and Verba attempted to define the concept of political culture in the first chapter of *The Civic Culture* did not lead to standardized usage but rather gave rise to a proliferation of definitions.[17] Similar results have characterized efforts to define and operationalize the most fundamental concepts of the field, including the state, the political system, power, and security.[18]

While many continue the quest for consensus over key concepts and their operational specification and even attempt to impose some measure of discipline on the discipline, in what follows I shall argue that the goal itself is illusory.[19] Concepts, whether used in everyday speech or for purposes of scientific communication, are *inherently* vague and ambiguous. Efforts to achieve a high degree of precision by stipulating definitions based on features or properties deemed essential or sufficient, which in turn are subject to operational specification, are usually little more than sleights of hand and therefore bound to fail.

Initial grounds for skepticism regarding the prospects for achieving a high degree of precision in the use of concepts arise from the fact that we employ a finite set of concepts to describe and explain objects and events in the world whose number is, in principle, endless. This basic fact points to a tension in orthodox understandings of the scientific method. For if science is about generalizing from the particular, then we must be willing to sacrifice some degree of precision. If, however, it is about precision, then the prospects for generalization are limited.

Efforts to achieve precision in the definition of scientific concepts rest on the assumption that a discrete set of necessary and/or sufficient properties or characteristics can be identified for purposes of demonstrating the existence of a phenomenon. Concepts are expected to establish sets of like individuals. Precise definitions should allow one to determine whether a given phenomenon does or does not constitute an example of the concept.

With reference to the empirical research of cognitive scientists, linguists, and anthropologists, as well as the philosophy of Wittgenstein, I will show that this fundamental assumption is problematic. Many concepts defy specification in terms of necessary and/or sufficient criteria that would allow for unproblematic judgments over their extension to a particular observation. Vagueness, I argue, is not necessarily a result of poor definitions, fallible perceptions, or the limitations of our measuring instruments. Rather, some of the most concrete data are by nature vague, and many empirical referents (e.g., for fog) are themselves vague.[20] Hence, the borders of concepts are often rather more fuzzy than discrete.

Finally, hopes for achieving precision and a high degree of uniformity in the use of empirical concepts rest on the assumption that all humans are capable of perceiving the world in the same, or at least a very similar, fashion, by virtue of shared sensory apparatus. In a strict sense, this is certainly true. But as cognitive science has begun to discover, despite our shared physiology, human beings are exposed to a diverse range of cultural and environmental stimuli, which structure the ways in which we perceive the world very early in the developmental process. By the age of two, individuals from different cultures and linguistic groups no longer experience basic optical or auditory stimuli in the same way, a claim to be elaborated in chapter 2.

These findings provide an explanation for the apparent inability of political scientists to settle basic debates over the definition of key terms and suggest that such debates are neither fruitless nor an indication of undisciplined scientific practice or theoretical underdevelopment. They also have important implications for efforts to construct precise and universally valid concepts as well as to develop more elaborate general theories.[21]

The Limitations of Logic

Proponents of a scientific approach to the study of social phenomena argue that theory development and empirical research should be guided by the rules of classical logic. Theories that purport to explain the social world, they argue, should be judged on the basis of their logical coherence and ability to produce deductions that predict (or retrodict) outcomes in the "real world." Theories that are logically incoherent or that lead to predictions that are falsified on the basis of observation should be rejected in favor of theories that are internally coherent and withstand the rigors of empirical tests.

By definition, a science based on the criterion of falsifiability excludes the undecided middle. The concepts and relationships that comprise social scientific theories must satisfy the criterion of a basic two-valued logic. In order to construct meaningful theories about the world, we need to be able to establish which states of the world are and are not consistent with the theory. In order to test our theories, we need to arrive at statements about the world that are either true or false. From this perspective, the job of social science is to bring us "closer to the truth."

Although it remains the dominant paradigm in the empirically oriented social sciences, philosophers of natural science have increasingly rejected this idealized conception of science. The fundamental problem is not a problem of logic, as I demonstrate in chapter 4, but of establishing the correspondence between theoretical and empirical statements.[22]

In practice, establishing the correspondence between even basic concepts and the "real world" is problematic. If even basic scientific concepts are fuzzy, and a neutral or universal observation language is beyond our reach (owing to the impact of culture on the development of our perceptual apparatus), then empirical statements are best thought of as being governed by a three-valued logic: they may be acknowledged to be true, false, or undecided. But if we grant that the logic of empirical statements is three-valued, then we are forced to reject the orthodox model of science.

Social Norms

Fundamental differences between the nature of logical and empirical statements have led philosophers of science to challenge basic claims made on behalf of the scientific method and provide grounds for questioning its adoption by the social sciences. Further grounds for skepticism particular to the onto-logical base of the subject matter of interest to most social scientists are pre-sented in chapter 5.

Specifically, I argue that a science built upon a two-value logic and the cri-teria of falsification is inadequate to the task of explaining the ways in which rules and norms inform individual choice and thereby shape human behavior. Because the meanings of general norms in specific cases are subject to inter-pretation, and because they can be extended and interpreted in novel ways, their effects cannot be captured a priori in terms of "if . . . then" statements, even if these are formulated probabilistically. There are two central problems. First, norms are counterfactually valid. Thus, a single instance of a norm's vio-lation does not refute its general validity. Second, because norms are applied to novel situations on the basis of analogy and judgments of similarity, they give rise to sets of cases that are neither homogeneous nor discrete. Hence, efforts to capture the effects of norms through statistical procedures are misplaced.

The Search for Useful Knowledge

Having raised doubts regarding the prospects for defining scientific con-cepts in terms of necessary and/or sufficient characteristics as well as the em-pirical status of relationships established on the basis of logical necessity, I turn to the problem of producing useful knowledge in chapter 6. Can we construct general theories if we cannot establish categories of equivalent individuals? If general theory is beyond our reach, how can we go about establishing the ex-istence of causal relationships? Moreover, how might we bring the practice of political science closer to the practice of politics itself?

The answer, I suggest, lies in abandoning the ideal of grand deductive the-orizing and moving toward a model of science closer to that of medical prac-tice. Acknowledging the limitations inherent in single-case or small-N analy-sis as well as inductively generated inferences, the practitioner nevertheless *can* develop explanations and understandings that are more than mere opinion. And she may do so in ways that suggest points and methods of intervention, either to promote or prevent outcomes that may recur.

What follows is admittedly idiosyncratic and draws on a wide range of em-pirical research and philosophical rumination. In addition to political science, I have consulted literature from the fields of anthropology, biology, law, linguistics, mathematics, medicine, psychology, physics, philosophy, and sociology. Many of the arguments are unorthodox and controversial, at least from the standpoint of mainstream political science. Some of them will undoubtedly turn out to be wrong. If they were well known, conventional, or self-evident, there would be no point to raising them.

CHAPTER TWO

Of Concepts and Conceptualization

> Language is the formative organ of thought. . . . Thought and language
> are . . . one and inseparable from each other.
>
> WILHELM VON HUMBOLDT

The typical book or essay on methodology in political science begins with a discussion of the various problems afflicting the enterprise, problems that are held to set the social sciences apart from the natural sciences more generally and that point up the discrepancy between the two branches of science with respect to theoretical progress and the cumulation of knowledge. Thus, various commentators lament that relatively few social scientists have recourse to experimental research designs, that the field is bedeviled by "too many variables and too few cases," or that political laws have a short half-life and consequently that humans enjoy plastic rather than "cast-iron" control over the social world.[1] Although these problems are real—even if, as I shall argue later, their importance has often been exaggerated or misconstrued—beginning a discussion of the practice of political science with such observations is putting the cart before the horse. For before we can begin to discuss questions of correlation, causation, explanation, or even *Verstehen,* we face a problem or task that unifies all scientific inquiry, social and natural, namely that of conceptualization.

In this chapter I argue that although the task of conceptualization is fundamental to the scientific enterprise, it has largely been ignored or treated as self-evident and unproblematic in the most influential works on political science. To the extent that the question of conceptualization has been addressed, it has generally been at the level of operationalization, the linking of concepts to empirical referents. Although of central importance for the conduct of empirical research, operationalization is neither the only nor the most important challenge in the process of conceptualization. Rather, a number of inherent problems remain under-explored and, I shall argue, are in no small measure responsible for the rather limited success of political science theories in generating general and cumulative knowledge, despite more than a half-century of "scientific" approaches to the study of politics.

The chapter is structured as follows. I begin with a discussion of concepts and conceptualization. The discussion centers around the language- and theory-dependence of conceptualization and thus draws on literature from the fields of psycholinguistics and the philosophy of science. Having established that there is no one-to-one correspondence between the physical world and the concepts humans use to represent it, and that the borders of most concepts are fuzzy rather than distinct, I suggest that the essence of scientific concepts is found in their capacity to convey *some* meaning. This unorthodox understanding of the nature of scientific concepts leads to a critical discussion of standard arguments asserting the necessity of "precision." The chapter ends with a brief comparison of scientific concepts and those informing other structures of meaning, of which religion is perhaps the most important and enduring. While I acknowledge that science and religion are different enterprises, the difference is not primarily found in the nature of the concepts each employs.

Conceptualization and the Development of Scientific Concepts

Conceptualization is the indispensable first step toward the generation of knowledge in general and is central to the scientific enterprise in particular. Our experience of "the world" is not direct. Rather, concepts both mediate and structure our experience of the world (apprehension) and our reflections on that experience (comprehension). We do not perceive each and every individual experience as a unique and independent event, but rather in terms of patterns and categories that comprise our cognitive apparatus. Conceptualization is the mental process of discovering patterns and commonalties in the world and of ordering phenomena and experience in terms of patterns and similar or common traits.

A concept is a mental representation of an element or phenomenon of the physical, social, or psychological world. Scientists often differentiate among categories, classes, cases, attributes, variables, and parameters, but because they all presuppose a parceling of experience, all constitute concepts, as here defined.[2] Concepts exist in our mind and do not reveal themselves directly to the mind-external world. Thus, it makes no sense to categorize concepts as "real" or "imaginary," they are all mental depictions. Rocks are not in our minds, rather mental depictions of rocks inform our thoughts. Fairies do not exist in the physical world, but depictions of fairies animate the dreams and fantasies of children and adults alike.[3] The mental boundedness of concepts becomes even more apparent if we consider concepts lacking in physical manifestation such as time, fairness, or love.

The capacity for symbolic representation is perhaps the most important distinctive feature of the human mind and sets us far apart from our closest living relatives, the apes. Through the course of human evolution, we not only developed larger brains with an expanded capacity for memory and the vocal apparatus for language, but also a new and highly complex system for representing reality.[4] Precisely how the brain engages in symbolic representation is a hotly debated question, with classical cognitive theorists tending to regard concepts as "virtual objects" that are manipulated by a set of mental rules and procedures, while connectionists and parallel distributed processing theorists consider representations to result from particular states of the "conceptual system" distributed across the neural networks of the brain.[5]

The physiology and biochemistry of the human mental apparatus, though crucial to the capacity for conceptualization, are not central to the analysis at hand. Rather, the analysis focuses on the links between processes of conceptualization and our ability to generate warranted knowledge about the world that can be communicated to others.

The Linguistic Origins of Concepts

Concepts are mental representations of elements or phenomena in the physical, social, or psychological world, but how are such representations constructed, and what is the relationship of concepts to the phenomenological world that inspires them? The traditional source for answers to these questions has been the philosophy of science. Increasingly, however, the arguments of philosophers of science have been augmented by the findings of empirically oriented researchers in the much newer field of cognitive science. In this section, I will briefly summarize some of the most important findings of cognitive science relating to the question of conceptualization and then turn to the arguments of philosophers of science. I will attempt to show that both approaches yield strikingly similar insights. Specifically, both suggest that most conceptualization takes place within complex preexisting yet evolving symbolic structures and bears no direct, one-to-one correspondence to mind-external phenomena.

Although cognitive science does not offer a single answer to questions of conceptualization, a growing body of evidence indicates that culture and in particular language play a central role in the cognitive development of children and that early cognitive development strongly structures subsequent processes of conceptualization and categorization.

That concepts are language-bound is clear to anyone who speaks more than one language and comes upon the common situation where an adequate translation (or even description) of a concept proves elusive. It is not only the terms that differ across languages, but more importantly, as Humboldt argued, a *worldview:* "There resides in every language a characteristic world view. As the individual sound stands between man and the object, so the entire language steps in between him and the nature that operates, both inwardly and outwardly, upon him. . . . Man lives primarily with objects, [but] he actually does so exclusively as language presents them to him."[6] Nonetheless, many contemporary social scientists either do not consider the degree to which concepts are language-bound or maintain that concepts can, at least in principle, apply universally. Such beliefs, however, have been convincingly refuted by strong and reliable cross-cultural empirical research that demonstrates the impossibility of "objective" and language-neutral conceptualization.

Take, for example, something as basic as color. How is it that humans develop the concept of color, and then categorize various colors as red, green, blue, and so on? Are colors objectively "out there"? If so, we would expect them to have been apprehended by members of every cultural and linguistic group— assuming their environment is rich enough to include examples of the various colors—and that every language would have developed words to represent the variety of colors present in the physical world. We might not be surprised to find that speakers of different languages have developed different terms for each color, but we would expect fundamental agreement on the range of colors in need of linguistic categorization.

In a classic study, Brent Berlin and Paul Kay discovered that there were similarities across languages with respect to the categorization of color, namely the universal existence of what they called "basic color terms."[7] Basic color terms are characterized by a single morpheme, such as *red,* rather than multiple morphemes, for example *dark red* or *blood red.*[8] Moreover, basic color terms are not contained within another color. Thus, *scarlet* is not basic, as it is contained within the color term *red.* A basic color term is generalizable, that is, its application is not restricted to a specific category or a small number of objects, as is the case with color terms such as *blond,* which is generally restricted to hair or wood. Finally, basic colors are common and generally known, for example *yellow* as opposed to *saffron.*[9]

Upon further examination, Berlin and Kay discovered that basic color terms reflect the existence of conceptual color categories that are characterized by focal, best, or purest examples. That is, for any given color category, there exists a shade or tone that a group of people would agree is the "best" example of that color. Eleven such *basic color categories* were identified, those corresponding to the English terms *black, white, red, yellow, green, blue, brown, purple, pink, orange,* and *gray.*

The universal existence of basic color categories and widespread agreement on what constitutes the best or purest example of a given color would appear to lend support to the notion that colors are indeed "out there" and that linguistic terms will come to reflect these natural phenomena in a more or less direct fashion. This, however, is not the case. For although some languages, such as English, make use of all eleven basic color categories, others use as few as two. Languages that categorize colors in terms of two basic terms differentiate between black (covering the English terms *black, blue, green,* and *gray*) and white (covering the English terms *white, yellow, orange,* and *red*). When a language utilizes three basic color terms, they are *black, white,* and *red.* When a fourth is included, it is either *yellow, blue,* or *green.* When there are fewer than eleven basic color terms, those terms represent unions of the eleven basic color categories.[10]

Languages differ not only with respect to the number of basic color terms they employ, but also with respect to the boundaries among color categories. The existence of focal colors—the best examples of given colors—reveals that color categories are not uniform. Rather, some members of a color category are generally acknowledged to be better examples of the category than others.

Berlin and Kay discovered a high degree of consistency across linguistic communities when individuals were asked to identify the best or focal example of a given color. They did not, however, find uniformity with respect to judgments over what constitutes the range of examples for any given color. For example, if a language has a basic color term for red, then the best example, called *focal red,* appears to be the same for everyone, regardless of which language they speak. But speakers of different languages for which there is a concept of red do not agree on its borders, that is, what constitutes an example of red.[11] Although color categories have central members (focal colors), there appears to be no general principle for predicting the application or extension of the term beyond the central members. The boundaries of basic color terms vary from language to language.[12]

Berlin and Kay's findings give rise to as many questions as they answer. In particular, why should there be a discrepancy among (1) the number of basic color categories all humans appear to be capable of apprehending, (2) the number of basic color terms employed in any given language, and (3) the borders of basic color terms across languages? The answer appears to be a combination of human physiology, cognition, and culture.

Human physiology would appear to account for the fact that most people are capable of apprehending the full range of primary colors. In a series of laboratory experiments with macaque monkeys, primates with a visual physiology very close to that of humans, DeValois and his associates found that the neural pathways between the eye and the brain are comprised of six types of cells. Four of these, the opponent response cells, were found to determine the hue of a particular stimulus, while the remaining two determined brightness. The opponent response cells are grouped into two pairs, one determining the perception of blue and yellow, the other red and green. Each opponent response cell was found to maintain a certain rate of activity or "firing" without any external stimulation, the base response rate. In the presence of a visual stimulus, the firing rates either increase or decrease, resulting in the brain's apprehension of color. For example, there are two types of red-green cells. The +G−R cells fire above their base rate in the presence of green and below the base rate in response to red, whereas the +R−G cells do the exact opposite. The two types of red-green cells jointly determine the brain's apprehension of red or green. The process is the same for blue and yellow. Focal blue, then, is the color perceived when the blue-yellow cells produce a blue response while the red-green cells are firing at their base rates.

Purple, a combination of blue and red, is seen when the blue-yellow cells produce a blue response and the red-green cells a red response. Pure primary colors are produced when either the red-green or blue-yellow cells are firing at their base rates, whereas nonprimary colors are characterized by situations where none of the opponent cells are firing at their base or neutral rates.

The remaining two cell types are sensitive to dark and light. Pure white, black, and gray are produced when the opponent response cells are all firing at their base rates (and thus producing no sensation of the basic colors blue, yellow, red, or green). Pure black results when the darkness-sensitive cells are firing at their maximum rate and the light-sensitive cells at their minimum rates. Pure white is seen when the darkness-sensitive cells are firing at their minimum rates while the light-sensitive cells are firing at their maximum.

Thus, our apprehension of colors would appear to be largely a function of neurophysiology. However, the apprehension of color does not produce uniformity of perception or categorization, as Berlin and Kay discovered. The neurophysical studies produce an account for why it is that humans should agree on the existence of the focal primary colors: black, white, red, yellow, blue, and green. However, they do not provide an adequate explanation for the categorization of nonfocal colors, such as turquoise, or nonprimary colors, such as purple, orange, or brown. Moreover, as Berlin and Kay demonstrated, although some languages use up to eleven basic color terms, each of which denotes a basic color category characterized by a focal member on which nearly all speakers agree, some languages make use of as few as two. What accounts for the conceptualization and categorization of color, that is, our ability to "see" in basic color categories?

Building on the work of Berlin and Kay, further empirical studies suggest that basic color categories are a function of both neurophysiology and cognitive processes that are at least in part culturally determined. That is, color categorization makes use of human physiology, but the interaction of human physiology with the physical world does not produce uniformity with respect to the conceptual categories humans use to order their thoughts about the world. For example, in certain Mesoamerican languages the color corresponding to the English term *brown* falls within the color category that has yellow at its center, whereas in others it falls within the category that centers on pure black. Similarly, the color we term *purple* is in some languages found within a single color, *cool,* with focal points at blue *and* green, whereas in others it falls on the boundary of cool and red.[13] Moreover, in cases where the English-language basic color categories of blue and green are conjoined, some language groups identify pure green as focal whereas for others, pure blue is identified as the best example for the blue-green color category. What these results indicate is not only that conjunctions and disjunctions of basic color categories exist, but also that they are not the same for all people. It is not just the names of "real" colors that are "out there" that vary from culture to culture, but also precisely the conceptual categories within which speakers of a given language "see." Colors, it seems, are products of both neurophysiology and culture.[14]

Culture, and more particularly language, not only influence the objects we "see" but also how we conceive these objects to relate to one another spatially. Language is much more than a tool through which preexisting or independent spatial concepts can be conveyed to others. By imposing a particular structure on physical space, language also structures cognition. Although space would appear to be a continuous and homogeneous phenomenon, "stretching without seam in three open-ended dimensions," to think or speak about location or motion requires that we parcel three-dimensional space into spatial categories. And these categories are given to us by language.[15]

Take, for example, a cookie that is in contact with the upper surface of a dish: "We must decide whether it is 'on' or 'in' the dish. The shape of the dish may be intermediate between a flat plate and a clear cut bowl, but in everyday English we cannot represent the relationship as intermediate between 'on' and 'in.'"[16]

Does it matter? One could certainly give a more detailed description of the spatial relationship of the cookie to the dish as well as of the shape of the dish itself, and thereby communicate more precisely the observed state of affairs. The "problem" in this case would be one of articulating a given observation for which a particular language may or may not have an adequate or appropriate linguistic term, not that the observed state of the world is in any sense "determined" by language.

In the 1960s and 1970s, studies of child development concerned themselves with how children come to identify linguistic terms to articulate spatial relationships that they already "know." That children learn about spatial relationships before they talk has been convincingly demonstrated.[17] Children often appear to be trying to convey spatially structured ideas before they enjoy command of a commensurate vocabulary. For example the words "sit" and "pool" might be combined in the utterance "sit pool" in an effort to convey the desire to sit *in* the pool. Moreover, children often play with objects in ways that demonstrate an appreciation of the spatial concepts of "containment" and "support" before they learn the words *in* and *on,* suggesting that these linguistic terms are mapped later to preexisting spatial concepts.[18]

Herbert Clark has argued that infant children possess prelinguistic knowledge of space and that their knowledge is strongly determined by human biology and the workings of the physical environment. In the process of language acquisition, linguistic terms are mapped onto these a priori cognitive concepts:

> The child is born into a flat world with gravity, and he himself is endowed with eyes, ears, an upright posture, and other biological structures. These structures alone lead him to develop a perceptual space, a **P**-space, with very specific properties. Later on, the child must learn how to apply English spatial terms to this perceptual space, and so the structure of **P**-space determines in large part what he learns and how quickly he learns it. The notion is that the child cannot apply some terms correctly if he does not already have the appropriate concept in his **P**-space. Since this is so, the concepts of space underlying the English spatial terms, to be called **L**-space, should coincide with **P**-space: any property found in **L**-space should also be found in **P**-space.[19]

Clark hypothesized that the infant child develops spatial understandings that are basically a function of perspective. Projecting from the human body leads to such mental concepts as top, bottom, front, and back.[20] Spatial language is thus conceived to be both conditioned by and isomorphic to this purely cognitive and nonlinguistic structuring of space.

If in fact spatial knowledge is determined by human biology and its interaction with the material world, and if human beings develop spatial knowledge prior to their acquisition of speech, then we would expect most cultures of the world to have developed similar linguistic concepts for these essentially "natural" spatial relationships. When confronted with the same state of affairs, speakers of different languages should make more or less the same categorical distinctions. The linguistic terms in which a given situation is articulated will differ by language, but they should all convey the same meaning with respect to a situation that itself is objective.[21]

This, however, is not the case. Although at first glance spatial relationships would appear to be "out there" and subject to apprehension and articulation by means of linguistic terms, and although most languages have parceled physical space in terms of spatial prepositions, they do so in very different ways.

And the differences are not limited to the linguistic labels attached to particular spatial relationships. Rather, the relationships themselves are perceived quite differently. When viewing the same state of affairs, representatives of different linguistic groupings often disagree on what precisely they "see," on whether a given state of affairs "counts" as a case of one or another spatial relationship.

Take for example the prepositions *in* and *on*. These prepositions (or their counterparts in other languages) are among the first spatial terms learned by children, often before the age of two. Proponents of the view that linguistic terms are essentially mapped onto nonlinguistic and universally learned semantic primitives generally analyze the meanings of *in* and *on* in terms of topological or functional notions such as "containment" and "inclusion" versus "support" and "contact."[22] If the spatial relationships we associate with *in* and *on* are nonlinguistic in terms of origin and reflect semantic primitives that are related to concepts such as "containment" or "contact," then speakers of various languages should more or less agree on what constitutes a case of *in* or *on*—that is, when an object is "contained" or "included" *in* another, and when by virtue of "contact" or "support," one object can be said to be *on* another.[23]

Now consider figure 2.1, which provides illustrations of four spatial activities.

If asked to group these actions in terms of like spatial relations, speakers of English would group (a) placing an apple *in* a bowl, together with (c) putting a cassette *in* its case, and group (b) placing a cup *on* the table together with (d) putting a lid *on* a container, as shown in figure 2.2. In English, appropriate categorization occurs by means of extending the term *in* according to the concepts of "containment" or "inclusion" and *on* according to the concepts of "contact" or "support."

The situation, however, is very different for speakers of Korean, as Choi and Bowerman have demonstrated.

When asked to categorize the four illustrations in terms of the spatial activity each represents, speakers of Korean place (b) and (d) together while (a) and (c) are accorded categories to themselves, as in figure 2.3. For Korean speakers, putting a cassette in its case (b) and a lid on a container (d) are grouped together as like activities (*kkita*) because each involves bringing an object together with another in a three-dimensional relationship of meshing or fit. Placing an apple in a bowl (a) is an example of putting something into or taking something out of a loose container (*nehta*), while placing a cup on a table

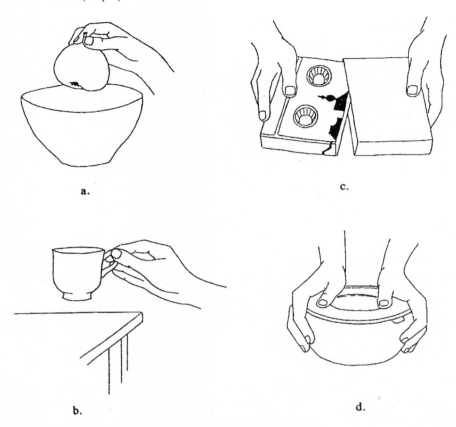

Fig. 2.1. Four spatial activities. From Bowerman (1996), 150.

(c) is an example of the broader class of putting something loosely on a surface (*nohta*).[24]

Now consider the static spatial configurations represented in figure 2.4. For English speakers, only the first illustration is an example of an object that is *in* another, that is, the apple is *in* the bowl. All of the others—(b) through (g)—constitute examples of objects that can be said to be located *on* other objects, that is, the handle is *on* the pan and the fly is *on* the door.

If asked to group like configurations together, English speakers will divide the seven illustrations into two groups, *in* and *on,* with (a) constituting the single example of *in,* and all of the others belonging to the category *on.* The characterization is remarkably different if we turn to speakers of Finnish. In Finnish, most locative relationships are indicated by suffixes added to the

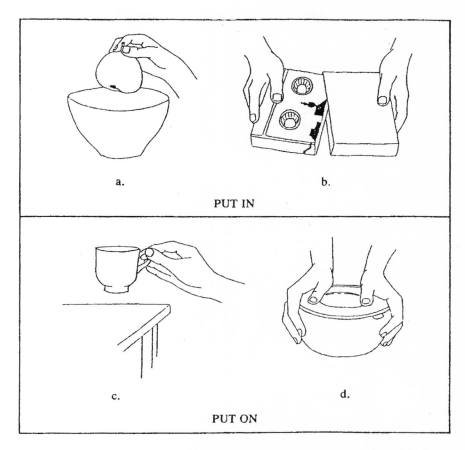

Fig. 2.2. Semantic classifications of four actions in English. From Bowerman (1996), 152.

nominal term, with the suffixes *-lla* and *-llä* corresponding roughly to the English prepositions *on, onto, off,* or *from,* and *-ssa* or *-ssä* translating roughly to *in, into,* and *out of.* Turning to figure 2.5, Finnish speakers will group illustrations (a) through (e) as belonging to the class *-ssa/-ssä,* leaving (f) and (g) as cases of *-lla/-llä.*[25]

In English, containment or location in the interior of an object is different from mere contact with an outer surface. Hence, the apple is *in* the pan whereas all other illustrations constitute examples of *on.* Moreover, English speakers do not immediately differentiate between objects that are intimately or loosely in contact with a surface. The handle is on the pan, much as the fly is on the door.

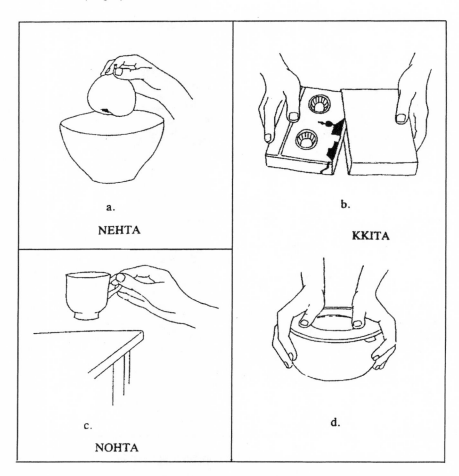

a.

NEHTA

b.

KKITA

c.

NOHTA

d.

Fig. 2.3. Semantic classifications of four actions in Korean. From Bowerman (1996), 153.

For speakers of Finnish, the relevant distinction to be made in figure 2.5 is between objects that are either interior to or in intimate contact with another (*-ssa/-ssä*) and those in loose contact (*-lla/-llä*). The most intimate relationship is that of the apple located in the interior of the bowl. Somewhat less intimate are objects that are affixed or attached to outer surfaces, such as the handle on the pan, the band-aid on the leg, the ring on the finger, or the fly on the door, but in Finnish both relationships (interior to and affixed to) are characterized by the suffix *-ssa*. Because the surface of the picture and that of the wall are in loose contact (that is, the nail is not part of the picture itself) and the cup is

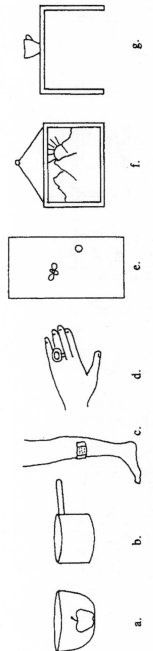

Fig. 2.4. Seven static spatial configurations. From Bowerman (1996), 154.

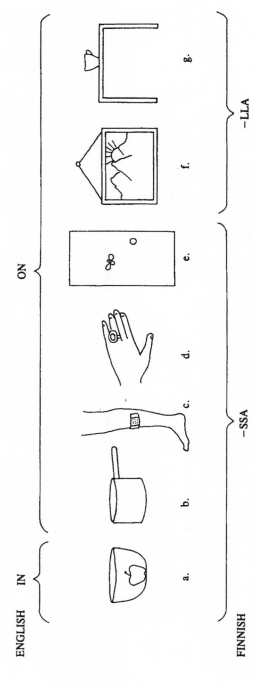

Fig. 2.5. Semantic classification of static spatial configurations in English and Finnish. From Bowerman (1996), 157.

not attached to the table, these relationships are, for Finnish speakers, essentially the same (*-lla*).

The situation for speakers of Mixtec, a language of western Mexico, is altogether different. For Mixtec speakers, spatial relationships are understood in terms of the metaphorical projection of body parts.[26] Thus, *He is on top of the mountain* would in Mixtec be *He is located on the mountain's head*. But the Mixtec concept *head* is not the precise equivalent of the English *on,* for the moon, were it to be seen over a mountain, would also be located on the mountain's *head*.[27] Moreover, should a bird choose to fly from the branch of a tree onto the roof of a house, the Mixtec speaker would say that it flew from the tree's *arm* to the house's *back*. Because houses in western Mexico have flat roofs, the term *head* is not appropriate for the location of the roof relative to the house. Instead, the term for the back of an animal is used, as animal backs are, in general, horizontal. For the Mixtec there is no such thing as that which speakers of English refer to as *on*. Rather, there is a variety of spatial locations conceptually organized in terms of relationships of body parts, relationships that intersect with the prepositional relationships of English in significant respects. To understand how the Mixtec parcel space, one needs more than a list of equivalent terms, one must immerse oneself in a conventional system of metaphorical projection and mapping.

The fact that various language groups conceive of spatial relationships in quite different ways alone gives rise to doubts as to the "naturalness" of spatial concepts and to the possibility of reducing them to universal prelinguistic spatial primitives. When observing a particular state of the world, for example an apple in contact with a dish, the human mind may be universally capable of perceiving such things as the shape of the dish and the nature of the contact. But an individual cannot know ahead of time which of these properties is essential for characterizing the situation as a case of one or another spatial relationship. This is language-specific and something the individual can only master with time through observation of and interaction with fluent speakers.

If spatial concepts are more cognitive than linguistic and based on more or less universal spatial primitives, then the meanings of the words children use to convey spatial information in the early phases of development should reflect language independence and either be universal or highly idiosyncratic.[28] Only with the mastery of speech would we expect language-specific references to spatial relationships. If, however, spatial concepts are largely products of linguistic systems, then we would expect children to employ language-specific terms early in development and to display relatively weak language-indepen-dent preferences in the classification of spatial relationships.[29]

In a series of cross-cultural studies, Bowerman and Choi found the latter to be the case. Examining early spontaneous speech data from English- and Korean-speaking children, they found that in both groups, children began us-ing spatial terms at fourteen to sixteen months and used them productively beginning at sixteen to twenty months. And children in both groups spoke about similar events, such as sitting down or standing up, putting on or tak-ing off articles of clothing, and manipulation of objects in a variety of ways. But although there was a high degree of similarity in preoccupations across the two groups, there were important differences in the categorizations employed by the speakers of English and Korean.

For example, by sixteen to twenty months, English-speaking children used prepositions such as *up, down, in, out, on,* and *off* for spontaneous as well as caused motion. Consistent with conventional English usage, they used the term *out* for such activities as climbing *out* of the bathtub as well as taking something *out* of a box. By contrast, in the same age period, Korean-speaking children differentiate between spontaneous and caused motion, using, for ex-ample, the term *kkenayta* ("take out of loose container") for taking blocks out of a box, but not for getting out of the bathtub. By eighteen to twenty months, English speakers differentiated between *in* and *on* and their opposites *out* and *off.* They used *on* and *off* for both surface attachment (such as lids on jars, or Lego pieces) and looser contact, such as climbing on or off a stool, and in and out for the inserting and removing of objects from containers, regardless of whether the fit was tight (e.g., placing shaped wooden objects into their proper hole on a puzzle-like board) or loose (e.g., placing toys in a box). In the same period, however, Korean speakers did not distinguish among spatial relation-ships and activities in terms of the global categories of "containment" or "sup-port." Rather, they used the term *kkita* (to fit) and its opposite *ppayta* (to unfit) with appropriate modifications for "tight" and "loose" for both those actions and relationships that English speakers characterized in terms of *in* or *out* as well as those that are characterized as *on* or *off.* Between sixteen and twenty months, English speakers used the terms *up* and *down* for a wide range of spon-taneous and caused vertical motion, such as going up or down the stairs, or asking to be picked up or put down. Korean children used verbs that classify these events according to criteria other than shared vertical motion.[30]

The Bowerman and Choi studies demonstrate that both Korean- and English-speaking children use the spatial terms of their language with a high degree of accuracy well before the age of two. English speakers extend the words *in* and *out* or *on* and *off* to new situations without regard to whether motion is spontaneous or caused, and they pay particular attention to vertical motion (*up* and *down*). Korean children use different words for spontaneous and caused motion, differentiate surface contact in terms of the type of fit in ways that cross-cut the concepts of containment and support, and they make distinctions among different types of vertical motion. Such early, language-specific references to spatial relationships and activities would appear to indicate that our perception and conceptualization of space is in large measure linguistically determined and not solely, or even primarily, cognitive. Infant children appear to be "hard-wired" to notice shape and motion, but they are not merely mapping linguistic terms onto preexisting spatial primitives. "From the beginning, they are paying close attention to the way adults use spatial words: across contexts, the word serves as a 'lure to cognition' . . . which draws the learner's attention to properties the referents share."[31]

The foregoing examples of color and space provide strong evidence to support the notion that observation is mediated by language. What we "see," although a function of human physiology, is also very much dependent on the language we learn. And language is first accessed by means of hearing. But what about our perception of sound? Is it direct—that is, free from the mediating effects of language and culture?

Studies of newborn infants have shown that they prefer the mother's voice to other voices and are more attuned to the language of their community than to other languages, indicating some prenatal development of the brain's language- or sound-processing faculties.[32] They are clearly sensitive to those acoustic properties that differentiate the phonemic segments of their native language.[33] However, a number of studies have shown that newborns are also capable of apprehending phonemes[34] that are not found in their native language and are sensitive to phonemic distinctions that adult speakers do not make and cannot discriminate.[35] For example, Japanese newborns can discriminate between the sounds associated with the letters /r/ and /l/, sounds that Japanese adults typically cannot distinguish. Similarly, babies born to English-speaking parents in Toronto could distinguish among phonetic contrasts in both English and Czech, whereas adult English speakers could not.[36]

However, speech perception requires not only the differentiation among phonemic segments but also the ability to recognize distinct sounds as members of the same category. The production of speech is not uniform. Rather, a given vowel or consonant will be pronounced in different ways by different speakers, and the same phonemic segment will be subject to variation in its production even by the same speaker. Yet, language is based on categorical structures, including phonemes, grammatical classes and word meanings.[37] Mastery of language and comprehension requires the ability to categorize a given phonemic segment correctly despite variations in the production of speech.[38]

The first source of variation in the production of speech arises from changes in such factors as speaker, rate of speech, or intonation. If meaningful communication is to take place, equivalence of phonemic segments must be established in spite of differences in pitch, rate of speech, or volume. Studies of infant children exposed to both natural and computer-generated speech have shown that they are able to make such distinctions and form mental classes of equivalent phonemic segments that correspond to adult phonemic categories by the age of six months. Because the stimuli are linguistically equivalent (e.g., all being examples of the same vowel sound) but acoustically very different (e.g., high pitch / low pitch, loud/soft), they are presumably highly discriminable on a variety of dimensions. For example, one might classify all loud sounds as members of the same group, or all quickly articulated sounds as generating a class. However, the evidence is strong that prelinguistic children engage in a particular form of categorization based on a recognition of similarities among sounds that will come to define linguistic categories. This conclusion is further supported by evidence that they have difficulty forming such categories when exposed to random samples of the same auditory stimuli.[39]

The second type of acoustic variation reflects the inherent variability in the production of a particular phonemic segment in a given context by a single speaker. If exposed to two exemplars corresponding to different syllables in a given language that nonetheless come from the same acoustic continuum, for example [da] and [tʰa] (from, say, the English words "dad" and "tad"), infant children show signs of discriminating the differences that become meaningful among proficient speakers.[40] If, however, they are exposed to acoustically different exemplars from the same category, for example, two instances of [da] or two of [tʰa], they typically do not show signs of discriminating between them.[41]

What the studies of speech perception in infancy demonstrate is that humans appear to be engaging in prelinguistic categorization with categories that are relevant to the phonemic distinctions of adult speech and make possible the later acquisition of the corresponding adult phonemic categories.[42] As Miller and Eimas note, however, two points need to be kept in mind. First, although there appears to be a close relationship between the prelinguistic categories of infants and adult phonemic categories, languages differ in terms of which phonemic categories they use and the location of the acoustic boundaries between those categories. If the human brain is predisposed toward certain linguistic perceptual categories, these will have to be modified as children come to master their native languages.[43] Second, the fact that infants do not appear to discriminate between exemplars of the same adult phonemic category (the example of the two instances of [da]) can give rise to more than one inference. It may be that they are unable to discriminate (at least under the parameters of the testing situation) among different exemplars of the same adult phonemic category, a finding that would point most strongly to fairly fixed prelinguistic perceptual categories. But the same data might also indicate that although the differences among exemplars of the same phonemic category are distinguishable, other dimensions are more salient for purposes of categorization. In either case, however, the data clearly indicate that there is no one-to-one correspondence between the various acoustic properties of a given segment of speech (volume, pitch, duration, etc.) and its categorization by prelinguistic infants. Rather, these categorizations appear to be highly dependent on exposure to language and are refined and perfected (as compared to the phonemic categories employed by proficient adult speakers) through experience.[44]

Physiologically, the first year of an infant's development is characterized by the rapid maturation of the central nervous system and the establishment of speech centers in the left hemisphere of the brain. What the various studies of speech perception in prelinguistic infants suggest is that in this period of cognitive development, environmental stimuli begin to structure the brain such that particular acoustic markers become salient for purposes of categorization, while others are ignored and with time may no longer be subject to apprehension (such as when Japanese speakers no longer "hear" the difference between the sounds associated with the letters /l/ and /r/). In a series of studies—both with groups of subjects at different ages and with the same group of subjects over time—infants lose the ability to distinguish among sounds not found in their own language at roughly eight to ten months of age.[45] The loss of perceptual capacity does not appear to reflect a loss of ear function, but rather a structuring of cognition that is necessary for the parceling of sound and the acquisition of speech.

For example, a study of English speakers exposed to Zulu "clicks"—sounds that are quite different from anything found in the English language—found that adult speakers were quite adept at apprehending "clicks" under a variety of conditions. Moreover, in contrast to the diminished capacity to discriminate among foreign sounds that resemble sounds used in their native language, children tested in early infancy and again at approximately one year of age did not suffer from a loss of sensitivity to Zulu clicks.[46] What the data appear to demonstrate is that the cognitive capacity to perceive features that compete with phonetic segments of the native language is lost in the first year of development, whereas the capacity to perceive sounds that have no equivalent in the native language remains intact.[47] As one's native language is learned, the ability to perceive certain sounds declines, or is "forgotten." Hence, much as language structures our perception of spatial relationships and colors, it also structures our perception of sound. By providing the necessary cues, language makes possible the parceling of sound into meaningful categories, the existence and boundaries of which are neither universal nor uniform.

Parceling or abstracting from the complexities of the physical, social, or psychological world is the essence of conceptualization and a prerequisite for human thought and action. The human organism is certainly capable of extralinguistic conceptualization; however, as the examples above demonstrate, language interacts with, shapes, and structures our cognition beginning in the earliest stages of mental development. Language gives us cues as to which dimensions or characteristics of the physical world are relevant or meaningful for purposes of classification in a particular cultural context. There is no one-to-one correspondence between even the most basic features of the physical world and the concepts we use to apprehend, describe, and comprehend it. Different linguistic traditions give rise to different ways of experiencing the world, which in turn affect the way we think about the world.

Abstraction is in the first instance about bracketing: the establishment of boundaries or borders. In the process of conceptualization, a given aspect of the endless medium of experience and thought is bracketed on the basis of linguistically implicated cues or markers and thereby identified as an "instance" or "case" of something. Language—itself a system of conceptualization and categorization—not only provides the cues according to which phenomena and relationships can be identified, it also provides the medium through which the culturally appropriate borders of concepts and categories are established. For example, through a process of trial and error during upbringing and education, the child learns which extensions of a given word are accepted as legitimate—that is, convey meaning.[48] Likewise, when efforts to communicate meaning fail, proficient speakers will become aware of the bounds of legitimate extension.

But the range of possible extensions for any given concept is never completely articulated in a given linguistic community, nor can it be known in advance, given that novel situations and applications by definition cannot be anticipated. The logic of concept extension is one of analogy based on the recognition of culturally relevant cues or dimensions in a novel observation or thought and thus the extension of a preexisting concept to the novel situation. However, the "test" of an extension's appropriateness is found in efforts to employ the concept in communication. Where usage proves ineffective at conveying meaning, the concept has been misapplied.

The studies of color, spatial, and phonemic perception demonstrate that the boundaries of categories are not universally valid, but vary across linguistic communities.[49] Thus, what counts as a case of /l/ will be different for adult speakers of English and Japanese. However, variability in the boundaries of concepts can also be found within linguistic communities. Because the dimensions according to which one might discriminate among visual, tactile, or acoustic experiences are many, and because a given phenomena might comprise more than one culturally relevant dimension, a variety of categorizations might be accepted as appropriate. Extending a concept to an object or experience may then be less than straightforward, the implication being that the boundaries of concepts and categories will often be fluid or fuzzy.

Family Resemblance, Prototype Effects, and "Fuzzy" Concepts

Classical notions of concept formation and categorization were based on the assumption, either explicit or implicit, that good conceptual categories are characterized by clear boundaries that are established by attributes or properties common to members of the category. Most students of the scientific method would also assert that concepts, the building blocks of larger classificatory schemes as well as the classes or categories of such larger frameworks, are characterized by complexes of essential attributes, properties, or relationships that constitute membership.[50] Moreover, the criteria of clearly defined and operationalized concepts are generally held to be necessary conditions for scientific investigations of the natural or social world.

Classical notions of the requisites for good scientific concepts are influential in the social sciences, and the failure of social scientists to adhere to rigorous standards in the formation of concepts is routinely identified as a primary cause of theoretical underdevelopment.[51] Thus, lamenting the fact that "comparative politics, indeed political science itself, suffers from ambiguity and imprecision of concepts," the author of an introduction to comparative politics asserts: "Conceptualization should be clear and well formulated, devoid of ambiguity and a multiplicity of different meanings which may obfuscate connotation."[52] Bruce Bueno de Mesquita posits the superiority of quantitative over qualitative studies of international politics because the former "insists on explicit rules for defining variables" as well as "precise coding criteria," both of which he holds to be essential for the discovery of "underlying truth."[53] Similarly, Anatol Rapoport argues: "Rigorous theory . . . involves strict operation, predominantly mathematical, definitions of terms and logically compelling deductions."[54] And in a now classic article, Giovanni Sartori reacted to the widespread practice of what he termed "conceptual stretching" by arguing the necessity of precision in the specification of the "totality of characteristics any thing must possess" to be considered an example of a given concept. Guided by classical notions of what constitutes a useful scientific concept, Sartori maintained that precision in connotation is a necessary precondition for empirical testing.[55]

The classical conception, however, and the notions of science that rely upon it, are flawed. First, even the seemingly unproblematic spatial boundaries of physical entities dissolve under the lens of microphysics and can make the specification of necessary attributes or properties problematic. Second, many concepts defy definition in terms that would generate the clear borders Sartori seeks.

Concepts serve to order life experiences. Novel observations or experiences are comprehended in terms of mental representations, which are here called concepts. The extension of concepts is thus an exercise in the establishment of similarities across a range of observations. But similarity is itself a tricky concept as Nelson Goodman has pointed out. First, we often regard several particulars to be alike, even though none of them share any single quality in common. That is, "similarity cannot be equated with, or measured in terms of, possession of common characteristics." Concepts, it seems, are often generated by chains of overlapping dyadic likenesses.[56]

Ludwig Wittgenstein pointed out the difficulties of defending the position that concepts can be defined in terms of traits common to all exemplars through a philosophical analysis of the concept of a "game." His discussion merits citation at length:

> Consider for example the proceedings that we call "games." I mean board-games, card-games, ball-games, Olympic games, and so on. What is common to them all?—Don't say: "There *must* be something common, or they would not be called 'games'"—but *look and see* whether there is anything common to all.—For if you look at them you will not see something that is common to *all,* but similarities, relationships, and a whole series of them at that. To repeat: don't think, but look!—Look for example at board-games, with their multifarious relationships. Now pass to card-games; here you might find many correspondences with the first group, but many common features drop out, and others appear. When we pass next to ball-games, much that is common is retained, but much is lost.—Are they all "amusing"? Compare chess with noughts and crosses. Or is there always winning and losing, or competition between players? Think of patience. In ball games there is winning and losing; but when a child throws his ball at the wall and catches it again, this feature has disappeared. Look at the parts played by skill and luck; and at the difference between skill in chess and skill in tennis. Think now of games like ring-a-round-the-roses; here is the element of amusement, but how many other characteristic features have disappeared! And we can go through the many, many other groups of games in the same way; can see how similarities crop up and disappear.
>
> And the result of this examination is: we see a complicated network of similarities overlapping and crisscrossing: sometimes overall similarities, sometimes similarities of detail.[57]

What for Wittgenstein connects these various enterprises and constitutes them all as exemplars of the concept of a game are "family resemblances." Games form a "family" of activities that defy any precise definition or operationalization on the basis of essential attributes, properties, or relationships. Moreover, the boundaries of the family are not fixed:

> How should we explain to someone what a game is? I imagine that we should describe games to him, and we might add: "This and similar things are called 'games.'" And do we know any more about it ourselves? Is it only other people whom we cannot tell exactly what a game is?—But this is not ignorance. We do not know the boundaries because none have been drawn. To repeat, we can draw

a boundary—for a special purpose. Does it take that to make the concept usable? Not at all! (Except for that special purpose.) No more than it took the definition: 1 pace = 75 cm. to make the measure of length "one pace" useable. And if you want to say "But still, before that it wasn't an exact measure," then I reply: very well, it was an inexact one.—Though you still owe me a definition of exactness. . . . One might say that the concept "game" is a concept with blurred edges.—"But is a blurred concept a concept at all?"—Is an indistinct photograph a picture of a person at all? Is it even always an advantage to replace an indistinct picture by a sharp one? Isn't the indistinct one often exactly what we need?[58]

Wittgenstein draws our attention to the blurred or "fuzzy" edges around concepts that prove useful in everyday life. One person might choose to draw a rather fixed boundary around a concept, but that boundary might not correspond to another's boundary, if she has one at all.[59] What facilitates meaningful communication between two or more individuals is not conceptual congruence but rather a resemblance between the idiosyncratic concepts each employs.[60]

Two implications of Wittgenstein's notion of "blurred concepts" warrant emphasis. First, the proposition that the boundaries of concepts are usually, perhaps always, extendable. Extendibility may result from the emergence of a novel phenomenon that resembles an extant class of phenomena, for example the emergence of video "games" in the 1970s. Or it may result from the novel employment of a given concept, extending a concept with an established meaning in an unconventional or original fashion to a new domain, perhaps the extension of the concept "game" to the field of international politics.[61] Second, some instances of a given concept will be better examples than others. That is, concepts or classes are characterized by central and noncentral or marginal members. Wittgenstein gives the example of dice: "Someone says to me, 'Show the children a game.' I teach them gaming with dice, and the other says, 'I didn't mean that sort of game.'"[62] The point is that some games are more characteristic or representative of the class than others. When concepts are generated by means of extension from central or prototypical members, one can imagine a statement: "If anything is a case of x, then *this* is a case of x." It is harder to imagine someone saying: "If anything is a game, then throwing dice is a game." The attributes of dice would not appear to be central to the concept of game, yet dice can be understood to be a game.

A wide range of empirical studies of categorization and classification across cultures provides evidence to support Wittgenstein's philosophical ruminations on the nature of concepts. For example, studies of American Indian kinship systems found that kinship categories are generally based on a focal member and then extended to other, nonfocal individuals by means of certain rules. Thus, for the Fox tribe, the concept covering what speakers of English refer to as a maternal uncle—that is, one's mother's mother's son—is the same as that denoting "one's mother's mother's son's son, one's mother's mother's father's son's son, one's mother's brother's son, one's mother's brother's son's son, and a host of other relatives."[63] Although English speakers would distinguish between uncles and great uncles, for the Fox they are all members of the same kinship category. It is the existence of the focal member that leads to the generation of the class. He or she is central whereas others are not. For purposes of establishing kinship relations for the Fox:

> Anyone's father's sister, as a linking relative, is equivalent to that person's sister.[64]
> Any person's sibling of the same sex, as a linking relative, is equivalent to that person himself.
> Any child of one of one's parents (half-sibling) is one's sibling.[65]
> Thus, a mother's mother's father's sister's son is the equivalent of:
> A mother's mother's sister's son
> A mother's mother's son
> A mother's brother

Moreover, some members of this category, e.g., a mother's mother's sister's son and a mother's mother's son, are also members of the category "mother's brother," that is, they belong to two kinship categories at once. Thus, kinship categories for the Fox Indians are not distinct, and given the nature of the rules that give rise to a given kinship class, establishing class boundaries as well as any features common to all members of a given class is difficult, if not impossible.[66]

Insofar as they are characterized by focal members that give rise to a larger class or category by means of boundary extension, Fox kinship categories are similar in structure to the color categories uncovered by Berlin and Kay. Indeed, they represent a particular instance of a more general empirical phenomenon, the existence of *prototype effects*.

In a series of studies, Eleanor Rosch and her associates discovered that categories are generally characterized by the existence of "best examples," or what she termed prototypes, as well as other, less representative members. For example, when asked to identify the most "birdlike" in a sampling of birds that included robins, chickens, ostriches, and penguins, an overwhelming number of subjects will identify the robin. Similarly, a desk chair will be judged to be more representative of the category chair than a rocking chair or a barber's chair.[67] Rosch constructed a series of experiments both to test for and to measure prototype effects. First, subjects were asked to rate various members of a category in terms of their representativeness. Then they were asked to press a button to indicate the veracity of a statement such as "X is an example of Y" (e.g., "A chicken is a bird."), and their response times were measured. Rosch found that response times were shorter when subjects were presented representative examples than when confronted with marginal examples. In a third experiment, subjects were asked to list or draw examples of a given concept. Again, they overwhelmingly listed or drew more representative examples.[68]

Rosch's findings have been replicated across cultures in a number of anthropological studies. For example, in a study of folk classification of pottery in Mexico, Willet Kempton found strong evidence of prototype effects. Through extensive interviews, Kempton established native categories of pottery (roughly corresponding to such English-language concepts as jar, pot, pitcher, mug, and vase), eliciting the definitional features of a given term. Such descriptions generally mentioned function and easily describable features such as a handle or spout. Thus, a *jarro* is characteristically described as a one-handled vessel used for drinking, a *jarra* has one handle and a spout and is used for pouring, and an *olla* is a vessel with either two handles or no handles that is used for cooking.[69] Based on these native definitions, sheets of line-drawings were designed in which the identified features varied systematically; for example, the overall shape, the existence of one or two handles, or the existence of a spout. Within each sheet, variations among the drawings was gradual and monotonic. Adjacent drawings changed gradually in the same direction across and down the sheet.

When presented with the sheets and asked to identify which drawings corresponded to a given native category, subject responses routinely converged on particular shapes as focal, or "best examples" (indicated by Kempton as solid black). Moreover, the boundaries of a given concept (indicated by a line drawn around the drawings identified by respondents as valid examples) demonstrated certain overall gestalt effects, one of which was the importance of height-to-width ratios. Finally, respondents often identified outliers, drawings beyond the boundary that might under certain conditions be considered examples of a particular vessel (indicated by a dotted line).[70] The responses of a typical subject can be seen in figure 2.7.

Most formal definitions of concepts or categories require the delimitation of necessary attributes or properties such that an observer can establish whether a given phenomenon "is" or "is not" an example of the concept; by extension, this rules out the possibility that any one example is "better" than any other. Membership in the category is established on the basis of common features, and every member is of equal status as a category member. However, as the studies summarized above indicate, membership in conceptual categories is often graded. Some members are focal, central, or prototypical. Others, located at the fuzzy boundaries of a concept, are less central, or perhaps are only identified as exemplars under particular conditions.[71] The widespread existence of fuzzy boundaries and prototype effects for taxonomical concepts from both the physical (bird) and social (kinship categories) worlds suggests that widely held notions of the nature of conceptual categories and concept extension are not empirically valid and, indeed, are violated routinely.[72]

A skeptic or indeed critic of this claim might point out that for some categories, such as "tall," graded membership is quite understandable, as is the lack of any clear boundary between "tall" and "short" other than perhaps the mathematical mean, which is taken to be "average." She might even go further and argue that all I have done is stumble upon a rather basic distinction, namely that between discrete and continuous variables. However, two lines of rebuttal suggest themselves.

First, the problem with graded category membership as I have outlined it here is not the fact that individual exemplars are distinguishable on any given dimension or composite measures representing a combination of otherwise distinct dimensions. Rather, the problem is that the relevant dimensions according to which judgments of similarity or difference are made are not constant across the set denoted by a given concept. That is, we are faced with a problem of connotation: the collection of properties that determine the things to which a concept applies.[73]

For example, in the fields of comparative and international politics, the concept of democracy often figures prominently as an independent variable in explanations of such outcomes as a state's level of economic development, its foreign economic policy, or even its propensity to engage in armed conflict. Yet efforts to establish the properties of a political system that are both necessary and sufficient for denotation as democratic have proven futile. Although con-

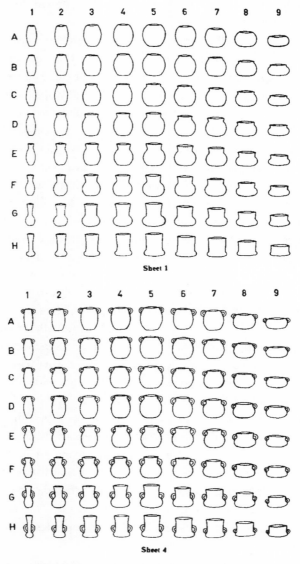

Fig. 2.6. Diagrams of vessels. From Kempton (1981), 44–45.

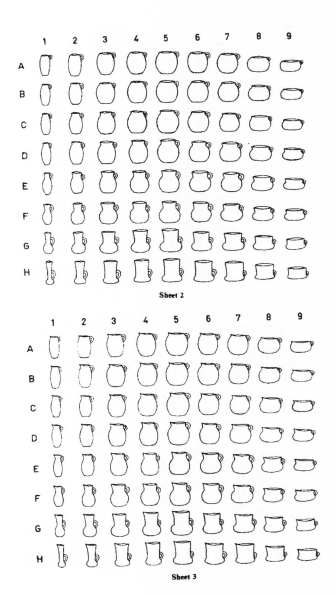

Sheet 2

Sheet 3

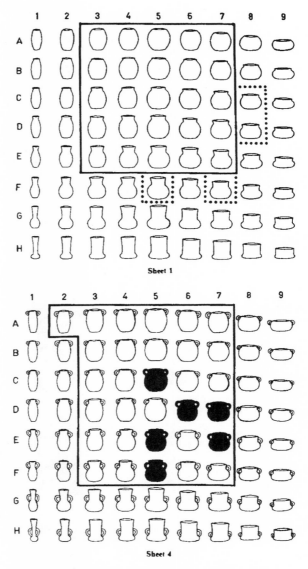

Fig. 2.7. Olla as identified by a 25-year-old factory worker from Axotla. From Kempton, (1981), 60–61.

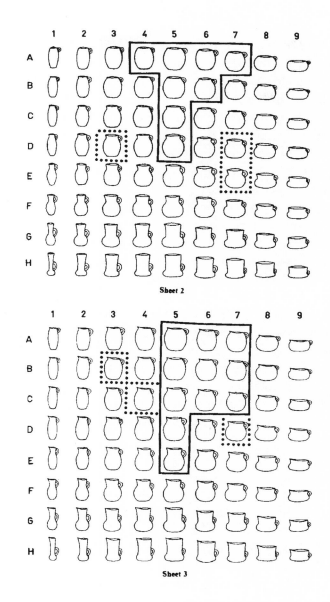

Sheet 2

Sheet 3

temporary debates over the definition and operationalization of democracy are the focus of detailed examination below, a simple illustration should suffice to make the more general point. Most contemporary democratic theorists would maintain that something approaching universal suffrage, competitive recruitment of candidates, competitive elections, and an independent judiciary are constitutive features of democratic systems. But the dimensions according to which polities constitute themselves are neither constant nor universal. Indeed, scholars are routinely confronted with systems that are clearly more democratic than not yet do not fit a "strict" operational definition. One need only mention the political system of Great Britain, where the remnants of feudalism persist in the form of a partially hereditary House of Lords.[74] As I will argue in the next chapter, an analysis of social scientific practice suggests that many scholars extend the concept of democracy on the basis of a given system's resemblance to an ideal or prototypical core.

The second objection is based on the relationship of conceptualization to the procedure of measurement. Establishing category membership (for example, the height requirements for inclusion in the category "tall") is logically prior to the question of measurement, as Sartori pointed out: "Measurement of what? We cannot measure unless we know first what it is that we are measuring. Nor can the degrees of something tell us what a thing is."[75] Conceptualization is the process of establishing what a thing is, and the "data" can never itself tell us what it is or where to draw the lines.

The Theory-Dependence of Concepts

As the foregoing discussion demonstrates, there is no one-to-one relationship between the phenomenological and the conceptual. Concepts do not result from direct access to the world but rather an experience of the world that is mediated by language. Observation may be possible in the absence of language, but conceptualization presupposes a system of meaning. The primary system for the construction of meaning is language. Higher-order systems of meaning are offered by substantive theories about the world, and thus many concepts arise from and are dependent on theory, which itself is embedded in and presupposes language.

Although the theory-dependence of both concepts and observation is widely accepted by philosophers of science, many empirically oriented social scientists have either missed or rejected these arguments. Some speak of "facts" and "events" as if they were self-evident and accessible to anyone who opens her eyes and looks for them. For example, in his examination of case study methods, Steven Van Evera speaks of "phenomena" and "cases," which theory can explain, but he never tells us what constitutes a case or how a given phenomenon is recognized as discrete, even as he claims to be concerned with "elementary points others omit."[76] And although they grant the theory-dependence of observation (or description), the authors of the most widely cited guide to methodology in the field of political science nonetheless assert that "description often comes first" and that "data collection efforts also differ in the degree to which researchers rigidly follow prior beliefs."[77]

Of course we always describe a situation *in terms of* preexisting concepts. And if scientists are not guided by some set of beliefs or criteria, on what basis can they select what is recorded as data or studied as a "case" from the universe of potential observations? Because the theory-dependence of concepts and observation will be central to subsequent discussion and analysis, its assertion requires some elaboration.

Let us begin the analysis once again with the concept of color, more precisely the color red. The standard inductivist notion of science—which is implicit in much social science writing—maintains that the origins of most of our basic scientific concepts are found in observations. Indeed, for the inductivist, the process of science starts with description or observation. When considering the genealogy of the concept "red," one inductivist argues: "From all the perceptual experiences of an observer arising from the sense of sight, a certain set of them (those corresponding to the perceptual experiences arising from sightings of red objects) will have something in common. The observer, by inspection of the set, is somehow able to discern the common element in these perceptions, and come to understand this common element as redness. In this way, the concept 'red' is arrived at through observation."[78] But as Chalmers points out, the construction is logically flawed, for it assumes that out of the endless number of perceptual experiences undergone by an individual, the set of experiences defined by the viewing of red objects is available for inspection. But how can this be so? The set of all red objects does not select itself. Rather, there must exist some criterion, according to which the observer parcels the infinite and creates a finite set. This criterion, of course, is the very concept of red whose origins the inductivist account seeks to explain.[79] Concepts are created, not found, and they are logically prior to observation.

Consider the flock of birds depicted in figure 2.8:

Fig. 2.8. Flock of birds. From Hanson (1958), 13.

For the scientist who believes that research is simply a matter of opening one's eyes and observing or collecting the "facts," the illustration depicts ten birds with rather long and open beaks. Consider now the animals depicted in figure 2.9:

Fig. 2.9. Herd of antelope? From Hanson (1958), 14.

What is one now to make of the proposition that figure 2.8 depicts a flock of birds? Is it perhaps a herd of antelope?[80]

Figures 2.8 and 2.9 demonstrate that observation is clearly more than just the collection of some brute "facts" that are "out there." A person who had never seen an antelope but had often seen birds *could not* see antelope in figure 2.9. And because most persons reading this text will have had more frequent exposure to birds than to antelope, I suspect that they would have seen birds upon first examination of figure 2.9 even had I refrained from providing a prior interpretive cue. In everyday life, context provides the cues that make observation possible amid complexity and ambiguity.

Observation is thus not merely a matter of apprehending lines and contours, colors, sounds, smells, tastes, or tactile sensations. Neither is it primarily about recognizing spatial and temporal connections. Rather, observation is a mental experience that requires the brain to organize, assemble, or integrate stimuli into a meaningful gestalt.[81] Thinking about how we recognize a broken chair (rather than a pile of wood) makes clear how the observation of a phenomenon is logically dependent on its prior existence as a mental construct.

In the first instance this is a function of language, for it is language that provides the basic concepts according to which we parcel our experience of the world. Such basic concepts, in turn, provide the building blocks for higher-order theories that help us make sense of experience by guiding observation toward putative relationships among concepts. These relationships may appear to be concrete or abstract. They may seem rather straightforward or relatively complex. But before we can observe the world at work, we need to know what we are looking for and how to observe it.

Observations of the world at work, and more importantly *observation statements,* are theory-dependent. Take, for example, the statement: "The tire is flat." Based on a rather simple observation, the statement is nonetheless theory-laden. It presupposes common knowledge of a particular class of rubber objects that are either flat or inflated depending on whether they contain a sufficient amount of air (or some other gaseous material). Even more theory is implied in the statement: "Look out, the wind is blowing the baby's buggy over the cliff!" The statement, both observation and prediction, assumes "that there is such a thing as wind, which has the property of being able to cause the motion of objects such as [buggies], which stand in its path. The sense of urgency conveyed by the 'Look out' indicates the expectation that the [buggy], complete with baby, will fall over the cliff and perhaps be dashed on the rocks beneath and it is further assumed that this will be deleterious for the baby."[82] That the buggy will indeed "fall" presupposes some understanding of physics, namely that most unsupported objects will fall to the earth's surface. Many observers of such an event would of course know that it is gravity that causes the buggy—once it has been blown over the cliff—to fall. But an account of motion that appeals to gravity is indeed theory-dependent, for gravity itself has never been directly observed.

The obvious objection to the claim that observation is theory-dependent is the notion that concepts must come from someplace, and if not from observation then where? In the social sciences the position is most evident among quantitatively oriented analysts guided by the measurement demands of statistical methods. Ferdinand Müller and Manfred Schmidt define concepts as "linguistic abstractions of observable phenomena."[83] And the belief that observation can somehow precede conceptualization is implied when in their "Rules for Constructing Causal Theories," King, Keohane, and Verba admonish scholars to "choose observable, rather than unobservable concepts whenever possible."[84]

In addition to the logical argument offered by Chalmers, three additional responses to such objections come to mind. First, the conceptual implications of experience are neither straightforward nor universal, as the examples from the discussion of spatial relationships make clear. There is no one-to-one relationship between what is "out there" and what different individuals or cultures perceive. Relatedly, the concept affixed to a particular worldly phenomenon is subject to change over time, even as the "observation" (here meant in the "Just open your eyes and see!" sense of the term) remains constant. Concepts and categories are evolving, continually emerging, and fading out. This is true for concepts relating to both "natural" and "social" kinds.

Consider the concept of species, which are (mistakenly, I believe) often taken to be an obvious example of natural kinds. But what precisely are *species*? The dominant view, the "biological species concept," is based on discriminations made by organisms themselves. Species are defined as clusters of populations of freely interbreeding organisms that are reproductively isolated from populations in other clusters.[85] Although it attempts to capture distinctions that are found in nature, the biological species concept is not without its shortcomings. First, it is difficult to identify a "population" independent of a preexisting species concept. Second, scholars differ on just how much interbreeding is compatible with the requirement of reproductive isolation. And finally, organisms whose reproduction is asexual or a function of hybridization are not captured by the definition.[86]

Since the eighteenth century, species have been named and categorized according to the system outlined by the Swedish botanist Carolus Linnaeus in *Systema Naturae*.[87] The Linnaean, or genus-species, system of biological classification, conceives of species in terms of family resemblances. Any given species is classified as belonging to a particular family or genus on the basis of its resemblance to a "type" specimen held to be most representative. For example, the common henbit weed (*Lamium amplexicaule*) is the genus type for the mint family. Any subfamily within the genus carries the name *Lamiodeae*. Over the course of four decades, however, *Lamium* has been reclassified three times. Reflecting changing judgments on the appropriate classification of henbit-like plants, three different subfamilies have borne the name *Lamiodeae* at one time or another.

Devised over a century prior to the publication of Darwin's theory of evolution, the Linnaean system more or less reflects a creationist view of the world.[88] Linnaeus regarded species as given and fixed entities and thus his classification system made no explicit provisions for within-species variation and evolution. But as acceptance of Darwinian theory has grown, so too has dissatisfaction with the Linnaean system. Biologists are now debating whether to drop the Linnaean system for one based on evolutionary or phylogenetic relationships wherein organisms would be grouped in "clades."[89] Under the new system, shared ancestry rather than morphology would determine category membership and the naming of species.[90] But as the focus of evolutionary analysis shifts to the level of the gene, determining clade membership turns out to be less than straightforward. Sometimes the analysis of one gene will lead to a different reconstruction of family heritage than will analysis of a different gene, with the result that organisms, perhaps even those specifying a clade, can shift in and out of clades accordingly.[91]

Social kinds—kinds of people, kinds of behavior, kinds of activity, kinds of acts—are likewise subject to evolution. Thus, Ian Hacking has chronicled how the Victorian concept of "cruelty to children," which produced a wide degree of social activism in late nineteenth-century Britain and America, faded from public notice by 1910. Owing to the influential and growing social work movement, attention shifted to the "root causes" of "neglected children." A man who beat his child was no longer considered "a wretch to be punished," but rather the member of a family in need of "family work." The contemporary concept of "child abuse" came about only in 1961–62, when a group of pediatricians in Denver, Colorado, used X-ray pictures of healed fractures that had gone unreported and unrecorded to argue that large numbers of children were being subjected to physical abuse. The gestalt shift had immediate repercussions. For example, what in a 1945 medical paper was termed "Infantile Cortical Hypertosis" was suddenly renamed "Battered Child Syndrome," a development with important medical, legal, and social implications.[92] One need go no further than the archaeological work of Michel Foucault to find further evidence that social kind concepts are subject to change, even as their empirical referents remain relatively constant.[93]

Second, many concepts for concrete or embodied entities—some of which are even cross-culturally valid—have no empirical referents. Terms for fairies, dragons, unicorns, and Martians are found in many languages, yet the claim of a "sighting" of any of them would most likely be greeted with a great deal of skepticism.[94]

Third, as the gravity example demonstrates, many of the most fruitful scientific concepts are not subject to direct (that is, merely language-mediated) observation. Newtonian concepts such as mass or force, Einstein's concept of energy, as well as concepts such as quantum states, all share the property of non-observability. The same is true of many social scientific concepts, including enmity, equity, affinity, loyalty, trust, interests, motives, intentions, preferences, or utility functions. These concepts are all derived from theory. They have their origins in and derive their meaning from theories of the world. That is, they are not properties of the world but properties of theories of the world. And as the multitude of competing theories makes clear, none of these theoretically derived concepts are directly implied by or reducible to observables.

That said, much of what constitutes scientific research is the identification of and empirical search for the *observable implications* of theories and theoretically derived concepts. It is the observable implications of theory-dependent concepts that we call "data" or "facts." Whereas members of a linguistic community may agree that a particular observation statement is an adequate description of a given situation (because they share a basic set of linguistically determined concepts), they still might disagree on its meaning, causes, or likely effects. That is, the same observations can be interpreted, or "coded," as one or more different kinds of data. Deciding what sort of data is represented in a particular observation statement is a matter of applying a theoretical concept to the statement. Data and facts are not found in the mind-external world, but rather in and via theories of the world.[95] The collection of data is always a theory-guided (or metatheory-guided) procedure.[96] Thus, the argument that "the best scientific way to organize facts is as observable implications of some theory" is not quite right.[97] It is the *only* way to organize facts!

Basic concepts are given to us through language and allow us to ask how the world hangs together. The answers to this question are theoretical and generate new theory-dependent concepts. These make possible new observations, which in turn generate new questions. Theories of complex processes or behaviors are built on foundations that are themselves theory- and/or language-dependent. Language and theory give us the concepts we use both to describe and to explain the world. In this sense, the world as it is understood through science is actually "created" by science. And science is made possible by language. Once the mind begins to construct a "world" on the basis of linguistic and theoretical concepts, thoughts and concepts cannot be disassociated from one another.[98] Thoughts and concepts become mutually constitutive.

Recognizing that even scientific concepts are often culturally bound, the anthropologist Clifford Geertz has sought to develop a method of analysis that, while being more than idiographic, is nevertheless not blatantly ethnocentric. Indeed, Geertz argues that through "thick description," concept and theory formation is possible:

> Ethnography is thick description. What the ethnographer is in fact faced with—except when (as, of course, he must do) he is pursuing the more automatized routines of fact collection—is a multiplicity of complex conceptual structures, many of them superimposed upon or knotted into one another, which are at once strange, irregular and inexplicit, and which he must contrive somehow first to grasp and then to render. And this is true at the most down-to-earth, jungle field work levels of his activity: interviewing informants, observing rituals, eliciting kin terms, tracing property lines, censusing households . . . writing his journal. Doing ethnography is like trying to read (in the sense of "construct a reading of") a manuscript—foreign, faded, full of ellipses, incoherencies, suspicious emendations, and tendentious commentaries, but written not in conventionalized graphs of sound but in transient examples of shaped behavior.[99]

The ethnographer of whom Geertz speaks is not engaged in thick description with the aim of generating *original* concepts. Rather, the goal is to uncover the conceptual categories already at play in a given subject culture, concepts which are only partially comprehensible to the observer, and only *in terms of* familiar (preexisting) concepts: "In finished anthropological writings, including those collected here, this fact—that what we call our data are really our own constructions of other people's constructions of what they and their compatriots are up to—is obscured because most of what we need to comprehend a particular event, ritual, custom, idea, or whatever, is insinuated as background information before the thing itself is directly examined."[100]

Anthropology is, of course, an artifact. It is usually written down. In writing down a passing event, the anthropologist is forced to translate his newly acquired understandings of foreign concepts into a language that is familiar to his colleagues. Geertz himself admits to resorting to a "repertoire of very general, made-in-the-academy concepts and systems of concepts—'integration,' 'rationalization,' 'symbol,' 'ideology,' 'ethos,' 'revolution'" in his own thick description of Indonesian and Moroccan culture, "in the hope of rendering mere occurrences scientifically eloquent. . . . Thus it is not only interpretation that goes all the way down to the most immediate observational level: the theory upon which such interpretation conceptually depends does so also."[101] Thus, even the interpretive social sciences, such as the anthropology practiced by Geertz and his students, is constrained (though also enabled) by extant theoretical concepts.[102]

Scientific Concepts

In the previous sections I argued that conceptualization is in the first instance a function of language and that higher-order concepts—those relating to the workings of the world—have their origins in and derive their meaning from theory. Cognitive science has provided us with strong and reliable cross-cultural evidence that nonverbal coding for memory and inference as well as verbal description are heavily influenced by first principles, which are internalized during the period of language acquisition. Infants confront a world that has both a physical and a social structure, some of which might appear quite patterned, other parts of which must seem highly variable. Implicit categorizations of prelinguistic children become explicit when expressed in language that itself is based on categorical structures. If infants had no extralinguistic capacity for categorization, then they could not learn language. However, the use of language requires a reparsing of experience into the categories of language, "effectively re-representing experience in a new culturally shared representational mode."[103]

In stressing the language- and theory-dependence of conceptualization, I do not mean to imply that cognitive and semantic representations are necessarily equivalent. Indeed, one can quite easily demonstrate that this cannot be the case.[104] What I am arguing, however, is that language and theory structure our thoughts in nontrivial ways and provide the media through which observation, communication, and the generation of knowledge become possible. Arbitrary experiences or conjectures that are remembered in terms of a private inner code, which cannot be translated into a public linguistic code, thus cannot be described at all. Hence the need or desire for communication on the part of human beings requires the coding of experience in terms that support linguistic description.

Concepts, being created rather than found, are mental representations of elements or experiences parceled from the limitless time and space of the physical, social, or psychological worlds. A *scientific concept* is the intersubjectively valid linguistic expression of a concept used to explain some aspect of human thought or experience. Because my claim is radical in its simplicity, let me be clear. The criteria for judging the scientific status of a concept are whether it can be given linguistic expression in a fashion that generates *some* shared meaning, and whether it is useful for making sense of the world we live in. Concepts that cannot be expressed in a way that generates a minimum degree of shared meaning or that cannot be used to help generate explanations of the world are unscientific.

My definition is unorthodox as the myriad objections to it will make clear. Surely there is more to "scientific" status than intersubjectivity. What about precision? What about operationalizability? What about the criteria of objectivity, generalizability, universality, and the like? And how are we to differentiate scientific concepts from nonscientific concepts found in religion or mythology? Let me address each of these objections in turn.

Most scientists would agree with the position that clearly defined concepts are prerequisites for good theory.[105] If we cannot define our concepts, we probably have not given enough thought to what we mean when we employ them. And though often undervalued as a contribution to scientific discourse, conceptual analysis, by exposing imprecision and incoherence in a given definition, can often move a stalled research program back on track.[106] Moreover, if we cannot define what we mean, we cannot communicate. Insofar as the goal of science is to discover and disseminate warranted knowledge, communication is central to the enterprise.

Elevating definitional clarity to evaluative status is not in and of itself a problem. Often, however, the invoked standards of clarity are themselves imprecise, implied to be unproblematic, or applied in idiosyncratic fashion. Thus, John Mearsheimer criticizes liberal and constructivist scholars for employing a concept of institutions defined so broadly that it has little "analytic bite," although the structural theory of international politics that he promotes has failed to produce consensus over the value of key variables or expected outcomes across a range of cases—even among the theory's strongest proponents.[107] Similarly, Michael Desch criticizes the use of culture as a variable in explanations of international outcomes because culture is "hard to clearly define and operationalize," even as he appeals to the explanatory leverage of the international structure and the notoriously nebulous concept of state power.[108]

The point is not so much to criticize one or the other group of scientists for imprecision. Rather I wish to forward the claim that definitions are better thought of as *imprecise,* their imprecision being a matter of degree. Definitions of a given concept are always provided *in terms of* other known concepts, the most basic of which are everyday language terms.[109] And as the application of these is never uniform or precise (e.g., because the borders of concepts are often fuzzy), apparent definitional precision always rests on a suspension of analysis.

In science, some things simply have to be left unexamined, for if they are not, infinite regress will cripple the entire enterprise.[110] "To take a straightforward example, suppose I am faced with the problem of justifying Kepler's first law, that planets move in ellipses around the sun. If I do this first by showing that its approximate validity follows from Newton's laws my justification is incomplete unless I can justify Newton's laws. If I attempt to justify Newton's laws by appeal to experimental evidence then the question of the validity of the experimental evidence arises, and so on. If the problem of the infinite regress is to be avoided, it would seem that what is needed is some set of statements that do not need to be justified by appeal to other statements but are in some sense self-justifying."[111] Because the search for ultimate foundations or self-justifying statements is futile, at some point we have to assume that a majority of colleagues "know what we mean." Only when we can assume that terms according to which any given scientific concept is defined are generally understood are we able to proceed with the business of theory construction and empirical research.[112]

It is worth noting that my definition of scientific concepts does allow one to reject as nonscientific what Sartori has referred to as self-contradictory "cat-dog" amalgams.[113] Concepts that are recognized to be internally incoherent or self-contradictory by proficient speakers cannot be said to convey meaning in any "meaningful" sense of the term.[114] Although I shall argue that the limits to, rather than possibilities for, operational precision and universality are of greater relevance to scientific practice, I do not mean to imply that efforts to reduce vagueness, ambiguity, and inconsistency in pursuit of conceptual coherence are misguided.[115]

Inherent Limits to Operational Precision

In a very thoughtful contribution to the discourse on social science methods, Arthur Stinchcombe argued that scientific concepts are those "which can take on various values such that we can tell by observation which value it has in a particular case."[116] Indeed, in order to move from definitions to empirical research, concepts need to be operationalized. An operational definition details the criteria by means of which an investigator can determine whether a concept does or does not apply in a given case.[117] This has sometimes been referred to as the "necessary knowledge" criterion. Following a common-sense form of logic, the investigator seeks to determine whether a given observation represents an instance of some concept or not: either x or not-x. To do so requires a catalogue of the observable features, traits, properties, or behaviors that represent the necessary and sufficient criteria for extension of a general concept to a particular instance.

Good operational definitions are held to produce high levels of reliability. That is, by providing clear guidelines according to which researchers can "code" a particular observation as a case of x or not-x, variance in coding does not diminish significantly as the number of independent observations increases. Inter-coder reliability is routinely held to be necessary for the replication of results, which proponents of both quantitative and qualitative methods regard as an evaluative criterion of good science.[118]

Alleged low degrees of inter-coder reliability have produced heated scholarly debates in the social sciences. For example, Richard Ned Lebow and Janice Gross Stein criticized a widely used dataset for the testing of propositions derived from models of the proponents of rational deterrence theory. Examining fifty-four cases of alleged deterrence encounters, Lebow and Stein found only nine to fit the definition as operationalized by Paul Huth and Bruce Russett, who compiled the original dataset.[119] Without a widely agreed-upon dataset, Lebow and Stein are skeptical that competing explanatory claims will ever be resolved.[120]

The problem is not limited to the social sciences. For example, the hypothesis that the relationship between economic growth and environmental degradation can be plotted as an inverted-U—rising at lower levels of income and falling at higher levels—has been challenged because "none of the pollutants unequivocally shows an inverted-U relationship where studies have been done by more than one group of researchers."[121] Similarly, low levels of inter-coder reliability plague the medical sciences and have frustrated efforts to formulate a consensus on issues relating to the spread and treatment of disease.[122]

The proposition that the prospects for cumulation of knowledge increases when scientific concepts are clearly operationalized seems persuasive enough. The question, however, is what is thereby understood. Because many of our most basic concepts refer to what are sometimes regarded as *natural kinds,* that is, objects or phenomena of the physical world that can be held to exist independent of human agency or thought, often we begin to believe that the world as apprehended by our concepts is *precisely so.* That is, we take the naturalness of our concepts so much for granted that we forget that their origins are found in linguistic or theoretical structures.

The problem is compounded when we introduce concepts that are not directly observable, or that reflect *social kinds,* which are the products of human thought and agency. No one has ever directly observed gravity, only its putative effects. The same is true of socially determined "structures," such as the market or the international balance of power. While we may be able to observe the effects of such structures on the behavior of actors, we cannot observe the structures themselves. Other concepts refer to inner and unobservable qualities or traits of observable social actors that are held to affect or be reflected in observable behavior. Examples include such concepts as love, compassion, fairness, envy, greed, or hate.

Operationalization is essentially yet another, although somewhat more specific, exercise in the definition of one concept in terms of other established concepts of generally accepted meaning. Whereas the operationalization of natural kinds may provide for more or less direct observation according to features accessible through our senses (directly or assisted by the use of measuring instruments), operational definitions of unobservables direct us to second-order observations, and may further obscure the cultural, linguistic, or theoretical boundedness of basic concepts or expectations.

Take the example of a "concerned" or "loving" mother. Whereas a dictionary might define concern as "regard for or interest in someone or something," and love as "an intense affectionate concern for another person," neither of these definitions lends itself to straightforward observation.[123] Thus one is forced to identify observable behaviors that would be consistent with "regard or interest" or "intense affectionate concern."

Now imagine for a moment an infant child is heard crying in its bedroom, where it had been sleeping in a crib. What would a concerned and loving mother do?

Almost everyone reading this text would expect the mother to check on the child and attempt to comfort it. Perhaps she will bring the child into another room with the rest of the family, change the diaper, or provide a bottle. That the ascription of concern or love to a particular mother should give rise to expectations along these lines would appear straightforward enough. Moreover, one might legitimately question the love and concern of a mother who remained aloof or unmoved by the cries of an infant left alone in another room, especially in the absence of some more pressing or immediate concern to inhibit her. If one were tasked with operationalizing the concept of a "loving mother," one might consider including precisely such behavioral indicators.

These operational criteria are not, however, universally valid. They are deeply rooted in a theory of behavior that is left unexamined. If one were to apply them to mothers in many Asian societies, the resulting codings would be erroneous. Anthropological studies have uncovered that whereas we in the West try to promote individuation and self-sufficiency in our young, many Asian cultures are devoted to fostering group identity over individuality, a goal not without implications for child-rearing. In most western societies, one of the first efforts to instill a sense of independence and individuality during infancy takes the form of moving the child as early as possible to its own room and leaving it to sleep on its own. A crying child is no longer asleep. Its cries alert the mother to some immediate need.

By contrast, in many Asian societies, the entire family sleeps together; during waking hours, infants are almost constantly bundled to their mothers. A person from such a society would most likely find it odd that a child was left to sleep alone. Indeed, the love and concern of the mother might be thereby called into question. But an Asian child who in the presence of his family begins to cry represents a threat to the group's tranquility and is likely to be promptly removed to a room and left alone until it is once again quiet. A loving mother in such a society shows concern insofar as she teaches her child the importance of not disturbing the group's repose.[124]

While this example points to the difficulties involved in the articulation of operational criteria with cross-cultural validity, the widespread finding of prototype effects suggests that reliable operationalization, measurement, and coding are often quite difficult within a single linguistic group. Rather than work their way through checklists of necessary and sufficient conditions for the application of a concept to a particular case (e.g., the application of the term *olla* in Mexican pottery classification), people often assimilate novel experiences or observations to the category generated by the prototype. The data find high levels of inter-coder reliability on prototypical or focal examples of a given concept but relatively low levels of inter-coder reliability in the extension of a concept beyond the focal core. Not only do codings vary across individuals from the same cultural or linguistic group, but there are relatively low levels of reliability with the same individual and same data when the data are presented in different environmental contexts.[125]

Although the widespread finding of graded category membership and prototype effects would appear to produce low levels of inter-coder reliability in the application of concepts, members of the same cultural or linguistic community rarely find this to be a significant obstacle to communication or industry. Similarly, there are good reasons to doubt that a high degree of operational precision is either a necessary or particularly useful criterion for the development of scientific concepts. Indeed, Hempel appears to have recognized this when he wrote: "It would be unreasonable to demand, however, that *all* the terms used in a given scientific discipline be given an operational specification of meaning; for then, the process of specifying meaning of the defining terms, and so forth, would lead to infinite regress. In any definitional context (quite independent of the issue of operationalism), some terms must be antecedently understood; and the objectivity of science demands that the terms which thus serve as a basis for the introduction of other scientific terms should be among those used with a high degree of uniformity by different investigators in the field."[126] Hempel is unclear as to how one would determine when investigators are using such operational terms with a high degree of uniformity. Indeed, I suspect we rarely stop and check. What matters is whether or not others appear to understand what we mean. Indeed, when speaking of "objectivity," Hempel means precisely that: "The objectivity, or intersubjectivity, here under discussion is of course a matter of degree, and it should be remembered that also the results of such 'operations' as observing an object by microscope or telescope, or a lung via fluoroscope or indirectly through an X-ray photograph, show intersubjective variation even among expert observers. What matters is, I think, to be aware of the extent to which subjective factors enter into the application of a given set of concepts, and to aim at gradual reduction of their influence."[127]

Hempel uses three terms. The first is "objectivity," which in the practice of science he equates with the second, "intersubjectivity." Intersubjectivity is the basis for scientific communication, but even "experts" are likely to employ a given concept in less than uniform fashion. Finally, he refers to "subjectivity." It is the influence of idiosyncratic or subjective opinions that Hempel seeks to minimize.

The precision and generalizability of operational definitions are limited by their linguistic and theoretical origins. The dogmatic position that high levels of inter-coder reliability are a prerequisite for scientific progress and can be achieved by the ever more precise operational definition of scientific concepts misconstrues the nature of definitions. It assumes that at some level, our basic concepts are defined by necessary and sufficient conditions that are "out there" and observable from some Archimedean position. But as Richard Rorty puts it, "no interesting descriptive term has any interesting necessary and sufficient conditions."[128] As is the case with first definitions, the specification of operational measures for our concepts requires that we at some point suspend analysis and accept that scientific concepts are "nested" in more basic and general conceptual categories given to the investigator through language.

The Virtues of Imprecision

Recent work in linguistic pragmatics suggests that, contrary to the widely held belief that precision promotes the effective conveyance of meaning, a certain degree of *imprecision* is essential for effective communication. Consider the example provided by Levinson:

> If I say *Some of my books are missing,* what I probably mean or intend is "some but not all of my books are missing." I don't need to spell that out given pragmatic principles governing quantifier interpretation. Of course I could have said *Some but not all of my books are missing,* but I might then have implied that there was a distinct corresponding thought, namely that it was possible or even likely that all of my books might have been missing. Similarly, I didn't spell out what the thought behind the expression "my books" was: I might have had in mind the

books I own, the books I wrote, the books I had on my bookshelf (some of which belonged to the library and to friends), etc. If I had said *Some of the books I own are missing,* I might have implied that the ones borrowed from the library are not missing, and so on. Thus not only do pragmatic principles allow us to be succinct—to say less than we think—they also make it difficult to be fully explicit, for then we invariably imply more than we intended. . . . The more explicit I try to be, the more unintended implicatures I will generate.[129]

Similar confusion often results from efforts to achieve precise operational measures of social scientific concepts, a point I shall return to.

The claim I am making is not that our concern for operational precision is completely misplaced. Rather, I am skeptical of the claim that through clearer definitions and more precise operationalization, competing claims about the world can be resolved and the "truth" thereby neared. The basic point is that behind operationalization, measurement, and coding lie theory and language. When we accept data we are accepting the limits of the theory and language behind it.[130] Because theory- and language-dependence imply the absence of generally valid, absolute, or neutral standards for judging the adequacy of a given operational definition, the labeling of a concept as "unscientific" on the allegation of its poor operationalizability is unjustified.

Science versus Religion

Finally, let me address a potential objection to my notion of scientific concepts arising from the proposition that science is significantly different from other structures of meaning, such as religion or myth, and thus that concepts anchored in scientific understandings of the world should be accorded a different status from nonscientific concepts.[131] One might start with the question of how it is that we differentiate between what constitutes religion on the one hand, and myth, on the other. The distinction, I would assert, is purely conventional and changes with time. Hence the religions of classical Greece and Rome are today taught in universities as studies in "mythology" whereas similar investigations into the tenets of Christian or Jewish religions constitute studies in "theology."

The same can be said of our differentiating science from nonscientific forms of inquiry. Naïve conceptions of science maintain that its claim to special status is based on it *method.* As Karl Pearson wrote: "The field of science is unlimited; its material is endless; every group of natural phenomena, every phase of social life, every stage of past or present development is material for science.

The unity of all science consists alone in its method, not its material."[132] Through adherence to specific rules of inference, fact can be distinguished from mere opinion, "truth" from speculation.

But because the set of all possible observations cannot be defined, there is no method of proving scientific theories to be true, or even probably true. Once one accepts the theory-dependence of observation—that "facts" and their measurement are functions of theory—then one is confronted with a situation wherein theories cannot be *disproved*. For how can we conclusively falsify a theory on the basis of observations that are themselves the products of fallible theory?[133] Hence it is difficult to sustain the claim that we can differentiate scientific from nonscientific bodies of knowledge on the basis of their falsifiability.

Moreover, as Thomas Kuhn discovered, the claim that the history of science is characterized by a rational process of methods-driven research and the cumulation of knowledge, one that brings us ever nearer to the truth, cannot be sustained. The major scientific advances—the innovations of Galileo, Newton, Darwin, and Einstein—were neither method-driven nor programmatic, but resulted from scientists asking questions "beyond the scope" of existing theoretical understandings.[134] Further, the acceptance of innovations by a wider community of scientists often has little to do with their correspondence to "empirical reality." Rather, paradigm shifts, and with them large-scale changes in the conceptual categories employed by researchers, come about through a process that resembles a religious conversion.[135]

A final and, I think, not insignificant response to the claim that scientific concepts are qualitatively different from concepts found in religion or myth is the undeniably intimate connection between science and religion. Thus, the emergence of Copernicus cannot be explained apart from the context of a Catholic Church in crisis and the discursive space opened by the Reformation.[136] But there is an even deeper connection.

Science shares some of the most basic assumptions of religion. Primary among these is the conviction that there is an order to the universe, one that is accessible and comprehensible. One need not accept the specificity of Carl von Weizsäcker's claim—that the incredible success of science rests on its Christian origins—to grant that many of the most basic concepts of science are secularized versions of preexisting religious terms.[137] At least since the writings of René Descartes, numerous concepts whose origins were previously understood to be located in divine revelation have been simply appropriated to the service of science and continue to inform scientific inquiry today.[138] Secularization, from this standpoint, is not the simple disintegration or dissolution of religion. Rather, it constitutes a transformation in which religious values are conserved through their incorporation in institutional ideologies, science among these.[139] The magisteria of science and religion overlap because they share a common heritage.[140]

The phenomenon is equally evident in political thought. The notion of the political equality of men, central to modern democratic theory, is directly traceable to the Christian conception of the equality of men before God. Kant's *telos* of "perpetual peace" under the rule of "pure reason" can be seen as a secularized formulation of Christian teachings regarding the relations of men in the "fullness of time."[141] The religious underpinnings of the constitutions and legal systems that give rise to the institutions of the modern state demonstrate that much institutionalist analysis is built on a conceptual foundation that is in part theological.[142] Recognizing the strong link between modern political science and religious ideas regarding the appropriate "order" of human relations, Carl Schmitt concluded: "The most fruitful concepts used in the modern study of the state are secularized theological concepts."[143]

Religion and myth exist independent of an individual's mental state or private beliefs. The same, however, cannot be said of all superstitions. What differentiates religion or myth from private superstition is a certain degree of intersubjectivity. Similarly, a paradigm, theory, or fact has scientific status by virtue of its acceptance by more than one member of the community of scientists. Scientific theories exist and have implications independent of any individual theorist, even the theorist who first articulates them.[144] Scientific concepts are no different.

Of course science and religion *are* different. But the principle difference is not found in the nature of the concepts each employs. Rather it is found in a basic orientation to the subject of inquiry. Science prospers on the skeptical search for meaning guided by the human capacity for reason. Religion challenges us to suspend disbelief and reason, and offers meaning in return.

CHAPTER THREE

Scientific Concepts and the Study of Politics

In chapter 2, I argued that scientific concepts are nothing more than linguistic expressions of mental constructs that generate some degree of shared meaning among individuals who use them in an effort to explain the world. They have their origins in theories of the world and, at a more basic level, the natural languages in terms of which they are ultimately defined. Languages, as we have seen, parcel the endless seam of space and time in very different ways. Robust cross-cultural studies suggest that our most basic concepts are formed around a prototype or focal "core" and extended as new exemplars are assimilated on the basis of resemblance. Because necessary and sufficient criteria for category membership are either lacking or ignored, the borders of concepts are not always, perhaps even rarely, distinct. Instead they frequently display a "fuzzy" character and fade as one moves further away from the prototypical core.

In this chapter, I explore some of the implications of my argument for the scientific study of politics. Because I stress the notion that concepts are created and not found, I begin with a discussion of constructivism and the constructivist turn in political science. Although constructivists have been quite successful in their efforts to persuade scholars of the conventional nature of scientific concepts, they have largely ignored the important question of whether concepts can be defined in terms of necessary and sufficient criteria. In a second step, I turn to an analysis of the arguments of those who, recognizing that many concepts cannot be operationalized in terms of necessary and sufficient conditions, have proposed gradation as a substitute for categorization with respect to the extension of concepts. The discussion then moves to an analysis of ideal types and prototypes. I will argue that the assimilation of new experiences or observations to concepts or categories that have ideal-typical or prototypical cores is common to both the study and praxis of politics. The chapter ends with a discussion of the implications of these arguments for claims regarding radical incommensurability in the social sciences and some thoughts on judgment.

The Constructivist Turn

The proposition that concepts are human inventions and bear no one-to-one correspondence to the mind-external world is a basic premise of constructivism, an epistemological position that—although implicit in older studies—has become increasingly influential and explicit in the study of politics since the mid-1980s.[1] For constructivists, the world as we experience it is largely "of our making."[2] And social constructivists are committed to the basic proposition that human behavior rests on an irreducible intersubjective base. Although some constructivists would argue that the material and social worlds are distinct and that constructivism is best limited to analyzing the class of "facts" that do not exist in the material world, many would go further, arguing that the material is important only insofar as humans accord it significance.[3]

With roots in the sociology of Emile Durkheim and Max Weber, social constructivism maintains that the wide range of human action cannot be reduced to the utilitarian calculations of unproblematic agents, but must be understood as resulting from identities and interests, which are themselves social products. In order to give an adequate account of behavior, we have to "go beyond the concept of utility" as related to an individual actor by uncovering the deeper collectively held and generated normative understandings of those ends.[4] Because they are *collective* understandings and not individual beliefs, interests and identities exist independent of and are not reducible to the properties or desires of any individual actor. As such, they constitute "social facts." Social facts comprise such diverse elements as moral norms, religious beliefs and practices, family structures, gender roles and identities, and language. In the field of international politics, nationalism, the state, as well as such concepts as sovereignty, legitimacy, and authority constitute social facts by virtue of their intersubjectivity and production or reproduction through practice.[5] Constructivist analyses have focused on the origins of sovereignty as a basic constitutive norm of the international system,[6] the ways in which international institutions socialize new states to the practices of the international system,[7] the collective understandings that gave rise to the post–World War II international economic order,[8] the construction of national identities,[9] and the ways the particular content of Arab nationalism interacts with the existence of a multiplicity of Arab states to produce foreign policy outcomes that are at variance with those of other regions.[10] Moreover, constructivist scholars have challenged the notion that the implications of the material features of international life are unproblematic and fixed. Thus, Alexander Wendt has argued that the nuclear arsenals of Britain or France do not have the same effects on the foreign policy of the United States as do the much smaller arsenals of states such as Iraq and North Korea.[11] Donald MacKenzie demonstrates that "accuracy" is not an inherent property of nuclear-armed ballistic missiles but must be viewed as an historical product and social construct that developed independent of strategic necessity.[12] And Geoffrey Herrera argues that the meaning of telecommunications technology for politics is neither straightforward nor fixed and will ultimately depend on its embeddedness in social practice.[13]

Because collective understandings and the significance actors attach to the material features of international politics are ideational phenomena, social constructivist explanations place great emphasis on the role of ideas in motivating behavior and thus seek to uncover the meanings, self-understandings, and reasons that produce any given outcome or pattern of interaction.[14] As concepts are ideational phenomena and scientific concepts the linguistic expression of intersubjective ideas, the origins, applications, and characteristics of scientific concepts should be of great interest to constructivists. Indeed, the processes of concept formation and their effects is what constructivism is all about.

In the field of international politics, the first wave of constructivist scholarship was largely devoted to demonstrating the limitations of materialist theories and demonstrating to a skeptical audience that social rules and norms are important to the explanation of human behavior.[15] This was largely accomplished by identifying behavior that was inconsistent with materialist theories and demonstrating how a rule-based understanding of human action could account for this residual variance. As constructivist scholarship has moved beyond this rather limited focus, analysis has increasingly been directed toward identifying the various pathways through which ideas come to shape international politics.[16] But constructivist scholars have only recently begun to analyze the critical question of how concepts are formed and transformed.[17]

Because they address the most basic feature of social construction, the findings of cognitive scientists should be of interest to constructivist scholars. Take, for example, the prevalence of graded concepts and prototype effects. The Berlin and Kay studies found that although there is cross-cultural variation in the ways in which the light spectrum is parceled into conceptual color units, the process is not entirely random. Basic color terms were found to exist in all languages, and the number of such terms never exceeds eleven, each corresponding to a color concept characterized by a best or focal example. Moreover, there exists a high degree of cross-cultural agreement on the focal core of basic colors. Although not every culture makes use of all eleven basic color terms, there are regularities with respect to which terms they do use. Hence, when languages divide the color spectrum into two categories, they correspond to the English terms black and white. When three are used, they correspond to black, white, and red. The pattern is systematic all the way up to those cultures that employ all eleven.

At least with respect to some features of the physical world, the range within which the construction of meaning through concept formation takes place appears to be bounded. The cross-cultural agreement on what constitutes a focal example or the patterned progression in the number of basic color terms employed across languages imply that the optical cues we term color have systematic effects on human physiology.[18] Although these effects are systematic, they are not uniform, as the variation in the number of basic colors recognized by different cultures demonstrates.

Equally important from the standpoint of constructivism is the finding that the boundaries of color categories vary. That is, even when two cultures have a concept "red" and even if there is a high level of agreement on what constitutes the "best," or focal, example of "red," there is a high degree of cross-cultural variation in what constitutes an example of "red" or where the borders of this color are located. Moreover, the borders of color concepts are not stable even with respect to a given individual, having been shown to vary according to context.[19]

The construction of meaning thus takes place at two points. First, with respect to the concepts with which a given culture will apprehend the world. Second, and I believe not fully appreciated by most constructivist scholars, in the application of preexisting concepts to new cases. Applying a general concept to a particular case is the first step in comprehension and a prerequisite for reflection, understanding, and ultimately goal-directed action, as it unites the practice and science of politics. The latter statement may be taken in one of two senses.

On the one hand, every student of politics is engaged in the application of concepts to particular cases in pursuit of explaining or understanding political outcomes. For positivist scholars, some of whom are constructivists, this involves the search for general laws that are held to govern political life.[20] Interpretivist or reflexivist scholars, having rejected the proposition that politics is a nomothetic domain, seek to uncover the ideas that governed actors' behavior in a particular case. Through empathy, the interpretivist seeks to understand the subject's application of a concept within the larger intersubjective systems of the collectivity of which he is a member. Both approaches, however, involve the evaluation of novel situations in terms of preexisting concepts.

The findings that concept extension involves assimilating novel observations or experiences on the basis of resemblance to prototypical or core exemplars and produces graded-membership and fuzzy borders and that there is considerable variability across individuals and contexts with respect to assimilating marginal exemplars, suggest that the least systematic construction of meaning is taking place at the margins of concepts rather than at the core.[21] I suspect that shifts in the focal core of a given concept are relatively rare, whereas extension of a given concept to new exemplars is quite common. Because there is a relatively high degree of inter-coder reliability with regard to what constitutes the prototypical or focal exemplars of concepts, but less reliability with respect to precisely where the borders of a given concept are drawn, understanding the processes of assimilation is key to uncovering underlying causes of behavior and will likely require an examination of psychological processes.

One suspects that the concepts informing the practice and study of international politics are characterized by similar dynamics. That political decision makers assimilate incoming information to preexisting images has been well established since Robert Jervis first brought widespread attention to the relevance of cognitive consistency models to the study of international politics.[22] Thus, during World War II, "British photographic analysts who thought that any German rockets would be huge and located next to a rail line saw only a vertical column in some pictures from Peenemünde, [whereas] another analyst who expected that the rockets would be smaller and more mobile recognized that the 'column' was an upright rocket."[23] Similarly, in the late 1980s, American leaders were slow to recognize the revolution in Soviet foreign policy that Mikhail Gorbachev had initiated. Even Gorbachev's December 1988 announcement of deep unilateral cuts in the Red Army's forward-deployed forces was regarded in Washington as consistent with a communist political system driven inexorably by expansionist aims.[24]

Even when not related to matters involving conscious political interpretation, cognitive consistency models infer the operation of mechanisms that are premised on at least middle-range theories about the world and generally have not been cast at the lower level of judgments over the extension of basic concepts to new observations. If prototype effects are widespread, then similar dynamics would appear to govern these more fundamental levels of perception and cognition. Although Jervis in fact says as much, there remains a tension between an argument based on the notion that perception is governed by preexisting concepts, which are themselves anchored in language or theory, and the notion that a given observation might constitute a "misperception."[25] Certainly there is no objective standpoint from which the analyst can differentiate "correct" or "true" perceptions from "misperceptions." Rather, "misperceptions" must be established vis-à-vis the intersubjective understandings that in general govern relationships of the collectivity under analysis. Arriving at a common, or at least similar, interpretation of a given stimulus is the prerequisite for appropriate or meaningful action and communication in a given social context.[26]

Further evidence suggesting that international politics should be thought of in terms of concepts or categories generated by extension from a prototypical member is found in a series of psychological studies conducted by Amos Tversky. For example, when presented with various groupings of countries—e.g., communist, capitalist, European, American—an overwhelming number of subjects converge on a particular country as the focal exemplar and rank others according to judgments of similarity. Much like Kempton's studies of

Mexican folk classifications, Tversky found similarity judgments to be context-dependent and strongly influenced by the particular makeup of the country groups, with the inclusion or deletion of a particular country changing the categorization of those remaining.[27] In general, individuals ignore like features across observations and base judgments of similarity on the proximity of a given exemplar to the prototype along dimensions on which they *differ*.[28]

Proponents of more orthodox understandings of the nature of scientific inquiry might object to the evidentiary status of such findings with regard to any arguments one might make vis-à-vis scientific practice. That the layperson might conceptualize nation states in some particular fashion or make judgments of similarity according to procedures that produce graded membership or prototype effects does not imply that social scientific judgments are governed by similar processes. But as a recent survey of scholarship on democracy demonstrates, this is precisely the case.

The Construction of Democracy

Despite the longstanding efforts of leading scholars to standardize usage of the term "democracy" in scholarly practice on the basis of precise operational definitions—or perhaps resulting from them?—David Collier and Steven Levitsky found a proliferation of subtypes, a phenomenon they refer to as "democracy with adjectives."[29] Efforts to define democracy in terms of a "procedural minimum," or those conditions necessary and sufficient to define a nation as a democracy, have not produced the intended uniformity of usage and high degrees of inter-coder reliability, but instead have led to the identification of hundreds of subtypes, of which "authoritarian democracy," "neopatrimonial democracy," "military-dominated democracy," and "protodemocracy" are but a handful.[30] As they see it, these findings confront scholars with a dilemma. On the one hand, there is an impulse to maximize *analytic differentiation* in order to capture the wide variety of democracies that have emerged across the globe. On the other, there is a necessary concern over *conceptual validity*. That is, a need to avoid what Giovanni Sartori has referred to as "conceptual stretching" or "conceptual straining." When a concept is applied to cases for which it is inappropriate, Sartori argued that any "gains in extensional coverage tend to be matched by losses in connotative precision."[31]

Having converged on a "procedural minimum" definition of democracy that requires fully contested elections, full suffrage, the absence of widespread fraud, and effective guarantees of civil liberties, scholars were soon confronted with a large number of cases in which one or another criterion was to some degree compromised.[32] Within the set of democratic states, various degrees of democracy are observable. The point is not that democracies are of different types, although this is also true. Rather, democracy appears to be a concept characterized by graded membership and fuzzy borders.

Democracies can be differentiated according to type, with each subtype constituting a full instance of the root definition of democracy. Hence, "parliamentary democracies," "presidential democracies," or "federal democracies" all can provide for fully contested elections, universal suffrage, the absence of widespread fraud, and effective guarantees of civil liberties, even as they do so in different ways. The essence of classical subtypes is that they allow one to distinguish among exemplars of a given concept along dimensions that are not essential to its definition. However, democracies can also be differentiated in terms directly related to the operational definition. Examples include "limited-suffrage democracy,"[33] "male democracy,"[34] and "illiberal democracy."[35] In contrast to classical subtypes, these "diminished subtypes" are distinguished by the fact they lack one or more of the defining attributes of democracy or enjoy these attributes at something less than "standard" or "ideal" levels. The distinctive feature of diminished subtypes is that they identify specific attributes of the case or observation that are *missing*.[36]

For example, Guatemala, a state in which the government is elected, does not fit the procedural minimum definition of democracy because civil liberties are not guaranteed. However, Guatemala can be assimilated to the concept of democracy once one allows for the existence of "illiberal" democracies: electoral regimes in which effective guarantees for civil liberties are missing.[37] Diminished subtypes have also been constructed to describe polities in which more than one attribute of the procedural minimum definition of democracy is missing. Once one allows for diminished subtypes, concept extension no longer follows the classical criteria of establishing the presence or absence of a uniform set of necessary and/or sufficient conditions but rather on the basis of judgments of similarity, resulting in concepts and categories with graded membership and fuzzy borders.

Moreover, because differences among individual observations are psychologically more salient than common features, comparisons between diminished subtypes and prototypical exemplars are likely to be characterized by directedness and asymmetry.[38] For example, if the United States serves as the conceptual prototype for a democratic system, we would not be surprised to find that significantly more people would agree to the statement "Guatemala's political system is similar to that of the United States" than would agree to the assertion "The United States' political system is similar to that of Guatemala." If true, this suggests that the borders of conceptual categories, or empirical datasets, will be strongly influenced by the choice of prototype. The set of all polities similar to the United States might be judged to include Guatemala, whereas the set of all polities similar to Guatemala might not be thought to include the United States, a situation inconsistent with orthodox understandings of the nature of scientific measurement and coding.

Diminished subtypes are common to the social sciences. For example, students of decision-making routinely distinguish between "full," "synoptic," or "complete" rationality on the one hand, and the diminished subtype of "bounded" rationality on the other. Whereas formal definitions of rationality require that the decision maker evaluate all possible choices and select the option that maximizes subjective expected utility, empirical studies found that actors routinely limit their search for alternatives and make incremental decisions producing outcomes that fall short of maximum utility.[39] Another example is found in the work of Robert Jackson. Whereas states of weak institutional capacity were historically denied a role in international society, Jackson argues that changes in the constitutive principles of the international system during the period of decolonization "brought into existence a community of states of unprecedented diversity of membership."[40] Enfranchised internationally, many of the former colonies that today constitute the Third World lack the institutional features that define sovereign statehood. These "quasi-states" are characterized by governments "deficient in the political will, institutional authority, and organized power" to accomplish the tasks of statehood, including the protection of human rights or provision of socioeconomic welfare.[41]

Collier and Levitsky argue that diminished subtypes "are a useful means to avoid conceptual stretching in cases that are less than fully democratic," and "provide differentiation by creating new analytic categories."[42] But recognizing or countenancing the resort to diminished subtypes in scholarly practice does not resolve the supposed dilemma from which their analysis begins. Diminished subtypes do allow for greater differentiation, but questions regarding validity remain, as their reference to the work of Bruce Bagley makes clear. Rejecting the diminished democracy subtypes that have been applied to the case of Colombia in the period 1958–74—e.g., "restricted," "controlled," "limited," "oligarchical," "elitist," and "elitist-pluralist"—Bagley characterizes Colombia as a subtype of authoritarianism![43]

Such arguments are precisely the stuff of concepts with graded membership and fuzzy borders. That the dilemma posed by the two values of analytic differentiation and conceptual validity is either false or beside the point is reflected in the response offered to Bagley's critique: "Scholars should be self-conscious about the analytic and normative implications of choosing to form subtypes in relation to democracy, as opposed to some other concept."[44] But having argued the virtues of analytic subtypes in terms of their relationship to root definitions, an appeal to the normative implications of "naming" is puzzling, to say the least.[45] It does, however, provide further evidence to support my contention that much of the "action" in the social construction of meaning is taking place at the boundaries of our concepts rather than their cores.

One might argue that the problem of fuzzy borders could be resolved through more precise operational definitions. But because scientific concepts are defined in terms of other concepts, the most basic of which are everyday language terms, this has the effect of shifting the borders of concepts but does not deal with the inherent imprecision of any definition. For example, studies of Central and South American "transitional" democracies found that one legacy of authoritarian rule is often the persistence of "reserved domains" where the military exercises power independent of political control.[46] The result has been the revision of the procedural minimum definition of democracy by some scholars to include the attribute of "effective power to rule," an attribute that many felt was already understood to be implied in the overall meaning of democracy even if it was not explicitly included in the definition.[47]

Rather than producing increased inter-coder reliability, efforts to increase operational precision have generated new lines of contention. "For example, in analyzing Chile in the post-1990 period, Rhoda Rabkin takes exception to the usage adopted by scholars who introduced the expanded procedural minimum definition. She argues that the problem of civilian control of the military does not represent a sufficient challenge to the democratically elected government to qualify Chile as a 'borderline' democracy."[48] By adding the condition "effective power to rule" to the definition of democracy, scholars have only shifted the borders of the dispute to questions of what constitutes "effective power to rule" or a "sufficient challenge to the democratically elected government." The example illustrates the futility of efforts to completely specify scientific concepts and the utility of taking some things for granted or assuming them to be antecedently understood.

With the end of the cold war, the impact of democracy on patterns of interstate conflict has become one of the dominant themes in the study of international politics. A series of systematic empirical studies has concluded that democratic states do not wage war against other democracies, a finding now routinely referred to as the "democratic peace."[49] The research program is interesting from the standpoint of this analysis because most of these studies have been conducted with the same data. Data on interstate conflicts is provided by the University of Michigan's Correlates of War Project, but regime-type data for the period 1800–1999 is provided by the Polity Project, directed by Ted Robert Gurr of the University of Maryland.[50] Both projects have gone to great lengths to develop operational definitions of key concepts and claim to have produced results with high degrees of inter-coder reliability.[51]

The exertions to formulate and apply precise definitions of "democracy" and "war" to the history of interstate conflict, however, have not prevented disputes over the coding of individual cases. Even as critics of the thesis have attacked the inclusion or exclusion of a particular state as democratic and/or a particular interstate conflict as a war, proponents of the democratic peace also confront an increasing number of results that run counter to commonly held beliefs, which they contend are best regarded as "unintended implicatures" of the operational specifications. Moreover, a close analysis of scholarly practice in the research program reveals that the coding process assimilates cases to a concept of democracy that is generated by a prototypical exemplar which is itself a product of culture and historical contingency. The claims require elaboration.

In an effort to facilitate cross-country regime comparisons, as well as to gauge regime transformations, the Polity Project has compiled yearly data on 161 contemporary states with longstanding members of the international system coded for every year beginning in 1800.[52] The primary units used in the analysis are polities, which are defined as "subsets of the class of authority patterns." An authority pattern is defined as "a set of asymmetric relations among hierarchically ordered members of a social unit that involves the direction of the unit. . . . The direction of a social unit involves the definition of its goals, the regulation of conduct of its members, and the allocation and coordination of goals within it."[53] Polities are coded along a number of dimensions designed to locate them on a continuum of regime types ranging from autocratic to democratic.

Democracy is operationalized in terms of "three essential, interdependent elements. One is the presence of institutions and procedures through which citizens can express effective preferences about alternative policies and leaders. Second is the existence of institutionalized constraints on the exercise of power by the executive. Third is the guarantee of civil liberties to all citizens in their daily lives and in acts of political participation." Each polity is given weighted scores along three dimensions: the competitiveness of political participation; the openness and competitiveness of executive recruitment; and the constraints on the chief executive. These scores are then added, resulting in a democracy score ranging from 0 to 10 (see table 3.1). A score of 10 would indicate a "mature and internally coherent democracy . . . one in which (a) political participation is fully competitive, (b) executive recruitment is elective, and (c) constraints on the chief executive are substantial."[54]

The application of these operational specifications produces a dataset that ranks polities over time, thereby allowing for temporal as well as cross-national comparisons. For example, the democracy scale discriminates among parliamentary and presidential systems on the basis of the constraints imposed on the chief executive. Consequently, for the early years of the Fifth Republic,

Table 3.1 Democracy scores

	Scale weight
Competitiveness of executive recruitment	
Election	+2
Transitional	+1
Openness of executive recruitment	
Dual election	+1
Election	+1
Constraints on chief executive	
Executive parity or subordination	+4
Intermediate category	+3
Substantial limitations	+2
Intermediate category	+1
Competitiveness of political participation	
Competitive	+3
Transitional	+2
Factional	+1

when de Gaulle enjoyed few constraints on his executive authority, France receives a lower democracy score than does the Federal Republic of Germany, where there were far more constraints on the executive. With the onset of "cohabitation" during the second phase of the first Mitterand presidency, France receives a higher score, reflecting the greater degree of parity within the various branches of the government.[55]

Autocracy refers to a distinctive set of authority patterns that are nondemocratic. "In mature form, autocracies sharply restrict or suppress competitive political participation. Their chief executives are chosen in a regularized process of selection within the political elite, and once in office they exercise power with few institutional restraints." As with democracy, an eleven-point autocracy scale is constructed additively, derived from codings of: the competitiveness of political participation, the regulation of participation, the openness and competitiveness of executive recruitment, and the constraints on the chief executive (see table 3.2).[56]

A single regime score, the Polity Score, is derived by subtracting the autocracy score from the democracy score. This procedure yields a continuum rang-

Table 3.2 Autocracy scores

	Scale weight
Competitiveness of executive recruitment	
Selection	+2
Openness of executive recruitment	
Closed	+1
Dual/designation	+1
Constraints on chief executive	
Unlimited authority	+3
Intermediate category	+2
Slight to moderate limitations	+1
Regulation of participation	
Restricted	+2
Factional/restricted	+1
Competitiveness of political participation	
Suppressed	+2
Restricted	+1

ing from +10, for "strongly democratic," to −10, indicating "strongly auto-cratic." But although a large number of scholars use the data generated by the Polity Project's operational definitions of democracy and autocracy, they do not agree on the cutoff point for the existence of a "democratic" state. That is, even if they judge polities according to their score on the 21-point Polity In-dex, they disagree as to the proper boundary between democracy and autoc-racy.[57] Moreover, the strict application of the coding protocols has produced results that offend conventional understandings of the concept. Thus, David Spiro questions the fact that using Zeev Maoz's threshold for democracy on the Polity II dataset, France "is not considered democratic after 1981 but El Sal-vador is, and Belgium was not a democracy until 1956, but for 1946 Colom-bia, Guatemala, and Turkey are coded as democracies."[58]

Some scholars combine the Polity data with other criteria, which they main-tain are implied or generally understood as constitutive to the concept of democracy. For example, Maoz and Russett delete Wilhelmine Germany from the Polity dataset, arguing that it was not a "stable" democracy, with stability operationalized by the number of years a polity meets the cutoff they regard as necessary for considering a state to be democratic.[59] Imperial Germany is ruled out of Doyle's dataset because the executive was not responsible to the Reichstag in questions of foreign policy, even though in both Britain and France foreign policy was insulated from the influence of the legislature.[60] Such moves have the effect of saving the thesis of the democratic peace from the rather embarrassing finding that World War I constituted a war between democracies (and a quite major one at that), but only change the border of contention to the question of what constitutes a "well established" or "en-trenched" democracy, as Spiro pointed out.[61] Examples of such "unintended implicatures" resulting from the over-specification of democracy abound, such as when the war between Peru and Ecuador is ruled out of one dataset because "the war came within one to three years after the establishment of a liberal regime, that is, before the pacifying effects of liberalism could become deeply ingrained."[62]

Proponents of the democratic peace thesis have tended to fall into one of two camps. On the one side are those who stress the effects of democratic struc-tures on the war proneness of states.[63] On the other are those who argue that the norms associated with democratic regime types are crucial.[64] If democratic structures are sufficient for pacific foreign policies, then democracies should be less war prone than other regime types. Yet this is not the case. The results of large-N studies suggest that democracies fight as many wars on average as nondemocratic states—it appears that they just don't fight other democracies.[65] Thus, in an effort to uncover an underlying mechanism behind the purported empirical finding of a democratic peace, scholars have increasingly shifted their focus from the institutional features of democracies to their normative underpinnings. For, as John Owen argues, if there is a zone of peace, it rests on a set of liberal norms, which has given rise to a Kantian "pacific union."[66]

Michael Doyle has been at the forefront of those stressing the existence of a pacific union among a group of nations, all of which adhere to three sets of liberal rights: freedom from arbitrary authority; protection and promotion of freedom; and democratic participation. According to Doyle: "Even though liberal states have become involved in numerous wars with nonliberal states, constitutionally secure liberal states have yet to engage in war with one another."[67] Emphasizing liberal norms rather than democratic structures, Doyle's list of liberal regimes is generated by a set of coding rules that assess whether a state has a private market-based economy, external sovereignty, citizens with juridical rights, and a republican representative government. Maoz and Russett, while remaining in the overall framework of the Polity II dataset, attempt to capture the normative features of democracy by including in their statistical analyses a proxy variable, namely political deaths, as compiled by the Conflict and Peace Data Bank.[68] If a government does not kill its citizens, it is coded as a liberal regime.

But again, efforts to increase definitional and operational precision for the concept of democracy produce rather odd results. For example, Doyle regards both the United States and Switzerland as liberal for the period of the eighteenth century, although women could not vote in either state and the United States maintained the institution of slavery.[69] In an effort to cope with the women's suffrage movement, Doyle classifies states as liberal if they grant female suffrage within a generation of its being demanded. Spiro counters: "If, as Doyle stresses, the normative aspects of liberalism are important, then the question of when illiberalism can be ignored seems to depend on the extent to which we tolerate the disenfranchisement of individuals other than wealthy white males at various points in recent history. It is disingenuous to claim that societies are liberal if unempowered groups are able to vote sometime after they get around to asking for it."[70]

What accounts for this conceptual confusion? More than one scholar has suggested that what is really driving the definitions of contemporary American political scientists is a concept of democracy that takes the contemporary United States as the prototype. As Ido Oren writes: "In all studies America receives virtually perfect scores on the democracy scale. America is the norm against which other polities are measured."[71] Moreover, this is also true for the last two hundred years despite manifest differences in the degree to which the population enjoyed the franchise and the state's protection of basic human rights.[72]

The datasets of democratic and autocratic regimes do not reflect the application of "neutral" and "precise" coding protocols. Indeed, on an alternative democracy index constructed by Finnish scholar Tatu Vanhanen, the United States ranked 30th, far behind the West European democracies, with Italy at the forefront.[73] What accounts for the differences between Vanhanen's dataset and those of his American colleagues is not so much the basic definition of democracy—indeed, he adopts the definition offered by the eminent American scholar Robert Dahl—but rather the method of operationalizing competition and participation. Clearly influenced by European models of proportional representation in which coalition governments are the rule, Vanhanen measures the degree to which an election is competitive according to the share of votes the smallest parties receive in major national elections. This is accomplished simply by subtracting the percentage of votes captured by the dominant party from 100. Participation is measured in terms of the proportion of the total population who actually vote.[74] The United States scores relatively low on both counts.

In American debates over the purported existence of a zone of democratic peace, whether the concept of democracy is extended to another state, contemporary or historical, is a function of the "degree of difference" when compared to the United States rather than its meeting a threshold generated by qualitative or index measures that reflect criteria held to be necessary and sufficient for category membership.[75] And shifting the analysis to liberal norms does nothing to change the underlying process of assimilation. In American scientific practice, "liberal" norms are merely those generally associated with the political system of the contemporary United States. These are then applied trans-historically to other political systems, if not the United States itself.[76]

Noting that even American definitions of democracy have changed over time, Oren argues: "Polities have numerous objective dimensions by which they can be measured. The dimensions captured by the current empirical measures of democracy came to be selected through a subtle historical process whereby objective dimensions on which America resembled its enemies were eliminated, whereas those on which America differed the most from its enemies became privileged. Thus, the coding rules defining democracy are better understood as a time bound product of America's historical international circumstances than as the timeless exogenous force that they are presumed to be."[77]

The democratic peace thesis rests not only on a coding of states as either democratic or nondemocratic, but also on establishing what constitutes a case of war. The most commonly used dataset for interstate wars is that of the Correlates of War (COW) Project initiated by Singer and Small.[78] The COW dataset includes all cases of interstate conflicts resulting in at least 1,000 battle-related fatalities between at least two members of the international system with populations of 500,000 or more.[79] A state is counted as a warring party if it committed at least 1,000 troops to the battlefield or suffered at least 100 battle-related deaths.[80] However, much as was the case with efforts to specify the precise operational indicators of democracy, the COW criteria have generated rather peculiar results and forced scholars to engage in any number of rhetorical contortions to explain away embarrassing findings.

Thus, critics point out that the 1969 "Football War" between El Salvador and Honduras, which lasted for four days and resulted in approximately 1,900 battle deaths, is counted as a case of interstate war, but Finland's participation on the side of the Axis Powers during World War II is not. Even though Great Britain bombed Finland at least once, Finland drops out of the dataset because there was no direct battlefield confrontation between Finland and the western democracies.[81] A more embarrassing case for those who argue that democracies rarely or never fight wars with one another is the 1999 war between India and Pakistan. Both states rate relatively high on the Polity Project's democracy scale, and battle deaths exceed the COW threshold for interstate war. However, as many of the deaths were Islamic guerrillas and not regular Pakistani troops, Russett concludes that the case does not qualify as a true interstate war.[82]

Arguably the most fruitful and influential research program in the field of international politics in the period following the cold war, the study of the "democratic peace," or the relationships between regime type and the war propensity of states, conforms to the expectations generated by the arguments on the nature of scientific concepts developed here.[83] First, efforts to refine and make the definitions of key concepts more precise have not produced consensus over data but merely shifted the borders of contention. Any definition establishes borders and gives rise to "borderline" cases. A large part of what constitutes scientific debate takes place at the borders of scientific concepts; ruling a particular empirical observation to be "inside" or "outside" of the concept's borders is an exercise in the social construction of meaning.

Establishing meaning—and thereby influencing judgments of appropriate behavior—through debates at the borders of concepts is not only the stuff of political science analysis, it also constitutes much of political practice itself. For example, whether a state is categorized as democratic or nondemocratic can affect its eligibility for bilateral and multilateral economic development assistance. In international legal affairs, the judiciaries of liberal states have been found generally to uphold and respect the validity of the judgments of courts in other liberal states while tending to subject the decisions of courts from nonliberal states to review.[84] Similarly, in the western democracies, individual applications for political asylum frequently hinge on judgments regarding the nature of the political and legal system of the applicant's home state.

Prototypes and Political Analysis

Endless debates over the appropriate extension of concepts demonstrate that, despite the best efforts of scholars, necessary and sufficient conditions for category membership often (or perhaps usually) cannot be specified. Instead, scientific concepts display many of the characteristics of concepts used in everyday language, in particular prototype effects and fuzzy borders. Scholars in both the United States and Europe have employed concepts of democracy that are typified by focal or core members and extended to other cases or observations on the basis of resemblance. And the exemplars that are regarded as central or core are those with which the various groups of scholars are most familiar. Thus, American scholars judge other states as democratic or nondemocratic on the basis of comparisons to the contemporary U.S. political system, whereas European scholars extend the concept of democracy on the basis of states' resemblance to a prototype characterized by proportional representation and the supremacy of parliament.[85]

Multiple and interrelated psychological processes contribute to such dynamics. A variety of findings would lead one to expect that conceptual prototypes are the exemplars with which a group is most familiar. For example, psychologists find that new observations are generally evaluated in terms of models, scripts, or exemplars that are readily available, easily remembered, and laden with emotional significance.[86] Although scholars would like to believe themselves to be free of the emotional attachments that generate biased interpretation of data by political decision makers, they presumably share the same cognitive dispositions that promote the use of familiar experiences or observations as conceptual prototypes.[87] Persuaded by the notions that the individual's psychological need for positive distinctiveness underlies processes of social identity formation and that the principles of everyday categorization can be extended to explain the categorization of people, students of social identity in the tradition of Henri Tajfel and John Turner would not be surprised by the finding that Americans judge other democracies on the basis of what they regard to be the unique and positive aspects of U.S. democracy, or the finding that similar behaviors exemplify the judgments of Europeans.[88]

Studies of analogical reasoning in foreign policy decision-making processes suggest that the origins of conceptual prototypes are often found in dramatic experiences of the individual's early adulthood. When such experiences are shared by a group or nation, the psychological processes at work give rise to strong generational effects.[89] Thus, in the wake of the 1990 Iraqi invasion of Kuwait, British Prime Minister Margaret Thatcher could implore President Bush to avoid "going wobbly" and repeating the errors of the Allied Powers in the run-up to World War II. Thatcher and Bush remembered the failures of the Munich accord and could readily assimilate Saddam Hussein to a conception of international aggressors with Adolf Hitler as its prototypical member.[90] Members of the government who had come of age during the Vietnam War—such as Secretary of Defense Richard Cheney and General Colin Powell, chairman of the U.S. Joint Chiefs of Staff—were far more reluctant to invest military resources to roll back the Iraqi forces.[91]

Although conceptual prototypes often reflect familiar or particularly vivid exemplars with bases in a group's common heritage or experience, scientific concepts are often generated by central members that are akin to Weber's notion of an "ideal type."[92] I say akin, because Weber was quite clear that he did not regard ideal types as true, either in the nominalist or realist sense of the term, and regarded them as ill-suited for purposes of categorization. For Weber, an ideal type is "a conceptual construct which is neither historical reality nor even the 'true' reality. It is even less fitted to serve as a schema under which a real situation or action is to be subsumed as one *instance*. It [is] a purely ideal *limiting* concept with which the real situation or action is *compared* and surveyed for the explication of certain of its significant components."[93]

In contemporary scientific practice, however, idealized types frequently do serve as the central or prototypical exemplars of scientific concepts, which are extended to observed or historical cases. And as with Weber's ideal types, they are created through the specification of postulates or theoretical relationships, often of a functionalist character.[94] Concepts such as perfect conductor, frictionless plane, perfect market, and balance of power connote idealized theoretical entities for which one does not expect to find any pure empirical examples. But they allow for the parceling of experience as novel observations are classified or named on the basis of resemblance to one or another ideal type. Because the prototype is an idealized abstraction, concept extension necessarily leads to graded membership, with any empirical case representing only an impure manifestation of the ideal type.

Weber argued that ideal types were useful for causal analysis of social outcomes. Through comparing the logic of an ideal type to concrete patterns and outcomes, the causes of the latter can be imputed.[95] The relationship is for Weber one-way, with the ideal type serving as a heuristic device in explaining why a particular historical instance was *so* and not *otherwise*. But when conceived as the central or prototypical exemplar of a given concept, the role of ideal types in producing general knowledge becomes clearer. By asking what accounts for the similarities and differences between observed and ideal types, a variety of relationships among various empirical instances may be uncovered, facilitating a fuller (though not necessarily precise) definition of the general concept itself. Seen from this perspective, graded membership—and borderline cases in particular—are not the obstacles to scientific explanation that dogmatic adherents to misguided notions of precision, inter-coder reliability, and validity claim them to be. Rather, they are the cases that are potentially the most informative. No one would regard the duck-billed platypus to be a prototypical mammal. However, by studying those characteristics of the platypus that are typically mammalian as well those that deviate, we are likely to learn a great deal more about the concept "mammal" than we are through the study of more typical exemplars, such as the common house cat.[96]

Summary

Before proceeding to some concluding remarks, a review of the major claims of the foregoing analysis is in order. First, rejecting the claims of those who maintain that we confront a world that is prepackaged into discrete units and that good scientific concepts—i.e., those that are most effective at generating explanations for processes or outcomes in the world—will ultimately correspond to those natural divisions, I have argued that scientific concepts, like the concepts of everyday language on which they are built, are created, not found. That is, there is no necessary or proper one-to-one correspondence between scientific concepts and the subject matter of science.

The latter point, however, does not imply that there is no correspondence or that "anything goes." If this were the case, then it would seem unlikely that we would find individuals from very different linguistic communities agreeing on what constitutes the best example of a given color even when they disagree about the borders of color concepts. Yet this is precisely the case, as Berlin and Kay discovered. The problem is somewhat more complex when we move from the physical to the social worlds, from so-called *natural* to *social* kinds, as the disagreement among political scientists over what constitutes the best example of democracy demonstrates. But some commonality exists, otherwise there would be nothing over which these scholars could *disagree*. Because scientific concepts are always defined in terms of other concepts, the most basic of which come from everyday language, the relevant correspondence for concepts referring to social kinds is at some level determined by the rules of language, conventional usage, and common sense—a topic I shall return to below.

Whereas a dogmatic realist would maintain that science has repeatedly demonstrated its capacity for discovering truths in the world and radical constructivists insist that the world is of our making, I seek to seize the middle ground.[97] Rejecting the strong realist claim, I am persuaded by the proposition that truth is not a property of "the world" but rather of statements *about* the world. And insofar as we are speaking here of science—that is, the systematic study of "the world"—contrary to the claims of radical constructivists, it is not the world itself that is made by our concepts but rather our representations of the world.[98] When one asks, "What is this a case of?" we are not constructing the experience or observation but rather a representation of it.[99] That our answers to such questions influence subsequent actions and thereby the nature of the world is not at issue here.

The classical notion of concepts as definable in terms of sets of necessary and/or sufficient conditions does not reflect scientific practice, nor could it. Scientific concepts are best understood as being generated by focal or prototypical core members and then extended to novel observations or experiences on the basis of perceived similarities. This process produces concepts characterized by graded membership and fuzzy borders, and it is precisely at the borders of our concepts that much of the "action" of science, and of the social construction of meaning, takes place. Efforts to solve the "problem" of borderline cases through better definitions and operational specifications have generated more heat than light. Rather than viewing such cases as problems to be solved, one should instead focus on the deliberative processes whereby an instance is ruled in or out of a given conceptual category. Not only are they informative vis-à-vis the assumptions, relationships, and theories that both imply and are implied by the concept (borderline cases are of particular interest in this respect), but also with regard to the normative, political, or deeper psychological processes that are always present in scientific practice.

Conclusions

The understanding of scientific concepts developed here helps make sense of contemporary social scientific practice and renders otherwise puzzling debates over such topics as "transitions to democracy" and the "democratic peace" both more intelligent and intelligible. It is not necessarily a lack of methodological discipline or intellectual effort that leads to conflicts over the application of a given concept, even those that are not "essentially contested" in the sense elucidated by Gallie.[100] Rather, such conflicts result from the very process of conceptualization and properties that are inherent to scientific concepts. Moreover, they do not pose the hindrance to scientific research that dogmatic adherents to the standards of "precision" maintain. Indeed, some of the most basic concepts, concepts that have given rise to large bodies of research, are among the most poorly defined and specified. This section is devoted to an elaboration of these points as well as some more speculative notions suggested by the foregoing discussion and analysis.

Resemblance, Not Congruence

Having pointed out the futility of efforts to define concepts in terms of some necessary and sufficient conditions that would give rise to clear boundaries and precise operational specification, I have defined scientific concepts as linguistic expressions of mental constructs that are intersubjectively valid in the sense that they serve to convey meaning between members of the scientific community. Using the field of international politics, I demonstrated that social scientific concepts exhibit prototype effects and fuzzy borders characteristic of everyday language terms. Scholars from different theoretical traditions or culturally determined contexts were shown to disagree both on where to draw the border between democratic and nondemocratic forms of rule as well as on what constitutes the "best" or purest example of a democratic regime. Nonetheless, and the point is not insignificant, debate goes on. Debate, that is communication, is possible, even though scholars are committed to, or guided by, somewhat different concepts of democracy. Whereas many in the scientific community adhere to the proposition that scientific progress demands precision in both the definition and employment of concepts, it strikes me that it is the resemblance, not the congruence, of concepts that characterizes fruitful research and indeed makes science possible. The point requires some elaboration.

Stressing the theory-dependence of concepts and the observations they make possible, many have followed Paul Feyerabend's lead in arguing that science is pervaded by incommensurability across theories and paradigms.[101] For Feyerabend, scientific theories, like natural languages, not only describe events, but by providing the mental constructs for apprehension and comprehension, serve to shape them. Like natural languages, theories are characterized by "subterranean" and "covert" assumptions and classifications, which by virtue of their interconnectedness form a "cosmology" or comprehensive view of the world. These deep or hidden assumptions may be quite subtle yet give rise to patterned resistances to alternative representations of the world. Moreover, sometimes even the claim that an alternative has been, or can be, presented is rejected: "If these resistances oppose not just the truth of the resisted alternatives but the presumption that an alternative has been presented, then we have an instance of incommensurability."[102] When theories are incommensurable, "every concept that occurs . . . is suspect, especially 'fundamental' concepts such as 'observation,' 'test,' and, of course, the concept 'theory' itself."[103]

In the study of international politics, the notion of incommensurability has gained some acceptance. For example, Stephen Krasner maintains that the comparison of research programs in the field is difficult because of "meaning incommensurability": the same terms have different meanings in different theories.[104] And after surveying the dominant paradigms in the study of international politics, Kal Holsti concluded that "there can be no meaningful synthesis, a 'super-field' of international theory, if the core concerns, units of analysis, key actors, and methodologies are different."[105]

I do not wish to challenge the proposition that there are or can be incommensurable worldviews. I am, however, skeptical of the claim that incommensurability pervades scientific practice, particularly the radical incommensurability asserted by the claim that translation between theories is impossible.[106] Not only is an adequate translation usually possible, quite often it is not even necessary.

As understood by Feyerabend, the problem of incommensurability is closely linked to the absence of an "independent observation language." Observation statements are always made in terms of some theory. Because modern scientific theories are sufficiently "deep," in the sense that they are built on covert classifications, Feyerabend contends that what counts as a fact in one theory cannot count as such in another. But it seems to me that Feyerabend mischaracterizes the subterranean foundations of scientific theories. Theories are indeed built on covert, or at least unexamined assumptions, as the discussion of definitions in this chapter makes clear. And we have already stipulated that concepts (and, by implication, observations and facts) do not exist independent of theory. The result, however, is not necessarily incommensurability.

With respect to scientific concepts, Feyerabend's argument must be turned around. Commensurability is not dependent on a neutral or independent observation language, rather it results from the fact that most scientific concepts share a common foundation in everyday language. Scientific concepts are always defined in terms of other concepts, the most basic of which are taken from everyday languages and assumed to be generally understood.[107] It is precisely this "subterranean" quality that makes resistance as well as fruitful debate possible.

Feyerabend himself appears to appreciate the role that everyday language plays in supporting the edifice of theory when he suggests that the degree of incommensurability between Newtonian and quantum mechanics is less than that separating ancient and modern cosmologies, because "the modern transition has left the arts, *ordinary language,* and perception unchanged."[108] But he fails to appreciate the implications of the admission. Thus, when suggesting that Catholics and Protestants hold incommensurable views, even though they "have the same book," he misses the point that theologians from each camp are quite active in debating the meaning of such concepts as "conscience," "justification," "authority," or "the church."[109] If congruence of terms were necessary for fruitful discourse, then we would be forced to conclude that the learned participants in "ecumenical dialogue" are cynical, delusional, or perhaps both.

Although institutionalized cynicism is not uncommon, it is more likely that communication, and indeed persuasion, can take place on the basis of concepts, which, although not identical, are sufficiently similar to convey meaning. Moreover, this condition is not unique to cross-theoretic or paradigmatic discussions but indeed is common to discussions among scientists working within the same theoretical tradition. Feyerabend's suspicion that the writings of quantum theorists von Neumann and Bohr betray different understandings of key theoretical terms is probably correct; however, it does not follow that they are somehow speaking a different language.[110] After all, one can never know whether a partner's understanding of *love* is quite the same as one's own, even as the utterance "I love you" proves indispensable to the relationship. In this sense, the proponents of incommensurability (or, for that matter, relativism) establish standards for understanding that are unrealistically high, which then serve to justify the claim that understanding is impossible.[111]

Scientific progress, by which I mean nothing more than socially valued, intersubjectively valid research, can occur through conceptual innovation, extension, elaboration, or revolution, in Kuhn's meaning of the term. Yet even radical revolutions will have a hard time sweeping aside every preexisting scientific concept, not to speak of more basic linguistic terms.[112] I suspect that the ruins created by scientific revolutions serve much the same function as those of ancient cities. They are the (perhaps unstable) foundations of modern constructions. If we dig deep enough, engage in the infinite regress of definition, we will discover that many a stone rejected now serves as a cornerstone.[113] Because substantive theories of the world are built on a foundation of basic linguistic terms, it is not at the level of theory but rather of language that we would expect incommensurability to emerge as an obstacle to meaningful communication.[114] But even Kuhn did not deny the possibility of translation, if only imperfect:

> Most readers of my text have supposed that when I spoke of theories as incommensurable, I meant that they could not be compared. But "incommensurability" is a term borrowed from mathematics, and it there has no such implication. The hypotenuse of an isosceles right triangle is incommensurable with its side, but the two can be compared to any required degree of precision. What is lacking is not comparability but a unit of length in terms of which both can be measured directly and exactly. In applying the term "incommensurability" to theories, I had intended only to insist that there was no common language within which both could be *fully expressed* and which could thereby be used in a point-by-point comparison between them.[115]

Arguments supporting the notion of incommensurability imply that communication among scientists of the same theory or paradigm depends on their using congruent concepts. Yet, as I have argued, scientific concepts are best thought of as fuzzy concepts characterized by individual empirical exemplars that display graded membership or degrees of membership. Thus, achieving congruence or "precision" through definition is impossible, as all definitions give rise to borders, and borders give rise to borderline cases. In practice, the extension of a given concept takes place on the basis of judgments of resemblance, rather than the strictures of operational specification. Different scholars will reach different judgments, especially at the margins, on the basis of features they regard to be most prominent or theoretically relevant. We can never be certain whether two researchers are employing concepts in precisely the same fashion, even when they are working within the same theoretical tradition. Often, we are quite certain that they are not. Nonetheless, fruitful discussion is possible, even if agreement remains elusive.[116]

By way of illustration, consider the concept of polarity, central to the scientific study of international politics. Understood in terms of the distribution of material capabilities across the major powers of the international system, it is the principal explanatory variable in one of the dominant (some would say *the* dominant) theories of international politics, the neorealist balance of power theory articulated by Kenneth Waltz.[117] For Waltz, polarity, or the number of great powers in the international system, defines the system's structure: international systems can be characterized as unipolar, bipolar, or multipolar.[118] Variations in polarity are held to produce systematic variations in the character of international politics, in particular stability understood in terms of the likelihood of system-wide war or a change in the number (and perhaps even identities) of the major powers. Building on insights from the theory of collective goods, Waltz maintains that bipolar systems are more stable than either uni- or multipolar systems.[119]

With polarity occupying a central position in neorealist theory, one might assume Waltz to have devoted quite a bit of effort to defining the term and to specifying those observable features of states' material capabilities that are sufficient for establishing both the number and identity of poles in any given system. Indeed, Waltz chides other scholars for employing "confused, vague, and fluctuating" definitions of polarity in quantitative studies whose results he views as meaningless with regard to advancing theory.[120] But anyone expecting a clearly defined and operationally specified concept of polarity will not find one in *Theory of International Politics*. Indeed, Waltz devotes but one paragraph to the subject:

> Counting the great powers of an era is about as difficult, or as easy, as saying how many major firms populate an oligopolistic sector of an economy. The question is an empirical one, and common sense can answer it. Economists agree that, even when the total number of firms in a sector is large, their interactions can be understood, though not fully predicted, through theories about oligopoly if the number of consequential firms reduces to a small number by virtue of the preeminence of a few of them. International politics can be viewed the same way. The 150-odd states in the world appear to form a system of fairly large numbers. Given the inequality of nations, however, the number of consequential states is small. From the Treaty of Westphalia to the present, eight major states at most have sought to coexist peacefully or have contended for mastery. Viewed as the politics of the powerful, international politics can be studied in terms of the logic of small number systems.[121]

From a critic of the imprecision with which others have used the concept of polarity, one might indeed have expected more. And given the vagueness of his own definition, it is not surprising that scholars working in a Waltzean framework have been unable to agree on the structure of the international system at any given time. For example, whereas Waltz argues that the international system at the time of World War II was multipolar, Randall Schweller makes the case for "tripolarity."[122] Similarly, in the wake of the cold war, neorealist scholars have variously described the international system as being unipolar, bipolar, or multipolar.[123] Nonetheless, having once again focused attention on polarity as a central feature of the international system, Waltz's theory has generated volumes of empirical research and an unprecedented discussion among the ranks of international relations scholars representing very different theoretical traditions or schools of thought.

Thus, Robert Keohane, a preeminent liberal scholar of international politics, has discussed the effects of changing polarity on international interdependence as well as the institutions to which interdependence has given rise.[124] Although Keohane's conception of power as "issue specific" runs counter to that of Waltz and thus might produce rather different descriptions of polarity, one does not come away from a reading of their works with the sense that they do not understand one another.[125] The situation is much the same with the work of prominent constructivist scholars. John Ruggie employs a readily understood and related concept of polarity, both in his critique of Waltz and in his more recent statements on international politics after the cold war, even as he finds the concept to offer little analytical leverage, whereas Alexander Wendt admits that Waltz's arguments about the greater stability of bipolar systems "sound an important cautionary note about the celebration surrounding the end of the cold war and the collapse of the Soviet Union."[126]

Even a cursory review of international relations literature betrays the fact that scholars working within the same neorealist framework use the concept of polarity in a less than uniform fashion. Even so, they appear to be cooperating in a larger research program devoted toward an understanding of the role of "structure" on international political outcomes. If concepts are in general theory-dependent or theory-laden, then the concepts of polarity used by scholars representing very different epistemological and theoretical traditions clearly cannot be congruent. Nonetheless, as the debates among neorealists, liberals, and constructivists demonstrate, the concepts' resemblance makes it possible for members of the scientific community to communicate with, and indeed to learn from, one another.[127] The situation resembles a conversation between persons who speak two dialects of the same language. Each might produce and use words in ways that the other could not—nonetheless, with enough effort and good will, they come to understand one another, although perhaps only incompletely.

Some might be willing to accept the above assertion but nonetheless maintain that congruence is necessary when the issue is one of "testing" a given hypothesis or theory. According to the logical empiricist conception of science, a particular observation statement is either derivable from a theory or it is not. The goal of science from this perspective is to construct hypotheses that are subject to falsification on the basis of observation. How is one to falsify a hypothesis on the basis of an uncertain observation or a fact over which, some might argue, the theory makes no claims?[128] Resemblance might foster dialogue across theories and research programs, but it is no substitute for rigorous and reliable measurement and coding when testing the implications of a single theory against the data.

Three responses to such arguments come to mind. First, even in the natural sciences it is often difficult to determine which observation statements are implied by a given theory.[129] Much of what constitutes scientific practice is concerned with debating what would count as a valid test. If concepts are characterized by graded membership and fuzzy boundaries, we should not be surprised to find scholars from the same theoretical tradition debating the meaning of cases or observations at the margins. Based on a study of debates among systematists over the proper classification of species, David Hull concluded that "no two scientists are ever in total agreement with each other, even in their areas of most concentrated investigation."[130] And as the discussion earlier in this chapter of the Polity dataset indicated, disputes over data and its meaning are often resolved not by agreement on *general* rules of evidence but rather a negotiated consensus on the coding of a *particular* borderline case.

Second, because the process of data collection is usually influenced by contextual features, frames of reference, and a multitude of small decisions, some of which may be obscure to the researcher herself, I am skeptical that a high degree of uniformity in the application of concepts characterizes the practice of even the most careful individual analyst. I suspect that most scholars would be hard-pressed to accurately reconstruct their own data-gathering and coding procedures, even as methodologists demand replicability across "the entire reasoning process used in producing conclusions."[131] I am not suggesting that sloppy research techniques should be promoted or even tolerated, only that even successful practice falls quite short of what are frequently held out to be near-minimal standards.

Finally, a certain degree of conceptual plasticity, especially in underdeveloped research programs, serves to guard against prematurely abandoning a line of inquiry that appears to be going nowhere. Although observation presupposes conceptual categories, these are not immutable and indeed are revised and refined in the light of additional data and the critical appraisals of colleagues:

> It would help, one might think, if scientists waited until they had their views fully developed before they publish, but this is not how the process of knowledge development in science works. Science is a conversation with nature, but it is also a conversation with other scientists. Not until scientists publish their views and discover the reactions of other scientists can they possibly appreciate what they have actually said. No matter how much one might write and rewrite one's work in anticipation of possible responses, it is impossible to avoid all possible misunderstandings, and not all such misunderstandings are plainly "misunderstandings." Frequently scientists do not know what they intended to say until they discover what it is that other scientists have taken them to be saying. Scientists show great facility in retrospective meaning change.[132]

Observations that do not conform to the expectations of theory may lead the investigator to revise the theory. But the reverse is also true. The concepts themselves, rather than any hypothesized relationships among them, might be changed.

The Role of Intuition and Common Sense

Admitting that actual scientific practice deviates from idealized notions is not, however, the same as embracing anarchy or suggesting that anything goes. First, the idiosyncratic usage of concepts is constrained by the need to communicate. If others cannot understand what is meant by a given concept, then it ceases to serve a scientific purpose. Moreover, because scientific concepts are at some level built upon a foundation of everyday language terms, a concept's core meaning will generally be anchored by standard usage. In most cases, language users conform to the rules of usage of their community. In some cases they do not, and important scientific advances are often characterized by the novel extension or adaptation of a preexisting concept. But as I have argued above, revolutions rarely sweep the slate entirely clean, and it is the debris of the old order that makes it possible to convey to others the intuitive "sense" of a novel application or at least convince them to temporarily suspend resistance or disbelief.[133]

The futility of efforts to "nail down" the meaning and use of scientific concepts by means of better operational specification is evidenced empirically by the increased number of unintended implicatures to which such measures give rise. Whether few or many, the unintended, if not outright embarrassing, implications of a given definition are seldom left unaddressed. But in resolving such cases, scientists are as likely to resort to intuition and "common sense" as they are to the rules of logic or strictures of methodologists.

Thus, a reconstruction of Rentz's field research on Australian *Tettigoniidae* (katydids) found that in developing his early classifications, he ignored observations that ran counter to his intuitive sense of how various insects were related to one another. Nonetheless, nearly all of Rentz's classifications turned out to be highly robust.[134]

The characteristics of common sense—apart from their "common-ness"—are certainly elusive. Yet it would appear that scientists are quite willing to appeal to common sense as a justification for apparently ad hoc adjustments in the application and extension of scientific concepts. For example, in response to David Spiro's call for regarding Finland's participation on the side of the Axis

Powers in World War II as a case of a war between democracies, Bruce Russett argues that "consistency in applying [the] definition" would only come "at some cost in good sense."[135] And remember Kenneth Waltz's views on counting the number of poles in the international system: "The question is an empirical one, and *common sense* can answer it."[136]

Whether or not an intuitive innovation or common sense deviation from a strict application of a term is sustained in subsequent practice is probably dependent on the ramifications of the move throughout the theoretical or linguistic system. That is, as logical, causal, and communicative systems develop and become more complex, important mistakes, errors, inconsistencies will tend to signal that something is wrong. As contradictions mount, the scientific community will be forced to revisit the definitions and extensions of concepts that have given rise to instability in the larger edifice.[137] But for reasons I shall discuss in the next chapter, such corrective signals do not come from "nature" or from the results of crucial tests. Rather, they emanate from and are resolved in communities of scientists committed to redressing common problems in a commonly accepted fashion.

CHAPTER FOUR

If . . . Maybe

Most people would agree with the proposition that a newborn infant is a young person. Moreover, the two-day-old infant is also young and remains young in the third, fourth, and fifth days of life. Indeed, in general, a person who was young yesterday is considered to be young today, the passing of a single day in no way relegating the individual to the ranks of the aged. And yet, by virtue of the passing of single days, the fortunate among us manage to become old! The paradox, made famous by the Greek philosopher Eubulides, would appear to arise from a rather straightforward desire to establish whether any given individual is or is not young.[1]

One need not turn to ancient Greek philosophers for a recognition of the problem of establishing when gradual shifts imply a shift in kind or essence—modern-day motorcyclists will do. The lead article in a bikers' newsletter asked: "Is it still a Harley" if you customize your bike yourself? The question, it seems, was raised by the Oregon Department of Motor Vehicles regulation, which states: "Anything that is not totally factory built will make it a reconstructed motorcycle, and it will be called 'assembled' on the title."[2] But is a Harley-Davidson motorbike that is repaired with a single nonfactory bolt "assembled"? The situation was rather much the same for the Papago farmworker who quit his job sorting fruit. He found it impossible to make up his mind between good and bad oranges.[3]

Owing to the nature of our concepts, contemporary science faces a paradox not unlike that of Eubulides. And many a practicing scientist has quit her job, either by embracing the radical extremes of postmodernism, and thus rejecting the proposition that there can be any standards for judging among competing truth claims, or by giving up on the scholarly pursuit of knowledge altogether. Science, we have been told, is demarcated from other bodies of thought in that it is built upon propositions that are, at least in principle, falsifiable. The purpose of science is to establish whether or not a given hypothesis or empirical statement is or is not false. Modern scientific practice is thus built upon a two-value logic; the undecided middle is excluded. But like the Papago farmworker, the contemporary scientist often finds the job of deciding whether something is or is not the case simply too frustrating.

In the previous two chapters I developed the argument that scientific concepts are characterized by core or focal exemplars and then extended to novel observations on the basis of resemblance. Whereas classical notions of category membership, based on the establishment of necessary and sufficient properties or attributes, rules out qualitative differences among members—that is, no one member of a conceptual category is a better example of the category than any other—the understanding developed here would lead one to expect that categories are characterized by graded membership and fuzzy borders. Because the fuzzy borders of concepts often overlap, it may be difficult or, indeed, impossible to establish consensus over the proper classification of a given observation on the basis of operational definitions. In the field of political science, even the most careful efforts to do so have failed. Even when all observers agree on definitions and would appear to be reliably following conventional measurement procedures, some observations seem to fit equally well—or in equally limited fashion—into more than one category. For example, in surveying the efforts of empirically oriented political scientists to define democratic political systems operationally, we found that efforts to increase precision through the construction of diminished subtypes produced a situation in which a given state could as easily be coded a marginal democracy as judged an example of a marginal authoritarian regime.[4]

If borderline cases are endemic and the possibility of multiple classifications common, then the two-value logic upon which the scientific method is based will prove inadequate to the task of grasping the empirical world it seeks to explain. The standard formulation of empirical hypothesis in terms of "if . . . then" statements becomes problematic when the veracity of observation statements is undecidable.

My aim in this chapter is to illustrate the shortcomings of a two-value logic as the basis, both for science in general and the social sciences in particular. The critique is based on two main lines of argument. First, I will attempt to point out the logical problems with the approach to causal explanation exemplified by figures such as Karl Popper and Carl Hempel. Special attention will be given to the status of the relationship between theoretical statements and empirical tests in their writings. Second, I shall discuss the challenge presented by concepts characterized by graded membership and fuzzy borders as well as efforts to confront the challenge through the resort to probabilistic statements. Before moving to the critiques, however, an introduction to the scientific method and the role of deductive logic in scientific explanations is in order.

Falsification and the Scientific Method

The proper content of what is commonly referred to as the "scientific method" is the subject of much fierce debate, both in the form of methods textbooks and in the writings of philosophers of science. Even a cursory survey of this literature or a summary of the various positions would require us to set aside the line of argument to be developed here. Thus, no effort will be made to summarize the myriad unresolved issues and points of ongoing contention.[5] Rather, I will focus on a particular theory of the scientific method in order to add yet another voice to the chorus of debate.

The aim of science is to make sense of the world; not just any—or even any logically possible—world, but what is commonly referred to as the "real world" or "the world of our experience."[6] Making sense of the world requires us to do more than merely describe or catalogue particular observations or occurrences in the world of our experience, but also to try and uncover relationships among the various elements of that world. For many, the goal is more specific. Scientific research, writes Hempel, "tries to discover regularities in the flux of events and thus to establish general laws which may be used for prediction, postdiction, and explanation."[7] And "the logic of scientific discovery," as Popper tells us, "should be identified with the theory of the scientific method."[8]

In an effort to make sense of that world, the scientist formulates hypotheses—statements of causal relationships among variables—and tests them against experience. The formulation of positive propositions about the world is the process of theorizing. The empirical sciences are thus theoretical systems, their theories likened to "nets cast to catch what we call 'the world': to rationalize, to explain, and to master it."[9] Successful theories are characterized by sets of logically related empirical statements that have stood up to the test of experience. Good science is thus a matter of logical form and method. Method is a matter of rules, and for Popper and other logical positivists, the rules of science aim at ensuring "the testability of scientific statements; which is to say, their falsifiability."[10]

Popper's ideas regarding the form and content of scientific explanations, as well as his assertion of falsifiability as the criterion of demarcation, have found a receptive audience in the social sciences, where they arguably constitute the dominant paradigm. With few exceptions, social science has accepted the proposition that an adequate explanation is a matter of establishing a causal relationship that can be logically deduced from a universal law and subjected to empirical testing and potential falsification. Jack Snyder is characteristic when he writes: "In a mature science, hypotheses are part of a logical, deductive framework, shaped like a pyramid. At the apex are theoretical assumptions and abstract theorems derived from them, at the base are empirically testable hypotheses stating the implications of these theorems in a variety of contexts."[11] Because of their widespread influence, I shall present Popper's arguments and the related ideas of Hempel in some detail. Of particular interest is the relationship Popper established between deduction and falsification, for it is here that the constraints of two-value logic emerge as central to his understanding of scientific explanation.

The fundamental question animating Popper's philosophy of science is that of the bases or warrants for knowledge about the world. More specifically, on what basis can we derive general or universal statements, and how are we to judge their validity? Immediate access to the world is provided to us via our sensory organs, and thus observation, meaning not only visual but also any sensory input, quite necessarily plays a central role in the generation of knowledge about the world. But moving from particular observations to general statements is a difficult, perhaps impossible, task. It is precisely the relationship of individual observations to universal statements or general "laws" that concerns him.

The Problem of Induction

To understand nature, Francis Bacon argued, we should not consult the writings of Aristotle, but rather must consult nature herself. This widely held notion of science—as a body of knowledge derived from the facts of experience—has its origins in a seventeenth-century reaction to what was perceived as an overreliance on the writings of the ancients in light of the dramatic successes of a new generation of empirical scientists, with Galileo and Newton at the forefront. Science, it is maintained, begins with observation, and observation provides a secure basis on which to build an edifice of truth by means of induction. For the inductivist, it is legitimate to generalize from a finite list of singular observation statements to universal propositions, provided that: the number of observations is large, the observations have been repeated under a wide variety of conditions, and no accepted observation statement contradicts the universal proposition.[12]

Rendered in a general form, the inductivist argument reads: "If a large number of *A*s have been observed under a wide variety of conditions, and if all those observed *A*s without exception possessed the property *B*, then all *A*s possess the property *B*."[13] The principle of induction is held to be derived from experience. Hence, the inductivist justifies his method with the following argument:

The principle of induction worked successfully on occasion x_1.
The principle of induction worked successfully on occasions $x_2, x_3, x_4, \ldots$
The principle of induction always works.

The circularity of such justifications, however, was already apparent to Hume.[14] One cannot justify inductivism through resort to the very kind of inductivist arguments the validity of which one seeks to justify![15] Moreover, one cannot defend induction by resort to logic. Inferring universal statements from particular observation statements, no matter how numerous and varied the conditions under which they were made, is logically problematic, because any conclusion derived in this fashion might turn out to be false.

Consider, for example, the hypothetical Texas prison inmate, who owing to diminished mental capacity did not understand that the state judge had sentenced him to execution. Upon arriving in the state penitentiary he discovers that he is fed breakfast every morning at 8 a.m. As his lawyers avail themselves of every opportunity in the state and federal courts to overturn his conviction, years pass, and our inmate is able to collect a large number of observations. Irrespective of the day of the week, season of the year, or weather, a prison guard appears at his cell at 8 a.m. with breakfast. Finally, he reaches the conclusion: "I am always fed breakfast at 8 a.m." Alas, when the United States Supreme Court rejects his lawyers' petition to review the decision of the lower courts and the governor of Texas denies an appeal for executive clemency, the prison guard appears one morning at 8 a.m. and leads our inmate to the electric chair. An inductive inference with true premises produced a manifestly false conclusion.[16]

The sophisticated inductivist will no doubt object that our hypothetical inmate did not have access to a number of observations sufficient to draw a valid conclusion. After all, in solitary confinement on death row, our inmate did not see what was happening to the inmates in neighboring cells. Nor could he observe what was taking place in prisons across the state of Texas. The circumstances of his observations were not varied enough.

But what constitutes sufficient variation? Would access to the daily lives of all Texas prisoners have led to a more valid inference? Or perhaps access to the lives of prison inmates in Maine or Iowa? Or should the sample have been broadened to include inmates in Germany, Israel, and China? What are the grounds for answering such questions?

If we are to avoid increasing the list of necessary variations indefinitely, we need some criterion by which we can eliminate irrelevant or superfluous observations. But when is the number of observations superfluous? To distinguish significant from superfluous observations presupposes theoretical knowledge of the situation, which is to admit that theory precedes observation. Yet the inductivist begins from precisely the opposite position.

The irresolvable problem of induction is this: On the basis of a finite number of observation statements, we can never conclude that a relationship is universally valid.[17]

Deduction and the Modus Tollens

The inductivist is confronted with a situation in which a conclusion derived from even a very large number of observations (for example, "All swans are white") can be refuted by a single accepted observation statement ("There is a black swan"). Although on the basis of a finite number of observations it is logically impossible to assert that in an infinite set of possible observation statements something *is* the case, a single observation statement can establish that something *is not* the case. Whereas one cannot move from the truth of singular statements to the truth of universal statements, it is possible "to argue from the truth of singular statements to the falsity of universal statements." This basic asymmetry between verifiability and falsifiability, an asymmetry resulting from the logical form of universal statements, was recognized by Popper and led him to conclude that falsifiability must be taken as the criterion of demarcation in the empirical sciences.[18] In shifting the inductivist's focus on the requirements of verification to those of falsification, Popper appears to solve the problem that occupied Hume:

> The root of this problem is the apparent contradiction between what may be called "the fundamental thesis of empiricism"—the thesis that experience alone can decide upon the truth or falsity of scientific statements—and Hume's realization of the inadmissibility of inductivist arguments. This contradiction arises only if it is assumed that all empirical scientific statements must be "conclusively decidable," i.e., that their verification and their falsification must both in principle be possible. If we renounce this requirement and admit as empirical also statements which are decidable in one sense only—unilaterally decidable and, more especially, falsifiable, and which may be tested by systematic attempts to falsify them, the contradiction disappears: the method of falsification presupposes no inductive inference, but only the tautological transformations of deductive logic whose validity is not in dispute.[19]

And in marrying the criterion of falsification to deductive logic, Popper proposes a theory of the scientific method.

Whereas the inductivist begins from singular observation statements and attempts to infer universal statements or empirical laws from them, logical positivists propose the theoretical assertion as the proper point of departure in the search for warranted knowledge. Observation may give rise to theories about the world, but inductive inferences from these observations provide no basis for belief in their veracity.[20] Rather, universal statements can be deduced from theories and subjected to tests through which they might be shown to be false:

> From a new idea, put up tentatively, and not yet justified in any way—an anticipation, a hypothesis, a theoretical system, or what you will—conclusions are drawn by means of logical deduction. . . . Next we seek a decision as regards these (and other) derived statements by comparing them with the results of practical

applications and experiments. If this decision is positive, that is, if the singular conclusions turn out to be acceptable, or *verified,* then the theory has, for the time being, passed its test: we have found no reason to discard it. But if the decision is a negative one, or in other words, if the conclusions have been *falsified,* then their falsification also falsifies the theory from which they were logically deduced.[21]

From this perspective, theories are never proven to be true. However, as long as they withstand a series of "hard" or "critical" tests, and pending their replacement with theories of greater empirical reach or elegance, they are held to have been corroborated by experience.

Often overlooked in this regard is Popper's conviction that the implications of theories are never tested against "the world" but rather against the competing implications of other theories. Objectivity thus is not a property of the world, but of systems of thought. "The *objectivity* of scientific statements lies in the fact that they are *inter-subjectively tested.*" Because we are testing not against the world, but against statements derived from other theoretical systems, "*inter-subjective* testing is merely a very important aspect of the more general idea of inter-subjective *criticism,* or in other words, of the idea of mutual rational control by critical discussion."[22] It follows, then, that any limits to intersubjectively valid criticism necessarily limit our ability to conduct valid tests and thereby adjudicate competing truth claims.

The mode of inference whereby the falsification of a logical conclusion implies the falsification of the theoretical system from which it was deduced is the *modus tollens* of classical logic. Stated simply: if p is a conclusion of a set of statements t, and p is false, then the set of statements t must also be false. Now let p be the implication of a system of statements t, which consists of theoretical assertions and initial conditions. If on the basis of an observation statement p is held to be false, then the entire system of theory and initial conditions represented by t is also false.[23] Note that it is the entire system of statements comprising t, rather than each individually, that is hereby falsified. We cannot know on the basis of the falsity of p whether any single statement of the system is or is not refuted, a point we shall revisit below.

For the logical positivist, theories cannot be proven to be true, but they can be falsified. The asymmetry lies again in the relationship between singular observation statements and general or universal claims. Tests of theories lead to singular observation statements (perhaps more than one) of the sort sometimes referred to as *strictly existential statements* (or "*there is*" statements). To say that "there are white swans" certainly does not falsify the hypothesis "all swans are white," but neither does it prove it to be true. To move from strictly existential statements to universal statements would be to commit the inductive fallacy. However, the singular statement "there exists at least one black swan," if accepted, would falsify the general proposition that all swans are white, although the statement "there exists at least one black swan" itself cannot be falsified. "We cannot search the whole world in order to establish that something does not exist, has never existed, and will never exist. It is for precisely the same reason that strictly universal statements are not verifiable. Again, we cannot search the whole world in order to make sure that nothing exists which the law forbids."[24]

Because no single statement of an observed event, nor indeed an infinitely large number of singular statements, can contradict a strictly existential statement, Popper argues them to be nonempirical or, indeed, metaphysical.[25] Universal statements, insofar as they are falsifiable, are both empirical and scientific. "Whenever it is found that something exists here or there, a strictly existential statement may thereby be verified, or a universal one falsified."[26] From the standpoint of scientific progress, singular observation statements are most useful when they provide grounds to reject a theory.

Properly understood, Popper's approach to deductive theorizing requires the formulation not so much of "if . . . then" propositions, but rather of statements that take the form of prohibitions or proscriptions:

> They do not assert that something exists or is the case; they deny it. They insist on the non-existence of certain things or states of affairs, proscribing or prohibiting, as it were, these things or states of affairs: they rule them out. And it is precisely because they do this that they are *falsifiable*. If we accept as true one singular statement which, as it were, infringes the prohibition by asserting the existence of a thing (or the occurrence of an event) ruled out by the law, then the law is refuted.[27]

When, on the basis of logic, a given state of affairs is ruled out by a set of laws and initial principles, a single observation to the contrary is held to give us warrant to reject the entire edifice!

The most important scientific discoveries are thus those that serve to falsify an assumed null hypothesis. To say that Christopher Columbus "discovered" America is to say that he falsified the hypothesis that there was nothing but ocean between Europe and China. Likewise, the discovery of pulsars by Anthony Hewish and Jocelyn Bell was important because it falsified an accepted hypothesis in the field of astrophysics, that the radio emissions of astronomical systems are due to random natural processes and therefore irregular in time and amplitude.[28]

Scientific theories, in the logical positivist's formulation, can never be proven to be absolutely true. But insofar as they give rise by means of deductive logic to universal statements that take the form of prohibitions—that is, they assert something cannot be the case—and assuming these universal prohibitions can be subjected to the test of experience, theories can be shown to be false. Whereas the veracity of the general or universal is undecidable, that of the individual observation statement must be decidable if it is to be used as a grounds for rejecting a general claim. That is, if the deductive logic of the modus tollens is to serve as a guide to empirical research, the results of individual tests must in principle be capable of producing clear-cut observation statements of the strictly existential sort.

The logical positivist's theory of science is thus a product of linking deductive logic to empirical observation statements in pursuit of general knowledge about the world. In an effort to discover why a particular state of the world exists, or why a particular event has come to pass, the logical positivist seeks a universal statement or general law and initial conditions from which the event can logically be deduced. Explanation thus becomes a matter of prediction, which, from the standpoint of the logical positivist, is simply a question of deductive entailment. As Hempel writes: "The customary distinction between explanation and prediction rests mainly on a pragmatic difference between the two: While in the case of an explanation, the final event is known to have happened, and its determining conditions have to be sought, the situation is reversed in the case of a prediction: here, the initial conditions are given, and their 'effect'—which, in the typical case, has not taken place—is to be determined."[29] To provide an explanation is, then, to show how a given observation statement can be derived from a set of statements regarding initial conditions given a particular set of universal statements or general laws.[30] To say that a given event or set of events caused another is to identify a general law that links the putative cause with the effect by means of deductive entailment. Recognizing both the necessity and limits of relying on experience as a warrant for truth claims, the logical positivist grants an explicit role to experience only insofar as experience can be used to test the veracity of those observation statements logically derived from universal laws or theories.

Logical Positivism and the Empirical Sciences

The incredible success of logical positivism, as measured by its acceptance in the community of practicing scientists, is, I would maintain, a function of four interrelated factors. First, the elegance of the approach. Owing to the axiomatic nature of logic, deduction allows one to generate a system of internally coherent propositions of increasing specificity (or ever more limited empirical reach) on the basis of a few very general assumptions. Logic rules out self- and/ or mutually contradictory propositions within an axiomatic system and thus provides an objective standard for evaluating theories. Theories that are demonstrably incoherent can be rejected without further consideration. Moreover, the hierarchical nature of axiomatic systems provides a clue as to which statements are fundamental to the theory and which are the derivations: the fundamental axioms of a theoretical system are those that are not deducible within the rest of the system. Hence, the criteria for establishing parsimony are given, as only those axioms necessary and sufficient for the deduction of all statements belonging to the theoretical system are to be included in the axiomatic core.[31] Finally, because axioms, theorems, and lower-level hypotheses can be fit into a coherent theoretical structure, the various relationships come to be seen as natural, lending credibility to the structure as a whole.[32]

Second, logical relationships, insofar as they can be conveyed in mathematical form, provide a precise and universal language with which to convey information. Because the goal of science is the discovery of objective—that is, intersubjectively valid or reproducible—knowledge, and because mathematics is (at least in most applied settings) unambiguous and universally valid, it provides, from the standpoint of universality, an "ideal language" for scientific communication. Using the method of Euclidean geometry, the scientist can build upon precisely formulated axioms and derive a series of theorems backed by proofs, and thereby construct an edifice of logical consequences that can be recorded, consulted, comprehended, or criticized by the mathematically literate at any place or time. Through the analytic or Cartesian method, he can exploit algebraic symbolism and conduct formal logical operations in much greater depth than would otherwise be possible. Although an entire deductive edifice might be too complex to be grasped by the human brain as a single gestalt, each sequence in a series of geometric theorems or algebraic manipulations can in turn be calculated and recalculated, and any doubts as to the validity of unpalatable conclusions or unexpected relationships thereby re-moved.[33]

The dramatic success of rational choice theory, which since the 1980s has spread across the social sciences and is the dominant paradigm in some sub-fields, is in large part a function of its susceptibility to formal mathematical manipulation. For example, Bruce Bueno de Mesquita and James Morrow ar-gue that formal rational choice models are superior to other forms of analysis because the rigor of mathematics leads to "the analyst using formal methods to confront logical problems that can be missed in purely verbal arguments."[34] Similarly, Peter Ordeshook argues that "understanding politics requires so-phisticated tools of deduction. . . . If mathematics is a necessary part of that analysis, then such mathematics is necessarily a part of political theory."[35] In the field of comparative politics, Robert Bates has heralded the arrival of ra-tional choice theory, suggesting that scholars are finally "becoming equipped to handle area knowledge in rigorous ways."[36] Indeed, I suspect that it is pre-cisely the dazzling rigor of sophisticated mathematical models—rather than their empirical validity—that gives them their allure.[37]

Third, and more controversially, the virtues of logic and mathematical no-tation lead many to study precisely those aspects of the world of experience that appear to be most readily expressible in precise mathematical terms. As the physicist John Ziman argues: "It is not simply good fortune that physics proves amenable to mathematical interpretation; it follows from careful choice of subject matter, phenomena and circumstances. Physics defines itself as the *science devoted to discovering, developing, and refining those aspects of reality that are amenable to mathematical analysis*."[38] The phenomenon is perhaps more pronounced in the physical sciences, but it extends beyond them. Thus, the mathematical economist Gerard Debreu warns that "the values imprinted on an economist by his study of mathematics . . . do not play a silent role: they may play a decisive role. The very choice of the question [a mathematical econ-omist] tries to find answers to is influenced by his mathematical background. Thus, the danger is ever present that the part of economics will become sec-ondary, if not marginal to that judgment."[39] Reflecting on the apparent suc-cess of economic theory, sociologist Paul Hirsch and his colleagues argue: "De-spite the stability and power of economists' core assumptions and the logical consistency they allow, there is a fatal flaw for sociologists in their deductive modeling: it leads them to ignore the empirical world around them."[40] Fur-thermore, "Pure elegance of models leads to sterility; unwillingness to abstract from and go beyond one's data leads to pure narrative. Our bias, if forced to choose, however, is that we already have too much of the former."[41]

Though behaviorism is no longer a driving force for methodological change, the behavioral revolution left deep impressions across the social sciences. One legacy is the widespread assumption that only those features of social life that lend themselves to quantification through measurement can be fully subjected to the "rigors" of scientific analysis.[42] In the view of David Easton, one of the most prominent participants in the behavioral revolution, scientific analysis requires "precision in the recording of data and the statement of findings," which presupposes "measurement and quantification."[43] Having left mathematics for the social sciences, Anatol Rapoport nonetheless argues that "rigorous theory . . . involves strict operational, predominantly mathematical, definitions of terms and logically compelling deductions."[44] Empirical science, he asserts, "looks askance at any 'theorizing' that is not supported by hard data . . . [and] the hardest data are quantitative data."[45] Such convictions are apparent in the writings of King, Keohane, and Verba on the question of summarizing historical detail, where the prior quantification of data is rather unproblematically assumed:

> After data are collected, the first step in any analysis is to provide summaries of the data. Summaries describe what may be a large amount of data but they are not directly related to inference. Since we are ultimately interested in generalization and explanation, a summary of the facts to be explained is usually a good place to start. . . . Our model of the process of summarizing historical detail is statistic. A statistic is an expression of data in abbreviated form. Its purpose is to display the appropriate characteristics of the data in a convenient format. For example, one statistic is the sample mean, or average.[46]

And this from authors whose intended reader is the qualitatively oriented social scientist![47]

Theories can be likened to nets created to catch the world, but we should not make the mistake of the inductivist fisherman and conclude that all fish are necessarily larger than the size of our mesh. Even if we successfully cast our nets in a variety of waters, we have no basis on which to infer that that which we catch comes anywhere close to representing the diversity of phenomena over which we might seek knowledge.

The fourth explanation for the widespread acceptance of the theory of science promoted by Popper and the other logical positivists is precisely the apparent success of the physical sciences. Of particular importance in this regard is the history of successful predictions generated by deductive theorizing. Who can claim to have been unimpressed by the story of Mendeleyev's successful prediction of the existence and properties of undiscovered elements on the basis of gaps in the Periodic Table? Similarly impressive were the independent predictions of the existence of the planet Neptune in the mid-nineteenth century by Urbain Leverrier in France and John Adams in England. When the recorded orbit of Uranus could not be reconciled with Newton's theory of gravitation given what was then known of the solar system, Leverrier and Adams inferred the existence of an as yet undetected planet and calculated the point in the heavens where, shortly thereafter, Neptune was indeed observed by Johann Galle in Berlin. The twentieth century was likewise marked by confirmations of incredible predictions: in the field of astronomy, the existence of quarks and black holes; in paleontology, the existence of elevated levels of iridium in the particular layer of the earth's sediment associated with the time of the dinosaurs' extinction.

Although "new facts," as Imre Lakatos has termed them, are not logically privileged in the evaluation of scientific theories, the ability to anticipate an as yet unknown or unexpected phenomenon or entity is, psychologically speaking, extremely significant.[48] Were we now to uncover that Mendeleyev had already discovered ekaaluminum before he developed the Periodic Table, we would no doubt be far less impressed by the achievement and might even have less faith in the underlying logic. By offering the prospect of prediction, science gives man some hope of control over his fate. We have no way of being certain that the universe is governed by timeless laws, that the future will in a very fundamental way be like the past. But successful prediction is taken as evidence of the existence of a larger transcendental order. Through science, it would seem, we gain the foundation and justification for a better future. Insofar as it assuages existential fears and generates a sense of control over the world, science can be seen as "an extension of the psyche in its conscious, rational dimension."[49]

The apparent success of the logical positivist theory of science in the natural sciences is in large part responsible for its popularity, and it predisposes many to embrace the argument that it is equally suitable to the study of human behavior. Through rigorous application of deductive logic, Hempel argues, human history can be explained in terms of general laws.[50] Similar convictions underlie efforts to promote logical positivism in sociology, psychology, and political science.[51]

The relevance of a covering law model of explanation for the social sciences has, however, come under increasing scrutiny. Some challenge the underlying assumption that the relationships governing social outcomes share the time-less quality of relationships between nonsentient entities in the physical world. Because social systems are ordered and function through changing structures of meaning rather than (or in addition to) physical or natural rela-tionships, the search for general laws is probably misguided and likely to fail.[52] By means of critical reflection, humans are capable of learning and change. They not only act within natural and social systems, they also strategically in-tervene to structure them in desirable directions. Because human beings often seek knowledge over a situation in order to transcend it, causal regularities in the social world will be historically bound.[53] Thus, it is argued, social scientists should spend less time trying to discover timeless laws and general theories to explain them and instead invest more effort in understanding contemporary relationships in service of the general welfare.[54]

In a related fashion, critical theorists, whether Marxist or postmodernist, ar-gue that the search for timeless laws stifles the social sciences and leads to a conservative bias. For example, in criticizing mainstream international rela-tions theory, Robert Cox has argued that despite its claims to objectivity, "it is value bound by virtue of the fact that it implicitly accepts the prevailing order as its own framework." Similarly, Richard Ashley has argued that the search for timeless laws leads to "a positivist structuralism that treats the given order as the natural order, limits rather than expands political discourse, negates or triv-ializes the significance of variety across time and place, subordinates all prac-tice to an interest in control, bows to the ideal of a social power beyond re-sponsibility, and thereby deprives political interaction of those practical capacities which make social learning and creative change possible."[55]

The remainder of this chapter is devoted to a third line of critique. Whereas mathematical systems and deductive structures are based on a two-valued logic—a given statement is either "true" or "false"—empirical statements are always subject to uncertainty. They obey a three-valued logic. That is, empiri-cal statements fall into one of three categories: "true," "false," or "undecided."[56] The implications of the claim extend to both the natural and the social sciences.

Owing to the theory-dependence of observation, many—some would argue all—observation statements are fallible. As I argued in chapter 2, even the most basic observations are theory-laden. Simple observation statements are made in terms of preexisting concepts and categories that are themselves embedded in theoretical understandings of the world, many of which are unexamined or taken for granted. Insofar as the logical positivist is committed to the proposition that theories can never be proven true but only tentatively corroborated, conclusively establishing the empirical validity of theoretically derived propositions on the basis of theory-laden observations is, as a matter of principle, impossible. Recalling that Popper's claim to have solved the problem of induction rests on the proposition that universal statements can be falsified on the basis of single observation statements, it becomes immediately clear that if individual observation statements, by virtue of their theory-dependence, are themselves fallible, then they cannot provide the basis for conclusive falsification. Without a perfectly secure observational base, conclusive falsification is ruled out.[57]

Recognizing the problem of establishing the correspondence between a statement and the fact or state of affairs it seeks to describe—the problem of the "empirical basis"—Popper makes a distinction between the private perceptual experiences of individuals and the public observation statements to which these give rise. The latter can be verified or challenged by others through independent observation. They come to be accepted or rejected "as the result of a decision or agreement; and to that extent they are conventions."[58] The empirical basis on which we are justified in falsifying a universal statement or theoretically derived proposition is thus intersubjective and inductive!

The basic problem of establishing the correspondence between states of the world and statements about the world produces skepticism with respect to the appropriateness of a two-value logic for empirical science. Consequently, many have concluded that all observation statements are equally implicated, their veracity, in principle, undecidable. Though in some respects related, the arguments I wish to make are more limited in scope. Two are based on the difficulties associated with evaluating the status of the results of "tests" and the problems arising from concepts with fuzzy borders and are common to both the natural and social sciences. A third arises from the nature of norm-governed behavior and efforts to explain it and is particular to the social sciences.

Moving from Deductive Logic to Empirical Tests

The goal of science is to provide warranted knowledge about the world (or, indeed, the universe). But because the world is unknowable in its complexity, the search for knowledge necessarily involves the parceling of experience. Scientific analysis requires the analyst to select from the infinite set of possible observations those phenomena she finds most interesting and believes most relevant to the explanation she seeks. The production of knowledge is thus akin to a radical dissection where all but the bare bones of the organism are discarded.

Having singled out particular phenomena as meaningful or important, the scientist then goes about trying to explain them. Through the process of theorizing, the scientist relates one set of phenomena to others in a systematic fashion with the goal of generating explanations.

For the logical positivist, an adequate account or explanation consists of showing how a statement describing a given phenomenon or state of the world can be derived from a statement of initial conditions using one or more general hypotheses or universal laws as premises. The logical structure of scientific prediction is essentially the same. In practice, however, explanation generally involves a known outcome and involves the search for initial conditions necessary and sufficient to have caused it in light of some general hypothesis. In the case of prediction, initial conditions are known or given and their effect, by virtue of the operation of a general law, is identified a priori.[59] And the logical positivist's understanding of explanation is held to apply to both natural and social phenomena: "Historical explanation, too, aims at showing that the event in question was not a 'matter of chance,' but was to be expected in view of certain antecedent or simultaneous conditions. The expectation referred to is not prophecy or divination, but rational scientific anticipation which rests on the assumption of general laws."[60]

Having identified general laws and generated theories to both link and explain them, science is necessarily concerned with the question of whether to accept or reject them. In general, this is accomplished through the construction of suitable tests. Empirical testing is the means by which the logical positivist seeks to establish the validity of a proposed hypothesis, and he admits as scientific only those hypothesis which on the basis of testing are, in principle, falsifiable.

The simplest tests are of single observation statements and based more or less on a direct "observation" of the pertinent "facts." Observations of this kind would most likely suffice as tests of the validity of statements such as, "It is raining outside," or "This dog has only three legs." Although even everyday observation statements such as these are theory-laden and thus fallible in the sense discussed above, a consensus regarding the correspondence of such observation statements with the observations they seek to describe usually can be established quite readily.

Often, however, general statements and theoretical conjectures are not amenable to testing by means of direct observation. In addition to the fact that we cannot directly observe the universe of cases over which a general relationship is held to obtain, many hypotheses involve relationships between nonobservable entities. The condition of nonobservability may reflect limits in the technology of observation and measurement and thus prove transient. However, it often reflects the fact that the hypothesized relationships involve theoretical entities—for example gravitational force—which are unobservable in principle. Moreover, many theoretical conjectures appeal to a hypothetical past in an effort to explain present conditions. Because we cannot "observe" directly whether the universe began with a big bang, whether *homo sapiens* evolved from *Australopithicus,* whether individuals engage in cost-benefit calculus prior to making decisions, or whether individuals feel regret or remorse for having violated social conventions, we are forced to rely on indirect methods of testing in an effort to reach a judgment on the empirical validity of such theories. Thus, "from the hypothesis under test, suitable other statements are inferred which describe certain directly observable phenomena that should be found to occur under specifiable circumstances if the hypothesis is true; then those inferred statements are tested directly; i.e., by checking whether the specified phenomena do in fact occur; finally, the proposed hypothesis is accepted or rejected in light of the outcome of these tests."[61]

For the logical positivist, the process of testing is merely the extension of the process of explanation. On the basis of certain initial conditions (cause) and a theoretical statement, hypothesis, or general law, a particular state of the world (effect) is predicted (or ruled out). The empirical validity of the predicted state is then established by means of observation.

The centrality of testing to the scientific enterprise is shown by the volumes devoted to research design and the construction of valid testing procedures. The art of testing consists of gaining maximum analytic leverage from what is necessarily a limited observational base. The ideal scientific test would take the form of a perfect experiment, where all relevant conditions are known and deliberately subjected to severe control. In its simplest form, the experimental method constructs two equivalent situations, one of which is exposed to a stimulus while the other (the control situation) is not. The two situations can then be compared and any differences between them attributed to the stimulus.

In practice, both the identification of relevant conditions and their susceptibility to investigator control vary greatly. Many hypotheses—in both the natural and social sciences—do not lend themselves to testing by means of controlled experiment. Hence, tests often take the form of comparing theoretically derived predictions to "naturally" occurring data.[62] The inferential value of such observations, sometimes referred to as *quasi-experiments,* is dependent upon the criteria according to which they are selected.[63] Whereas in true experiments subjects are randomly assigned to the conditions under study:

> The task confronting persons who try to interpret the results from quasi-experiments is basically one of separating the effects of a treatment from those due to the initial noncomparability between the average units in each treatment group; only the effects of the treatment are of research interest. To achieve this separation of effects, the researcher has to explicate the specific threats to valid causal inference that random assignment rules out and then in some way deal with these threats. In a sense, quasi-experiments require making explicit the irrelevant causal forces hidden within the ceteris paribus of random assignment.[64]

When the analyst has access to a large number of random or representative observations, statistical analysis can be employed to manipulate and compare the values assigned to theoretically derived variables in an effort to determine whether any partial correlations deviate systematically from those predicted merely by chance.[65] Often, however, the number of available observations is too small to allow for reliable statistical manipulation. Thus, analysts have developed a number of strategies for testing hypotheses through comparative and single-case analysis.

Although individual historical episodes are always in some sense unique, science is based on the grouping of discrete events into classes or categories that are subject to comparison.[66] Even when deliberate investigator control is impossible, the logic of experimental design suggests ways of grouping and comparing individuals from a given class or category in an effort to discover or test for relationships among variables. Through the identification of historical constellations or cases where the values of theoretically relevant initial conditions are similar along most dimensions but vary along some dimension or dimensions believed to be responsible for the operation of a hypothesized general law, the analyst manipulates and compares historical data in an admittedly imperfect effort to control across variables and thereby strengthen the inferential value of any differences observed in the historical trajectories of each case.[67]

When structured and focused comparison of multiple cases is either impossible or impractical, single-case analysis has been used as a means of testing general laws and theories. Of particular interest in this regard are the claims made for the evidentiary value of "critical" or "crucial" case studies. According to Eckstein, "The essential abstract characteristic of a crucial case can be deduced from its function as a test of a theory. It is a case that *must closely fit* a theory if one is to have confidence in the theory's validity, or, conversely *must not fit* equally well any rule contrary to that proposed. . . . Generally speaking, 'must fit' cases are those that naturally have the characteristics of a well-designed experiment, so that mere forecasts must be as accurate as concrete, or even experimental, predictions."[68] A case can be said to be a "must fit" when it is comprised of a set of initial conditions which the theory under analysis maintains are necessary and sufficient to produce (or rule out) a given outcome.

Further removed from the experimental ideal, if more common, are "most likely" and "least likely" case analyses. "Most likely" cases are characterized by a set of initial conditions which lead to the strong expectation that evidence in favor of a hypothesized relationship should be present. A "least likely" case is one which would appear to be adequately accounted for by a competing or already accepted explanation and where the expectation that evidence will support a novel explanation is weak.[69]

Thinking in terms of most likely and least likely cases sharpens one's awareness of the fact that the empirical sciences involve testing theories and the hypotheses deduced from them against expectations generated by other theories, and not against nature or "empirical reality," as is often asserted.[70] It is precisely because a novel prediction is unexpected from the standpoint of accepted theory that its subsequent confirmation has a strong impact on existing understandings and further research. For example, in the field of international political economy, established trade theory maintains that rising levels of import penetration produce demands for protectionist trade policies by those industries most severely impacted by foreign imports. Challenging the conventional wisdom, Helen Milner argued that increased levels of cross-border intra-firm trade in industries that have moved toward globalized production should produce relatively stable preferences for free trade, even in periods of increased import penetration. To test her hypothesis, Milner concentrated on hard cases from the standpoint of established trade theory. That is, she studied the formation of firm trade preferences in industries facing high increases in import penetration, rising unemployment, declining profits, and excess production capacity. Because firms in such distressed industries were presumed to have a strong interest in increased protection in the home market, her finding that firms with strong ties to the international economy continued to favor free trade proved to be a strong challenge to the conventional wisdom.[71]

Advocates of crucial case studies argue that because they are identified on the basis of logical deductions, they can (at least in principle) produce the sort of falsification of which Popper spoke. The beauty of the modus tollens, Popper argued, is that it allows one to reject an entire theoretical framework on the basis of a single observation statement, if such a statement affirms a state of affairs that is logically prohibited given the initial conditions and a universal law. If the evidence gleaned from a careful analysis of a "must fit" or "most likely" case affirms a state of affairs logically inconsistent with the theory being tested, then the investigator has solid grounds for rejecting it.[72] Moreover, if a novel proposition appears to be confirmed under conditions where, in light of all that we think we know of the world, it "must not fit" or should be "least likely" to obtain, then the investigator has strong grounds for questioning the validity of prevailing understandings and for deciding to proceed toward the development of an alternative theory.

Limits to Falsifiability

There is, however, a problem with Popper's claim to have resolved the question of how to employ singular observation statements in pursuit of general knowledge in a logically coherent fashion. Although logically sound, both the criterion of falsification and the methodology of testing associated with it are flawed. In scientific practice almost every theory turns out to be falsified to some degree by the world of experience. That is, when tested, most theories cannot provide complete or perfect accounts of all relevant observations. The question confronting the researcher, then, is how to treat the discrepant or unexpected "variance."[73] For this, logical positivism provides precious little guidance. The problem is most pronounced when a "crucial experiment" or "critical case" produces empirical evidence that appears to contradict the theory under consideration, as logic alone cannot provide an indication of whether the "error" is a refutation of the basic theoretical assumptions and axioms or the result of a failure to establish and control initial conditions or a function of faulty or inadequate measurement.[74]

A basic problem concerns the relationship of logic to observation. As Ziman argues, "the identification of ideal with empirical statements is not deductive."[75] What is logically compelling need not be empirically valid. However, the difficulties associated with establishing the veracity of even simple observation statements are not insignificant and might indeed prove consequential to progress in any given research program. Consider the statement:

> "The distance from London to Bristol is 120 miles." What do we mean by "London" and "Bristol"? Does "London" mean the City of London, or the area covered by the Greater London Council? Is Avonmouth part of Bristol for this purpose? Does the measurement refer to the distance between the centres of the areas of the two regions, or to certain conventional points such as the Post Office Tower? Even if these points were defined, could we determine the distance to an accuracy of 10^{-8} cm? Does the measurement allow for thermal expansion, the microscopic movements of the earth's surface, the influence of the tides, the phases of the moon, the behaviour of the local population and other conceivable interfering factors? The point is that this sort of statement—or any other empirical statement—could not be made indefinitely precise. We would eventually be forced to admit that a statement of the form "the distance from London to Bristol is less than (say) 193.6142857 km," is undecided and cannot be taken to be true or false.[76]

Indeed, moving from the ideal to the empirical is an exercise in operationalization and is subject to all of the limitations of operationalism discussed in the previous chapters.[77] Because the logical positivist account of science requires the linking of covering laws to initial conditions, which must be empirically established in order to conduct a valid "test," and because the establishment of initial conditions is subject to the uncertainties inherent to operationalization, we can never know whether the results of our tests truly have bearing on theoretically established relationships.

Such uncertainties are of little moment when the results of empirical investigations appear to conform to theory-grounded expectations. In daily scientific practice, apparent corroborating evidence is almost always taken as unproblematic "confirmation" of—or considered to be "harmonious" with—the theory under consideration, even when the evidence is not sufficiently strong to rule out alternative explanations or would be consistent with a variety of theories. Thus, although widely accepted as having confirmed that the gravitational field of the sun bends light rays, as predicted by Einstein's general theory of relativity, Eddington's photographs of the 1919 solar eclipse were later found to be as inconsistent with the predictions of Einstein's theory as they were with the Newtonian theory they were hailed as having falsified.[78]

When, however, tests produce results that are ambiguous or that would appear to contradict conclusions that are logically necessary from the standpoint of theory, questions of measurement error are immediately raised, or the results ignored altogether.[79] As one practitioner put it:

> The process of explaining away deviations is in fact quite indispensable to the daily routine of research. In my laboratory I find the laws of nature formally contradicted at every hour, but I explain this away by the assumption of experimental error. I know that this may cause me one day to explain away a fundamentally new phenomenon and to miss a great discovery. Such things have often happened in the history of science. Yet I shall continue to explain away my odd results, for if every anomaly observed in my laboratory were taken at its face value, research would instantly degenerate into a wild-goose chase after imaginary fundamental novelties.[80]

Consider, for example, the prediction of a large flux of neutrinos emanating from nuclear reactions at the core of the sun, which should be observable as they come into contact with the earth. Neutrinos, the lightest and least reactive of the elementary particles in the standard model of physics, are elusive but can be observed with highly sophisticated equipment. For decades, scientists have been searching for solar neutrinos but have only observed them in numbers far lower than predicted by theory.[81] Whereas this has led some astrophysicists to reject the underlying theory of the sun's source of energy, others have devoted their efforts to "explain away" the anomaly, either by challenging the astronomy or the radiochemistry that produced the data.[82]

Neutrinos come in one of three forms: electron, muon, and tau. A possible explanation for the low numbers of observable neutrinos is the hypothesis that electron-neutrinos produced by nuclear fusion in the sun's core mutate to either muon or tau neutrinos, which are much harder to detect. Technical advances in detection appear to confirm that such mutations—known as neutrino oscillations—indeed are occurring.[83] But in rescuing the dominant theory of the sun's energy source, the findings call into question more fundamental assumptions of the nature of the universe. Like photons, neutrinos are assumed to be massless. But neutrino oscillations would be possible only if neutrinos have mass. If one is to accept the empirical statement that neutrinos can assume various forms, then one is forced to reject core elements of the

dominant paradigm in physics. Yet if one rejects the finding of neutrino oscillations, one is forced to question the validity of the theory of fusion derived
from the very same paradigm. Deductive logic alone cannot direct us toward
a solution to the dilemma.

Although by comparison the supporting theoretical edifice in political science is far less developed, a similar controversy concerns the absence of a coalition of states devoted to balancing against the United States as the dominant
power in the post–cold war international system. Realist balance of power theory maintains that the absence of world empire is best explained by the historical formation and re-formation of systemwide balances of power. Because
there is no authority above the individual states that can provide for law and
order and thereby guarantee their continued sovereignty, states create alliances
to aggregate capabilities in order to deter attacks and enhance territorial defense in a system comprised of other powerful states and coalitions.[84]

Apart from balancing the military capabilities of a common enemy, however, states are held to have few incentives to cooperate with one another, even
in pursuit of joint gains, as the distribution of such gains presents a potential
source of conflict and threat to the existing balance of power.[85] In the wake of
large-scale conflict, the balance of power in the international system is expected to favor the members of the winning coalition. And with the defeat of
the common enemy, a state's erstwhile allies constitute the only remaining
threats to its own security. Mutual uncertainty among the members of the winning coalition produces new alignments and leads to the collapse of the vic-
torious alliance:

> In a competition for the position of leader, balancing is sensible behavior where
> the victory of one coalition over another leaves a weaker members of the winning
> coalition at the mercy of the stronger ones. Nobody wants anyone else to win;
> none of the great powers wants one of their number to emerge as the leader. If
> two coalitions form and one of them weakens, perhaps because of political disor-
> der of a member, we expect the extent of the other coalition's military prepara-
> tion to slacken or its unity to lessen. The classic example of the later effect is the
> breaking apart of a war winning coalition in or just after the moment of victory.[86]

Indeed, the shadow of any postwar balance of power often colors intra-alliance
debates over strategy and methods for prosecuting the war and produces a
weakening of alliance cohesion even before victory has been secured: "The
various ways of winning rarely lead to the same results for all the partners.

Logically, each state desires to contribute to the victory, but without weakening itself in relation to its allies. These rivalries fatally diminish the effectiveness of the coalition."[87] Thus, an alliance is not expected to survive the defeat or demise of the common threat it was created to address. Deprived of a common enemy, balance of power theory predicts that an existing alliance will collapse and a new alignment will form, as states react to a new distribution of capabilities across the system.[88]

Following the logic of balance of power theory, leading analysts of international security affairs predicted that in the wake of the cold war, the NATO alliance would collapse and new alliances aimed at balancing the hegemony of the United States would take its place.[89] Yet over a decade after the collapse of the Soviet Union and the Warsaw Pact, NATO not only persists but is expanding, both in terms of reach and missions. And although the gap between the military and economic capabilities of the United States and the remaining great powers continues to increase, there is no coalition of states devoted to balancing American hegemony in the international system. True, the French denounce the *hyperpuissance* enjoyed by the United States, and the leaders of Russia and China routinely speak of the need to reestablish multipolarity, but such rhetoric has to date failed to generate the action necessary to effectively balance American primacy.[90]

Widely regarded as providing a critical test of the balance of power theory, the history of international politics since the end of the cold war has provoked intense theoretical controversy.[91] The persistence of NATO as well as the nonexistence of a coalition of great powers directed against the United States are recognized as theoretical anomalies by both the proponents of balance of power theory as well as its longstanding critics. But the empirical data have led remarkably few balance of power theorists to conclude that the theory is flawed.[92] Whereas liberal scholars such as Celeste Wallander and Robert Keohane have used the data to argue that balance of power theory has failed to take account of the multiple functions alliances perform and to develop a competing institutionalist theory of international security, realists have tended instead to argue that the data itself is flawed.[93] Most extreme in this regard is, not surprisingly, Kenneth Waltz, who argues that as a alliance, NATO has indeed disappeared: "I expected NATO to dwindle at the Cold War's end and ultimately disappear. In a basic sense, the expectation has been borne out. NATO is no longer even a treaty of guarantee because one cannot answer the question, guarantee against whom?"[94] Other realists are somewhat less categorical.

Rather than reject balance of power theory on the basis of the apparent failure of states to balance and thereby constrain American power, Feaver pleads for better data, by which he means more precise operational measures: "Has the United States been 'punished' for post–cold war adventurism? It is hard to say because realists have yet to provide a clearly defined way of measuring punishment or system constraints."[95]

The controversies surrounding the "missing" neutrinos or the balancing behavior of states in anarchy demonstrate that the results of experiments or the implications of observation statements for purposes of evaluating theories are often indeterminate. Because we cannot be certain that our observations are reliable, Popper's criterion of demarcation is of no guidance to the individual analyst in deciding whether or not to reject a given theory or instead question the very evidence that apparently falsifies it. Whereas deductive logic requires the exclusion of the undecidable case, and the modus tollens presupposes the ability to establish the veracity of a purely existential statement, the logic of scientific practice is three-valued, with many statements falling into the category of "undecidable."

The claim can be justified on purely practical grounds. Because theory and evidence are intimately linked, science could not progress if the practitioner were to discard a theory on the basis of a single observation or even a series of observations appearing to contradict it. In the early phases of a research program, when theory is weakest, grounds for rejecting both theory and evidence are likely to be numerous. And although both the quality and evidentiary status of the data is likely to improve with the development of theory,

> it would be unwise and even irrational for the scientist to drop or significantly modify a well-established theory to conform to a small amount of discrepant information. Instead he must follow the implications of the weight of the evidence. This will necessarily involve ignoring or twisting bits of evidence that seem to contradict the theory he thinks is correct. To a person who holds a new theory, it will seem obvious that the proponents of the established theory are ignoring crucial evidence and devising unnecessarily complex and ad hoc explanations to try to save it. But the alternative to this way of treating evidence is to abandon any attempt to understand the world.[96]

The problems associated with relating theory and data for purposes of testing and ultimately falsification are common to both natural and social scientific practice. For a variety of reasons, however, they are more pronounced in the social sciences. First, the links between theory and data are in general more removed.[97] Moreover, although the natural sciences have not developed an observation language that is theory-independent, much measurement knowledge can be said to be theory-neutral in that it is anchored in broader paradigms common to the variety of competing theories. For example, each of the many ways of measuring temperature is based on known physical principles accepted by every practicing physicist. This facilitates testing, as the same data can be used to adjudicate among competing theoretical claims. By contrast, the social sciences lack widely accepted measurement protocols grounded in theory-neutral observation language. Individual researchers frequently choose measurement procedures that seem to work on pragmatic, if not intuitive, grounds.[98] In the absence of generally accepted substantive theories on which to base measurement procedures, it is not surprising that we often cannot agree on the evidentiary status of a given set of data for purposes of testing theoretical claims.[99]

Further undermining our confidence in rejecting a theory on the basis of a single observation or even a series of observations is the fact that the subjects of social science research—be they individuals, groups, organizations, societies, or nation states—are not homogeneous. Grounded in the metaphysical assumption that nature is both continuous and homogeneous, the physicist "can be confident that the light waves observed from a nonrandom set of stars tell us something of a general nature." By contrast, the sociologist's "typical questions cannot be answered with much confidence by interviewing any 12 people."[100] Because ceteris paribus conditions are never guaranteed in the social sciences, test results in principle are always subject to perturbations arising from relationships among variables for which—even if they are known— there is inadequate control.

Whereas the laws of nature are held to be timeless, as soon as one accords human beings the capacity for reflection and learning, one is forced to admit that social laws—to the extent that they can be identified at all—are most likely timebound. Thus, when a given test produces results that would appear to falsify a theory, the social scientist faces the daunting task of establishing whether it is the data, the initial conditions, the covering law, or perhaps only its temporal scope that is implicated. But perhaps the task is inappropriate. As Cronbach argues:

> All this begins to suggest that general, lasting, definite "laws" are in principle beyond the reach of social science, that sheer empirical generalization is doomed as

a research strategy. Extrapolation to new circumstances apparently has to rest on a rhetorical argument, one that relies on *qualitative* beliefs about the processes at work in the old and new situation. . . . Skepticism regarding generalizations that reach beyond time, place, population expresses a constructive attitude, not nihilism. The sooner all social scientists are aware that data never speak for themselves, that without a carefully framed statement of boundary conditions generalizations are misleading or trivially vague, and that forecasts depend on substantive conjectures, the sooner will social science be consistently a source of enlightenment.[101]

As one moves from the realm of logic to that of empirical tests, Popper's claim to have solved the problem of induction—the justification of universal claims on the basis of a finite number of observations—becomes increasingly unconvincing. Owing to the problematic status of observations, falsification of theories cannot proceed according to a straightforward mechanical procedure whereby the "fit" between theory and empirical evidence is established. Rather, it must turn on the expert judgments of communities of scientists who must interpret the meaning of test results in light of what is held to be settled or understood, given the uncertainties associated with the data and the idealizations of mathematical analysis.[102] From this perspective, knowledge of the empirical world should not be regarded as resting on objective "facts," but rather on linked complexes of theoretically informed conventions on what *may be*.[103]

Graded Membership and Fuzzy Logic

Classical logic rests on discrete categories and the principle of the excluded middle: a given statement must be either true or false. But much of our daily experience and knowledge does not conform to the strictures of mathematical logic. As the discussions in the previous chapters illustrated, humans interact with a world in which the boundaries between things often are not distinct. The existence of concepts comprised of a focal or prototypical core member and extended on the basis of resemblance for which there are no clearly defined borders thus presents a problem for classical logic. When concepts are conceived as sets with fuzzy boundaries, a given individual, object, case, event, or observation may defy clear and concise categorization.

For example, in the United States, the categorization of persons according to race has become increasingly difficult as historical taboos against interracial marriage have decayed. Whereas persons were traditionally classified as Caucasian, Black, Native-American, Asian, or Mixed, with the later addition of Hispanic, in recent years many surveys have chosen to add a catch-all category: "Other." What precisely constitutes this "other" is, however, unclear. Many individuals choose to mark more than one category and thereby render their data invalid for purposes of statistical analysis. The golf phenomenon Tiger Woods is characteristic. Leaving the amateur circuit to play his first U.S. Open, he released a statement on the question of his racial background, which—owing to the fact that golf has traditionally been a rather "white" sport—had so preoccupied the press: "The various media have portrayed me as African-American, sometimes Asian. In fact I am both. . . . On my father's side I am African-American, on my mother's side I am Thai. Truthfully, I feel very fortunate and equally proud, to be both African-American and Asian. . . . The bottom line is that I am American."[104]

Graded membership produces not only concepts with fuzzy borders but also fuzzy truth statements. To say that a person with Asian, European, and African ancestors is "Caucasian" is—given most people's understanding of the concept of Caucasian—true, to a certain degree. But it is also to some degree false. The same could be said of a statement that the person is "Black" or "Asian."[105] Although fuzzy truth claims would appear to constitute inexact information, the problem is not one that is amenable to solution by means of probabilistic statements. Probability is a property relating to uncertainty over the occurrence of events in the world. Fuzzy truth claims result from gradations of membership in sets. Whereas a probabilistic statement is a statement that is likely (to some degree) to be completely true, a fuzzy logical statement is true (under a given set of conditions or in a given context) to some particular fixed degree. "The statement that a whale is sort of a fish does not mean that if you randomly sample a whale there is a chance it will be a fish. Rather it means that it is partly true of each and every whale that it is a fish."[106]

Moreover, the issue is not one of the distinction between discrete and continuous variation. Based on the proposition that concepts and categories are comprised of individuals that can be characterized as enjoying varying degrees of membership, the dimensions according to which they vary are not uniform across the set. For example, most persons would consider an ostrich to be less of a bird than a robin owing primarily to its size and the fact that it cannot fly. But how would a penguin rank in terms of "birdness" as compared to an ostrich? On certain dimensions (size, for example) it would rank closer to the prototypical bird than an ostrich, but on others (habitat and the fact that it swims under water) it deviates more.

The difference between ordinal scales and graded membership can also be grasped when one considers that two individuals might each be full members of a set even though they deviate from a prototypical or focal member in varying degrees. Charles Ragin considers the problem for multidimensional concepts for which there exists a composite index:

> Consider the contrast between a conventional measure of degree of Protestantism, applied to individuals, and the fuzzy set of Protestants. Imagine that the conventional measure is based on a variety of indicators of Protestant behaviors, attitudes, and beliefs, and that these different indicators strongly correlate with each other, justifying their combination into a single index of degree of Protestantism. Assume further that this scale is both valid and reliable. But where on this scale is the cut-off value (or values) separating those who are more in the set of Protestants from those who are more in the set of non-Protestants?
>
> To answer these questions, the researcher needs not only an index of Protestantism, the fine-grained measure just described, but also a good base of substantive knowledge about Protestantism and a solid grasp of its theoretical relevance—why degree of membership in the set of Protestants matters and how it should be assessed. . . .
>
> This infusion of knowledge transforms rankings that are almost entirely relative in nature (e.g., degree of Protestantism) to ones that show degree of membership in a well-defined set (e.g., degree of membership in the set of Protestants) . . . [and] often redefines portions of the range of a conventional continuous variable as irrelevant. For example, the range of variation in the Protestantism index above a certain value may be irrelevant to membership in the set—scores of 1.0. Likewise the range of variation in this index below a certain value also may be irrelevant to the fuzzy set of Protestants because these scores may all signal full nonmembership in the set—scores of 0.[107]

Ragin's example makes clear the theory-dependence of concepts and categories. Full-fledged members of the group "Protestant" might still display variation in the degree to which they are Protestant in terms of a composite index, but these variations might well be unimportant from the standpoint of degree of membership in a theoretically defined set. Similarly, one might be able to identify and differentiate among degrees of Protestant behavior in non-Protestants, even if such variance has no bearing on the question of whether or not such individuals should be considered members of the set of all Protestants.

If the issue were merely a function of identifying the proper cutoff point for membership, however, it would not necessarily constitute a fundamental obstacle to the application of classical logic, which only demands that categories be discrete.[108] The problem, however, is that the dimensions according to which members of a category vary are often open-ended and therefore not subject to composition. Even in cases where one might conceive of a fuzzy set in terms of a simple three-valued logic—with the score of 1 constituting items which are clearly "in" the set, 0 representing those that are "out," and 0.5 those that are neither fully in nor fully out—the criterion according to which one would assign a given observation a 0.5 score often cannot be identified a priori.

The assertion is based on the proposition that many scientific concepts refer to classes of objects, events, or ideas that are characterized by diverse complexes of features, many of which are integral or constitutive of the individual case, even if none is shared by all members of the set.[109] Often one simply cannot construct categories with crisp boundaries in terms of necessary or sufficient properties. Rather, as was argued in chapters 2 and 3, concept extension occurs according to judgments of similarity. The argument both grants and challenges central claims of two opposing epistemological positions.[110] On the one hand, it grants that every observation is to some degree a unique and individual construction of reality, a proposition that increasingly unites rather than divides the natural and social sciences.[111] Efforts to construct concepts or categories on the basis of equivalent observations thus cannot rest on the presumption of complete homogeneity. On the other hand, judgments of similarity do allow us to construct concepts and generate sets, even if the borders of these are not distinct. Because, however, the universe of all possible observations is neither temporally nor spatially fixed, the range of diversity in both the number and form of features according to which judgments of similarity—and thus concept extension and set membership—might be made is unknowable.

When concepts are characterized by graded membership and fuzzy borders, standard methods of scientific testing become problematic. First, the relevant population of cases is underspecified. Large-N statistical studies require that populations be clearly defined and delimited so that the strength of correlations among variables across the set can be computed. Because much natural and social scientific research is conducted with populations that appear to be given by nature, the concept of population is rarely problematized.[112] For example, social scientists often study organizationally or territorially defined human populations that appear to be empirically given or "preconstituted." Examples include the member states of an international organization such as the United Nations; citizens of a given country, county, or city; members of a particular political party or labor union; representatives in a legislature; delegates to a convention; employees of a given firm; or members of a particular household. Medical science studies the effects of therapeutic regimes on populations that are constituted by individuals who suffer from a given disease.

Even in nature, however, defining and delimiting populations is fraught with conceptual and empirical difficulties. Consider one of the most influential concepts in the field of evolutionary biology, the "biological species concept." Articulated by the German biologist Ernst Mayr, the biological species concept regards species as "groups of interbreeding natural populations that are reproductively isolated from other such groups."[113] Natural populations are further specified as "a group of individuals so situated that any two of them have equal probability of mating with each other and producing offspring, providing . . . that they are sexually mature, of opposite sex and equivalent with respect to sexual selection. The local population is by definition and ideally a panmictic (randomly interbreeding) unit. An actual local population will, of course, always deviate more or less from the stated ideal."[114]

Leaving aside the problems posed by the existence of organisms that reproduce asexually, empirical applications of the concept give rise to serious doubts about its adequacy.[115] As Philip Kitcher has pointed out:

> In some cases there will be organisms that are not among the most probable mates of their most probable mates. If a male bird of paradise has dull plumage, his potential mates will include females who do not include him among their potential mates. Examples like this—and it is easy to see that they are legion—prompt Mayr's suggestion that we treat the notion of population as an ideal, abstracting from the actual differences in sexual selection. Of course, once we demand that mating must involve not only copulation but production of viable offspring, then we encounter troubles with those organisms carrying alleles that are not concordant with the alleles found in members of the opposite sex. If we do not make the demand, then we shall have trouble with populations in which males have the propensity to copulate with females of closely related species as well as their conspecifics.[116]

Because the variety of scenarios affecting the probability that any two organisms might mate are not known and would appear to be less than uniform, it is difficult to see how one can distinguish between species existing in marginal or less than ideal conditions and species comprised of a substantial number of organisms that routinely mate with members of other species (a finding that would suggest Mayr's definition rests on faulty theoretical assumptions).[117]

Whereas Mayr's definition treats species basically as temporally restricted populations, Hull has proposed the delineation of species as populations of organisms historically connected with one another on the basis of *actual* (rather than modal) mating patterns.[118] At first glance, Hull's approach would appear to solve the problem posed by the existence of organisms at the margins of Mayr's population of randomly breeding individuals. But in shifting the focus from the *possibility* of gene exchange to *actual* matings between organisms, Hull raises a new set of conceptual conundrums: "One obvious trouble results from the fact that, in many species, vast numbers of organisms belonging to the same population do not mate at all. This difficulty could be overcome by supposing that organisms whose parents belong to the same population and that inhabit the same region belong to the same population. Unfortunately, that supposition would debar *by fiat* the possibility of instant speciation, and would yield counterintuitive results in the known cases in which polyploidy results from a single generation event."[119] Moreover, given the existence of individual organisms that only mate with members of different species (especially when these have relatives that engage in matings with conspecifics), as well as other naturally occurring forms of hybridization, the delimitation of populations on the basis of actual descent could produce assemblages comprised "of members of different species—perhaps even species that are quite distantly related but connected by a chain of close relatives."[120]

Although species, conceived as populations of like organisms, are generally held to be real and given by nature, biologists have not been able to construct an operational concept that produces generally accepted data.[121] Whether conceived in terms of temporally bound populations or as populations constituted on the basis of genealogy, the borders between species are not distinct. And without a readily deployable concept of species, the testability of evolutionary theory as well as its utility for research in fields such as paleontology and neontology is compromised.[122] "How is it possible to claim that one species descended from another . . . before having first demonstrated the existence of those particular species or taxa?"[123]

Owing to the pervasiveness of concepts and categories characterized by graded membership and fuzzy borders, the problem of underspecified populations is perhaps even more pronounced in the social sciences, where most populations are clearly not given by nature. As I argued in chapter 3, debates over the proper composition of datasets are inherent to the social scientific enterprise and cannot be resolved by appeals to "the facts" or through more precise operational measures. Because the delimitation of populations is not straightforward, differences in theoretical predilections or observational perspective will lead individual scholars to different judgments, especially at the margins.

Changing the composition of the set of relevant cases or observations renders testing extremely difficult. First, such shifts can alter relationships between putative causal variables across the set of positive cases. Second, shifting judgments over the proper borders of concepts also affect the composition of the set of negative cases, which for purposes of causal and/or statistical analysis is equally significant. For example, assume that the recent spate of ethnically based civil wars occurred in a substantial subset of former Warsaw Pact countries but not in other multiethnic countries undergoing democratic transitions. If the investigator were to define the relevant population of observations as "all multiethnic countries undergoing democratic transition"—a group that would include a large number of Latin American, Asian, and African states—then one of the best predictors, and perhaps the only strong predictor, of ethnic civil strife would be the status of having been a member of the Warsaw Pact.

In this example, by defining the population of relevant cases as all multiethnic states undergoing democratic transition, the analyst predetermines a major finding. But is a country's communist past a predictor of ethnic civil war, or should it be used to delimit a smaller, more uniform population of observations (all former members of the Warsaw Pact, or perhaps only those former Warsaw Pact countries that are multiethnic in composition)? If the population of relevant cases were defined in terms of a shared communist past, other factors—for example, the pace of economic reform, the presence and scope of economic inequalities, or perhaps the effectiveness and degree of openness of political institutions—would emerge as strongly correlated with levels of political stability.[124]

Sophisticated analysts will no doubt argue that there are technical solutions to such problems, that they are essentially problems of research design. Even if it were possible to reach consensus on the population of known cases, however, social science shares a problem with evolutionary science that raises additional doubts regarding the assumption of, and/or the prospects for, generating populations of equivalent individuals. In much of social science, what constitutes the individual cases, instances, or observations are complexes or configurations of features, a nonuniform subset of which provide the grounds for similarity judgments and categorization or concept extension.[125] And without the assumption of homogeneity, one cannot generalize to the universe of cases on the basis of individual case studies (in the negative sense of falsifying a claim on the basis of a critical or crucial case) or even a large-N statistical study (as when one infers properties of the whole on the basis of statistically significant relationships among a representative subset). When the range of features that could give rise to a judgment of similarity is unknown, we do not even know what would constitute a representative sample and thus cannot assume that relationships in any given sample will hold across all members of the set.[126] And owing to the progress of time and the capacity of human beings to learn and adapt, the set of all possible configurations or complexes in social life is potentially infinite.

The assumption that it is possible to delimit populations comprised of members that are essentially equivalent and interchangeable is closely linked to a strong assumption that the universe is characterized by *causal homogeneity*. In its strongest form, the assumption of causal homogeneity maintains that any given causal factor will have the same effects across a given population (a statement sometimes moderated by a probability estimate).[127] The assumption often extends beyond the effects of environmental stimuli on members of the population to the effects and functions of features constitutive of the individuals themselves.

For example, proceeding from the knowledge that wings are in general conducive to flight, many have suggested that the emergence of winged insects presents a problem for proponents of evolutionary theory. Because incipient or rudimentary wings would not have conferred an advantage in terms of mobility, critics of evolutionary theory suggest that wings must have emerged all at once, fully formed.[128] But as Stephen Jay Gould has pointed out, Darwinian theory provides an elegant answer to the dilemma of wings in the hypothesis of *functional shift*. Whereas many researchers have spent years trying to uncover how the incipient stages of insect wings contributed to flight or preflight, Gould suggests the more appropriate focus is on the ways in which the rudimentary structures associated with what eventually evolved into what we today refer to as wings were related to thermo-regulation. Because of high ratios of surface area to volume, small animals tend to lose heat rapidly. Presenting a large surface area to the sun for quick heating, modern insect wings turn out to be quite effective supplementary devices for thermo-regulation. As incipient wings grew in size, they not only became better collectors of solar heat, but they began to convey aerodynamic benefits.[129]

That shared morphological features do not necessarily imply similar function has long been appreciated by anthropologists and is increasingly recognized by political scientists. Thus, Martha Finnemore found that although almost every state has a science bureaucracy, the functions and effects of these vary greatly. She argues that the driving force behind the spread of science bureaucracies in the second half of the twentieth century was essentially normative. International organizations such as UNESCO concluded that since the formation of science bureaucracies was successful in promoting economic and technological advancement in the West, their effects would be the same in the developing world, so they set out on a campaign to promote the development of science at the national level by helping states to create, organize, and expand scientific institutions. Science bureaucracies did not emerge out of the domestic conditions and challenges facing the developing world. Rather, "states adopted these bureaucracies because of a new understanding of necessary and appropriate state behavior rather than any functional need."[130]

The phenomenon of functional shift is also evidenced in social life. Recognizing that "structures originally developed for one purpose may ultimately come to serve another," Stephen Krasner has argued that the institution of state sovereignty is essentially a product of functional shift.[131] Returning for a moment to a case discussed above, although NATO as an institution was conceived and grew in response to the threat posed by the Soviet Union and its Warsaw Pact allies, its persistence in the wake of the cold war has confounded many political realists who predicted its rapid demise. But as cooperation and coordination among NATO member states both deepened and widened over the course of the cold war, the institution increasingly came to take on functions relating to the management of political and security relations among member states and not only the aggregation of their capabilities in the event of an attack from without. It is the capacity for managing political and security relations among the member states themselves that institutionalist scholars maintain accounts for the continued existence and expansion of the erstwhile cold war alliance.[132] Similarly, students of German domestic politics have noted that although the institutions of vocational training in Germany are marked by striking continuity over the past century, their function in the labor market has undergone a radical transformation. Whereas the system of vocational training was originally established to weaken a nascent social democratic labor movement, by the 1990s vocational training institutions constituted one of the chief sources of strength for organized labor.[133]

The potential for functional shift is of course central to functionalist and neofunctionalist theories of political integration. Through "spillover" effects, cooperation in one issue area is expected to produce incentives to cooperate in others, over time shifting the nature of accompanying institutions. At first limited to facilitating economic cooperation, such institutions are expected eventually to assume legitimate political authority at the expense of the sovereign state.[134] Without an understanding of how institutions have evolved—that is, how they have both shaped and been shaped by their environments—the existence of functional heterogeneity despite shared morphology is difficult to explain.[135]

When guided by the assumption that the effects of constitutive features or exogenous causes across any given population will be uniform, the analyst, confronted with significant variance in a large-N study, must decide whether to reject a hypothesized relationship or adjust the borders of the population to ensure uniformity. Owing to the theory-dependence of observation, there will always be some interplay between the constitution of populations and the theory being investigated. Nonetheless, standard scientific practice proscribes adjusting the borders of a population on the basis of effects or outcomes. Such adjustments are tautological: they rescue the proposition of homogeneity at the expense of the scientific criterion of falsifiability.[136] If, however, populations are not given by nature, then there are no obvious criteria, logical or objective, according to which the analyst can decide whether it is the hypothesized relationship or the composition of the population that is in need of revision or rejection.

When populations are delimited on the basis of judgments of similarity or resemblance rather than necessary and sufficient properties or features, a certain degree of heterogeneity is taken for granted or, indeed, seen as a guide to potentially fruitful research. While open to the prospect of causal homogeneity, the researcher does not proceed from the assumption that this necessarily will be (or that one could definitively establish it to be) the case. In this regard, borderline cases are often more informative than prototypical or core exemplars, as they are more likely to provide an indication of the degree to which the effects of a given process or feature vary in the presence or absence of other constitutive features.[137]

For example, scholars have often taken the history of economic and political development in late nineteenth- and early twentieth-century Imperial Germany either as evidence that the claims of modernization theorists regarding the democratizing effects of economic development are faulty or that Imperial Germany did not constitute a valid case for purposes of testing the theory.[138] By contrast, Sheri Berman has recently argued that Imperial Germany constitutes a particularly informative case for modernization theory precisely because of its marginal status in the population of states subjected to historical processes of economic and political development. Moreover, "from a contemporary perspective Imperial Germany appears less a gross deviation from a benign historical pattern than an early sojourner on the path many rapidly developing countries are treading today. Several features of Germany's past that were previously considered abnormal or pathological can be found elsewhere . . . and while economic development may not have brought about a full transition to democracy before the First World War, it did influence German political development in relatively clear and predictable ways."[139]

Berman's analysis is suggestive of the benefits of fuzzy over classically defined discrete concepts as well as of the limits fuzzy concepts imply with regard to claims for definitive falsification. Allowing for the existence of marginal cases may heighten the analyst's sensitivity to important contextual features or variables that condition the effects of general processes, patterns, or relationships. Through the analysis of marginal cases, the analyst might develop a more precise specification of theoretically informed speculations. For example, through the analysis of marginal democracies—e.g., new, weakly institutionalized democracies—Edward Mansfield and Jack Snyder were able to specify more clearly the links between democratic forms of government and the empirical phenomenon of the democratic peace.[140] But insofar as the ultimate bounds of fuzzy concepts are unknowable by their very nature—because concept extension is based on judgments of similarity rather than the presence of necessary and/or sufficient conditions—the status of relationships among variables across a fuzzy set is always provisional. As individual instances of a phenomenon are moved in and out of the set, the status of any previous "tests" for which they constituted data—whether corroborating or falsifying— is subject to reevaluation. Thus, as the set of states subjected to processes of modernization increased in the late twentieth and early twenty-first centuries, the inferential value of Imperial Germany's rapid industrialization and problematic political development has changed. Rather than constituting evidence against modernization theory, in the new context of the expanded set, the case appears to conform—at least partially—to theoretically generated expectations.

Because the dimensions according to which judgments of similarity are made are not exclusive to any single set—that is, certain features can be shared by members of different sets—some things may be subject to a variety of classifications. Indeed, many categories that are assumed to be mutually exclusive are, upon closer examination, discovered to be rather fuzzy. Such is often the case in biology and paleontology. Many microscopic organisms, including some that are self-propelling and derive energy both through digestive and photosynthetic processes, defy clear classification as plant or animal. Although it clearly belonged to the animal kingdom, *Archaeopteryx* was a complex assemblage of avian and reptilian features. To take an example from the field of political science, Great Britain would almost universally be accorded membership in the set of democratic states. But it might also be classified as a monarchy. It is unlikely that anyone would argue Great Britain to be prototypical of either set, but it shares enough features with prototypical exemplars to be included in each.[141] Although multiple codings of an individual phenomenon are generally held to pose a hindrance to scientific progress, this is not necessarily the case.

Consider another example, this one from the field of biology. In contrast to adherents to the biological species concept, biologists and botanists, who study organisms in which reproduction is asexual or in which hybridization is common; microbiologists, who study bacteria and viruses; as well as paleontologists, for whom the fossil record is often the only source of "hard" data—all tend to delineate species on the basis of shared morphology. Although in many cases the morphological and biological species approaches produce equivalent results, this is not always the case. Some organisms will be grouped together using one method of classification and divided using another.

Such was the case with two groups of mosquitoes that were held to represent a vector for malaria. For years, biomedical researchers were puzzled by the fact that malaria is present in some mosquito-infested areas yet absent in others. In terms of morphology, the mosquitoes were indistinguishable, so they were regarded as a single species. The puzzle was resolved once researchers shifted from a morphological to a behavioral definition of species. Although the two groups were indistinguishable in appearance, they constituted two distinct populations of interbreeding individuals—two *unique* species, when defined by Mayr's biological species concept. The reverse has proven to be the case in the study of AIDS and Lyme disease, where the grouping of viruses and bacteria according to morphology has led researchers both to the structures that make it possible for these disease vectors to attack the human organism as well as to the drugs that can block them.[142]

Although it is possible that researchers might have discovered the subclass of malaria-carrying mosquitoes without the biological species concept, it is certainly possible that they might have missed it. Such examples demonstrate that the question of whether or not a certain individual should be considered a member of one or another population cannot be answered by a simple appeal to nature, even if the criterion according to which such distinctions are made seems perfectly "natural" or "real." Rather, the extension of a particular concept or category membership to an individual phenomenon is a function of the theoretically determined interests, goals, and capacities of human beings.

CHAPTER FIVE

Social Behavior and the Indeterminacy of Norms

The previous chapter demonstrated that the covering-law approach to explanation as well as the two-value logic of falsification upon which logical positivists have constructed a theory of science break down as soon as one moves from the realm of logic to that of empirical observation. Skepticism regarding the utility of logical positivism for the social sciences and efforts to formulate general explanations for human behavior would be warranted on these grounds alone. Additional grounds are suggested by the assertion that much of social life is constituted by norm- and rule-guided behavior, the analysis and explanation of which requires resort to a three-valued logic.

Highlighting the importance of intersubjective meanings as well as the discursive processes whereby such meanings are established, in this chapter I argue that classical understandings of conceptual categories—as being defined by necessary and/or sufficient membership criteria—are misplaced when applied to the categorical judgments that both give rise to human behavior and are necessary for its satisfactory explanation and evaluation. Because the application of general norms to particular circumstances proceeds according to judgments of similarity and family resemblance, the set of all cases to which a particular norm or rule can be said to apply is neither uniform nor distinct. Hence, efforts to apply conventional social science methods to the study of norms are misguided and, not surprisingly, have led to a great many confused discussions and produced invalid research results. Because it is the field I know best, the discussion will center on studies in international politics, although the general argument is, I maintain, valid for efforts to explain behavior in other social domains.

Social Norms and Individual Choice

Human behavior is neither exclusively instinctual nor the product of reflex but also results from decisions in situations of choice. Whether I decide to spend a free day reading a book, taking a walk through the city, or visiting a museum is a product of choice. Similar decisions govern my behavior in the marketplace: given any particular supply of goods, I am confronted with the choice of how to allocate the limited financial resources I have at my disposal. Accounting for behavioral choice is thus central to the social science enterprise, and, as these rather simple examples suggest, the explanation of individual choice is often cast in terms of idiosyncratic tastes or "preferences." For some purposes, explaining individual choice in terms of preferences is perfectly reasonable, even at the expense of a deeper understanding of the origins of preferences or the social conventions that create the possibility of choice. In many situations, however, an adequate explanation for behavior cannot be constructed merely in terms of individual preferences and must be supplemented with an analysis of social norms.

Because social actors, by which I mean both individuals and collectivities, not only face the scarcity inherent to the natural world but must also interact with other social actors whose preferences might not coincide with their own, "rational" action will not only reflect egoistic preferences but also some estimation of the effects of any given choice on future interactions with others. Hence, the communicative component of action—at a basic level, the signaling of hostile or pacific intent—must be of central concern to actors engaged in rational decision-making.[1] By providing meanings shared by both actors and observers, norms provide the medium for linking individual autonomy to collective sociality.

When behavior takes place against the background of norms embodied in rules and conventions, not only must individual actors refer to them prior to making choices, but observers must understand the normative structures un-derlying action if they hope to adequately interpret and evaluate it.[2] Under-stood as "prescriptions for action in situations of choice,"[3] social norms serve to direct both actors and observers to the factors that they should take into consideration in identifying and appraising options and evaluating the choices and behavior of others in a world of infinite complexity: "First, by 'ruling out' certain methods of individual goal-seeking through the stipulation of forbear-ances, norms define the area within which conflict can be bounded. Second, within the restricted set of permissible goals and strategies, rules which take the actors' goals as given can create schemes or schedules for individual or joint enjoyment of scarce objects. Third, norms enable the parties whose goals and/ or strategies conflict to sustain a 'discourse' on their grievances, to negotiate a solution, or to ask a third party for a decision on the basis of commonly ac-cepted rules, norms, and principles."[4] To claim that much behavior is governed by social norms is not to deny the existence of other "causal" factors. Begin-ning from the assumption of a baseline of what is expected, acceptable, or "normal" in terms of social norms and conventions, however, allows us to identify and evaluate other sources of human behavior.

For example, most people would accept the proposition that the human or-ganism is subject to certain physical drives, among them a drive for sexual sat-isfaction. And yet, an appeal to "natural instincts" will explain neither the sex-ual behavior of individuals in society nor the reaction of observers to it. Although nature is replete with examples of regular matings between the males of a species and their female offspring, in almost every human society such be-havior is considered "unnatural" and abominable. It is only against the back-drop of the assumption that sexual relations are governed by social norms, such as those relating to majority and consent, that we can identify cases of sexual misconduct and investigate their general and/or particular causes and effects in a given society. Similarly, only when we understand that sex is in general a norm-governed behavior are we in a position to examine the conditions that make rape an effective tool of terror in interstate warfare and ethnic conflict and ask why some soldiers participate in such behavior and others try to stop it.[5]

The example of rape, while discomforting, is particularly informative for pur-poses of illustrating the role of norms in explanations of human behavior. What becomes immediately clear when one considers the existence of rape is the in-direct relationship between social norms and human behavior. Although they guide, shape, inform, and condition, norms cannot be said to "cause" behavior in a direct fashion. Thus, norms can be counterfactually valid: even widespread violations do not necessarily imply that a norm is weak or no longer operative. The fact that newspapers routinely report cases of rape and incest does not necessarily imply that societal norms governing the appropriate pursuit of sexual satisfaction are inoperative. Rather paradoxically, it is precisely when norms are violated that we are able to establish their precise scope and meaning in a particular social context. Unless a suspected rapist can convincingly argue that his accuser did in fact grant consent, he will be severely punished and treated as a pariah.[6] Punishment may be less severe for the rapist who can convincingly plead temporary diminished capacity owing to a drug addiction or the effects of alcohol; however, repeat offenders will most likely be regarded as morally deficient and subject to permanent removal from society and/or castration.[7]

Because compliance with norms is often explicitly linked to the provision of sanctions—punishments for noncompliance and rewards for compliance—many have mistakenly argued norm-guided behavior to be merely utilitarian, a matter of cost-benefit calculation in light of beliefs over the probable existence and effectiveness of enforcement mechanisms. In the field of political science, this tendency has its roots in a particular interpretation of the writings of prominent contractarian theorists and historically has been most pronounced in the subfield devoted to the study of international politics, where the dominant school of realism regards the absence of an international sovereign to be constitutive of an international anarchy devoid of the rule-following behaviors characteristic of domestic society.[8] At most, realists accord a role for rules and rule-guided behavior in hegemonic systems where rules are conceived as constraints on behavior promulgated and enforced by the most powerful state in the international system.[9]

The many inadequacies of such approaches to the analysis of norm-guided behavior have been persuasively argued by others.[10] Nonetheless, four issues deserve brief mention. First, even when amenable to explanation in utilitarian terms, many norms tend to be self-enforcing. This is particularly true with respect to coordination norms, a classic example being the norm directing vehicles to drive on the right or left side of the road.[11] Second, even when enforcement is an issue, there is no necessary relationship between the existence of a normative order and centralized or hierarchical institutions of authority: compliance with social norms is often promoted by means of threatened or actual exclusion and other forms of unilateral or decentralized enforcement.[12] Third, many norms enjoy deontic force. That is, they give rise to feelings of right and obligation and, when violated, engender feelings of unease and re-gret. Rule-following under such circumstances may have very little to do with material self-interest defined in terms of material gain or loss, but with images of self.[13] Finally, many norms do not prescribe or proscribe behavior in any di-rect fashion but are enabling of choice in the first instance; they constitute the rules of the game.[14] Before one can speak of the economic interests, for ex-ample, one requires the institution of the market, the normative underpin-nings of which are clearly reflected in conventions regarding money, property rights, and contracts.

Norms and the Construction of Facts

Although much of social life would appear to be norm-governed, social sci-ence has not proven particularly adept at developing norm-based explanations of human behavior in terms of generally valid covering laws that are subject to falsification by means of empirical tests. A central problem concerns the sta-tus of observable behavior in evaluating the effects of norms. First, many norms are not explicitly codified in law or formal institutions but nonetheless serve as "tacit" guides to behavior to which actors may become socialized.[15] When norms of a proscriptive nature are internalized by actors, there may be no outward behavioral traces on which to infer their existence.[16] But to infer the existence of a norm on the basis of every behavioral regularity would be to deny that behavior may indeed result from habit or environmental con-straints. Moreover, as the example of rape makes clear, the existence and gen-eral status of a norm are not necessarily challenged by recognized violations, even if they are regular and repeated.

The problem results from the fact that although norms influence both be-havior and its evaluation, the conditions under which any given norm can be said to be applicable are not a priori given but instead are established through practice. Although norms, whether constitutive of social situations or regula-tive of individual behavior therein, enjoy general claims to validity across a given class of situations, they rarely provide definitive criteria according to which the boundaries of the class can be established. By contrast, individual action as well as collective evaluative judgments in the first instance are con-cerned necessarily with the facts of a particular situation.

Insofar as norms are constitutive as well as regulative, much of norm-governed argument and reasoning is not surprisingly focused on defining the nature of the problem or issue with which the parties to a particular discourse are confronted. Before we can ask which rules should apply in a given context, we must first answer the question: "What is this a case of?" Because, however, actors confront social situations that are neither objective—in the sense of being naturally given and existing independent of subjective experience—nor unambiguous, the effects of norms on behavior and its evaluation in any given case will hinge on the results of diagnostic processes.

The diagnostic process is one of establishing category membership: of moving from the particular case to the class of events or situations over which certain norms can be argued to apply in general. Often, however, a case can be argued to be governed by multiple norms, each of which might direct behavior in rather different directions, making it impossible to subsume directly the facts of the case under a single norm. Thus, the diagnostic function is rather more akin to analogic reasoning, where actors and observers try to establish a best *fit* between the "facts" of the situation and prototypical or archetypal scenarios, of which legal precedents present a special case. The process of reasoning from case to case results in a set that is not characterized by uniformity or congruence, but by family resemblance, graded membership, and fuzzy borders. Moreover, because norms are often extended to novel situations, the universe of all cases that would belong to any given norm-constituted set is, in principle, unknowable.

The philosophical issue here at stake is not the status of any warrants that serve to link data to conclusions (although these too are problematic), but rather that of the premises from which an argument is to proceed.[17] Consider the following argument presented in the form of a classical syllogism:

All murderers are criminals subject to punishment by life imprisonment.
Mr. Smith is a murderer.
Mr. Smith is a criminal to be punished by life imprisonment.

The argument might well form the basis of a prosecutor's claim before a court of law. But even if the judge and jury accept the proposition that all murderers are criminals and should be punished by life imprisonment, it is incumbent upon the prosecutor to present the "facts" of the case in such a fashion as to convince them that Mr. Smith indeed has committed "murder." In support of his argument, the prosecuting attorney may produce eyewitness accounts of how Mr. Smith was seen to pull out a gun and kill the victim, and these eyewitness accounts may be corroborated by a coroner's report. His goal is to provide an account of the case that is persuasive if not compelling.

Of course in most cases, the defense attorney will do her best to convince the jury that the case before them is a rather different one from that presented by the prosecutor. She may try to establish that Mr. Smith was engaged in "self-defense" or perhaps that his gun misfired, the death, therefore, an "accident." The simple point is that the facts of the case must first be established, a result which is achieved by placing them in a context that is generated or constituted by norms, behind which are usually ethical values. Establishing the nature of the case is antecedent to evaluating the appropriateness of Mr. Smith's behavior and/ or any punishment implied by the existence of a general rule, and such questions cannot be answered by formal logic. Rather, they rest on a choice over the appropriate narrative account.[18] And in both legal and nonlegal situations, such choices typically involve a combination of rational and nonrational elements.[19]

Of particular relevance to the line of argument we are developing is the generative potential of general norms or principles articulated or implied in past decisions when applied to novel situations in an effort to determine an appropriate construction of the "facts." As every student of the law knows, the domain of cases over which statutory laws or legal principles that have been established through precedent can be said to apply is rarely (if ever) fixed.

Consider the classic case of common law jurisprudence known as *Donoghue v. Stevenson,* in which the plaintiff was awarded damages for injuries she suffered after consuming part of the contents of an opaque bottle of ginger beer, which was contaminated by the decomposed remains of a snail, but purchased and served to her by a friend.[20] Crucial to the outcome of the case was the nature of the relationship (if any) between the plaintiff and the manufacturer. Counsel for the defendant argued that insofar as the plaintiff had not herself purchased the bottle of ginger beer, she was merely a third party to a contract and therefore had no claim to damages. But the arguments of the plaintiff's counsel proved to be more persuasive. In the words of Lord Atkin:

> At present I content myself with pointing out that in English law there must be, and is, some general conception of relations giving rise to a duty of care, of which the particular cases found in the books are but instances. The liability for negligence, whether you style it such or treat it as in other systems as a species of "culpa," is no doubt based upon a general public sentiment of moral wrongdoing for which the offender must pay. But acts or omissions which any moral code would censure cannot in a practical world be treated so as to give a right to every person injured by them to demand relief. In this way rules of law arise which limit the range of complaints and the extent of their remedy. The rule that you are to

love your neighbour becomes in law, you must not injure your neighbour; and the lawyer's question, Who is my neighbour? receives a restricted reply. You must take reasonable care to avoid acts or omission which you can reasonably foresee would be likely to injure your neighbour. Who then in law is my neighbor? The answer seems to be—persons who are so closely and directly affected by my act that I ought reasonably to have them in contemplation as being so affected when I am directing my mind to the acts or omissions which are called in question.[21]

In characterizing Donoghue as Stevenson's "neighbor," Atkin offered a construction of the material facts of the case, which made possible a decision in favor of the plaintiff on the basis of a general principle of law "you must not injure your neighbor."[22]

It is not the legal implications of the argument that are of importance here. Rather, what is important is the fact that, through argument and the construction of a particular narrative, the concept of "neighbor" could be extended in a novel fashion to persons previously not so designated. Indeed, a person might now be considered to be my "neighbor" even though she does not reside in the "neighborhood" and despite the fact that we have never had direct contact with one another.

Similar diagnostic processes are at work in international politics. Only after one has established the nature of the question at hand is it possible to devise an appropriate response. As with legal reasoning, the "facts" of any particular case must usually be established through reference to general norms or treaty obligations that constitute the "rules of the game." But as in legal reasoning, the meaning of such norms is neither straightforward nor fixed. Because they can be extended in new and previously unanticipated ways, general principles and norms give rise to classes or categories of behavior with borders that are more fuzzy than distinct.

Thus, Louis Henkin argued that the United Nations General Assembly's failure to condemn India's invasion of the Portuguese colony Goa in 1961 removed the stigma of a violation of Article 2 of the U.N. Charter (prohibition against unilateral resort to force) "by suggesting that the Charter provision, properly interpreted, was not violated" and may have had the effect of modifying, *pro tanto,* the Charter itself.[23] The Indian argument that the Charter and General Assembly Resolutions permit unilateral force to be used against "colonialism" could in the future be extended "to justify force against racism, and even beyond."[24] By appealing to General Assembly resolutions demanding decolonization and the Charter's guarantee of the right of peoples to self-determination, India successfully constructed the facts such that the invasion was not regarded by the majority of states as a violation of international law. As a result, Portugal's appeals for assistance from the international community were unsuccessful.

A more recent example of the ways in which norms and principles generate categories or classes that cannot be defined a priori is NATO's response to the terrorist attacks in New York and Washington, D.C., on September 11, 2001. It is doubtful that any of the signatories to the Washington Treaty ever imagined that NATO would first invoke Article 5—the principle that an attack on one member will be considered an attack on all—in response to an attack on the continental United States. But certainly no one contemplated that Article 5 would be invoked in response to an attack by a nonstate terrorist network. Invoking Article 5 in response to a terrorist attack not only increased the set of cases in which the alliance may come to play a role, it also had the immediate effect of expanding the alliance's geographic focus beyond its historical focus on the North Atlantic and rendered obsolete the discussions over "out of area" operations, which had been of central concern since the end of the cold war.

If they are to serve as a guide to further action or choice, the accounts or interpretations of events or processes cannot be arbitrary. But insofar as proponents of a particular narrative can advance good reasons for their characterizations, they are not arbitrary. Even if the cumulative effect of arguments in support of one interpretation would appear to be greater than that of the arguments in support of an alternative, it may nevertheless not be logically compelling. What one is left with is a fuzzy set of interpretations enjoying varying degrees of reasonableness (see fig. 5.1).[25]

Clearly Unreasonable

Reasonable

Clear Cut

Reasonable

Clearly Unreasonable

Fig. 5.1. Fuzzy set generated by the application of general norms to specific cases

The fact that norm-generated classes of events are often characterized by graded membership is evidenced in the very language used to refer to specific cases or events. Whether a particular action or development is characterized as a "clear-cut violation" of a norm, a "classic," "unambiguous," or "borderline" case, is often important in determining whether and how others will respond. For example, during the Cuban Missile Crisis, lawyers in the U.S. State Department argued that although the deployment by the Soviet Union of medium-range ballistic missiles in Cuba posed a serious security threat to the United States, it did not constitute a clear-cut case of aggression sufficient to trigger the right to self-defense under Article 51 of the United Nations Charter, an argument that contributed to President Kennedy's decision to respond with a naval quarantine rather than an air strike.[26]

Implications for Social Science Explanations

Despite frequent assertions to the contrary, behavior rarely "speaks for itself." As Christopher Stone put it, "People not only walk and punch, they trespass and commit battery."[27] But what constitutes a case of trespass, and when should it be punished? If I were to cross into my neighbor's yard while running from a loose pit bull terrier, it is unlikely that anyone would hold me liable for trespass. In hot pursuit of my own runaway dog, I might knowingly ignore a "No Trespassing" sign, but it does not follow that I deny a general obligation to comply with the injunction. Moreover, we cannot merely appeal to the "facts of the case" in order to explain and appraise behavior. Owing to the complexity of even the most routine social situations as well as conflicting interests, actors and observers often will disagree on which—if any—situational features were compelling.[28] To return to my example, a property owner who had just seeded his lawn might reasonably have expected me to go around his property in my efforts to retrieve my faithful—if wayward—canine friend.

In order to explain and evaluate adequately the particular choices social actors make, the justifications and excuses offered for action must be taken seriously. Of course justifications and excuses can be manipulated and are sometimes mere ex post facto rationalizations for decisions taken on other grounds, but disregarding them in favor of overt behavior will not take us very far.[29] In an effort to establish the veracity of the actor's claim to have perceived the facts of the situation in a certain fashion, one might try to test the implications of the putative appraisal for other fields of behavior. If a particular justification is true, a high degree of consistency across related areas would be expected. Similarly, if an actor apologizes for violating a norm and justifies noncompliance in terms of extenuating circumstances, then we would expect other observable behaviors and conditions to be consistent with the requirement of the particular exigencies identified.[30] Mere rationalizations can be distinguished from forthright justifications because the justifications can reasonably be fit into a larger pattern of behavior and reconciled with prominent contextual factors, whereas rationalizations cannot.

Often, the appraisal of an excuse or justification will lead observers to issue queries or demands for additional information. Through the process of claim and counterclaim (or the "pleadings" of parties to a legal process), observation becomes intelligible and a satisfactory explanation and appraisal of behavior possible.[31] Charles Peirce has referred to this form of interrogative reasoning as the process of "abduction." Through the successive adjustment of facts and conjectured ordering schemes, one aims toward providing a satisfactory account and appraisal of the facts of a given "case."[32] Such appraisals presuppose a shared frame of reference based on a high degree of intersubjectivity or the form of cultural understanding on which Weber's notion of *Verstehen* rests. Only against a background of common understandings and patterns of reasoning is it possible to evaluate the veracity of justificatory claims and reach consensus on the "proper" framing of the facts.[33] As John Ruggie argues: "The aim is to produce results that are verisimilar and believable to others looking over the same events."[34]

Discourse

The appropriate unit or level of analysis for judging the effects of norms is thus discourse, by which I mean not only speech but also nonlinguistic forms of communicative behavior, such as signaling. Whereas much of the literature on rhetorical and persuasive processes proceeds from the assumption of "ideal speech situations" and thus fails to adequately confront real power disparities among parties involved in political discourse, the literature on signaling, while stressing power, overlooks the fact that even threatening is a norm-governed behavior and requires a high degree of intersubjectivity if it is to prove effective.[35] An adequate explanation of political behavior requires an approach to analysis that anchors *both* signaling and speech in a broader context of intersubjectivity. For example, Jervis's arguments on the strategic uses of signaling rest on the assumption that actors and observers can coordinate their interpretations of behavior given particular situational factors: "The actor's explanation may present a pattern into which others can satisfactorily put much of his behavior. . . . Actors can use the fact that explanations can alter the inferences drawn from indices to project desired images. What you say about your goals, motives, and calculations is apt to be easier to control cheaply than what you actually do and may produce a relatively large pay-off in terms of the interpretations others make."[36] Similarly, the need to incorporate both signals and speech in a discourse-analytic theory of international politics animates Maja Zehfuss's critique of Alexander Wendt's efforts to develop a constructivist (or social) theory of international politics: "Wendt's actors do not speak. They only signal. Social behavior is characterized by the sending of a signal, its interpretation, and the formulation of an answer based on that interpretation. . . . But to reflect and interpret, actors must be capable of speech. Wendt, however, fails to analyze the role of speech in this context. He never mentions it."[37]

That intersubjective understandings underlie both the cognitive and social psychological processes whereby environmental stimuli are apprehended, sifted, and transformed into a "case" is often overlooked. They are, however, central both to the explanation of individual behavior and its appraisal—as intelligible, "correct," or "deviant"—whether the onlooker is another social actor or, indeed, a social scientist.[38] It seems clear, for example, that Schelling's notion of "focal point" solutions to coordination games with multiple equilibria rests both on the particular features of a given coordination problem as well as a backdrop of intersubjectivity. The fact that two commuters from New Haven who agreed to meet on a given date in New York City but forgot to set a time and location should converge at noon on the information booth at Grand Central Station seems intelligible to anyone who has ever spent an extended period of time in the greater New York metropolitan region. But the example tells us little about how two Korean tourists might try to find each other under identical circumstances.[39]

Fuzzy Sets

It should now be clear why standard social science methods have proven incapable of capturing the effects of social norms on human behavior in terms of explanation schemes based on the identification of initial conditions and the application of a covering law. First, though general, normative injunctions cannot be reduced to the two categories "allowed" and "not allowed" that would make it possible to construct hierarchies of deductively linked observation statements. Rather, a third category—call it "tolerated" or "permitted"— is required. And because the class of tolerated or permitted actions cannot be established a priori on the basis of logical necessity, but rather is established by means of deliberation, that is through processes of persuasion within the context of particular cases, single cases cannot serve as the basis for rejecting claims regarding the general applicability of any given norm. Hence, the problem is not that social scientists have failed to specify adequately their variables or the relationships among them, but rather, as Aristotle argued, that norm-governed behavior is contingent, and its appraisal is not amenable to logical analysis.[40]

The problems associated with efforts to apply deductive modes of reasoning to norm-governed fields of behavior are apparent in the many rather confused discussions of the effects of regimes in international relations, as Kratochwil and Ruggie have repeatedly pointed out. Defined as "principles, norms, rules, and decision-making procedures around which actor expectations converge in a given issue area," many have sought to "test" their effects by applying standard social science methods, essentially seeking to measure levels of "compliance" on the basis of observable behavior.[41] When observable behavior is discovered to be less than fully compliant with the regulative features of the regime, the regime is held either to be "weak" or "in decay."

The rather embarrassing survival of many putative regimes in the wake of terminal diagnoses, however, has led many to criticize the regime concept itself. As Susan Strange argued, without clearly defined boundary conditions and identifiable standards of appropriate behavior, the notion of regimes is imprecise and "woolly" at best.[42]

Regimes are indeed woolly, but the imprecision is inherent and not a function of poor definition or inadequate attention to operational measures. Rather, the boundaries of regimes and their meaning in specific contexts cannot be determined a priori. "International regimes," Ruggie tells us, "are akin to language." The constituent elements of a regime, while providing guidance, do not in and of themselves define their domain: "We know international regimes not simply by some descriptive inventory of their concrete elements, but also by their generative grammar, the underlying principles of order and meaning that shape the manner of their formation and transformation. Likewise, we know deviations from regimes not simply by a categorical description of the acts that are undertaken, but also by the intentionality and acceptability others attribute to those acts in the context of an intersubjective framework of meaning."[43] Because the meaning of a regime—its scope, domain, and what constitutes acceptable behavior—is established and modified over time through the practices of the actors themselves, there exists no fixed and objective standard against which the analyst can judge behavior to be "compliant" or "noncompliant."[44] Even when regimes emerge by design, as in the case of negotiated treaties, it is usually impossible to determine a priori what would constitute definitive evidence that the regime no longer serves as a guide to behavior.

Consider, for example, the Anti-Ballistic Missile Treaty signed by the United States and the Soviet Union in 1971. Part of the larger Strategic Arms Limitation Treaty (SALT) regime, the ABM treaty limits the deployments of missile defenses in the United States and Russia to strategically insignificant numbers.[45] Moreover, through Article VI the treaty bans the development and testing of new weapons technologies "in an ABM mode." But because the universe of all possible ABM systems was not known in 1971 (nor can it be known today), the meaning of this general prohibition is unclear when applied to specific cases of weapons research, development, and testing. Such was the case in the mid-1980s with a number of developments relating to President Reagan's Strategic Defense Initiative (SDI) as well as renewed Soviet testing of intercontinental ballistic missiles (ICBMs) with surface-to-air missile (SAM) radar tracking. Despite the renewal of cold war rhetoric that came to characterize superpower relations, both sides were able to use the Standing Consultative Commission—an institution created under SALT I to resolve questions of interpretation—to reach agreement on the specific meaning of "testing in an ABM mode" under the new circumstances.[46] Although the Americans were not successful in arguing that SDI was completely consistent with the spirit of the ABM Treaty, neither could the Soviets argue that every aspect of the program was expressly forbidden. Hence, certain developments and tests were tolerated, allowing both sides to put off a decision on whether to withdraw from the treaty altogether.[47]

Practical Reasoning and Path Dependency

The process of applying general norms to particular cases is one of *practical* reasoning. And although we can trace the paths according to which judgments regarding appropriate behavior are made,

> following them is not reducible to clear algorithms, or to subsumptions of the particular norms and rules under the more general principles or higher level norms.

Such an interpretation is faulty if for no other reason than the fact that at each turning-point a "practical judgement" is required as to how a certain factual situation is to be appraised. . . . It seems therefore that the specification of purely formal criteria, such as the yardstick that one has to treat similar cases alike, is important but of limited utility as opposed to the appraisal of the more substantive criteria embodied in precedents and institutional history.[48]

For example, beginning in the 1990s, Germany, Denmark, and the Netherlands all recognized a need to reform the welfare state, which has come under increasing financial strain owing to aging populations and the competitive pressures of globalization. Held to be similar in terms of political culture, history, and domestic political institutions, students of comparative politics have been puzzled by the fact that the Netherlands and Denmark have become model cases of welfare reform whereas welfare reform has been ineffective in Germany.[49] But although the three political systems are similar in terms of domestic interest groups and institutions, the rhetorical strategies employed by the reform movements in Denmark and the Netherlands were quite different from those of German reformers. Proponents of welfare reform in Denmark and the Netherlands framed their arguments in terms of the need to support a broader range of widely accepted societal norms and values. In Germany, by contrast, reformers spoke of the need to increase Germany's competitiveness in global markets for capital and labor.[50] Whereas the "objective" situation was the same for all three states, the choice of frame in each case structured subsequent debates with the result that a societal consensus for welfare reform emerged in Denmark and the Netherlands but not in Germany. Had German reformers framed the issues in terms of job security rather than competitiveness, they might have proven more effective.[51]

When the paths along which political processes proceed are shaped by norm-governed discourse as well as preexisting interests and institutional and material constraints, efforts to predict political outcomes solely on the basis of nomothetical regularities are misplaced and doomed to failure.[52] Starting from similar initial conditions, a wide range of outcomes may be possible. Sometimes a different framing of the "facts" will suffice to produce a different outcome. Hence, explaining outcomes—or predicting the range of possible future outcomes—will require an analysis of rhetorical processes where the sequencing and timing of claims and counterclaims is important and not the establishment of correlations between initial conditions (or even arguments) and outcomes.[53] The effect of an argument or justification raised early in a politi-

cal process may be quite different from that produced by the very same argument in a later phase, even if all of the other conditions or features of the "case"
are the same.[54]

Returning to the example of welfare reform, after a failed attempt to generate support for reform on the basis of arguments relating to the need for increased economic competitiveness, it is unlikely that efforts of the German reform movement to recast their arguments in terms similar to those initially
employed by reformers in Denmark would produce similar effects. Indeed, one
would not be surprised if such arguments were judged by German labor to be
less than sincere and greeted with more than a hint of skepticism.[55]

Path dependency often produces (equilibrium) outcomes that are relatively
stable and self-reproducing, especially when "communities of discourse" develop shared representations of the world and appraisals of what constitutes
appropriate behavior.[56] Identifying the processes whereby shared meanings
are reproduced and reinforced "helps us to understand why organizational and
institutional practices are often extremely persistent—and this is crucial, because these continuities are a striking feature of the social world."[57] But even
when widely shared normative understandings are stable, they do not provide
a basis for causal generalizations of the "if . . . then" sort, even if these are formulated probabilistically.

Probabilities can only be established with respect to a well-defined set with
members that are assumed to be interchangeable—that is, no member of the
set is considered to be more or less representative than any another, and adding
or subtracting members from the set is not expected to change the values of
correlations among key variables. Insofar as the set is conceived as a zone of
homogeneity, relationships established across a representative subset or sample are expected to remain constant across the population as a whole.[58] But
the ultimate borders of norm-generated categories are unknown. Through
processes of analogical reasoning and judgments of similarity, norms are extended to novel situations that resemble but are not congruent with other
members of the set. Moreover, individual cases are not interchangeable. As argued above, any individual social situation will generally be amenable to multiple categorizations. Owing to the existence of extenuating or special circumstances, the general applicability of a given norm may be suspended with
respect to a particular case, even though it resembles a "typical" case on many
dimensions. The range of reasonable exceptions to a rule is often much larger
than may appear on the surface, as they may be based on rules or principles

that are themselves not fixed in written or verbal form or may not even have existed at the time the rule was formulated.[59] When the members of a set are not "substitutable instances of the same thing," efforts to capture causal relationships through standard statistical models produce results of dubious validity.[60]

Consider, for example, Beth Simmons's attempts to "test" the effects of international legal commitments on levels of "compliance" with international norms through statistical analysis.[61] Specifically, she tried to establish whether a state's formal commitment to Article VIII of the International Monetary Fund's Articles of Agreement has a significant effect on the probability that it will comply with the prohibitions on current account restrictions detailed in Section 2 of the Agreement. "Controlling for every likely macroeconomic influence on the decision to implement current account restrictions," Simmons finds "a formal declaration of adherence to Article VIII obligations consistently has a strong negative effect on the probability of imposing restrictions. In fact, controlling for all other economic variables as well as for policy inertia, countries that continue to live under the transitional Article XIV regime have an estimated probability of .87 . . . the corresponding probability for an identically situated Article VIII country is only .69. Thus, commitment accounts for a percentage point difference of about 18 in the probability of imposing restrictions on current accounts for the sample of cases as a whole."[62]

The validity of Simmons's conclusions, however, is undermined by the problematic nature of the indicators she uses as evidence of noncompliance. Focusing on cases in which governments have committed to Article VIII, any imposition of restrictions on the state's current account is taken a "a priori evidence of noncompliance."[63] But by her own admission, she "does not examine the technical question as to whether the IMF Executive Board approved the restrictions in place, rendering them 'legal' temporarily."[64] The question, however, is more fundamental than technical. The issue at stake is not the probability that a norm will be observed across a given population, but rather the question of to which population a given "case" belongs. For the applicability and meaning of any general rule or norm may not be straightforward when applied to particular cases, and it is precisely through deliberative processes that a judgment regarding appropriate behavior will be made. The function of such processes is not to establish how everyone in the group will or should act (in this case, all Article VIII members of the IMF), but rather what can be expected from an *individual* member given its particular circumstances.[65] Considering the fact that the IMF has traditionally recommended "transitional arrangements" under Article XIV and a delay in committing to Article VIII for countries that are experiencing balance of payments difficulties, one might reasonably expect the IMF Executive Board to tolerate temporary restrictions on current accounts and/or exchange rates when Article VIII members come under strong balance of payments pressures.

In fact, the IMF Executive's surveillance procedures have rarely produced judgments leading to enforcement measures or sanctions. Rather, the "emphasis is on getting a clear picture of developments in the member's monetary and overall economic situation and identifying potential or emerging problems in time to take corrective action."[66] With respect to developing countries, noncompliance is often a problem more of limited capacity than of ill intent: "Often economic events are simply beyond the party's control. Export prices may slide or the cost of essential imports—oil—rise precipitously. Bureaucratic and administrative incapacity is endemic. And national politics in developing countries, as elsewhere, are notoriously resistant to economic austerity measures." Through "monitoring what are essentially best-efforts undertakings," the IMF engages member states "in an ongoing process of negotiation that exerts continuing pressure to bring developing country monetary and economic policy into line with the fund's notions of what is desirable."[67]

With respect to Article VIII commitments and the likelihood that states will refrain from imposing current account and exchange rate restrictions, a focus on discourse would have produced a dataset indicating lower levels of noncompliance than that suggested by a focus on behavioral indicators alone.[68] And because the set of all economic conditions that might give rise to "legitimate" justifications for temporary current account restrictions cannot be identified by means of straightforward deduction, we can delimit neither the set of cases constituting compliance nor that of noncompliance. As a result, we cannot "test" for the "causal effects" of norms on behavior, and even probabilistic statements must be judged to rest on false premises.

Establishing the Effects of Norms on Political Behavior

Because norm-generated classes of events or cases are established not by identifying features held to be necessary and/or sufficient for category membership, but rather by extending norms to novel situations through processes of practical reasoning and judgments of similarity, we cannot know when a prevailing set of understandings will give way to new characterizations and thereby open the way to new patterns of behavior. Could anyone have predicted whether, how, and when society would converge on the notion that women should be guaranteed the right to vote? And where will the demands of homosexuals for "equal rights" lead? Extending liberal norms regarding the proper relationship of the state to public persons (citizens) to the field of gender, Andrew Sullivan argues that the state must put

> an end to sodomy laws that apply only to homosexuals; a recourse to the courts if there is not equal protection of heterosexuals and homosexuals in law enforcement; an equal legal age of consent to sexual activity for heterosexuals and homosexuals where such restrictions apply; inclusion of the facts about homosexuality in the curriculum of every government-funded school, in terms no more and no less clear than those applied to heterosexuality (although almost certainly with far less emphasis, because of homosexuality's relative rareness when compared with heterosexuality); recourse to the courts if any governmental body or agency can be proven to be engaged in discrimination against homosexual employees; equal opportunity and inclusion in the military; and legal homosexual marriage and divorce.[69]

But the issues involved can be framed in other, perhaps equally liberal, terms.[70] Whether, when, and precisely how societal conventions on issues of gender will change cannot be predicted on the basis of even a very complete understanding of the contemporary conditions that both enable and block social change.[71]

Because apparent correlations between the existence of norms and norm-consistent behavior explain neither how general norms are interpreted in particular cases nor when and how a society's prevailing normative understandings are subject to change, and because we can never know actors' private motives, empirical research aimed at capturing the effects of norms on political outcomes must look beyond behavior (which includes choice) to discourse, which is pervaded by normative appeals. Governmental officials and state actors routinely invoke norms in an effort to further their own particularistic interests in policy debates. By invoking the validity of a norm in a particular case, they seek to justify their preferences and actions or to call into question the appropriateness of the preferences of others.

Elsewhere I have demonstrated how societal and state actors use *international* norms to shape the terms of *domestic* political debates. The research makes clear, however, that not all international norms resonate in domestic debates. Rather, an international norm's "salience" in domestic political debates requires a durable set of societal attitudes toward its legitimacy.[72] When a norm is salient in a particular social discourse, its invocation by relevant actors legitimates a particular behavior or action. By creating a prima facie obligation, salient norms shift and raise the burden of justification necessary to overcome the claimant's position in favor of competing options or interpretations.[73]

Subsequent research on the mechanisms that lead to increasing or decreasing salience has pointed to the importance of socialization and political rhetoric.[74] Rhetoric, or persuasive discourse, is an important mechanism for generating collective understandings regarding the legitimacy of norms. Although the effects of rhetoric on political decision-making are only beginning to attract the attention of scholars, the effectiveness of normative appeals appears to be conditioned both by the identity of the actors engaged in debate and their ability to frame the debate in terms of broader, often material, interests.[75]

The pronouncements of authoritative national leaders illustrate how domestic understandings about the legitimacy of a particular norm can evolve. Repeated declarations by state leaders on the legitimacy of the obligations that an international norm places on states have been shown to set precedents and standards that restrict the leaders' future range of choice. A political leader's initial embrace of a norm may be merely instrumental, even cynical, yet it still leads to its enhanced salience in the domestic political arena.

Thus, President George Bush's repeated appeal to the norm of collective security and the principles embodied in the United Nations Charter in the days following Iraq's August 1990 invasion of Kuwait constrained his ability to pursue unilateral action over the next several months. Members of the Congress who were opposed to an American military response or to unilateral action used the earlier declarations to limit the American response to those actions approved by the United Nations Security Council.[76] Such effects extend beyond the domestic politics of liberal or democratic states. For example, Thomas Risse documents cases in which authoritarian leaders have adopted the language of universal human rights norms as part of a political strategy aimed at relieving outside pressures for domestic political reform or for securing foreign economic assistance, only to discover that they had enhanced the salience of these norms at home.[77]

The salience of any given norm is also likely to be a function of its perceived relationship to other societal interests, whether they be normative or material. Researchers have found that international norms are more likely to become salient in domestic political debates if they are perceived to support important domestic economic or security interests. It is not enough merely to invoke an international norm in connection with a narrow domestic material interest. Rather, one must connect the particular interest with the nation's more general beliefs and durable national priorities. For example, G. John Ikenberry argues that the Bretton Woods system was successful and politically feasible because its norms "allowed political leaders and social groups across the political spectrum to envisage a postwar economic order in which multiple and otherwise competing political objectives could be combined."[78] Indeed, the most salient norms are those that "bridge domestic rifts, allowing for the convergence of diverse material and ideal interests into a national interest."[79]

Conclusions

Because social norms both give rise to desires and "interests" and prescribe the means appropriate for their pursuit or maximization, efforts to explain social life in purely utilitarian terms are bound to fail.[80] But to grant that social behavior is guided by the normative understandings of individual actors as well as the societies of which they are members requires one to take leave of deductive and nomothetic approaches to explanation.

First, because norms can be counterfactually valid, the two-valued logic of deductive models is inappropriate for generating testable propositions of the "if . . . then" sort. The behavioral implications of a general norm for specific cases cannot be established a priori through the application of logic. Rather, they result from processes of practical reasoning, which at best are accessible through the analysis of discourse, which itself is a path-dependent process.

Second, because the process of practical reasoning proceeds by means of the construction of analogies and judgments of similarity, it gives rise to classes of events or behaviors that are characterized by fuzzy borders and graded membership. Through the extension of norms to new circumstances, the borders of a given category of behavior are subject to expansion. Sometimes, however, appeals to special or extenuating circumstances justified in terms of other norms or higher-order principles will serve to call into question the applicability of a general norm to a particular case, and the case may ultimately be judged to lie beyond the borders of a set comprised of otherwise quite similar cases. Because the borders of norm-governed sets are not fixed and significant morphological heterogeneity is possible within the set, efforts to uncover nomothetic regularities through the resort to statistical analysis will likewise produce results of quite dubious validity.

The crucial question in norm-based explanations is not "What is generally true?" but rather, "What are the facts of this particular case?" Whereas most social science research tries to deduce from a general theory the implications for a particular case (given certain initial conditions and a covering law), the implication of the analysis developed here is that we need to think about how we can move from specific cases to more general claims. If, however, we cannot generalize on the basis of regularities established across a finite set (that is, through the process of induction) and if deductive theorizing is inappropriate (both for its reliance on two-valued logic and the impossibility of conclusive falsification through empirical tests), how are we to generate warranted knowledge in the social sciences? The question constitutes the point of departure for chapter 6.

CHAPTER SIX

Methods for the Production of Practical Knowledge

The discussions of the previous chapters raise important issues relating to idealized conceptions of the empirical sciences. In particular, they challenge the widespread and deep-seated belief that through the application of proper methods, something approximating "the truth" can be discovered. But if science in general, and the social sciences in particular, cannot achieve the conceptual precision, deductive elegance, and nomothetic generality characterizing the idealized notions cherished by so many, on what basis should scientific discovery proceed? More fundamentally, what is the nature of the scientific warrant?

A satisfactory—not to mention comprehensive—answer to these questions is beyond both the scope of this study and, I suspect, my own faculties of reason. Nonetheless, I shall endeavor to elaborate on some of the implications of the arguments developed in the previous chapters for the scientific enterprise. Again, the primary focus will be on the social sciences, and on political science in particular, although I would argue that many of the issues addressed are of broader relevance.

I begin with a discussion of the relationship of "cases" as units of scientific analysis to the understanding of scientific concepts developed in chapters 2 and 3. The analysis then turns to the relationship of general to particular knowledge and the difficulties in moving from the latter to the former when ceteris paribus comparisons are impossible. The possibilities for redressing the problem of control by means of counterfactual and within-case process tracing analysis draw our attention to the ways in which single-case studies can aid in the development of typological theory, which, I argue in the concluding section, can serve to relink the study and practice of politics.

Cases and Concepts

"Social science methodology," writes Charles Ragin, "is anchored by a number of basic precepts that are rarely questioned by practitioners. One precept that is central to the logic of analysis is the idea of having *cases*. Social scientists use terms like '*N* of cases,' 'case study,' and 'sample of cases' with relatively little consideration of the possible theories and metatheories embedded in these terms or in the methods that use cases and make conventional forms of analysis possible." Of course implicit in any reference to cases is the conviction that the objects of scientific investigation can usefully be grouped into classes or categories "similar enough and separate enough to permit treating them as comparable instances of the same general phenomenon."[1]

In designating a particular object, event, thought, or process as a "case" of something, social scientists are employing a concept. The concept used to identify the case logically must be prior to any discussions of populations, samples, or variance. Although I would not want to go so far as claim to have articulated (let alone developed) a theory or metatheory of concepts and processes of conceptualization, the arguments and analyses of the preceding chapters have implications for our understanding of what constitutes a "case" in the social sciences.

To recapitulate a fundamental point, concepts are not found in nature but rather are created by humans in their efforts to make sense of experience. They are mental representations of elements or experiences parceled from the limitless time and space of the physical, social, or psychological worlds. *Scientific concepts,* I have suggested, are the intersubjectively valid linguistic expressions of these mental representations. That is, a concept's claim to scientific status rests on its ability to convey some meaning.

The same, it would seem, must apply to cases. Cases represent the extension of preexisting concepts and should be judged in terms of their ability to convey some meaning among the members of a scientific community. As representations of some parcel of human thought or experience, they must be articulated in terms of preexisting linguistic or theoretical terms. And because both theories and language are governed by a particular grammar, the articulation of cases necessarily proceeds through adherence to certain rules and conventions. Cases then are not empirical entities but rather social conventions: they are linguistic constructions that enjoy intersubjective validity.

Conceiving of cases as conventions raises a number of issues that cross-cut a number of otherwise competing epistemological and methodological positions. For example, much statistical, quantitative, or large-N research proceeds from the assumption that what constitutes a case or observation is straightforward and naturally given. Empirical data is regarded as "out there," just waiting to be discovered and measured. Many qualitatively oriented scholars share the basic conviction that data is given in the "real world," even though they would probably disagree with the quantitatively oriented researcher on the nature and origins of "the world" to be studied. The conviction extends even to some interpretivist scholars who, through an inductive approach grounded in the perspectives of the actors comprising the system or society of interest, aim to establish the empirical boundaries of "real" cases, which then may be subjected to further, perhaps even statistical, analysis.[2]

Asserting the conventional nature of cases also challenges the position of those postmodernist scholars who would accord subjective or idiosyncratic perspectives or accounts of the world scientific status or perhaps assert that the "truth" claims of such perspectives are no less valid than those that enjoy some degree of intersubjectivity. Although I do not wish to push the argument too far, there are important differences between storytelling or even the diary of an historical individual, on the one hand, and an analytic narrative, on the other. A diary may (or may not) be empirically real and bounded, but these properties afford it no particular scientific status. Rather, the linguistic terms with which individuals make reference to the diary and the subjective accounts and opinions it records may enjoy the status of scientific concepts.

From this perspective it is not the empirical entity that is central to science, but rather the concepts that are used to apprehend it. Properly understood, the process of identifying cases is a matter of concept extension and not of identifying real or natural empirical borders. To the extent that we are engaged in establishing borders, we establish them with respect to our concepts and not some "real" world, which exists external to language and scientific theory.

Because the goal of science is the production of generally accessible knowledge, however, any genuinely scientific concept is necessarily external to any particular researcher. Given a particular conceptual system, the research of any given individual might suggest the existence of a new case or set of cases. More likely, she will entertain slightly different versions of the cases identified, playing one against the other in an effort to establish the best fit between the cases and the larger conceptual system. As she confronts other researchers, the variety of case constructions only increases—some versions will be eliminated while still others are added. But what ultimately (or, more likely, only temporarily) emerges is not the result of a personal dialogue with reality but rather the product of collective scholarly work and interaction. Insofar as cases emerge from social processes, their content and meaning cannot be specified without reference to the community of scientists who formulate them.[3] In stressing the conventional nature of cases, however, one is able to reject the position that objectivity in science is achieved by means of testing hypotheses against the world without accepting the claim that "anything goes."[4]

Although I stress the conventional nature of cases and their emergence through processes of communication within communities of scholars, it does not follow that all scholars—even those working in the same research program—will agree on the borders or meaning of every case. As argued in chapter 2, universal agreement on the meaning of concepts is almost always lacking. Nonetheless, people usually can communicate with one another well enough. Moreover, because cases emerge from conceptual systems—linguistic or theoretical—insisting on fixed and congruent understandings as a criterion for scientific status would be to foreclose the opportunity for conceptual systems to evolve and grow. And yet as David Hull's research demonstrates, it is precisely through the evolution of theories and theoretical terms that research programs progress.[5]

If the meaning of cases is to be found in their relationship to evolving conceptual systems rather than their relationship to "the world," archaeological excavations in search of the ultimate epistemic foundations upon which the edifice of scientific truth can be built are misguided. At most, such explorations will discover that the roots of scientific concepts are found in basic language terms. But as we discovered in chapter 2, basic language terms, such as those for colors or spatial relationships, are not universal. And even when languages share basic terms, the range of cases to which these are generally held to apply are far from uniform.[6]

Because one is always confronted with the question of where to "cut in" to complex and evolving conceptual systems, science is conducted in medias res. And owing to the evolving nature of concepts and more encompassing conceptual systems—both at the level of the individual researcher and of collective research programs—the group of cases and sets of cases are likely to change over time.[7] Even when scientific analysis is suspended, the resting place is rarely, if ever, final.[8]

Diversity, Complexity, and Similarity

The conviction that physical as well as conceptual entities are possessed of essences is persistent and widespread.[9] In discussions of scientific method, this conviction emerges in the form of an overriding concern with "precision." Concepts, we are repeatedly told, must be precisely defined and operationalized. And these procedures are understood to require the identification of features held to be necessary and sufficient for category membership. Without the precise specification of a concept's essences, true scientific discourse and progress is, it is argued, impossible.

In chapter 2 I presented arguments of philosophers of language as well as empirically oriented anthropologists and linguists that suggest that these notions are misguided. "Cases" of a given concept often cannot be established on the basis of shared essences. There simply are no features common to all members of the set. Rather, concepts are formed around prototypical or ideal-typical core members and extended to new observations on the basis of similarity judgments. New observations are assimilated to the set insofar as they can be seen to resemble the prototype. The extension of concepts on the basis of resemblance produces sets that are characterized by graded membership and fuzzy borders. Some exemplars of a given concept are clearly better or more representative than others. Some, located at the fuzzy borders, are marginal.

This conception of concepts (as a "concept" is also a concept) proceeds from the assumption that diversity and complexity are ubiquitous and pervasive. Uniform or homogeneous sets of cases—whether such cases are individual physical, biological, or theoretical entities—are in practice rarely, if ever, delimited. They certainly are not given by nature.[10]

The assumption of pervasive diversity leads to a certain degree of skepticism with respect to arguments that the primary goal of science is the establishment of general laws of the "if . . . then" sort, leaving quite aside any claims of such discoveries. When sets are created through the extension of concepts to novel observations on the basis of similarity judgments, individual members may not be equivalent in the sense that they share common features, and the ultimate borders of the set may be unknowable. As argued in chapters 4 and 5, when neither the homogeneity of cases forming a set nor its ultimate borders can be guaranteed, both assertions of causal regularities and claims to have falsified such assertions are suspect.

General versus Particular

Skepticism regarding the status of general laws leads to the suggestion that science should at least show as much concern for the identification of the particular as it does for the general. The two tasks are, of course, quite related. At some level the particular cannot be known apart from the general, and vice versa. But the search for general laws has led scientists to focus on classes at the expense of particular knowledge about individuals.[11] Indeed, some prominent voices have argued that true social science research is concerned only with classes and therefore should avoid reference to individuals and proper names altogether.[12]

Often, however, it is precisely the individual case that is of interest rather than what is, or might be, true *in general*. Thus, the social worker assigned to a delinquent teenager will be interested in the specific circumstances that might be implicated in the problematic behavior of his "case." An allergist will try to isolate the specific antigen responsible for repeated outbreaks of skin rash in her patient. And a business consultant brought in to help turn around a failing firm will look for the specific deficits in management, production, distribution, or marketing that account for the diminished fortunes of his client.

One need not question the importance of large-N quantitative studies to also recognize that many social scientists are interested in the qualitative study of particular cases. A particular event—for example, a political revolution, global economic depression, or world war—may produce effects of such importance, both for contemporaries and future generations, that its specific causes are of inherent interest. Moreover, historically unique or novel occurrences may be of interest for policymakers who seek to either promote or forestall their recurrence. Often, however, the single case is interesting precisely because it suggests and relates to more general phenomena, processes, or mechanisms. Finally—and often less recognized as legitimate subjects of study—are cases that are merely hypothetical constructions, a point to which we shall return.

In pointing to the importance of studying the particular in addition to the general, the scholar is immediately confronted with the question of how to do so. Recent years have witnessed a renewed interest in the methodological imperatives of qualitative small-N case studies, and a number of considered works on the subject have been published by political scientists, sociologists, and historians.[13] It cannot be my task to review all of these works here, but insofar as the arguments developed in the previous chapters bear on important themes in ongoing methodological discussions and indeed offer somewhat unique perspectives on some enduring questions, I shall refer to them.

Ceteris Paribus

Social science methodologists routinely argue that one of the principle obstacles to the discovery of strong causal laws is the fact that controlled experiments are rarely available for the testing of hypotheses.[14] Social scientists, it is argued, can rarely establish the ceteris paribus conditions necessary to establish the effects of putative causal variables.[15]

Ideal experimental research designs afford the investigator control over both the selection of observations as well as initial conditions. Through the construction of two situations where all initial conditions are equivalent except for the value assigned to a variable under investigation, here referred to as α, any variance in outcomes is attributed to α. When measurement techniques are precise, "crucial" or "critical" experiments are held to provide strong methods of testing—and potentially falsifying—general theories.[16]

In the social sciences, however, we rarely have the sort of control necessary for experimental research designs. The values of putative independent variables are usually given, either by history or nature. Control in nonexperimental design is thus dependent on the researcher's selection of cases and observations. In an effort to approximate the control of the laboratory setting, investigators seek naturally occurring cases that are similar on all dimensions except for the dimension defined by the independent variable under analysis. For example, to test for whether or not a university education affects a person's political affiliation, one would look for individuals who are alike in every way except for their level of education and then observe whether differences in this dimension correlate with differences in political affiliation.

In actual social scientific practice, the number of cases (N) selected and observed varies greatly with the proponents of large-N statistical analyses and small-N case study researchers engaging in never-ending debates over the merits of each approach.[17] One issue of contention is which approach offers a better opportunity to control for initial conditions across a set of cases selected for comparison. The issue is usually cast in terms of the problem of omitted variables or of "degrees of freedom."

The problem of omitted variables, or "omitted variable bias" as it is sometimes called, is perhaps best demonstrated by a simple example. Let us assume that someone articulates the hypothesis that higher levels of economic development as measured in terms of Gross Domestic Product (GDP) per capita is causally connected with increasing levels of democracy. And let us assume that a dataset is constructed of all member states of the United Nations. For each state, GDP per capita is measured, as is its level of democracy (leaving aside the question of how it is measured). Finally, let us assume that higher levels of GDP per capita are found to correlate with higher levels of democracy in 80 percent of the cases.

Is the finding strong evidence in support of the hypothesis? Because correlation does not imply causation, the investigator would first try to establish causal direction. Did increases in GDP per capita precede or follow increasing levels of democratization? Although some would insist on the need to test this proposition across classes of states over time, others might indeed grant the qualitatively oriented researcher the study of individual states over time. Now let us assume that strong evidence is discovered to support the proposition that increasing levels of democracy follow increases in GDP per capita. Are we now justified in concluding that increasing levels of economic development promote democracy? The problem of omitted variable bias is raised as soon as someone suggests that the correlation between GDP per capita and level of democracy is a spurious correlation and suggests that, in fact, increasing levels of education explain both rising economic fortunes and transitions to democratic governance.[18]

The "degrees of freedom" problem arises when the number of cases or outcomes available for analysis is smaller than the number of potential causes That is, the researcher is confronted with more independent variables than observations. In order to control for the effects of any single variable, one generally needs at least two observations. By comparing outcomes in two situations where initial conditions are identical except for the value assumed by the independent variable, one seeks to establish or control for any causal effect. As the number of variables held to produce a given outcome increases, the number of observations required to control for the effects of each increases. The problem is particularly acute when the outcomes we are interested in appear to be produced by the convergence or interaction of a number of factors, which appear to be correlated with one another.[19] If the number of observations is insufficient to control for the effects of each independent variable, the researcher is confronted with an indeterminate research design.

In statistical terms, the number of degrees of freedom for any research design is defined as "the number of quantities that are unknown minus the number of independent equations linking these unknowns."[20] In a simpler formulation, if a dataset is comprised of N number of cases, then the researcher can at most control for N-1 independent variables.[21]

Qualitative case study research has often relied on John Stuart Mill's "method of agreement" and "method of difference" as proxies for the strict control of experimental settings, even though Mill himself was skeptical of their utility for social science inquiry.[22] Briefly summarized, Mill's method of agreement attempts to identify causal relationships by comparing cases with a common outcome, whereas the method of difference attempts to do so by comparing cases where the outcome was different. Both strategies employ a logic that Mill referred to as a method of "elimination." For Mill: "This term (employed in the theory of equations to denote the process by which one after another of the elements of a question is excluded, and the solution made to depend on the relation between the remaining elements only) is well suited to express the operation, analogous to this, which has been understood since the time of Bacon to be the foundation of experimental inquiry, namely, the successive exclusion of the various circumstances which are found to accompany a phenomenon in a given instance, in order to ascertain what are those among them which can be absent consistently with the existence of the phenomenon."[23]

When using the method of agreement, investigators compare two or more cases characterized by a common outcome or value on the dependent variable and eliminate as potential causes those conditions or independent variables that are not present in both cases. Variables that survive this method of elimination can be regarded as possible necessary conditions for the outcome in question.

The method of difference exploits the same logic of elimination to exclude as possible causes for the variance across a set of observations any conditions or independent variables that are present across cases with varying outcomes. The logic behind the procedure would appear to be quite straightforward: a condition present both when an outcome occurs and does not occur cannot account for the difference in the outcomes. Any condition that survives this method of elimination, however, can be regarded as possibly being associated with the outcome under investigation.

By comparing cases along similar dimensions, Mill's methods of agreement and difference structure analysis with the goal of achieving some measure of control over initial conditions.[24] But both methods are plagued by the inherent weakness of inductive inference. For example, when using the method of agreement, an investigator might indeed identify a factor common to all outcomes, but this does not rule out the possibility that there exists a case in which it is absent. Similarly, by using the method of difference, one might identify a cause that seems sufficient for producing a certain outcome, but one cannot conclude on the basis of a finite number of observations that there does not exist an instance of the outcome for which the relationship does not hold.

Because we can never know whether the sample of cases we have examined is representative of all possible cases and because we do not know whether we have identified and "controlled" all possible independent variables, the method of elimination can lead to spurious and invalid results. On the one hand, as a result of too narrow a sample, we may falsely conclude that a certain condition or combination of conditions is necessary to produce a particular outcome.[25] On the other hand, a form of omitted variable bias may lead one to prematurely eliminate certain features from the list of candidate causes. Such "false negatives" are likely to result when the eliminated condition is associated with an outcome *if and only if* an additional condition or set of conditions is present, the identity of which was unknown at the time of the original investigation. But as the number of conditions or variables reputed to be necessary for the production of any given outcome increases, the number of cases needed to control adequately for the independent effects of each independent variable also increases. Whereas statistical research design is often more self-conscious of the data requirements for the testing of multivariate relationships, sometimes the number of naturally occurring cases of a phenomenon is simply too small to allow for statistical control. For some research questions the problem of "too many variables, too few cases" cannot be addressed by resorting to the logic of elimination or statistical control.

Large-N statistical analyses offer no inherent advantages over small-N comparative studies with respect to the question of omitted variable bias. The problem confronting both approaches is the same: the universe of potential variables is in principle limitless. Hence, deciding what measures to include or not include in a regression analysis is always a question of theory.[26] Without a theoretical model linking putative causal variables with the outcome at issue, trivial explanatory variables might turn out to be the most significant in a multivariate regression analysis.[27]

In scientific practice, we can only control for variables that are known to us. Moreover, if only because our resources are limited, we should only control for variables that we have reason to believe are likely to be linked to the outcomes we seek to explain and avoid including in our analyses an endless number of factors under the mistaken belief that we are thereby increasing the validity of our results.[28] If the selection of independent variables is theory-dependent, then ceteris paribus is a condition that relates to *theoretical terms* and not "the empirical world." And if this is true, then the prospects for acceptable levels of control in the social sciences are not as bleak as they at first glance appeared. Even in the experimental sciences, the only variables over which investigators can achieve some measure of control are those that are identified either by assumption or theory, as Paul Diesing recognized: "Thus we assume that college sophomores [standard subjects for laboratory experiments conducted by American psychologists] are not affected by phases of the moon, so it is not necessary to control for that. But flatworms are so affected! We used to assume that experimenters' knees, like the moon's phases, are irrelevant—until Rosenthal discovered that knees can convey the experimenter's expectations. Since then, experimenters have had to be aware of kinesic communication in the experimental situation."[29]

The foregoing discussion directs attention toward one of the critical and most often unacknowledged foundations upon which the experimental sciences are built, namely the metaphysical assumptions of the constancy and homogeneity of the natural universe. Because the influence of the outside universe on the controlled setting of the laboratory is taken to be constant, one can proceed from the assumption of ceteris paribus once control has been established over all theoretically relevant factors. Random fluctuations in the influence of nature on the laboratory setting are expected to "wash out" as experiments are repeated; over the course of time, experimental results are expected to converge, increase in verisimilitude, and bring us "closer to the truth." Moreover, owing to the assumption of homogeneity, relationships that appear to obtain in the laboratory are expected to obtain throughout the universe wherever and whenever equivalent conditions obtain.

I wish to challenge neither the metaphysics nor the practicality of such assumptions as they relate to the natural sciences. Indeed, more competent observers have already done so.[30] The arguments developed in preceding chapters, however, do move me to suggest that the assumptions are more problematic when applied to the world of social relationships.

First, if social science concepts are extended to novel observations on the basis of judgments of similarity to a prototypical or core exemplar (family resemblance) rather than on the basis of essential (necessary and sufficient) features or properties, then we cannot proceed from the assumption of unit homogeneity. If the assumption of unit homogeneity cannot be sustained, then methods for establishing the existence of general relationships or laws applicable across the set that are premised upon the condition of ceteris paribus become problematic.

Insofar as I have argued that the ceteris paribus condition is best understood to apply to theoretically relevant conditions or features, the problem is not insurmountable. But the argument does suggest that far more attention must be paid to the unique or specific features of individual members of conceptual categories rather than the usual focus on supposed common features whose functions or effects are assumed to be constant across the set. When judgments of similarity produce sets of individuals that display graded membership—that is, some individuals are judged to be better exemplars of the concept than are others—Max Weber's arguments on the uses of ideal types in causal analysis may provide a better starting point for generating theoretical insights than a commitment to the existence of generally applicable covering laws.

Second, as the discussion of path dependency suggests, even when individual cases may appear identical or similar enough to be classified as instances of a particular concept, they may have reached that status via very different historical processes. These unique individual histories may, in turn, have important implications for present or future developments. When an individual's past exerts a pull on the present, the effects of a particular feature or variable may not be constant across a set of two or more cases that might otherwise appear equivalent on all relevant theoretical dimensions.

Of course, one could argue that when similar cases have resulted from different historical processes, initial conditions only appear to be constant, meaning that the ceteris paribus criterion has not in fact been fulfilled. But this is precisely the point. A physicist can argue that carbon dioxide will behave like carbon dioxide, regardless of whether it was "created" in the laboratory, from decaying plant material, animal metabolic processes, or released from calcium deposits that come into contact with ammonia. But a social scientist will have a much more difficult time convincing colleagues of the claim that democracies will act alike independent of the unique historical circumstances from which they have emerged. Yet as intuitive as this might sound, most social science research—and this is especially true for large-N statistical studies—does not proceed from the assumption that the unique or individual historical trajectories of the particular units of analysis condition the effects of causal variables or processes in meaningful ways.

If we grant, however, that many of the outcomes we are interested in explaining are products of goal-oriented human behavior, and if we assume that humans are capable of reflecting upon and learning from the past, then we should not be surprised when social actors facing the same conditions choose to react in very different ways. Moreover, when behavior reflects decisions that result from processes of rhetoric and practical reasoning—I would argue that most political behavior falls into this category—then the cases used to construct datasets do not exhibit the independence necessary for controlled comparison. Precisely because what happens in the present is a function of what happened in the past and not the other way around, we cannot treat two seemingly equivalent cases as if they were interchangeable.[31]

Once one accepts the proposition that human beings reason and learn, one must necessarily view the search for general and timeless covering laws with a great deal of skepticism. But to reject the search for timeless laws held to govern social life is not to reject the search for explanations or the identification of causal processes. But if the social scientist cannot resort to experimental procedures or achieve ceteris paribus through the use of statistical or small-N comparative case studies, on what basis can he proceed?

Learning from Cases of One or Fewer[32]

In chapter 4 we learned that for logical positivists, to provide an explanation is to show how a given observation statement (*explanandum*) can be derived from the *explanans*, a set of statements regarding initial conditions and a particular set of universal statements or general laws.[33] To say that a given event or set of events caused another is to identify a general law that links the putative cause with the effect by means of deductive entailment. In the social sciences, however, we often seek explanations for singular events in the absence of well-established general laws. Indeed, most of the time general laws are lacking even as the number of cases proliferates.

The discussion of the proceeding section suggests that we should not be surprised that this is the case. Because conceptual categories are often generated on the basis of assimilating new observations to a set on the basis of judgments of similarity vis-à-vis a core or prototypical exemplar, individuals will display varying or graded degrees of category membership and may be only rarely interchangeable. Without unit homogeneity, relationships that are found to obtain for some individuals of the set are unlikely to apply across the entire population. And because the individual cases we are interested in often times cannot be assumed to be causally independent of one another, any correlations we discover are likely to be biased and to lead to invalid inferences.

If science is defined as the search for valid general laws, and if explanation presupposes the existence of such laws, then it would seem that the prospects for discovering explanations of social phenomena are bleak. As a prominent proponent of statistical approaches to the study of politics noted:

> To be comparative, we are told, we must look for generalizations or covering laws that apply to all cases of a particular type. But where are the general laws? Generalizations fade when we look at particular cases. We add intervening variable after intervening variable. Since the cases are few in number, we end up with an explanation tailored to each case. The result begins to sound quite idiographic or configurative. . . . As we bring more and more variables into our analysis in order to arrive at any generalizations that hold up across a series of political systems, we bring so much that we have a "unique" case in its configurative whole.[34]

Concluding that the enterprise is indeed hopeless, some logical empiricists argue that the social sciences should be abolished all together and replaced by sociobiology.[35] But to debate the merits of such conclusions would be to accept a premise that is itself untenable.

Contrary to the claims of many methodologists, cases are not identified by subsuming them under general laws or by a mechanistic process of matching observations to checklists of conditions held to be necessary and sufficient for inclusion in the dataset. Rather, they proceed along the basis of judgments of similarity. As we discovered in our analysis of the datasets for democracies and interstate wars, even when scholars rigorously attempt to apply precise operational criteria for the coding of cases, they routinely confront borderline cases that can be resolved only by making informed judgments. Conceiving of cases as being constructed by judgments of similarity, family resemblance, prototype effects, and fuzzy borders acknowledges that members of any given set will differ on a number of dimensions, some of which may have implications for the operation of previously documented relationships and mechanisms. Hence, the qualitative investigation of individual cases is recognized to be as important to the scientific enterprise as is the search for general laws across classes.

Critical Junctures and the Role of Counterfactual Scenarios

The proposition that only universally valid laws are scientific has been challenged by Paul Diesing, who writes:

> To reject the relevance of the logical empiricist scheme does not mean to reject the goal of achieving valid general laws; it means that there are other goals as well and that generality is a matter of degree. Generalizations about U.S. voting behavior can be valid even though they apply only between 1948 and 1972 and only to Americans. Truth does not have to be timeless. Logical empiricists have a derogatory name for such changing truths (relativism); but such truths are real, while the absolute, fully axiomized truth is imaginary.[36]

In arguing that social science produces results of relative generality and relative validity, Diesing implies that the validity of a statement is not linked to its generality. That is, the generality and validity of scientific explanations should be regarded as independent of one another. Thus, Donald Davidson, a philosopher generally acknowledged to be continuing in the tradition of Hume, writes:

> Ignorance of competent predictive laws does not inhibit valid causal explanations, or few causal explanations could be made. I am certain the window broke because it was struck by a rock—I saw it all happen; but I am not (is anyone?) in command of laws on the basis of which I can predict what blows will break which windows. A generalization like, "Windows are fragile, and fragile things tend to break when struck hard enough, other conditions being right" is not a predictive law in the rough—the predictive law, if we had it, would be quantitative and would use very different concepts. The generalization, like our generalizations about behavior, serves a different function: it provides evidence for the existence of a causal law covering the case at hand.

We are usually far more certain of a singular causal connection than we are of any causal law governing the case. . . . It is an error to think no explanation has been given until a law has been produced.[37]

Taken together, these critiques of covering law approaches suggest the need to direct our focus toward single-case causal analysis and the possibilities for analyzing causal processes in purely hypothetical cases. For even if one were to grant that general laws might exist, as Davidson appears to do, we are not forced to suspend causal analysis pending their discovery.

When searching for an explanation for a given social outcome, we are usually interested in identifying its antecedent causes—even though when the unit of analysis is human behavior, the "causes" in play are often best conceived of as *reasons* for goal-oriented action. As the discussion of norm-governed behavior in the previous chapter demonstrated, reason-based explanations are amenable neither to deterministic nor probabilistic explanations that take the form of "if . . . then" statements. Identifying a particular social norm may be necessary in explaining a given behavior or even a set of behaviors, but the norm itself may not be sufficient for producing such behaviors. Moreover, the norm may not be universally necessary, that is, the behavior thus explained might also occur as a result of very different circumstances. The same, however, is also true of some causes, as Alasdair MacIntyre recognized:

For very often we speak of "the" cause of an event, for instance at a coroner's court in assigning responsibility for an accident, we point to a condition, by itself necessary but not sufficient for the occurrence of the accident. We do so when *events were in train* such that without the condition in question being satisfied the event would not have occurred. Taken by itself the condition was necessary but not sufficient. Taken in conjunction with all the other prior events, its satisfaction was sufficient to bring about the accident. So it is with the ice patch on the otherwise safe road.[38]

MacIntyre's example of the ice patch on an otherwise safe road is reminiscent of our discussion of norm-generated sets. "Taken in conjunction with all the prior events," the ice patch was sufficient to cause an accident. But we know that accidents can occur in the absence of ice patches, and even if we could identify the prior events that produced the accident in this specific case, we would still know precious little about the set of all possible conditions that, together with the existence of an ice patch, will lead to an accident. Even if we had prior knowledge of the conditions prevailing in the moments leading up to the accident at hand, we most likely could not have predicted it with a high degree of reliability. Yet common sense tells us that had there been no ice patch, things would have come out differently. And this common-sense notion of causality suggests a first cut at the question of how to conduct causal analysis in single-case studies.

For followers of Hempel, or indeed of Hume, a cause is usually conceived as something that regularly precedes events of a certain type. But the notion of causality implied in the example above is more akin to a "lever that brings about a *particular* effect," as "something that intervene[s] in a process" to produce "an alteration in an outcome."[39] In the example above, it is the counterfactual assertion that the accident would not have occurred in the absence of the ice patch that identifies the ice patch as the cause of the accident. *If only* the road had been clear of ice, the car would have passed the curve without incident.[40]

Causes can thus be thought of as branching points in historical processes. By identifying critical junctures, we learn something about the course of future events even though we may not be in a position to predict or control similar events in the future.[41]

Conceiving of causes in this fashion allows us to identify relationships in individual cases while bypassing the more difficult question of whether the causes so identified are truly necessary and/or sufficient in the universal or even boundedly general sense. To do so is to make no claims with regard to the ultimate possibility of identifying generally valid relationships; indeed, this approach to analysis denies the proposition that general laws are necessary for an adequate explanation of the individual case.

Of course the counterfactual upon which such explanations rest is itself a product of generalizations that are used to predict the course events would have taken absent the perturbation we identify as causal. Such generalizations may be derived from well-developed theories, but they also are often provided by "imperfectly universal but practically convincing propositions about ordinary happenings."[42] For example, the proposition that absent ice patches automobiles will pass curves without experiencing an accident is far from universally valid, but experience tells us that it is not unreasonable.

The general proposition that automobiles will pass curves without accident would most likely be accepted by a majority of observers, but some will argue that it should first be established through resort to statistical analysis. By collecting a large enough sample of observations on the independent variable (automobiles navigating curves in the road), the probability of an accident across the population of cars driving on curved roads can be established. Although helpful for establishing the reasonability of the general proposition giving rise to the counterfactual, the statistical results alone do not constitute nor can they provide a theory or explanation for why a particular car crashed while trying to pass a particular curve.

The counterfactual scenario is based on the presumed normal course of events or the prevailing historical trend, and any intervening condition or process is held to be the cause of some alteration in the otherwise expected outcome. Of course such established trends are themselves the products of underlying causal features, each of which in some sense contributed to the historical outcome as it actually occurred. And had one of these not been present, the ultimate outcome might also have turned out differently. For example, returning to the case of the automobile crash, it is certainly true that had the automobile run out of gas prior to having reached the ice patch, then the accident would not have occurred. So why do we identify the ice patch as the cause of the accident and not the gasoline? The answer, I believe, is twofold.

First, in the scenario of a car navigating a curve in the road, a tank with gasoline is considered part of the normal course of events, a generally applicable condition. Such conditions, while perhaps necessary to the outcome in question, are also consistent with a wide range of alternative outcomes. That is, a full tank of gas is also consistent with the car successfully navigating the curve. Absent the ice patch, a full tank of gas is not a sufficient explanation for the accident.

But the argument can be turned around: absent the gasoline, the ice patch loses its significance entirely. This brings me to my second point. Imagining an empty tank prior to the ice patch requires us to change more in our counterfactual analysis than just the fact of the accident. Indeed, it requires us to change the counterfactual outcome itself. Without gasoline, the car cannot reach the curve, let alone successfully navigate it.

The above discussion points out that our basic understandings of causal processes are intimately linked with counterfactual scenarios and expected futures. It also suggests that what we consider to be the most important causes of historical outcomes are those conditions whose absence would produce the fewest number of changes in both the actual train of events as well as the counterfactual scenario. Because removing the ice patch from the train of events requires us to change less of the actual or "factual" history and leads to a simpler counterfactual scenario than imagining the car to have run out of gas prior to reaching the ice patch, the ice patch is more appealing as the ultimate cause of the accident.[43]

Likewise, several scholars have proposed a "minimum rewrite" criterion as both a constraint on counterfactual reasoning and as a guide to the identification and selection of "causes" from the myriad antecedent conditions that were necessary for the production of the outcome under analysis.[44] For example, James Fearon writes: "When we say that '*A* caused *B*' we seem to mean not only that if *A* had not occurred, *B* would not have occurred. Rather, we mean that if *A* had not occurred, *B* would not have occurred and the world would otherwise be similar to the world that did occur."[45] In constructing counterfactual scenarios, scholars should begin with the world as it was otherwise known before asserting the counterfactual, avoid long rewrites of history, and avoid changing what we otherwise know about the original actors and their goals and beliefs.[46]

For example, the minimum rewrite rule has been used to dismiss the assertion of some deterrence theorists that the Cuban Missile Crisis could have been avoided if President Kennedy had only sent a credible and timely warning to the Soviet premier Nikita Khrushchev in the spring of 1962 rather than in September, when the missile deployments were already underway.[47] Examining the documentary record, Lebow and Stein conclude that President Kennedy's September warnings were issued in response to intelligence reports of increases in Soviet conventional forces on Cuba. Hence, "in April, before the conventional buildup began, Kennedy had no reason to suspect a missile deployment, and months away from an election campaign, had no strong political incentive to issue a warning." The argument that the failure of Kennedy to issue a timely threat was an important cause of the Cuban Missile crisis is implausible, because it requires us to change too much of what we know about the political incentives confronting Kennedy and the information that was available to him.[48]

The critical reader might agree that conceiving of causation in terms of crucial junctures or turning points in historical processes is legitimate for some purposes but deny that it is appropriate for the social scientist. Social science, after all, is supposed to be different from history. The former, we are told, is nomothetic and general. The latter is idiographic and particular.

Bruce Bueno de Mesquita reflects the views of many political scientists when he argues that most historians "are primarily interested in explanations that emphasize particularistic factors that distinguish one event, one sequence, one location from another. The meaning or explanation of events and actions is often assumed to be revealed through culturally and temporally bounded interpretations."[49] Similarly, sociologist Robert Bierstedt wrote, "History, as idiographic, is interested in the unique, the particular, the individual; sociology, as nomothetic, in the recurrent, the general, the universal."[50]

Such distinctions and the debates to which they give rise, though interesting in and of themselves, are both separate from—and not necessarily connected to—the question of how we should conceive of causation or try to establish the existence of causal relationships and mechanisms. The question of whether one seeks to explain singular events in terms of unique processes or attempts to use particular cases to identify relationships and processes that might indeed recur relates to the product of scholarly analysis. It is quite different from the question of whether causal processes are best identified through qualitative analysis of individual cases or through appeals to general laws and deductive logic.[51]

Counterfactual scenarios help us to learn from individual events, but they can also be used to generate insights into nonevents: events that might have occurred in a specific historical context but were avoided, or events we can imagine but have not yet experienced. Near-histories or hypothetical histories exploit the data contained in analyses of historical processes to provide a more complete assessment of the possibility that future distributions might diverge from past experience. Thus, well in advance of the explosion of the American space shuttle Challenger in 1987, some NASA engineers argued that although the shuttle had flown a number of successful missions in the past, careful study of successful missions revealed that they represented lucky draws from a distribution of possible outcomes for which the prospects of disaster were quite high.[52] In the field of international politics, Scott Sagan has argued that a careful examination of the history of the command and control of U.S. and Soviet nuclear weapons arsenals suggests that the prospects for accidental nuclear war are much higher than is generally believed, a finding that has important implications both for the management of existing weapons stockpiles and the question of proliferation.[53] And although we have never experienced a war between two nuclear-armed states, through the analysis of a multitude of hypothetical scenarios physicians, physicists, biologists, mathematicians, meteorologists, military strategists, and political scientists have all generated useful insights into the possible courses and outcomes of such a conflict.

Although counterfactual, nonevents can nonetheless generate knowledge that is more than speculative. When our interest is in avoiding catastrophic events—such as an all-out nuclear war or the destruction of the planet through ecological degradation—to insist that we suspend goal-directed action in the absence of "hard" data would be folly. Even if we judge the probability of a particular outcome to be quite low, the payoffs (positive or negative) of such an outcome might be of sufficient size to warrant intense counterfactual analysis.[54] Moreover, if we ignore the potential for learning from the analysis of counterfactual scenarios, we may misinterpret what hard evidence we have. For example, even though some NASA engineers were warning of the possibility of a catastrophic system failure, others, including key decision makers, rejected their arguments as exaggerated: in the experienced history of the shuttle program the system had demonstrated it was robust enough to tolerate such problems.[55]

Psychological processes contribute to the systematic overweighting of experienced history in the development of theory and the formulation of possible future scenarios. People tend to recall vivid first-hand experiences much more readily than they remember other types of stored knowledge.[56] As time progresses, memory centers on the event itself rather than the range of near or hypothetical outcomes. This is especially true when past decisions and policies appear to have been successful, as perceived success produces fewer psychological incentives for self-examination and reflection than failure.[57] Evidence from a variety of psychological studies indicates that retrospective assessments of the probability of events are affected by knowledge of whether or not these events have actually taken place, a phenomenon referred to as "creeping determinism."[58] Memories of vivid past events and the systematic overweighting of the probability that they would reoccur reduce the prospects that near-histories will be used for generating future contingencies.[59]

Even if we can control for biases with roots in psychological processes, we will still need to focus on the question of how to discipline the generation and use of counterfactual scenarios in the absence of general or universally valid covering laws. The "minimum rewrite" rule suggests we accord more credibility to near-histories that change fewer aspects of the known course of events than we do to alternative scenarios that arise from imagining a broader range of changes and/or changes that are projected into a distant past. The logic can be extended to processes of forward reasoning and the generation of future scenarios. Although the obstacles to accurate prediction in complex social systems are many and significant, if social scientists are called upon not only to explain the past but also to think critically and analytically about the future, if *only* to help avert catastrophe, then we need to develop methods for coping with them.[60]

Process Tracing

If the extension of scientific concepts to novel observations produces sets of cases that are characterized neither by unit homogeneity nor the less demanding condition of membership defined in terms of necessary and/or sufficient attributes or properties, then many of the assumptions on which both large- and small-N comparative studies proceed are problematic. When concept extension on the basis of similarity judgments and family resemblance produces sets of cases that are characterized by graded membership and fuzzy borders, then the qualitative analysis of causal (and constitutive) processes giving rise to the individual case would appear to be a legitimate, perhaps even an indispensable, method of investigation.[61]

Well-known criticisms of single-case studies claim that they are at best little more than "thick descriptions" of historical events and processes. But do the logical problems associated with efforts to base general claims on inductively derived propositions render single-case studies meaningless from the standpoint of theory development and the creation of general knowledge? Are single-case studies necessarily idiographic? Although I recognize that there are serious limitations associated with inductive procedures and single-case analysis, I nonetheless argue that they can and do contribute to the creation of knowledge that is general, more than speculative, and useful for both theory development and purposeful social action. Although the arguments concerning how to conduct rigorous single-case or "within case" analysis I will summarize here are not new, the justification I have offered for turning to such methods is.

Characterizing the social world as a collection of cases understood in terms of discrete events or outcomes may lead us to overlook the wealth of historical experiences that are represented in each individual case. Although for some purposes it might make sense to conceive of cases as discrete empirical entities that permit only a single observation for measurement and coding, this is not always true. Rather, for some purposes it makes more sense to think of cases as complex phenomena, each of which comes with a history. When history or nature are less than generous in providing cases of the phenomenon we seek to explain or understand, or when we have reason to believe that the set of cases is not uniform in the sense that it can be delimited by reference to necessary and/or sufficient membership criteria, we can compensate for limitations in experimental or statistical control by directing our analysis to the histories of individual cases. By experiencing these more richly, we can increase the number of observations associated with each case: "Every unique historical event is a collection of micro events, each of which can be experienced. In this sense, the learning potential of any historical event is indeterminate. Because both the scope of an event and the depth of its decomposition into elements are arbitrary, so also is the richness of experience."[62] By breaking down the single case into a series of events and observations, we can evaluate the degree to which the broader pattern appears to "fit" with putative explanations or understandings.[63]

The most theoretically informed approach to the rigorous analysis of single cases through decomposition is the method of "process tracing," developed by Alexander George and his associates.[64] Process tracing is an effort to identify causal or constitutive processes and mechanisms that link a set of initial conditions and one or more variables with a particular outcome. Although he recognizes the difficulties associated with generalizing from a paucity of cases, George argues that even unique cases can contribute to theory development provided we "formulate the idiosyncratic aspects of the explanation for each case in terms of general variables."[65] What differentiates a purely historical account or description of a given event or outcome from a social science explanation is that the latter converts historical data into a suitable theoretical or "analytic" vocabulary that, at least in principle, can be applied to other cases.

When applied to the analysis of behavior, process tracing looks to uncover the structures and stimuli confronting social actors and the ways in which actors make use of these factors to arrive at decisions regarding the necessary or appropriate response.[66] As George and McKeown put it: "The framework within which actors' perceptions and actions are described is given by the researcher, not the actors themselves. However, because that framework often is revised after observations of behavior (in fact, the original framework itself may be based on previous observations of behavior), the externally imposed theoretical framework is certainly shaped by actors' self-definitions, even if it is not designed specifically to capture such self-definitions."[67] Thus, process tracing steers a course between the two poles represented by extreme objectivist and interpretivist conceptions of social science, each of which was challenged by the arguments developed in chapters 2 and 3. Although I argued that universally valid concepts are rare, I nonetheless maintained that translation and interpretation are possible and proceed from a partially shared empirical world and the assumption of a partially shared rationality. Although I am skeptical of the prospects for developing objective and universally valid theories, intersubjectively valid middle-range theories are indeed within our grasp.[68]

In process tracing, the analyst engages in the construction of explanations by assembling bits and pieces of evidence into a larger pattern or network, often resorting to counterfactual analysis of the sort described above. Only those items that are necessary for an account of the final outcome and that are consistent with the broader pattern of data are included. When a modification of the existing pattern is inconsistent with or weakens the structure as already developed, it is rejected. When, however, a modification both increases the precision of an existing account and leads to the discovery of new pieces of the larger network, it can be accepted. From this perspective, the "case" is no longer seen as a single data point, as it is in controlled small- or large-N comparisons, but rather as a pattern of relationships or a "stream of behavior" through time. A satisfactory explanation will account not only for the final outcome (the dependent variable), but for the entire stream of behavior.[69]

When the constituent features of a given historical outcome are constant (even if the concepts used to apprehend them are subject to change), the larger pattern of historical facts that constitutes the case can to some degree serve as its own "control."[70] Because other potentially relevant features of the case remain constant, the independent impact of a given stimulus can be established by comparing the broader state of affairs before its introduction into the train of events to the wider pattern of relationships as they exist after exposure to the stimulus.[71] As we observe changes in the values associated with theoretical variables, any changes in the broader network of relationships and behaviors that we observe should be predictable or at least compatible with the general explanatory framework.[72] Owing to the well-documented tendency of humans to impose patterns on data even when the data have been generated by random processes or are otherwise ambiguous, systematic efforts to "test" the interpretation or explanation through extension to other aspects of the case are necessary, even if they are subject to many of the limitations discussed in chapter 4.[73] However, under conditions that may come closer to ceteris paribus than comparative case study research designs, the inferential value of any hypothesized causal path is weakened to the extent that the wider set of data does not conform to expected patterns, or when such evidence is lacking altogether.[74]

The goal of process tracing is not merely or even primarily to provide an explanation for the individual case, although this too is important, but rather to uncover general mechanisms and processes that *might* recur and that might contribute to the development of more encompassing theory. Though not necessarily nomological, process tracing explanations can nevertheless be causal. And insofar as the constellations or mechanisms uncovered can be recast in terms of analytical or theoretical terms, their occurrence is no longer seen as merely accidental and unique, but general in the sense that they are likely to recur.[75]

Though analytic, the method of process tracing is inductive when used for purposes of theory building. Hence, we are not in a position to make final judgments on whether any variables uncovered through the analysis of a single case is necessary or sufficient for producing the outcome of interest (recall, however, that our analysis began with the proposition that necessary and/or sufficient conditions are often lacking). Moreover, we may confront cases for which a number of hypothesized causal mechanisms appear to account equally well for the data uncovered through process tracing. But although the available data may turn out to be inadequate to the task of judging among alternative explanations for the individual case,[76] because the focus of analysis is on causal mechanisms (why things happened) rather than correlations (that they happened) and is conducted in terms of abstract general concepts rather than idiosyncratic terms, we nevertheless have confidence that analyses will cumulate and lead to better theory.[77] From this perspective theory development is seen as open-ended, with theories being built from the "bottom up" rather than "top down."[78]

One of the best examples of how the results of process tracing across a number of cases can cumulate in support of theory development is found, not surprisingly, in George's own research on deterrence.[79] Dissatisfied with the deductive approach that characterized the development of deterrence theory amid the cold war crises of the 1950s and 1960s, George and his collaborator Richard Smoke undertook an inductive analysis of eleven cases of attempted or contemplated deterrence between 1948 and 1963 in an effort to uncover the processes that led to success or failure.[80] By converting the unique historical circumstances of each case into more general analytic terms and mapping out the relationships among them, George and Smoke were able to identify three general patterns of deterrence failure and thereby improve upon the overly simplistic (and sometimes erroneous) insights offered by the prevailing highly stylized rationalist-deductive models, which were assumed to embrace the essential analytical and policy issues.[81] Through process tracing they were able to identify contextual features, which although external to deductive models were critical both to decisions over whether to challenge the international status quo and over the appropriate strategy for doing so.[82] In suggesting that a more differentiated theory of deterrence was both necessary and possible, George and Smoke opened the door to a new wave of process-oriented case study research, which over time has led to a theory of international influence that is at once more differentiated in terms of discriminating among varieties and patterns of international crisis and more encompassing in terms of the range of situations over which it provides analytic leverage.[83]

Process tracing has also proven to be especially well suited to the analysis of norm-governed behavior, which, as we discovered in the previous chapter, is not subject to deductive entailment based on the identification of initial conditions and the existence of a covering law. Particularly problematic from the standpoint of deductive theorizing is the fact that norms can be counterfactually valid. That is, even generally valid norms may be legitimately violated in a particular case. Hence there is no one-to-one correspondence between the existence of a norm, on the one hand, and observable behavior, on the other. Moreover, because both the range of cases to which norms can be argued to apply as well as the contextual features that would give rise to legitimate grounds for the violation of an otherwise applicable norm cannot be determined a priori but emerge through processes of practical and analogical reasoning, we cannot turn to statistics in search of probabilistic statements.

To gauge the impact of norms on behavior thus requires an analysis of the reasons actors give for their actions and a judgment of how the these reasons fit the larger framework of the case. Because, however, justifications and excuses can be manipulated and are sometimes mere ex post facto rationalizations for decisions taken on other grounds, the analyst makes a judgment of the veracity of such claims by evaluating the degree to which a broader range of behaviors appears to be consistent with them. Mere rationalizations can be distinguished from forthright justifications because the justifications can be reasonably fit into a larger pattern of behavior and reconciled with prominent contextual factors whereas rationalizations cannot.

Although the potential for learning from single cases through the method of process tracing is high, in practice the utility of process tracing is limited by its substantial data requirements: "Documenting the process by which inputs are converted to outputs requires much more evidence than does simply noting the inputs and the outputs and treating what lies between them as a black box."[84] George and McKeown have suggested that because behavior is a social phenomenon and usually requires that individual social agents communicate with one another, the documented content of this communication should facilitate process-oriented research and analysis.

For a variety of reasons, however, available historical materials may be inadequate to the task. Because institutions and individuals have an interest in presenting themselves and their decisions in the best terms possible, an interest that colors both their documentation of the present as well as their accounts and recollections of the past, data regarding social processes and outcomes must always be regarded with a healthy degree of skepticism. Societal and institutional incentives can produce systematic biases in recorded data: certain data are recorded in a certain fashion while other data is ignored, discarded, or suppressed.

Thus, the data on aviation accidents and near-accidents was discovered to be heavily compromised by legal and financial contexts that give individuals and organizations incentives for uncovering certain facts and mechanisms at the expense of others.[85] Similarly, the national data reported and compiled in the International Classifications of Diseases (ICD), a dataset used to study the effectiveness of medical systems, treatments, and public health measures on the incidence and spread of disease, has been shown to reflect both social mores and incentives created by national insurance systems and principles of medical liability.[86]

And the ways in which political and budgetary incentives can bias the production of data were colorfully detailed by a former U.S. assistant secretary of defense: "I first encountered the problem of military readiness 30 years ago when I was a Naval flight officer in the Far East. One Sunday afternoon, in response to a call from the Seventh Fleet, I reported that only 3 of our 12 planes were ready for combat. For my honesty, I received a severe tongue-lashing from my commanding officer, who informed me that whenever headquarters called we were always ready." But in the wake of the Iran crisis and the Soviet invasion of Afghanistan, the atmosphere in Washington had changed: "Military leaders were quick to grasp the political potential of readiness scares. In the late '70s word went out that reports of readiness problems would be *welcomed* by headquarters."[87] Whereas the effects of such biases in the available data may be argued to "wash out" in large-N statistical analyses, they will tend to undermine the validity and generalizability of conclusions reached by process tracing in the single case.

Equifinality

Standard statistical methods attempt to identify conditions sufficient for the production of a given outcome by randomly selecting cases from a population that is characterized by unit homogeneity and independence. Because both assumptions are often problematic, process tracing emerges as a means of "within case" testing that helps deal with problems of control. An additional justification for process tracing and the qualitative analysis of individual cases is found in the pervasiveness of equifinality in social life.

The search for necessary and sufficient causes that characterizes most statistical and small-N comparative case research is rooted in an often implicit and unexamined assumption that similar outcomes are the most likely products of similar or common causes. The fact that similar outcomes can be produced by very different causal processes and mechanisms—the condition of equifinality—challenges this assumption and raises important issues relating to the development and testing of theory. Rather than focusing on the discovery of features common to a set of cases, the task of scientific inquiry becomes one of mapping out the range of different causal and constitutive patterns that can give rise to similar outcomes.

When the analyst suspects that there exist multiple sufficient causal mechanisms leading from a given set of initial conditions to the outcome under question, or when the same outcome can be arrived at from a wide range of initial conditions, deductive approaches to theory development won't take us very far, as logic will give us very little grounds for moving beyond relationships that can be inferred from initial assumptions. When a phenomenon is governed by equifinality, theory development is more likely to result from inductive process-oriented case studies.

Because the analyst is interested in identifying the variety of different causal or configurative patterns leading to the phenomenon under investigation, cases are not chosen because they are representative of the broader category or class but precisely *because they differ from one another even though they belong to the same class.* Whereas the statistician is frustrated by "deviant" cases or "statistical outliers" that reduce the value of his r^2 and is likely to attribute them to measurement error, researchers suspecting equifinality will regard such cases as potential opportunities for theory building. Through careful controlled comparison of heterogeneous cases, some of which may be causally linked, the process-oriented analyst seeks to develop a set of conditional rather than probabilistic generalizations. The ultimate goal is "to identify the conditions under which each distinctive type of causal pattern occurs," rather than the establishment of frequency distributions.[88]

Ongoing research on the ways in which international norms affect states' foreign policies affirms the need to consider alternative paths to similar outcomes and the value of process tracing for theory development. Whereas a first wave of scholarship on international norms was cast at the level of the international system, with states treated more or less as unitary actors, cross-national variation in the effects of international norms on state behavior has led a second wave of scholars to argue that international norms have important effects on state behavior via domestic political processes.[89] Through process tracing in a variety of national contexts, two domestic-level factors have been shown to condition the effects of international norms on state policies: the domestic salience or legitimacy of the international norms and the structure of the decision-making process conceived in terms of state-society relations. These discoveries have in turn led to the development of more precisely specified hypotheses with respect to when and how international norms will have an impact on foreign policy decision-making and to new efforts devoted to mapping out the various mechanisms whereby international norms are introduced into the domestic political arena and come to be regarded as legitimate guides to behavior.[90]

Typologies and Typological Theory

When we observe similar processes leading to similar phenomena in a variety of social contexts (temporal and/or spatial) and can cast these in terms of general scientific concepts, the natural tendency of science is to conclude that the similarity is more than just a function of accident or chance.[91] Because we are speaking here of causal or constitutive mechanisms and not mere correlations among lists of variables, the conclusion is justified even when the number of observations is quite limited. And when a variety of recurring patterns leads to similar outcomes, we naturally begin to differentiate among them and to classify them according to "type."

Although the construction of typologies is common in both the natural and social sciences, their status in the development and evaluation of theories is contested. For example, Gary King and his colleagues suggest that typologies "are useful as temporary devices when we are collecting data but have no clear hypothesis to be evaluated. However, in general, we encourage researchers not to organize their data in this way. Instead, we need only the organizing concept inherent in our theory. That is, our observations are either implications of our theory or irrelevant."[92] But as I have argued elsewhere, the development of typologies, particularly in underdeveloped areas of theorizing, may lead the analyst to see things she otherwise might overlook. The identification of recurrent clusters of features or mechanisms can spur the search for explanations for why they appear to "hang together."[93] If outcomes are path-dependent and/or governed by equifinality, then organizing data in terms of individual variables is less likely to contribute to explanation than a division based on different patterns of interactions among them. When formulated in general analytical terms, a typology allows one to acknowledge similarities across types while identifying important differences that may be of theoretical importance. Hence, the development of analytic typologies is an independent and potentially worthwhile form of theorizing.[94]

Recent years have witnessed a renewed interest in the uses of typological theory in the social sciences, particularly among scholars engaged in small-N qualitative case study analysis.[95] In contrast to those typologies that merely partition events or entities into types that share specific combinations of features, *typological theories* are defined as typologies "specified in terms of theoretical independent and dependent variables, which are defined in turn by an underlying theory or set of theories that address not only how these variables act singly but how they behave in specified conjunctive combinations."[96]

Given the understanding of scientific concepts developed in this study, it should come as no surprise that I agree with the general proposition that typologies and typological theories are worthwhile pursuits in the systematic study of social life. Precisely because the extension of concepts to novel observations—or the novel application of norms in processes of practical reasoning—often produces sets that are characterized by graded membership or family resemblance, discovering diversity among individual phenomena or processes that are otherwise acknowledged to be of a given type as well as uncovering the broader implications of such diversity are important contributions to the development of a more comprehensive understanding of a phenomenon.

But whereas many methodologists maintain that, to be useful for purposes of theory development, the individual categories of a typology must be mutually exclusive—that is, a given pattern or cluster cannot be representative of more than one type—the arguments developed in chapters 2 and 3 suggest otherwise.[97] Because typologies are nothing more than complex concepts—analytical constructs defined in terms of configurations of other scientific concepts—and because the borders of most scientific concepts are fuzzy, we should not expect that the borders of type-concepts will be distinct.[98] Indeed, as we discovered in chapter 3, one of the most fruitful typologies in the study of politics, e.g., regime type, has yet to be operationalized in terms that would allow for the unambiguous and exclusive coding of individual polities. Individual regimes, we discovered, often are best conceived in terms of overlapping membership.[99]

A healthy tolerance for fuzzy concepts and classificatory schemes will help to constrain the proliferation of types and subtypes whenever we find an instance of some phenomenon that exhibits some new or unique feature or combination thereof. Because the dimensions according to which individual exemplars of a given type could be further differentiated is unknowable and potentially limitless, the criteria according to which judgments regarding the appropriate number of types are reached are prudential rather than logical or objective. In daily scientific practice, the proliferation of types will be disciplined by the need to reconcile them with the available analytical variables in terms of which the type must be cast. Nonetheless, when similar outcomes are suspected to result from a multitude of processes, the development of typologies must be open-ended as investigators set about cataloguing the range of types and the "repertoire of causal mechanisms." The development of a differentiated typological theory and the articulation of contingent generalizations is dependent on the accumulation of knowledge and a better understanding of the characteristics of the specific types.[100]

Knowledge for Policy: Relinking the Study and Practice of Politics

I began this study with the observation that a half-century of the "scientific study of politics" has failed to generate a widespread sense of progress or optimism that such is anywhere in the offing. Partisans of a logical positivist conception of science would no doubt argue that the problem resides in the failure of the majority of social scientists to adhere to rigorous methodological strictures.

As I have tried to point out, however, the problem is not that social scientists are in general sloppy thinkers or undisciplined in the construction of theory and/or the conduct of empirical research (even if this is frequently the case). If the practice of social science were nothing more than the derivation of theorems from axioms, then we certainly would have constructed a much more impressive edifice of statements generally accorded the status of truth. The problem, it seems, is rather one of moving from the logical to the psychological and empirical. If neither the human brain nor the social and "natural" worlds can be comprehensively, or even adequately, apprehended or described in terms that correspond to the laws of logic, then we should not be surprised to see our efforts to construct grand edifices of deductively linked propositions frustrated. Once we begin to operationalize scientific concepts and ideal statements derived from initial assumptions on the basis of logic, theory becomes a metaphor, characterized as much by uncertainty as necessity.[101]

The problems confronting the search for generally valid causal laws in the social sciences are not limited to those associated with the nature of our concepts and the ambiguities inherent in the results of empirical tests. Because social action by definition takes place within social systems, most of which are characterized by complex interactions among a variety of actors and structures, outcomes may not be easily reducible to straightforward cause and effect relationships.[102] Many of the outcomes we are interested in explaining are produced by nonlinear relationships and best conceived as properties of the system rather than its constituent parts.[103] Even closed systems comprised solely of inanimate elements can be of sufficient complexity that the outcomes they produce are contingent, rendering explanation in terms of law-like relationships among independent and dependent variables impossible.[104] And if only because human agents are capable of reflection and learning, social systems must be regarded as open, making their evolution and change even less predictable.[105]

Although I am skeptical with respect to the prospects for developing robust and universally valid theories in the social sciences, the arguments developed above nonetheless provide some grounds for optimism. Recognizing the limitations inherent in the empirical sciences in general, and the nonexperimental sciences in particular, I have argued that analytically oriented case study research can contribute to the production of general knowledge, which in turn can serve as the basis for middle-range theories useful for guiding both research and policy.

Through systematic analysis of patterns and mechanisms associated with important problems held to be generic—a term that does not render single cases or nonevents meaningless—social science research can produce catalogues of causal and constitutive processes that, insofar as they are cast in general (rather than case-specific) terms, are theoretically useful. But the sort of theory I have in mind is built over time from the bottom up rather than the top down. Although I do not deny that important insights can be generated through the logical deduction of propositions on the basis of initial assumptions and our knowledge thereby increased, the efforts of social scientists to replicate the success of physics have led us to ignore other success stories, modern medicine among them.

I raise the example of modern medicine because it exemplifies a model of science that is characterized by a strong link between theory and practice as well as diversity in both its modes of theorizing and methods of empirical analysis.[106] Rather than doggedly asserting that science is governed by a single logic of inference or that the development of warranted knowledge must proceed through means of deductive theorizing, modern medical science progresses through an amalgam of deductive and inductive theorizing, as inferences are generated and tested on the basis of controlled experiments in laboratory and clinical settings, large-N statistical studies, and day-to-day medical practice dictated by the needs of the individual case. And as even a cursory review of modern medical history makes clear, important medical breakthroughs have resulted both from the deduction of counterintuitive propositions from established general principles and from the intuitions and observations of skilled practitioners.

Understanding *illness*, which remains the central focus of medical science despite the pleas of many to replace it with *health*, is in the first instance a function of recognizing particular clusters of symptoms as constituting similar instances or occurrences. And interestingly enough, many diseases cannot be defined in terms of a single symptom or cluster of symptoms held to be necessary or sufficient for a correct diagnosis. Rather, clusters of symptoms give rise to medical judgments on the basis of similarity to a pattern or case that serves as a prototype.[107] Once an illness is recognized as such, laboratory researchers as well as clinical practitioners turn to the business of tracing the etiology and cataloging vectors of transmission in hopes of devising both methods for early diagnosis and intervention strategies designed to prevent and/or cure it.

In similar fashion, we can imagine a political science that, devoted to the identification and analysis of generic outcomes or problems of importance to both individuals and collectivities, seeks to catalogue the repertoire of mechanisms that appear to produce them. In the course of tracing processes that lead from a given set of initial conditions to the outcome of concern, analysts should focus on the identification of critical junctures that may provide actors a point of access for purposes of intervention.[108] Although probabilistic generalizations can contribute to goal-directed behavior and effective policy-making, they often provide very little guidance for deciding how to deal with the specific case at hand. Not only do they leave the decision maker "with the difficult task of deciding whether the probabilistic relationship in question applies to the particular case . . . but their value is often sharply reduced because such studies seldom include causal variables over which the decision maker has some control."[109]

The foregoing highlights the importance of diagnostics. Because we are unlikely to develop theories that allow us to make predictions with any degree of certainty but are still capable of mapping out the variety of mechanisms that produce social outcomes, social science should also be directed toward the development of techniques that would contribute to their early recognition. We may not be able to forecast a single "most probable" future, but well-developed middle-range theories should allow the construction of a handful of likely or possible scenarios, positive or negative contingencies, which, when coupled with adequate diagnostic procedures, would allow us to act in ways consistent with our underlying values and goals.[110]

But what are the important questions that should guide the development of social science theory? And which policy responses would be consistent with our values? The answers to these questions cannot be delivered by an empirical social science limited to the search for explanations of causal regularities.[111] For such answers, we need to rediscover and acknowledge the centrality of philosophy and religion to the practice of science. For if social science has a foundation, it will be found in collectively held beliefs about what constitutes the good life.

Notes

ONE: Introduction

Epigraph: Gary King, Robert O. Keohane, and Sidney Verba, *Designing Social Inquiry: Scientific Inference in Qualitative Research* (Princeton: Princeton University Press, 1994), 229.

1. This is particularly true for the United States, the largest producer and consumer of social science.

2. Although I cannot here provide a comprehensive history of the movement from the idiographic and normative focus that characterized the prewar academic study of international politics to the deductive-nomothetical focus that dominates today, see E. H. Carr, *The Twenty-Years' Crisis, 1919–1939: An Introduction to the Study of International Relations* (London: Macmillan, 1939); David Easton, *The Political System* (New York: Knopf, 1953); Alan Isaak, *The Scope and Method of Political Science* (Homewood, IL: Dorsey, 1969); Hedley Bull, "International Theory: The Case for a Classical Approach," *World Politics* 18 (April 1966): 361–77; Morton Kaplan, "The New Great Debate: Traditionalism vs. Science in International Relations," *World Politics* 19 (October 1966): 1–20; Oran Young, "Professor Russett: Industrious Tailor to a Naked Emperor," *World Politics* 21 (April 1969): 486–511; Bruce Russett, "The Young Science of International Politics," *World Politics* 22 (October 1969); and more recently Michael Banks, "The Inter-Paradigm Debate," in *International Relations: A Handbook of Current Theory,* ed. Margot Light and A. J. R. Groom (London: Pinter, 1985), 7–26, and Yosef Lapid, "The Third Debate: On the Prospects of International Theory in a Post-Positivist Era," *International Studies Quarterly* 33 (September 1989): 235–54.

3. In keeping with Anglo-Saxon usage, the term *science* as used here refers to those methods associated with the search for regularities and ultimately generally valid causal laws in the world of empirical observation. From this perspective, scientific explanation means the deductive subsumption of individual events under a covering law. *Science* is thus in English usage a much more restrictive term than the German term *Wissenschaft,* which refers to the systematic study of a given phenomenon by any of a number of methods.

4. The term *normal science* comes from Thomas Kuhn, *The Structure of Scientific Revolutions* (Chicago: University of Chicago Press, 1962). For the argument that cumulation is a criterion of progressive research programs, see Imre Lakatos, "Falsification and the Methodology of Scientific Research Programmes," in *Criticism and the Growth of Knowledge,* ed. Imre Lakatos and Alan Musgrave (Cambridge: Cambridge University Press, 1970), 91–195, esp. 116–22.

5. See Richard Ned Lebow and Thomas Risse-Kappen, "Introduction: International Relations Theory and the End of the Cold War," in *International Relations Theory and the End of the Cold War,* ed. Lebow and Risse-Kappen (New York: Columbia University Press, 1995), 1–21.

6. See Joseph Lepgold, "Is Anyone Listening? International Relations Theory and the Problem of Policy Relevance," *Political Science Quarterly* 113 (Spring 1998): 43–62; and David D. Newsom, "Foreign Policy and Academia," *Foreign Policy* 101 (Winter 1995–96): 52–67.

7. See Joseph Kruzel, "More a Chasm than a Gap, but Do Scholars Want to Bridge It?" *Mershon International Studies Review* (April 1994): 179–81.

8. King, Keohane, and Verba, *Designing Social Inquiry,* ix.

9. For a general introduction to postmodernism, see Madan Sarup, *An Introductory Guide to Post-Structuralism and Postmodernism* (New York: Harvester Wheatsheaf, 1993). For a sampling of postmodern arguments applied to the study of international politics, see Richard K. Ashley, "The Poverty of Neorealism," in *Neorealism and Its Critics,* ed. Robert O. Keohane (New York: Columbia University Press, 1986), 255–300; Richard K. Ashley, "The Geopolitics of Geopolitical Space: Toward a Critical Social Theory of International Politics," *Alternatives* 12 (October 1987): 403–34; James Der Derian and Michael J. Shapiro, eds., *International/Intertextual Relations: Postmodern Readings of World Politics* (Toronto: Lexington Books, 1989); and Bradley Klein, *Strategic Studies and World Order* (Cambridge: Cambridge University Press, 1994).

10. See James A. Caporaso, "Research Design, Falsification, and the Qualitative-Quantitative Divide," *American Political Science Review* 89 (June 1995): 457–60. An argument in support of interpretivist or "reflexivist" analysis is developed in Mark Neufeld, *The Restructuring of International Relations Theory* (Cambridge: Cambridge University Press, 1995), esp. 39–70. For excellent examples of historically grounded analysis characteristic of the best traditionalist work, see Richard N. Haass, *Intervention: The Use of American Military Force in the Post–Cold War World* (Washington, DC: Carnegie Endowment, 1999); and Richard Ned Lebow and Janice Gross Stein, *We All Lost the Cold War* (Princeton: Princeton University Press, 1994).

11. Although the point was made eloquently by Almond and Genco a quarter century ago, the field all too often continues to treat social outcomes as natural or mechanical events. See Gabriel A. Almond and Stephen J. Genco, "Clouds, Clocks, and the Study of Politics," *World Politics* 29 (July 1977): 489–522.

12. See Ernst Haas, "The Balance of Power: Prescription, Concept, or Propaganda?" *World Politics* 5 (July 1953): 422–77; and Martin Wight, "The Balance of Power," in *Diplomatic Investigations: Essays in the Theory of International Politics,* ed. H. Butterfield and Martin Wight (London: Allen and Unwin, 1966), 132–48.

13. See, for example, the arguments in George J. Graham, *Methodological Foundations for Political Analysis* (Waltham, MA: Xerox College Publishing, 1971), 36–109.

14. Scientific observation is often mediated, such as when air pressure is measured by means of a barometer.

15. The classical statement on the dictates of operationalization is Percy W. Bridgman, *The Logic of Modern Physics* (New York: Macmillan, 1927), 1–32.

16. Harold D. Lasswell and Abraham Kaplan, *Power and Society: A Framework for Political Inquiry* (New Haven: Yale University Press, 1950).

17. See, for example, Gabriel A. Almond and Sidney Verba, *The Civic Culture: Politi-*

cal Attitudes and Democracy in Five Nations (Princeton: Princeton University Press, 1963); Lucian Pye and Sidney Verba, *Political Culture and Political Development* (Princeton: Princeton University Press, 1966); Robert A. Dahl, *Political Oppositions in Western Democracies* (New Haven: Yale University Press, 1966); Philip Converse, "The Nature of Mass Belief Systems," in *Ideology and Discontent,* ed. David Apter (New York: Free Press, 1964); Richard Fagan, *The Transformation of Political Culture in Cuba* (Stanford: Stanford University Press, 1969); and Donald Devine, *The Political Culture of the United States* (Boston: Little, Brown, 1972). The concept of political culture has recently undergone a revival, renewing old debates as to its meaning. See Lucian W. Pye, "Political Culture Revisited," *Political Psychology* 12 (September 1991): 487–508; Michael C. Desch, "Culture Clash: Assessing the Importance of Ideas in Security Studies," *International Security* 23 (Summer 1998): 141–70; John S. Duffield et al., "Correspondence. Isms and Schisms: Culturalism versus Realism in Security Studies," *International Security* 24 (Summer 1999): 156–80; Ido Oren, "Is Culture Independent of National Security? How America's National Security Concerns Shaped 'Political Culture' Research," *European Journal of International Relations* 6 (December 2000): 543–73; and Gabriel A. Almond et al., "Forum: Responses to Ido Oren," *European Journal of International Relations* 7 (September 2001): 399–408.

18. For various conceptions of the state, see Jean Bodin, *The Six Bookes of a Commonweale* (1576; repr. Cambridge, MA: Harvard University Press, 1962); Jean Jacques Rousseau, *Social Contract* (1762; repr. London: Dent, 1961); Max Weber, *Wirtschaft und Gesellschaft: Grundriss der verstehenden Soziologie,* 5th rev. ed. (1921; repr. Tübingen: Mohr, 1976); Harold J. Laski, *The State in Theory and Practice* (London: Allen and Unwin, 1956); and Ernst-Wolfgang "Die Bedeutung der Unterscheidung von Staat und Gesellschaft in demokratischen Sozialstaat der Gegenwart," in Böckenförde, *Staat, Gesellschaft, Freiheit: Studien zur Staatstheorie und zum Verfassungsrecht* (Frankfurt: Suhrkamp, 1976), 185–220. For a sampling of the various attempts to define the concept of the political system, see Gabriel A. Almond, "Comparative Political Systems," *Journal of Politics* 18, no. 2 (1956): 391–409; David Easton, *A Systems Analysis of Political Life* (New York: Wiley, 1965); Morton A. Kaplan, *System and Process in International Politics* (New York: Wiley, 1964); and William C. Mitchell, "Political Systems," in *International Encyclopedia of the Social Sciences,* vol. 15, ed. David L. Sills (New York: Macmillan Co. and Free Press, 1968), 473–79. The literature on the concept of power is immense. Among the most important modern works are Weber, *Wirtschaft und Gesellschaft;* Lasswell and Kaplan, *Power and Society,* 74–102; Robert A. Dahl, "The Concept of Power," *Behavioral Science* 2 (July 1957): 201–15; Robert A. Dahl, "Power," *International Encyclopedia of the Social Sciences,* vol. 12, 404–15; Talcott Parsons, "On the Concept of Political Power," *Proceedings of the American Philosophical Society* 107 (June 1963): 232–62; John C. Harsanyi, "Measurement of Social Power, Opportunity Costs, and the Theory of Two-person Bargaining Games," *Behavioral Science* 7 (January 1962): 67–80; Peter Bachrach and Morton S. Baratz, "Decisions and Nondecisions: An Analytical Framework," *American Political Science Review* 57 (September 1963): 632–42; Steven Lukes, *Power: A Radical View* (New York: Macmillan, 1974); David A. Baldwin, *Paradoxes of Power* (New York: Basil Blackwell, 1989). The concept of security was recognized by Arnold Wolfers to be ambiguous; it continues to defy consensus. See Wolfers, "National Security as Ambiguous Symbol," in Wolfers, *Discord and Collaboration: Essays on International Politics* (Baltimore: Johns Hopkins University Press, 1962), 147–66; David A. Baldwin, "The Concept of Security," *Review of International Studies* 23 (January 1997): 5–26; J. Ann Tickner, "Re-visioning Security," in *International Re-*

lations Theory Today, ed. Ken Booth and Steve Smith (Oxford: Oxford University Press, 1995), 175–97; Helga Haftendorn, "Das Sicherheitspuzzel," in *Regionalisierung der Sicherheitspolitik,* ed. Christopher Daase (Baden-Baden: Nomos, 1993), 13–38; and Ole Wæver, "Securitization and Desecuritization," in *On Security,* ed. Ronnie D. Lipschutz (New York: Columbia University Press, 1995), 46–86.

19. The authors of *Designing Social Inquiry* have admitted that their goal is to "discipline political science." See Gary King, Robert O. Keohane, and Sidney Verba, "The Importance of Research Design in Political Science," *American Political Science Review* 89 (June 1995): 476.

20. William Labov, "The Boundaries of Words and their Meanings," in *New Ways of Analyzing Variations in English,* ed. C. J. Bailey and R. W. Shuy (Washington, DC: Georgetown University Press, 1973), 352–53.

21. It is something of a paradox that a number of fundamental assumptions of empirical science have themselves been called into question through the application of standard scientific methods.

22. John Ziman, *Reliable Knowledge: An Exploration of the Grounds for Belief in Science* (Cambridge: Cambridge University Press, 1978), 26–27.

TWO: Of Concepts and Conceptualization

Epigraph: Wilhelm von Humboldt, *Über die Verschiedenheit des menschlichen Sprachbauens und ihren Einfluß auf die geistige Entwicklung des Menschengeschlechts* (Berlin: Dümmlers Verlag, 1836). English translation by P. Heath, *On Language: The Diversity of Human Language-Structure and Its Influence on the Mental Development of Mankind* (Cambridge: Cambridge University Press, 1988). Quotation found on page 54 of the English version.

1. See, for example, Arend Lijphart, "Comparative Politics and Comparative Method," *American Political Science Review* 65 (September 1971), 685; and Gabriel A. Almond and Stephen J. Genco, "Clouds, Clocks, and the Study of Politics," *World Politics* 29 (July 1977), 489–522.

2. See, for example, Gary King, Robert O. Keohane, and Sidney Verba, *Designing Social Inquiry: Scientific Inference in Qualitative Research* (Princeton: Princeton University Press, 1994), 47.

3. Even the concept of the "mind" would appear to mediate between the mind as it is and the mind as we think of it. For philosophical reflections on the relationship, see G. W. F. Hegel, *The Phenomenology of Mind,* J. B. Baille, trans. (New York: Harper, 1967), 229–32, 338–72.

4. See Merlin Donald, *Origins of the Modern Mind: Three Stages in the Evolution of Culture and Cognition* (Cambridge: Harvard University Press, 1991), 3.

5. See Eric Pederson and Jan Nuyts, "Overview: On the Relationship between Language and Conceptualization," in *Language and Conceptualization,* ed. J. Nuyts and E. Pederson (Cambridge: Cambridge University Press, 1997), 1–2; Jan Nuyts, "Linguistic Representation and Conceptual Knowledge Representation," in *Layers and Levels of Representation in Language Theory,* ed. J. Nuyts, A. M. Bolkenstein, and C. Vet (Amsterdam: Benjamins, 1990), 263–93; D. Rumelhart, J. McClelland et al., eds., *Parallel Distributed Processing,* vol. 1 (Cambridge: MIT Press, 1986); and J. McClelland, D. Rumelhart et al., eds., *Parallel Distributed Processing,* vol. 2 (Cambridge: MIT Press, 1986).

6. As cited in Dan I. Slobin, "From 'Thought and Language' to 'Thinking for Speaking,'" in John J. Gumperz and Stephen C. Levinson, *Rethinking Linguistic Relativity* (Cambridge: Cambridge University Press, 1996), 70.

7. Brent Berlin and Paul Kay, *Basic Color Terms: Their Universality and Evolution* (Berkeley: University of California Press, 1969).

8. A morpheme is a minimum unit of speech that is both recurrent and meaningful. See Herbert H. Clark and Eve V. Clark, *Psychology and Language: An Introduction to Psycholinguistics* (New York: Harcourt Brace Jovanovich, 1977), 564.

9. The discussion here follows George Lakoff, *Women, Fire, and Dangerous Things: What Categories Reveal About the Mind* (Chicago: University of Chicago Press, 1987), 24–30.

10. Berlin and Kay, *Basic Color Terms,* 2–3, 22–23.

11. Berlin and Kay conducted their experiments with a standardized chart of 320 small color squares and asked the speakers of various languages to group them into basic color categories. See ibid., 5–14.

12. The boundaries of color terms also varied in their application by the same individual across contexts. See ibid., 13–14.

13. See Robert E. MacLaury, *Color Cognition in Mesoamerica: Constructing Categories as Vantages* (Austin: University of Texas Press, 1997), esp. chs. 4–8.

14. The cultural origins and social effects of color categorization are well known to students of race. For example, whereas in the United States children of mixed European and African heritage are generally considered "black," and thereby suffer the effects of racism, in Brazil they are regarded as mulatto and enjoy somewhat more social mobility than "black" Brazilians with darker skin. In the United States, the term *white* has been reserved for persons of no (known) non-Caucasian heritage. However, the situation was somewhat different in apartheid South Africa. According to one analyst: "South Africa, in short, classes with the white any person who can conceivably pass as white, where America classes with the Negro any person who can conceivably pass as Negro." See James F. Davis, *Who Is Black? One Nation's Definition* (University Park: Pennsylvania State University Press, 1991); and Anthony W. Marx, *Making Race and Nation: A Comparison of South Africa, the United States, and Brazil* (Cambridge: Cambridge University Press, 1998), 65–79, quotation 73.

15. E. Bialystok and D. R. Olson, "Spatial Categories: The Perception and Conceptualization of Spatial Relations," in *Categorical Perception: The Groundwork of Cognition,* ed. Stevan R. Harnad (Cambridge: Cambridge University Press, 1987), 511–31, quotation 511.

16. The discussion here largely follows Melissa Bowerman, "The Origins of Children's Spatial Semantic Categories: Cognitive versus Linguistic Determinants," in *Rethinking Linguistic Relativity,* ed. John J. Gumperz and Stephen C. Levinson (Cambridge: Cambridge University Press, 1996), 145.

17. For a review of the data, see Paul Van Geert, "In, On, Under: An Essay on the Modularity of Infant Spatial Competence," *First Language* 6 (1985/86): 7–28.

18. See Bowerman, "The Origins of Children's Spatial Semantic Categories," 148–49; M. Bowerman, *Early Syntactic Development: A Cross-linguistic Study with Special Reference to Finnish* (Cambridge: Cambridge University Press, 1973); and Eve V. Clark, "Nonlinguistic Strategies and the Acquisition of Word Meanings," *Cognition* 2 (1973): 161–82.

19. Herbert H. Clark, "Space, Time, Semantics, and the Child," in *Cognitive Develop-*

ment and the Acquisition of Language, ed. Timothy E. Moore (New York: Academic Press, 1973), 27–63, quotation 28.

20. Ibid., 30–35.

21. The meanings of terms need not be identical but would be expected to be consistent with hypothesized "spatial primitives." See Bowerman, "The Origins of Children's Spatial Semantic Categories," 150; Clark, "Nonlinguistic Strategies and the Acquisition of Word Meanings"; and David R. Olson and Ellen Bialystok, eds., *Spatial Cognition: The Structure and Development of the Mental Representation of Spatial Relations* (Hillsdale, NJ: Lawrence Erlbaum, 1983), ix–xii, 54–77. For a related discussion that focuses on the neurology of the mind, see Anatonio R. Damasio, *Descartes' Error: Emotion, Reason, and the Human Brain* (New York: Putnam, 1994), ch. 10.

22. See Bowerman, "The Origins of Children's Spatial Semantic Categories," 170, note 4. Also, Clark and Clark, *Psychology and Language* (New York: Harcourt, Brace, Jovanovich, 1977), 502–4.

23. See, for example, Lorraine McCune-Nicolich, "The Cognitive Bases of Relational Words in the Single Word Period," *Journal of Child Language* 8 (February 1981): 18; and Lois Bloom, *One Word at a Time* (The Hague: Mouton, 1973), ch. 2.

24. See S. Choi and Melissa Bowerman, "Learning to Express Motion Events in English and Korean: The Influence of Language-Specific Lexicalization Patterns," *Cognition* 41 (1991): 83–121; and Melissa Bowerman, "Learning a Semantic System: What Role Do Cognitive Predispositions Play?" in *The Teachability of Language,* ed. M. L. Rice and R. L. Schiefelbusch (Baltimore: Paul H. Brookes, 1989), 133–69.

25. Bowerman, "The Origins of Children's Spatial Semantic Categories," 156–58.

26. The discussion here follows Lakoff, *Women, Fire, and Dangerous Things,* 313–17. But see also Claudia Brugman, "The Use of Body-Part Terms as Locatives in Chaltcatongo Mixtec," in Report No. 4: *Survey of California and Other Indian Languages* (Berkeley: University of California, Berkeley, 1983), 235–90. Body-part spatial systems are not unique to the Mixtec but are widespread among Meso-American and African languages. See B. Heine, "Adpositions in African Languages," *Linguistique Africaine* 2 (1989): 77–127; and R. E. MacLaury, "Zapotec Body-Part Locatives: Prototypes and Metaphoric Extensions," *International Journal of American Linguistics* 55 (1989): 119–54.

27. Whereas the English concept *on* requires contact, many spatial systems, including Korean, Japanese, and Chinese, routinely use the same term to refer to relationships that in English would be broken down into *on* and *above.* See Bowerman, "The Origins of Children's Spatial Semantic Categories," 171, note 13.

28. See Bloom, *One Word at a Time;* and McCune-Nicolich, "The Cognitive Bases of Relational Words in the Single Word Period."

29. Bowerman, "The Origins of Children's Spatial Semantic Categories," 160–61.

30. Ibid., 165–66.

31. Ibid., 168.

32. See L. E. Bahrick and J. N. Pickens, "Classification of Bimodal English and Spanish Language Passages by Infants," *Infant Behavior and Development* 11 (July–September 1988): 277–96; and M. J. Spence and A. J. DeCasper, "Prenatal Experience with Low-frequency Maternal-voice Sounds Influences Neonatal Perception of Maternal Voice Samples," *Infant Behavior and Development* 10 (April–June 1987): 133–42.

33. Joanne L. Miller and Peter D. Eimas, "Studies on the Categorization of Speech by Infants," *Cognition* 13 (January 1983): 135–65.

34. A basic distinction in the study of linguistics is made between a phone, a unit of speech sound, and a phoneme, a perception occurring at a higher level of cognition than usually represents a phone. As Lakoff writes: "English has the phoneme /k/ . . . which occurs in the cords *cool, keel, key, school,* and *flak.* If attention is paid to details of pronunciation, it turns out that /k/ is pronounced differently in these words: aspirated velar [kʰ] in *cool,* aspirated palatal [k'ʰ] in *keel,* unaspirated velar [k] in *school,* and unaspirated palatal [k'] in *ski.* English speakers perceive these, despite their differences in pronunciation, as being instances of the same phoneme /k/. However, there are other languages in which [kʰ] and [k] are different phonemes, and others still in which [k'] and [k] are instances of different phonemes." Lakoff, *Women, Fire, and Dangerous Things,* 61.

35. See Katherine Nelson, *Language in Cognitive Development: Emergence of the Mediated Mind* (Cambridge: Cambridge University Press, 1996), 106–7; Jacques Mehler and Emmanuel Dupoux, *What Infants Know* (Cambridge: Blackwell, 1994), 51–53, 67–69, and 151–73; Miller and Eimas, "Studies on the Categorization of Speech by Infants," 136; and J. Mehler and J. Bertoncini, "Infants' Perception of Speech and Other Acoustic Stimuli," in *Psycholinguistics 2: Structures and Processes,* ed. John Morton and John C. Marshall (Cambridge: MIT Press, 1979), 67–105.

36. Mehler and Dupoux, *What Infants Know,* 168. These findings are not universally accepted. For an argument that exposure to phonetic distinctions of the native language induces a "speech mode" of listening, see Bruno H. Repp and Alvin M. Libermann, "Phonetic Category Boundaries Are Flexible," in *Categorical Perception: The Groundwork of Cognition,* ed. Stevan Harnad (Cambridge: Cambridge University Press, 1987), 106.

37. Nelson, *Language in Cognitive Development,* 107.

38. The discussion here follows Miller and Eimas, "Studies in the Categorization of Speech by Infants."

39. Patricia. K. Kuhl, "Perceptual Constancy for Speech-Sound Categories in Early Infancy," in *Child Phonology,* vol. 2, *Perception,* ed. Grace H. Yeni-Komshian, James F. Kavanagh, and Charles A. Ferguson (New York: Academic Press, 1989); K. Hirsh-Pasek et al., "Clauses Are Perceptual Units for Young Infants," *Cognition* 26 (1987): 269–86; and J. A. Fodor, M. F. Garrett, and S. L. Brill, "Pi Ka Pu: The Perception of Speech Sounds by Prelinguistic Infants," *Perception and Psychophysics* 18, no. 2 (1975): 74–78.

40. The relevant acoustic distinction is referred to as the "voice-onset-time" (VOT), which has been shown to differentiate voicing categories in a number of languages. In acoustic terms, VOT is defined by the time between the release of the lips and the onset of voicing and is particularly useful for distinguishing between voiced and voiceless consonants. For example, the typical speaker produces the linguistic segment corresponding to [d] with a VOT in the vicinity of 0 to 20 msec, whereas [tʰ] is typically produced with a VOT value of 30 to 100 msec. See Miller and Eimas, "Studies on the Categorization of Speech by Infants," 137.

41. Here, although the two chosen exemplars of [da] are acoustically as distinct on the VOT scale as are the [da]-[tʰa] exemplars, infants discriminate and categorize on the linguistic as opposed to acoustic dimension. See Miller and Eimas, "Studies on the Categorization of Speech by Infants," 137–39; and P. D. Eimas, "Speech Perception in Early Infancy," in *Infant Perception: From Sensation to Cognition,* vol. 2, ed. L. B. Cohen and P. Salapatek (New York: Academic Press, 1975), 193–231.

42. Peter W. Jusczyk, "Infant Speech Perception: A Critical Appraisal," in *Perspectives*

on the Study of Speech, ed. Peter D. Eimas and Joanne L. Miller (Hillsdale, NJ: Erlbaum, 1981), 113–64.

43. See Richard N. Aslin and David B. Pisoni, "Some Developmental Processes in Speech Perception," in *Child Phonology,* vol. 2, *Perception,* ed. G. N. Yeni-Komshain et al., 77–79.

44. Nelson, *Language in Cognitive Development,* 106–7.

45. Mehler and Dupoux, *What Infants Know,* 168.

46. C. T. Best, G. W. McRoberts and N. M. Sithole, "Examination of Perceptual Reorganization for Nonnative Speech Contrasts: Zulu Click Discrimination by English-Speaking Adults and Infants," *Journal of Experimental Psychology: Human Perception and Performance* 14 (August 1988): 345–60.

47. Mehler and Dupoux, *What Infants Know,* 168–69.

48. Nelson, *Language in Cognitive Development,* 113–16.

49. The findings are the same for cross-cultural studies of emotions. Thus, although the English terms for seven basic emotions (anger, fear, sadness, joy, disgust, shame, and guilt) were translated to the satisfaction of locals in 37 linguistic communities, major divergences in connotations and application were discovered, even between closely related languages such as German and Swiss German. See Klaus R. Scherer, "Toward a Concept of 'Modal Emotions,'" in *The Nature of Emotion: Fundamental Questions,* ed. Paul Ekman and Richard Davidson (New York: Oxford University Press, 1994), 25–31.

50. We will turn to a discussion of ideal types below.

51. See, for example, Dina A. Zines, *Contemporary Research in International Relations: A Perspective and a Critical Appraisal* (New York: Free Press, 1976), esp. ch. 1.

52. Ronald H. Chilcote, *Theories of Comparative Politics: The Search for a Paradigm* (Boulder, CO: Westview Press, 1981), 16–17. Such pronouncements are standard in methods textbooks. See, for example, Ferdinand Müller and Manfred Schmidt, *Empirische Politikwissenschaft* (Stuttgart: Kohlhammer, 1979), 11–12, 30–31.

53. Bruce Bueno de Mesquita, "Toward a Scientific Understanding of International Conflict," *International Studies Quarterly* 29 (June 1985): 121–36, quotations 126, 133.

54. Anatol Rapoport, "Mathematical Methods in Theories of International Relations: Expectations, Caveats, and Opportunities," in *Mathematical Models in International Relations,* ed. Dina A. Zinnes and John V. Gillespie (New York: Praeger Publishers, 1976), 11.

55. Giovanni Sartori, "Concept Misinformation in Comparative Politics," *American Political Science Review* 64 (December 1970): 1033–53.

56. See Nelson Goodman, "Seven Strictures on Similarity," in *How Classification Works: Nelson Goodman among the Social Sciences,* ed. Mary Douglas and David Hull (Edinburgh: Edinburgh University Press, 1992), 13–23, quotation 19.

57. Ludwig Wittgenstein, *Philosophical Investigations* (New York: Macmillan, 1958), 31–32, emphasis in original.

58. Ibid., 33–34.

59. Ibid., 36.

60. See the discussion of incommensurability in chapter 3.

61. Friedrich V. Kratochwil, *Rules, Norms, and Decisions: On the Conditions of Practical and Legal Reasoning in International Relations and Domestic Affairs* (Cambridge: Cambridge University Press, 1989), esp. 81–91.

62. Wittgenstein, *Philosophical Investigations,* 33.

63. The discussion here follows Lakoff, *Women, Fire, and Dangerous Things,* 22–23. For

the relevant studies in the field of cognitive anthropology, see Floyd Lounsbury, "A Formal Account of the Crow- and Omaha-Type Kinship Terminologies," in *Explorations in Cultural Anthropology*, ed. W. H. Goodenough (New York: McGraw Hill, 1964), 351–94.

64. This rule has as its corollary: the child of the brother of any female linking relative is equivalent to the sibling of that female linking relative (e.g., the daughter of a mother's brother is the equivalent of the mother's sister).

65. The concept of "linking relative" prevents the rule from applying directly. It requires there to be an intermediate relative between the reference individual and the person being described. Thus a person's paternal aunt is not equivalent to his sister whereas his father's paternal aunt is equivalent to his father's sister.

66. The fuzzy nature of kinship boundaries is not specific to the Fox. For example, the decision of whether a given individual is or is not a kinsman is, in general, far from categorical for Americans: "One cannot say that all second cousins are kinsmen, but all third cousins are not." See David M. Schneider, "American Kin Terms and Terms for Kinsmen: A Critique of Goodenough's Componential Analysis of Yankee Kinship Terminology," in *Cognitive Anthropology*, ed. Stephen Tylor (New York: Holt, Rinehart and Winston, 1969), 289.

67. Some of the more important findings are detailed in Eleanor Rosch, "Natural Categories," *Cognitive Psychology* 4, no. 3 (1973): 328–50; E. Rosch, "Cognitive Reference Points," *Cognitive Psychology* 7, no. 4 (1975): 532–47; E. Rosch, "Prototype Classification and Logical Classification: The Two Systems," in *New Trends in Conceptual Representation: Challenges to Piaget's Theory*, ed. E. Scholnick (Hillsdale, NJ: Erlbaum, 1983), 73–86; and E. Rosch, "Coherences and Categorization: A Classical View," in *Festschrift for Roger Brown* (Hillsdale, NJ: Erlbaum, 1988), 379–92.

68. For an argument that the finding of gradedness is an artifact of experimental design and not indicative of cognitive structures, see Sharon Lee Armstrong, Lila R. Gleitman, and Henry Gleitman, "What Some Concepts Might Not Be," *Cognition* 13 (January 1983): 263–308.

69. The eliciting technique is outlined in Willett Kempton, *The Folk Classification of Ceramics: A Study of Cognitive Prototypes* (New York: Academic Press, 1981), ch. 2. The examples are taken from page 36.

70. Kempton, *The Folk Classification of Ceramics*, ch. 3.

71. In related research, Amos Tversky found that people systematically judge prototypical exemplars to be less similar to variants than those same variants are judged similar to the prototype. That is, psychologically speaking, similarity is not a symmetrical relationship. Distinctive features of the variant are weighted more heavily in similarity judgments than are the distinctive features of the prototype. See Amos Tversky, "Features of Similarity," *Psychological Review* 84 (1977): 327–52. See also Tversky, "Elimination by Aspects: A Theory of Choice," *Psychological Review* 79 (1972): 281–99.

72. Moreover, prototype effects appear to extend to processes of reasoning in ways that violate basic criteria of rationality. For example, less representative or marginal examples are generally considered to be more like prototypical or central category members than prototypical members are considered similar to the less representative or marginal examples. See Amos Tversky and I. Gati, "Studies of Similarity," in *Cognition and Categorization*, ed. Eleanor Rosch and B. B. Lloyd (Hillsdale, NJ: Erlbaum, 1978), 79–98. And new information about a prototypical category member is more likely to be generalized to marginal members than vice versa. For example, one study demonstrated that

subjects thought it was more likely that a newly discovered disease would spread from robins to ducks than from ducks to robins. See Lance J. Rips, "Inductive Judgements about Natural Categories," *Journal of Verbal Learning and Verbal Behavior* 14, no. 6 (1975): 665–81.

73. For a standard treatment of connotation and denotation, see Wesley C. Salmon, *Logic* (Englewood Cliffs, NJ: Prentice Hall, 1963), 90–91.

74. In 1999, British Prime Minister Tony Blair successfully engineered a reform in the constitution of the House of Lords and reduced the number of hereditary members to 92. Prior to the Blair reforms, over 750 of the nearly 1,300 members owed their position to right of birth. However, insofar as the "life peers" owe their position to the patronage of either the Blair government or its predecessors, the upper house remains a curious institution from the standpoint of modern conceptions of democracy.

75. Sartori, "Concept Misinformation in Comparative Politics," 1038.

76. Steven Van Evera, *Guide to Methods for Students of Political Science* (Ithaca, NY: Cornell University Press, 1997), 3.

77. King, Keohane, and Verba, *Designing Social Inquiry,* 34 and 47n.

78. This example is taken from A. F. Chalmers, *What Is This Thing Called Science?* (Indianapolis: Hackett, 1982), 29.

79. Chalmers, *What Is This Thing Called Science?* 30.

80. The discussion here follows Norwood Russell Hanson, *Patterns of Discovery: An Inquiry into the Conceptual Foundations of Science* (Cambridge: Cambridge University Press, 1958), 4–30.

81. See Hermann von Helmholtz, *Handbuch der physiologischen Optik,* vol. 3 (Leipzig: Voss, 1867), 239.

82. Chalmers, *What Is This Thing Called Science?* 28–29.

83. Müller and Schmidt, *Empirische Politikwissenschaft,* 11, translation mine.

84. King, Keohane, and Verba, *Designing Social Inquiry,* 99, 109–10.

85. See Ernst Mayr, *Systematics and the Origin of Species* (New York: Columbia University Press, 1942).

86. For extended discussions of these issues, see Philip Kitcher, "Species," *Philosophy of Science* 51, no. 2 (1984): 308–33; and Kitcher, "Some Puzzles About Species," in *What the Philosophy of Biology Is,* ed. Michael Ruse (Dordrecht, Holland: Reidel, 1989), 183–208.

87. Carl von Linne [Carolus Linnaeus], *Systema Naturae* (1735; repr. Niewkoop, Holland: B. de Graaf, 1964).

88. Charles Darwin, *On the Origin of Species by Means of Natural Selection* (1859; repr. Chicago: Encyclopaedia Britannica, 1955).

89. E. Pennisi, "Linnaeus's Last Stand?" *Science* 291 (23 March 2001): 2304–7.

90. Among the earliest to work on phylogenetics was the East German entomologist Willi Hennig. His pathbreaking book, *Gründzüge einer Theorie der Phylogenetischen Systematik* (Berlin: Deutscher Zentralverlag, 1950), however, was at first largely ignored by the scientific community and received widespread attention only some decades after its publication. The basic elements of the PhyloCode system of classification were developed in the 1980s by Kevin de Queiroz and Jacques Gauthier and presented in a series of publications in the 1990s. See Queiroz and Gauthier, "Phylogeny as a Central Principle in Taxonomy: Phylogenetic Definitions of Taxon Names," *Systematic Zoology* 39 (1990): 307–22; Queiroz and Gauthier, "Phylogenetic Taxonomy," *Annual Review of Ecol-*

ogy and Systematics 23 (1992): 449–80; and Queiroz and Gauthier, "Toward a Phylogenetic System of Biological Nomenclature," *Trends in Ecology and Evolution* 9 (1994): 27–31. The PhyloCode classification system can be found at www.ohiou.edu/phylocode. For an introduction to cladistics, see Eugene S. Gaffney, "An Introduction to the Logic of Phylogeny Reconstruction," in *Phylogenetic Analysis and Paleontology,* ed. Joel Cracraft and Niles Eldredge (New York: Columbia University Press, 1979), 79–111.

91. Pennisi, "Linnaeus's Last Stand?" 2307.

92. See Ian Hacking, "World-Making by Kind-Making: Child Abuse for Example," in *How Classification Works,* ed. Mary Douglas and David Hull (Edinburgh: University of Edinburgh Press, 1992), 180–238.

93. Michel Foucault, *Discipline and Punish: The Birth of the Prison* (New York: Vintage, 1979); Foucault, *The Birth of the Clinic: An Archaeology of Medical Perception* (New York: Pantheon, 1973); and Foucault, *The History of Sexuality* (New York: Vintage, 1980).

94. Interestingly, however, depictions of such mythical creatures can be readily graded as more or less realistic with high degrees of inter-coder reliability. See Goodman, "Seven Strictures on Similarity," 14.

95. Here I take issue with the position of those who maintain that the goal of science is to "learn facts about the real world." King, Keohane, and Verba, *Designing Social Inquiry,* 6.

96. See Clyde H. Coombs, *A Theory of Data* (New York: John Wiley and Sons, 1967), 4–5.

97. King, Keohane, and Verba, *Designing Social Inquiry,* 46.

98. See Merlin Donald, *Origins of the Modern Mind: Three Stages in the Evolution of Culture and Cognition* (Cambridge: Harvard University Press, 1991), 253. Donald's central thesis is that human thought is not a product of biological evolution but rather a cultural invention.

99. Clifford Geertz, *The Interpretation of Cultures* (New York: Basic Books, 1973), 10. Interpretive theory based on thick description is neither nomothetic nor strongly predictive. See pages 24 through 28.

100. Ibid., 9.

101. Ibid., 28.

102. Ibid., 15–20.

103. Nelson, *Language in Cognitive Development,* 111.

104. On this point, see Stephen C. Levinson, "From Outer to Inner Space: Linguistic Categories and Non-linguistic Thinking," in *Language and Conceptualization,* ed. Nuyts and Pederson, 13–45.

105. See Van Evera, *Guide to Methods for Students of Political Science,* 19.

106. In the field of international politics, David Baldwin has been a frequent champion of conceptual analysis. See, for example, David A. Baldwin, "Interdependence and Power: A Conceptual Analysis," in Baldwin, *Paradoxes of Power* (New York: Basil Blackwell, 1989), 169–215; and Baldwin, "The Concept of Security," *Review of International Studies* 23 (January 1997): 5–26.

107. John J. Mearsheimer, "The False Promise of International Institutions," *International Security* 19 (Winter 1994/95): 8. For a sampling of the contradictory claims of structural realists, see John J. Mearsheimer, "Back to the Future: Instability in Europe After the Cold War," *International Security* 15 (Summer 1990): 5–56; Charles L. Glaser, "Realists as Optimists: Cooperation as Self Help," *International Security* 19 (Winter 1994/95):

50–90; Christopher Layne, "The Unipolar Illusion: Why New Great Powers Will Arise," *International Security* 17 (Spring 1993): 5–51; Layne, "From Preponderance to Offshore Balancing: America's Future Grand Strategy," *International Security* 22 (Summer 1997): 86–124; and William C. Wohlforth, "The Stability of a Unipolar World," *International Security* 24 (Summer 1999): 5–41.

108. Michael C. Desch, "Culture Clash: Assessing the Importance of Ideas in Security Studies," *International Security* 23 (Summer 1998): 141–70, quotation 150. See also the responses and rebuttal in John S. Duffield, Theo Farrell, Richard Price, and Michael C. Desch, "Correspondence. Isms and Schisms: Culturalism versus Realism in Security Studies," *International Security* 24 (Summer 1999): 156–80.

109. Hempel refers to the early stages of a research program as the "natural history stage" where everyday language terms predominate to facilitate observation and description. See Carl G. Hempel, *Aspects of Scientific Explanation* (New York: Free Press, 1965), 140. For a similar discussion, see Arthur L. Stinchcombe, *Constructing Social Theories* (Chicago: University of Chicago Press, 1968), 41.

110. The problematic nature of ultimate foundations is not restricted to the empirical sciences, as judges and lawyers well know. In American legal practice, the danger of infinite regress is limited by the canon that the courts are "never to anticipate a question of constitutional law in advance of the necessity of deciding it." *Liverpool, New York and Philadelphia Steamship Co. v. Commissioners of Emigration,* 113 U.S. 33, 39 (1885), quoted in *Communist Party v. Subversive Activities Control Board,* 367 U.S. 1, 71–72 (1962). See also Justice Brandeis's separate opinion in *Ashwander v. Tennessee Valley Authority,* 297 U.S. 288, 341, 346–47 (1936).

111. Chalmers, *What is This Thing Called Science?* 114.

112. For an extended discussion of the problem in the context of social constructivism, see Friedrich Kratochwil, "Constructing a New Orthodoxy? Wendt's 'Social Theory of International Politics' and the Constructivist Challenge," *Millennium* 29, no. 1 (2000): esp. 94–100.

113. Giovanni Sartori, "Comparing and Miscomparing," *Journal of Theoretical Politics* 3 (July 1991): 243–57.

114. The crucial point is that coherence is a function internal to the language of science and not the correspondence of our concepts to some external "real world."

115. On this point, see Alexander J. Motyl, *Revolutions, Nations, Empires: Conceptual Limits and Theoretical Possibilities* (New York: Columbia University Press, 1999), 4–6.

116. Stinchcombe, *Constructing Social Theories,* 38.

117. Hempel, *Aspects of Scientific Explanation,* 141; Percy W. Bridgman, *The Logic of Modern Physics* (New York: Macmillan, 1927), 1–32.

118. See, King, Keohane, and Verba, *Designing Social Inquiry,* 26–27; Müller and Schmidt, *Empirische Politikwissenschaft,* 30; Bueno de Mesquita, "Toward a Scientific Understanding of International Conflict," 133; and Jack Snyder, "Richness, Rigor, and Relevance in the Study of Soviet Foreign Policy," *International Security* 9 (Winter 1985/6): 89–108.

119. For the debate, see Richard Ned Lebow and Janice Gross Stein, "Deterrence: The Elusive Dependent Variable," *World Politics* 42 (April 1990): 336–69; Paul Huth and Bruce Russett, "Testing Deterrence Theory: Rigor Makes a Difference," *World Politics* 42 (July 1990): 466–501. The Huth and Russett dataset was originally presented in "What Makes Deterrence Work? Cases from 1900 to 1980," *World Politics* 36 (July 1984): 496–526; and

Huth and Russett, "Deterrence Failure and Crisis Escalation," *International Studies Quarterly* 32 (March 1988): 29–46.

120. Lebow and Stein, "Deterrence," 340.

121. P. Ekins, "The Kuznets Curve for the Environment and Economic Growth: Examining the Evidence," *Environmental Planning* 29 (1997), as quoted in Dale S. Rothmann and Sander M. de Bruyn, "Probing into the Environmental Kuznets Curve Hypothesis," *Ecological Economics* 25 (1998): 144. See also S. M. de Bruyn and J. B. Opschoor, "Developments in the Throughput-Income Relationship: Theoretical and Empirical Observations," *Ecological Economics* 20 (1997): 255–68.

122. For example, owing to ongoing debates over the reliability of the datasets, there is no consensus over the risk of HIV transmission from certain sexual practices (in particular oral sex), despite some two decades of research. See Giuseppina Liuzzi et al., "Analysis of HIV-1 Load in Blood, Semen and Saliva: Evidence for Different Viral Compartments in a Cross-Sectional and Longitudinal Study," *AIDS* 10 (December 1996): F51–56; Warren Winkelstein Jr. et al., "Sexual Practices and Risk of Infection by the Human Immunodeficiency Virus," *Journal of the American Medical Association* 257 (January 1987): 321–25; I. P. Keet et al., "Orogenital Sex and the Transmission of HIV," *AIDS* 6 (February 1992): 223–26; J. Levy, "The Transmission of HIV and Factors Influencing Progression to AIDS," *American Journal of Medicine* 95 (July 1993): 86–100; and David G. Ostrow et al., "A Case Control Study of Human Immunodeficiency Virus Type 1 Seroconversion and Risk Related Behaviors in the Chicago MACS/CCS Cohort, 1984–1992," *American Journal of Epidemiology* 142, no. 8 (1995): 875–83.

123. Definitions taken from William Morris, ed., *The American Heritage Dictionary of the English Language* (Boston: Houghton Mifflin, 1969).

124. Magnus Suseni, "Wandel in Indonesien," Lecture delivered 8 March 1999, at the Hochschule für Philosophie München, Munich, Germany.

125. See Berlin and Kay, *Basic Color Terms*, 10–14; and Kempton, *The Folk Classification of Ceramics*, 105–20.

126. Hempel, *Aspects of Scientific Explanation*, 143–44.

127. Ibid., 146.

128. Richard Rorty, *Philosophy and the Mirror of Nature* (Princeton: Princeton University Press, 1980), 307.

129. Levinson, "From Outer to Inner Space," 17–18.

130. Coombs, *A Theory of Data*, 5.

131. For one version of the argument, see Bronislaw Malinowski, *Magic, Science and Religion and Other Essays* (1925; repr. Garden City, NY: Doubleday Anchor, 1948). See also Stephen Jay Gould, *Rocks of Ages* (New York: Ballantine, 1999).

132. Karl Pearson, *The Grammar of Science* (London: J. M. Dent and Sons, 1892), 16. As cited in King, Keohane, and Verba, *Designing Social Inquiry*, 9.

133. A more detailed discussion of this problem is presented in chapter 2.

134. A widely held image represents truth as a circle whose borders we near through scientific progress. Leaving aside the argument that truth is a property of statements and not of the world, most major advances in science can be conceived as taking place outside the bounds of the circle.

135. Thomas S. Kuhn, *The Structure of Scientific Revolutions* (Chicago: University of Chicago Press, 1970), 92–159; Kuhn, *The Copernican Revolution: Planetary Astronomy and the Development of Western Thought* (Cambridge: Harvard University Press, 1957), 185–

228. See also Paul K. Feyerabend, "Philosophy of Science: A Subject with a Great Past," in *Historical and Philosophical Perspectives of Science, Minnesota Studies in Philosophy of Science,* vol. 5, ed. Roger H. Stuewer (Minneapolis: University of Minnesota Press, 1970), 172–83.

136. For an argument that the historical context was a necessary condition for the emergence of the theories of Copernicus, see Hans Blumenberg, *Die Genesis der kopernikanischen Welt* (Frankfurt: Suhrkamp, 1975), 147–300. Because the ideas of Copernicus challenged not only the authority of the Catholic Church but also of the Bible itself, they were rejected by the leaders of the Reformation.

137. See Carl F. von Weizsäcker, *Tragweite der Wissenschaft. I. Schöpfung und Weltenstehung. Die Geschichte zweier Begriffe* (Stuttgart: Hirzel, 1964), 196.

138. See Hans Blumenberg, *Die Legitimität der Neuzeit* (Frankfurt: Suhrkamp, 1966), 9–74. Blumenberg argues that Christian concepts were from the outset strongly influenced by Hellenic ideas, their secularization in the modern period therefore representing something of a *resecularization.* See also M. Stallmann, *Was ist Säkularisierung?* (Tübingen, Germany: Mohr, 1960), 33.

139. Thomas Luckmann, *Das Problem der Religion in der modernen Gesellschaft* (Freiburg, Germany: Rombach, 1963), 65.

140. The thesis of non-overlapping magisteria is put forward in Gould, *Rocks of Ages.*

141. Blumenberg, *Die Legitimität der Neuzeit,* 18.

142. On the religious origins of legal concepts, see Anthony G. Amsterdam and Jerome Bruner, *Minding the Law* (Cambridge: Harvard University Press, 2000), 32.

143. Carl Schmitt, *Politische Theologie. Vier Kapitel zur Lehre von der Souveränität* (1922; repr. Munich: Duncker and Humblot, 1932), 25.

144. This is sometimes referred to as the "objectivist" position on theory. See Chalmers, *What Is This Thing Called Science?* 113–23.

THREE: Scientific Concepts and the Study of Politics

1. Because we lack a general theory of the social construction of reality or a fully developed constructivist theory of politics, I characterize constructivism as an epistemological position. A leading constructivist scholar of international politics suggests that "constructivism remains more of a philosophically and theoretically informed perspective on and approach to the empirical study of international relations." See John Gerard Ruggie, "What Makes the World Hang Together? Neo-utilitarianism and the Social Constructivist Challenge," *International Organization* 52 (Autumn 1998): 855–85. Although constructivist scholarship is found in all subfields of the discipline, the examples here are taken from international politics, the field I know best.

2. This is the central claim of one of the first self-conscious works of constructivist scholarship in the field of international politics. See Nicholas G. Onuf, *World of Our Making: Rules and Rule in Social Theory and International Relations* (Columbia: University of South Carolina Press, 1989).

3. The argument is in part based on a denial of the proposition that naturally occurring objects are possessed of essences. To the extent that we identify necessary and sufficient conditions for purposes of categorization, these are propositions derived from theory.

4. Wolfgang Schluchter, *Rationalism, Religion and Domination: A Weberian Perspective*

(Berkeley: University of California Press, 1989), 9. As cited in Ruggie, "What Makes the World Hang Together?" 860.

5. Important theoretical constructivist works in the field of international politics include Onuf, *World of Our Making;* Friedrich V. Kratochwil, *Rules, Norms, and Decisions;* and Alexander Wendt, *Social Theory of International Politics* (Cambridge: Cambridge University Press, 1999).

6. John Gerard Ruggie, "Continuity and Transformation in the World Polity," in *Neorealism and Its Critics,* ed. Robert O. Keohane (New York: Columbia University Press, 1986), 131–57; Friedrich V. Kratochwil, "Of Systems, Boundaries, and Territoriality: An Inquiry into the Foundations of the State System," *World Politics* 39 (October 1986): 27–52; and Kratochwil, "Sovereignty as *Dominium:* Is There a Right to International Humanitarian Intervention?" in *Beyond Westphalia,* ed. G. Lyons and Michael Mastanduno (Baltimore: Johns Hopkins University Press, 1995), 21–42.

7. Martha Finnemore, *National Interests in International Society* (Ithaca, NY: Cornell University Press, 1996).

8. John Gerard Ruggie, "International Regimes, Transactions, and Change: Embedded Liberalism in the Postwar Economic Order," in *International Regimes,* ed. Stephen D. Krasner (Ithaca, NY: Cornell University Press, 1983), 195–231.

9. Paul Kowert, "Agent versus Structure in the Construction of National Identity," in *International Relations in a Constructed World,* ed. Vendulka Kubálková, Nicholas Onuf, and Paul Kowert (Armonk, NY: M. E. Sharpe, 1988), 101–22; and Yosef Lapid and Friedrich Kratochwil, eds., *The Return of Culture and Identity in IR Theory* (Boulder, CO: Lynne Rienner, 1996).

10. Michael Barnett, *Dialogues in Arab Politics: Negotiations in Regional Order* (New York: Columbia University Press, 1998).

11. Alexander Wendt, "Anarchy Is What States Make of It: The Social Construction of Power Politics," *International Organization* 46 (Spring 1992): 391–425.

12. Donald MacKenzie, *Inventing Accuracy: An Historical Sociology of Nuclear Missile Guidance* (Cambridge: MIT Press, 1990). The same can be said of the concept of "reliability" as applied to the U.S. nuclear stockpile. See Hugh Gusterson, "Nuclear Weapons Testing: Scientific Experiment as Political Ritual," in *Naked Science: Anthropological Inquiry into Boundaries, Power, and Knowledge,* ed. Laura Nader (New York: Routledge, 1996), 131–47.

13. Geoffrey L. Herrera, "The Politics of Bandwidth: International Politics Implications of a Digital Information Infrastructure," *Review of International Studies* 28, no. 1 (2002): 93–122.

14. Most are thus oriented toward hermeneutics or some form of the method Weber termed *Verstehen.*

15. See, for example, Peter M. Haas, "Do Regimes Matter? Epistemic Communities and Mediterranean Pollution Control," *International Organization* 43 (Summer 1989): 377–405; Peter M. Haas, "Introduction: Epistemic Communities and International Policy Coordination," *International Organization* 46 (Winter 1992): 1–35; Peter A. Hall, ed., *The Political Power of Economic Ideas: Keynesianism Across Nations* (Princeton: Princeton University Press, 1989); Kratochwil, *Rules, Norms, and Decisions;* Ruggie, "International Regimes, Transactions, and Change"; and Wendt, "Anarchy Is What States Make of It."

16. For a sampling of the literature from this growing field, see Michael N. Barnett, "Sovereignty, Nationalism, and Regional Order in the Arab States System," *International*

Organization 49 (Summer 1995): 479–510; Andrew P. Cortell and James W. Davis Jr., "How Do International Institutions Matter? The Domestic Impact of International Rules and Norms," *International Studies Quarterly* 40 (December 1996): 451–78; Audie Klotz, "Norms Reconstituting Interests: Global Racial Equality and U.S. Sanctions against South Africa," *International Organization* 49 (December 1995): 451–78; Thomas Risse-Kappen, "Ideas Do Not Float Freely: Transnational Coalitions, Domestic Structures and the End of the Cold War," *International Organization* 48 (Spring 1994): 185–214; Jeffrey T. Checkel, "Norms, Institutions, and National Identity in Contemporary Europe," *International Studies Quarterly* 43 (March 1999): 83–114; and Kathryn Sikkink, "Human Rights, Principled Issue-Networks, and Sovereignty in Latin America," *International Organization* 47 (Summer 1993): 411–41.

17. See, for example, Nina Tannenwald, "The Nuclear Taboo: The United States and the Normative Basis of Nuclear Non-Use," *International Organization* 53 (Summer 1999): 433–68; Jens Bartleson, *A Genealogy of Sovereignty* (Cambridge: Cambridge University Press, 1995); Richard Price, *The Chemical Weapons Taboo* (Ithaca, NY: Cornell University Press, 1997); Gearóid Ó Tuathail, *Critical Geopolitics: The Politics of Writing Global Space* (Minneapolis: University of Minnesota Press, 1996); and Ethan Nadelmann, "Global Prohibition Regimes: The Evolution of Norms in International Society," *International Organization* 44 (Fall 1990): 479–526.

18. For similar evidence relating to acoustic perception, see Bruno H. Repp and Alvin M. Libermann, "Phonetic Category Boundaries Are Flexible," in Harnad, ed., *Categorical Perception,* 107.

19. Berlin and Kay, *Basic Color Terms,* 13–14. See also Kempton, *The Folk Classification of Ceramics,* 105–20.

20. Although I do not find his arguments to be persuasive, Alexander Wendt is perhaps the most prominent scholar of international politics who has tried to marry a constructivist ontology to a positivist epistemology and method. See Alexander Wendt, *Social Theory of International Politics,* esp. 47–91.

21. For a similar argument from the field of linguistics, see Repp and Libermann, "Phonetic Category Boundaries Are Flexible," 89–112.

22. Robert Jervis, *Perception and Misperception in International Politics* (Princeton: Princeton University Press, 1976), esp. 143–64.

23. Ibid., 163.

24. See George Bush and Brent Scowcroft, *A World Transformed* (New York: Knopf, 1988), 13–14, 154–55.

25. Jervis, *Perception and Misperception,* 156–65.

26. The difficulties of achieving a common interpretation of behavioral signals is demonstrated in Robert Jervis, *The Logic of Images in International Relations* (Princeton: Princeton University Press, 1971). Although he does not make the claim, I believe a constructivist analysis is consistent with and holds the potential to unite many of the ideas developed in *Perception and Misperception* with those of *The Logic of Images,* which Jervis himself believes to be opposite sides of the same coin. See Robert Jervis, "Signaling and Perception: Drawing Inferences and Projecting Images," in *Political Psychology,* ed. Kristen Monroe (Hillsdale, NJ: Lawrence Erlbaum, 2001), 293–312. The potential for fruitful interchange between cognitivists and constructivists has also been suggested by others. See, for example, Andrew Bennett, *Condemned to Repetition? The Rise, Fall, and Reprise of Soviet-Russian Military Interventionism, 1973–1996* (Cambridge: MIT Press, 1999), 7;

Wendt, "Anarchy Is What States Make of It," 394; and Emmanuel Adler, "Seizing the Middle Ground: Constructivism in World Politics," *European Journal of International Relations* 3 (September 1997): 319–63.

27. Amos Tversky, "Features of Similarity," *Psychological Review* 84, no. 4 (1977): 327–52.

28. Tversky, "Features of Similarity"; and Tversky, "Elimination by Aspects: A Theory of Choice," *Psychological Review* 79 (1972): 281–99.

29. David Collier and Steven Levitsky, "Democracy with Adjectives: Conceptual Innovation in Comparative Research," *World Politics* 49 (April 1997): 430–51.

30. Ibid., 431.

31. Giovanni Sartori, "Concept Misinformation in Comparative Politics," *American Political Science Review* 64 (December 1970): 1033–53, quotation 1035. See also David Collier and James E. Mahon Jr., "Conceptual 'Stretching' Revisited: Adapting Categories in Comparative Analysis," *American Political Science Review* 87 (December 1993): 845–55.

32. For discussions of procedural definitions of democracy, see Collier and Levitsky, "Democracy with Adjectives," 434; Guillermo O'Donnell and Philippe C. Schmitter, *Transitions from Authoritarian Rule: Tentative Conclusions about Uncertain Democracies* (Baltimore: Johns Hopkins University Press, 1986); Samuel P. Huntington, "The Modest Meaning of Democracy," in *Democracy in the Americas: Stopping the Pendulum,* ed. Robert A. Pastor (New York: Holmes and Meier, 1989), 11–28; and Robert A. Dahl, *Polyarchy: Participation and Opposition* (New Haven: Yale University Press, 1971).

33. Ronald P. Archer, "Party Strength and Weakness in Colombia's Besieged Democracy," in *Building Democratic Institutions: Party Systems in Latin America,* ed. Scott Mainwaring and Timothy R. Scully (Stanford: Stanford University Press, 1993), 166.

34. Georg Sorensen, *Democracy and Democratization: Process and Prospects in a Changing World* (Boulder, CO: Westview Press, 1993), 20.

35. Donald Emmerson, "Region and Recalcitrance: Questioning Democracy in Southeast Asia," paper presented at the World Congress of the International Political Science Association, Berlin, Germany, 1994, 14.

36. Collier and Levitsky, "Democracy with Adjectives," 435–39. See also Collier and Mahon, "Conceptual 'Stretching' Revisited," 850–52.

37. Collier and Levitsky, "Democracy with Adjectives," 438.

38. See Tversky, "Features of Similarity"; and Tversky, "Elimination by Aspects."

39. Early studies include James March and Herbert Simon, *Organizations* (New York: Wiley, 1958); Herbert Simon, *Administrative Behavior,* (New York: Free Press, 1947); Charles Lindblom, "The Science of Muddling Through," *Public Administration Review* 19 (Spring 1959): 74–88; David Braybrooke and Charles Lindblom, *A Strategy of Decision* (New York: Free Press, 1963); and Charles Lindblom, *The Intelligence of Democracy* (New York: Free Press, 1965). More recent contributions include James March, "Bounded Rationality, Ambiguity, and the Engineering of Choice," *Bell Journal of Economics* 9, no. 2 (1978): 587–608. For a survey of the latest research, see Daniel Kahneman, "New Challenges to the Rationality Assumption," *Journal of Institutional and Theoretical Economics* 150/1 (1994): 18–36.

40. Robert H. Jackson, *Quasi-States: Sovereignty, International Relations, and the Third World* (Cambridge: Cambridge University Press, 1990), 24.

41. Ibid., 21

42. Collier and Levitsky, "Democracy with Adjectives," 441.

43. Ibid., 441–42; Bagley codes Colombia as an "inclusionary authoritarian regime." See Bruce Bagley, "Colombia: National Front and Economic Development," in *Politics, Policies, and Economic Development in Latin America,* ed. Robert Wesson (Stanford: Hoover Institution Press, 1984), 124–60. For a discussion of "inclusionary authoritarianism," see Susan Kaufman Purcell, *The Mexican Profit-Sharing Decision: Politics in an Authoritarian Regime* (Berkeley: University of California Press, 1977).

44. Collier and Levitsky, "Democracy with Adjectives," 442.

45. The politics of naming is the focus of much postmodernist scholarship. See, for example, Sandra Harding, Elvira Scheich, and Maria Osietzki, "'Multiple Subject': Feminist Perspectives on Postmodernism, Epistemology, and Science," Discussion Paper (Hamburg: Hamburger Institut für Sozialforschung, 1991); and Urban Wråkberg, "The Politics of Naming: Contested Observations and the Shaping of Geographical Knowledge," in *Narrating the Arctic: A Cultural History of Nordic Scientific Practice,* ed. Michael Bravo and Sverker Sörlin (Canton, MA: Watson Pub. International, 2002), 155–97.

46. J. Samuel Valenzuela, "Democratic Consolidation in Post-Transitional Settings: Notion, Process, and Facilitating Conditions," in *Issues in Democratic Consolidation: The New South American Democracies in Comparative Perspective,* ed. Scott Mainwaring, Guillermo O'Donnell, and J. Samuel Valenzuela (Notre Dame: University of Notre Dame Press, 1992).

47. Collier and Levitsky, "Democracy with Adjectives," 442–45.

48. Ibid., 443. The referenced study is Rhoda Rabkin, "The Aylwin Government and 'Tutelary' Democracy: A Concept in Search of a Case?" *Journal of Interamerican Studies and World Affairs* 35 (Winter 1992–93): 119–94.

49. The studies are too numerous to list. For a sampling, see Michael Doyle, "Liberalism and World Politics," *American Political Science Review* 80 (December 1986): 1151–69; Zeev Maoz and Nasrin Abdulali, "Regime Types and International Conflict, 1815–1876," *Journal of Conflict Resolution* 33 (March 1989): 3–35; Zeev Maoz and Bruce M. Russett, "Normative and Structural Causes of Democratic Peace, 1946–1986," *American Political Science Review* 87 (September 1993): 624–38; Bruce M. Russett, *Controlling the Sword: The Democratic Governance of National Security* (Cambridge: Harvard University Press, 1990); Russett, *Grasping the Democratic Peace: Principles for a Post–Cold War World* (Princeton: Princeton University Press, 1993); Russett, "The Democratic Peace: 'And Yet It Moves,'" *International Security* 19 (Spring 1995): 164–75; James Lee Ray, "Wars between Democracies: Rare or Nonexistent?" *International Interactions* 18 (Spring 1988): 251–76; David A. Lake, "Powerful Pacifists: Democratic States and War," *American Political Science Review* 86 (March 1992): 24–37; and T. Clifton Morgan and Sally Howard Campbell, "Domestic Structure, Decisional Constraints and War: So Why Kant Democracies Fight?" *Journal of Conflict Resolution* 35 (June 1991): 187–211. Recognizing the cumulative impact of these studies, Jack Levy has called the democratic peace "the closest thing we have to an empirical law in the study of international relations." See Jack S. Levy, "Domestic Politics and War," in *The Origin and Prevention of Major Wars,* ed. Robert I. Rotberg and Theodore K. Rabb (New York: Cambridge University Press, 1989), quotation 88. Critiques of both the empirical studies and theoretical bases of the proposition abound. See, for example, David Spiro, "The Insignificance of the Liberal Peace," *International Security* 19 (Fall 1994): 50–86; Melvin Small and J. David Singer, "The War-proneness of Democratic Regimes," *Jerusalem Journal of International Relations* 1 (Summer 1976): 50–69; Joanne Gowa, "Democratic States and International Disputes," *International Organization*

49 (Summer 1995): 511–22; and Gowa, *Ballots and Bullets: The Elusive Democratic Peace* (Princeton: Princeton University Press, 1999).

50. For the data on interstate wars, see Melvin J. Small and J. David Singer, *Resort to Arms: International and Civil Wars, 1816–1980* (Beverly Hills, CA: Sage, 1982). See also J. David Singer and Melvin Small, "Wages of War, 1816–1980: Augmented with Disputes and Civil War Data," Inter-university Consortium for Political and Social Research (ICPSR), Study I9044 (Winter 1984). Most of the studies cited above use data taken from Ted Robert Gurr, "Polity II: Political Structures and Regime Change, 1800–1986," ICPSR, Study I9263 (1990). The most recent data on regime types can be found in Monty G. Marshall and Keith Jaggers, "Polity IV Project: Political Regime Characteristics and Transitions, 1800–1999," Integrated Network for Societal Conflict Research (INSCR) Program (December 2000), www.cidcm.umd.edu/inscr/polity.

51. A close reading of the procedures adopted by the Polity program for measuring levels of inter-coder reliability, however, leads to some reservations. For example, claims for a high degree of inter-coder reliability for the Polity IV data are based in large part on a comparison of the 1999 scores to those of the previous year for polities that experienced no change of regime. Because the vast majority of polities showed coding differentiations from year to year of one point or less, the principal investigators conclude that inter-coder reliability is high. But if the aim of the dataset is to measure year-to-year changes along a variety of dimensions relating to regime type, basing judgments of inter-coder reliability on the assumption that regimes *will not* undergo significant change is odd, to say the least. See Marshall and Jaggers, "Polity IV Project," 6–8.

Although I cannot address the problems here, the COW project's dataset on "Militarized Interstate Disputes," or MIDs, which are disputes that fail to meet the COW definition of interstate war, is riddled with problems of inter-coder reliability and non-replicability. See Charles S. Gochman and Zeev Maoz, "Militarized Interstate Disputes, 1816–1976: Procedures, Patterns, Insights," *Journal of Conflict Resolution* 29 (December 1984): 585–615.

52. The dataset covers every country in the contemporary international system that in 1998 had a population in excess of 500,000.

53. Monty G. Marshall and Keith Jaggers, *Polity IV Project: Dataset Users Manual* (College Park, MD: Integrated Network for Societal Conflict Research Program, 2000), 1.

54. Marshall and Jaggers, *Dataset Users Manual*, 12–13. The operational criteria for the component variables of both the democracy and autocracy scores are more fully detailed on pages 15 through 26. For example, when coding for the regulation of executive recruitment, investigators first establish whether there are any established rules governing the selection of the chief executive. Regulation, or the extent to which a polity has institutionalized procedures for the transfer of executive authority, is then coded as "unregulated," "transitional," or "regulated." Competitiveness of executive recruitment looks to the degree to which subordinates enjoy equal opportunity to become superordinates, with polities coded as either "selective" (where chief executives are determined by hereditary succession, designation, or a combination of both), "dual/transitional" (where one executive is chosen by hereditary succession and the other by competitive election, or for transitional arrangements between selection and competitive election), and "election" (for cases where executives are chosen through competitive elections, either by popular vote or an assembly).

55. Marshall and Jaggers, *Dataset Users Manual*, 13.

56. Ibid., 13–14.

57. For example, whereas Farber and Gowa code states as democratic if their Polity Score is 6 or higher, others combine additional factors with the Polity data to construct their own regime-type scales. Russett codes regimes according to an index defined as: PCON (DEM−AUT), where PCON is a measure (with values ranging from 0 to 10) of the degree to which power in a given polity is concentrated in the hands of state authorities; DEM is the state's democracy score and AUT its ranking on the autocracy scale. States with total values ranging from 30 to 100 are coded as democratic, those with scores ranging from −25 to 29 as anocratic, and those below −25 as autocratic. See Henry Farber and Joanne Gowa, "Polities and Peace," *International Security* 20 (Fall 1995): 123–46; and Russett, *Grasping the Democratic Peace*, 76–80, 121–22.

58. Spiro, "The Insignificance of the Liberal Peace," 56. Zeev Maoz's codings of states' regime types for the years 1946–86 are reprinted in Russett, *Grasping the Democratic Peace*, 94–98.

59. Maoz and Russett, "Normative and Structural Causes of Democratic Peace," appendix.

60. Christopher Layne, "Kant or Can't: The Myth of the Democratic Peace," *International Security* 19 (Fall 1994): 41–42.

61. David Spiro, "The Insignificance of the Liberal Peace," 56. Although I use them to make a somewhat different point, the arguments in this section are largely taken from Spiro's critique.

62. Michael Doyle, "Kant, Liberal Legacies, and Foreign Affairs, Part I," *Philosophy and Public Affairs* 12 (Summer 1983): 213.

63. For example, Alex Mintz and Nehmia Geva, "Why Don't Democracies Fight Each Other? An Experimental Assessment of the 'Political Incentive' Explanation," *Journal of Conflict Resolution* 37 (September 1992): 484–503; Randall L. Schweller, "Domestic Structure and Preventive War: Are Democracies More Pacific?" *World Politics* 44 (January 1992): 207–13; Bruce Bueno de Mesquita, *War and Reason: Domestic and International Imperatives* (New Haven: Yale University Press, 1992); and Harvey Starr, "Why Don't Democracies Fight One Another? Evaluating the Theory-Findings Feedback Loop," *Jerusalem Journal of International Relations* 14 (December 1992): 41–59.

64. See Anne Marie Slaughter, "Law among Liberal States: Liberal Internationalism and the Act of State Doctrine," *Columbia Law Review* 92, no. 8 (1992): 1907–96; William J. Dixon, "Democracy and the Peaceful Settlement of International Conflict," *American Political Science Review* 88 (March 1994): 14–32; and Michael W. Doyle, "Liberalism and the Peaceful Settlement of International Conflict," *American Political Science Review* 88 (March 1994): 14–32.

65. Small and Singer, "The War-proneness of Democratic Regimes"; David Garnham, "War Proneness," *Journal of Peace Research* 23 (September 1986): 279–89; and Maoz and Abdolali, "Regime Types and International Conflict."

66. John M. Owen, "How Liberalism Produces Democratic Peace," *International Security* 19 (Fall 1994): 87–125. On the "pacific union," see Immanuel Kant, *Perpetual Peace* (1795; repr. Indianapolis: Liberal Arts Press, 1957), 17.

67. Doyle, "Kant, Liberal Legacies, and Foreign Affairs, Part I," 213.

68. Edward E. Azar, "Conflict and Peace Data Bank (COPDAB), 1948–1978: Daily Events File," ICPSR Study I7767.

69. In a footnote of a later work, he writes: "There are domestic variations within

these Liberal regimes. For example, Switzerland was Liberal only in certain cantons; the United States was Liberal only north of the Mason-Dixon line until 1865, when it became Liberal throughout." Michael W. Doyle, *Ways of War and Peace: Realism, Liberalism, and Socialism* (New York: W. W. Norton, 1997), 264n.

70. Spiro, "The Insignificance of the Liberal Peace," 57.

71. Ido Oren, "The Subjectivity of the 'Democratic' Peace: Changing U.S. Perceptions of Imperial Germany," *International Security* 20 (Fall 1995): 150.

72. Ibid., 266.

73. Tatu Vanhanen, *The Process of Democratization: A Comparative Study of 147 States* (New York: Crane Russak, 1990), 27–28.

74. Ibid., 17–24.

75. For a similar conclusion, see Spiro, "The Insignificance of the Democratic Peace," 9.

76. For arguments justifying the coding of ancient republics as illiberal, see Russett, *Controlling the Sword,* 123; and Doyle, "Kant, Liberal Legacies, and Foreign Affairs, Part I," 212. Clearly rooting his definition of liberalism in the political philosophy of Kant, John Owen comes closest to avoiding this contemporary bias. Nonetheless, in his effort to identify the mechanisms whereby democratic or liberal states come to identify one another—a necessary condition for the operation of the mechanisms generally held to connect liberalism to pacific resolutions of interstate crises—Owen employs an a priori concept of liberalism in order to generate a class of cases to study. A truly interpretive research design would have started with the question of "Which states have considered themselves to be liberal?" See Owen, "How Liberalism Produces Democratic Peace." For a critique of Owen's argument, see Oren, "The Subjectivity of the 'Democratic' Peace," 150n.

77. Oren, "The Subjectivity of the 'Democratic' Peace," 152.

78. For an overview, see Small and Singer, *Resort to War.* For a comparison of the most important datasets on interstate wars and the degree to which statistical regularities vary across them, see Edward D. Mansfield, "The Distribution of Wars over Time," *World Politics* 41 (October 1988): 21–51.

79. A state is coded as a member of the international system prior to World War I if it met the 500,000 cutoff for population and enjoyed British and French diplomatic representation on its soil at or above the rank of *chargé d'affaires*. After World War I, a state is coded as a member of the international system if at any time it was a member of the League of Nations or the United Nations. See Small and Singer, *Resort to War,* 40–41.

80. Ibid., 55–56.

81. Spiro, "The Insignificance of the Liberal Peace," 211–14. But, as Russett notes, Spiro is less than consistent in applying standards for counting allies in multilateral wars. See Russett, "The Democratic Peace—And Yet It Moves," 168–69.

82. Bruce Russett and John R. O'Neal, *Triangulating Peace: Democracy, Interdependence, and International Organization* (New York: W. W. Norton, 2001), 48.

83. The administrations of the elder George Bush and his successor William Clinton appear to have been influenced by research on the democratic peace. For example, in February 1992 U.S. Secretary of State James Baker declared: "The Cold War has ended, and we now have a chance to forge a democratic peace—an enduring peace built on shared values—democracy and political and economic freedom. The strength of these values in Russia and the other new independent states will be the surest foundation for

peace—and the strongest guarantee of our national security—for decades to come." Quoted in Owen, "How Liberalism Produces Democratic Peace," 97–98. And noting the absence of war between democracies, President Clinton used the occasion of his 1994 State of the Union Address to announce the promotion of democracy around the world as a goal of U.S. foreign policy. "Transcript of Clinton's Address," *New York Times,* 26 January 1994, A17.

84. See Anne-Marie Slaughter, "International Law in a World of Liberal States," *European Journal of International Law* 6 (1995): 503–38; and Anne-Marie (Slaughter) Burley, "Law among Liberal States: Liberalism and the Act of State Doctrine," *Columbia Law Review* 92 (December 1992): 1907–46.

85. In the aftermath of the U.S. presidential elections in November 2000, during which it became clear that George W. Bush would win the presidency in the electoral college even though he had received a smaller percentage of the popular vote than had the outgoing vice president Albert Gore, many of my European students, accustomed to systems of proportional representation, asserted that this aspect of the American electoral system was "undemocratic."

86. See Amos Tversky and Daniel Kahneman, "Availability: A Heuristic for Judging Frequency and Probability," *Cognitive Psychology* 5 (1973): 207–32; Tversky and Kahneman, "Judgement Under Uncertainty: Heuristics and Biases," *Science* 185 (1981): 453–58; Eugene Borgida and Richard Nisbett, "Differential Impact of Abstract versus Concrete Information in Decisions," *Journal of Applied Social Psychology* 7 (1977): 258–71; Sarah Lichtenstein et al., "Judged Frequency of Lethal Events," *Journal of Experimental Psychology: Human Learning and Memory* 4 (1978): 551–78; Antonio Damasio, *Descartes' Error: Emotion, Reason, and the Human Brain* (New York: Putnam, 1994).

87. See Oren, "The Subjectivity of the 'Democratic' Peace"; also Oren, "Is Culture Independent of National Security? How America's National Security Concerns Shaped 'Political Culture' Research," *European Journal of International Relations* 6 (December 2000): 543–73.

88. The basic studies giving rise to Social Identity Theory (SIT) are Henri Tajfel and John C. Turner, "An Integrative Theory of Intergroup Conflict," in *The Social Psychology of Intergroup Relations,* ed. W. Austin and S. Worchel (Monterey, CA: Brooks/Cole, 1979), 33–47; and Henri Tajfel, *Human Groups and Social Categories: Studies in Social Psychology* (Cambridge: Cambridge University Press, 1981). On the political implications of these findings, see the contributions to "Symposium on Social Identity," *Political Psychology* 22 (March 2001): 111–98.

89. Studies of analogical reasoning in the field of international politics include Ernest May, *Lessons of the Past* (New York: Oxford University Press, 1973); Richard Herrmann, "The Power of Perceptions in Foreign Policy Decision-Making: Do Views of the Soviet Union Determine the Policy Choices of American Leaders?" *American Journal of Political Science* 30 (November 1986): 841–75; and Yuen Foong Khong, *Analogies at War* (Princeton: Princeton University Press, 1992). For analyses that stress generational effects, see Michael Roskin, "From Pearl Harbor to Vietnam: Shifting Generational Paradigms," *Political Science Quarterly* 89 (Fall 1974): 563–88; Richard Ned Lebow, "Generational Learning and Conflict Management," *International Journal* 40 (Autumn 1985): 555–85; and Jervis, *Perception and Misperception,* 253–57.

90. See Margaret Thatcher, *The Downing Street Years* (London: Harper Collins, 1993), 816–22. In his memoirs, George Bush recounts that in the early hours after the Iraqi in-

vasion of Kuwait, even Saudi King Fahd suggested that Saddam Hussein was following in the footsteps of Adolf Hitler. See Bush and Scowcroft, *A World Transformed,* 320.

91. See Colin Powell with Joseph E. Perisco, *My American Journey* (New York: Ballentine, 1995), 451, 456, 465–67; Bob Woodward, *The Commanders* (New York: Simon and Schuster, 1991), esp. 290–321; Bush and Scowcroft, *A World Transformed,* 326–33, 380–81.

92. As with the Berlin and Kay color studies, Daniel Kahneman and Amos Tversky found a high level of agreement among group members over what constitutes the best or most representative example of a given concept or class. See Kahneman and Tversky, "Subjective Probability: A Judgement of Representativeness," *Cognitive Psychology* 3 (1972): 430–54.

93. Max Weber, "'Objectivity' in Social Science and Social Policy," in *The Methodology of the Social Sciences,* by Max Weber, trans. and ed. Edward A. Schils and Henry A. Finch (Glencoe, IL: Free Press, 1949), 93, emphasis in original.

94. Formalists would argue that although they are idealized abstractions, "ideal types" are nonetheless *real types* in that they have dynamics of their own, which are operative even in impure empirical manifestations. Nominalists or empiricists would of course reject this claim, reserving the term *real* for empirically occurring types. See Paul Diesing, *Patterns of Discovery in the Social Sciences* (New York: Aldine, 1971), 198–99.

95. Weber, "'Objectivity' in Social Science and Social Policy," 90, 103.

96. The example is taken from a similar discussion in Paul Ekman and Richard J. Davidson, *The Nature of Emotion: Fundamental Questions* (New York: Oxford University Press, 1994), 9.

97. I am speaking here of scientific realism, not the school of political thought known by the same term.

98. See Philip Kitcher, *Science, Truth, and Democracy* (Oxford: Oxford University Press, 2001), 11–28.

99. In this regard, science resembles the practice of law, where a "case" is not regarded as self-evident but rather as something that must be defined and constructed through language: "A case is the written memorandum of a dispute or controversy between persons, telling with varying degrees of completeness and accuracy, what happened, what each of the parties did about it, what some supposedly impartial judge or other tribunal did in the way of bringing the dispute or controversy to an end, and the avowed reasons of the judge or tribunal for doing what was done." N. Dowling, E. Patterson, and R. Powell, *Materials for Legal Method,* 2d ed. 1952, 34–35, as cited by William Twining and David Miers, *How To Do Things with Rules* (London: Weidenfeld and Nicolson, 1976), 160.

100. W. B. Gallie, "Essentially Contested Concepts," *Proceedings of the Aristotelian Society* 56 (1956): 167–98.

101. Paul Feyerabend, *Against Method* (London: Verso, 1975), 221–85.

102. Ibid., 224.

103. Ibid., 230.

104. Stephen D. Krasner, "Toward Understanding in International Relations," *International Studies Quarterly* 29 (June 1985): 139.

105. For Holsti, the sources of incommensurability are ultimately found in the deeper normative underpinnings of theories, which their adherents often leave unexamined or whose very existence may be denied. See K. J. Holsti, *The Dividing Discipline: Hegemony and Diversity in International Theory* (Boston: Allen and Unwin, 1987), quotation 80.

106. Feyerabend, *Against Method,* 270–71, 274.

107. Indeed, Malthus enjoined scholars to retain meanings associated with common usage whenever possible. See T. R. Malthus, *Definitions in Political Economy, preceded by An Inquiry into the Rules Which Ought to Guide Political Economists in the Definition and Use of their Terms; with Remarks on the Deviations from these Rules in their Writings* (London: J. Murray, 1827), ch. 1. For similar statements, see Fritz Machlup, *Essays on Economic Semantics* (Englewood Cliffs, NJ: Prentice-Hall, 1963), ch. 1; and Baldwin, "Interdependence and Power."

108. Feyerabend, *Against Method,* 271, emphasis mine.

109. Ibid., 254.

110. Ibid., 253.

111. Karl R. Popper, *The Myth of the Framework: In Defence of Science and Rationality* (London: Routledge, 1994), 33–34. See also Richard J. Bernstein, *Beyond Objectivism and Relativism: Science, Hermeneutics, and Practice* (New York: Basil Blackwell, 1983), 51–108.

112. Not only the preexisting concepts but also the debates of the old paradigm often survive the revolution. Thus, disputes among pre-Darwinian biologists strongly influenced the evolutionary research program after it emerged. See David L. Hull, *Science as a Process: An Evolutionary Account of the Social and Conceptual Development of Science* (Chicago: University of Chicago Press, 1988), 506–7.

113. The phenomenon is characteristic of political revolutions. The iconography and mythology of the ancien régime can either be appropriated and imbued with new meaning; possibly its original meaning is preserved as the revolution asserts the claim to recovering a lost or "true" version of the national ideal. See, for example, Jan Assmann, *Das kulturelle Gedächtnis: Schrift, Erinnerung und politische Identität in frühen Hochkulturen* (Munich: Beck, 1997), 32–48.

True to character, Bismarck turned the relationship around by appropriating many of the symbols and rhetoric of nationalist revolutionaries to the cause of conservatism and the establishment of the Kaiserreich. See Henry A. Kissinger, "The White Revolutionary: Reflections on Bismarck," *Dædalus* 97, no. 2 (1968): 888–924.

114. Samuel Huntington's argument that international politics will increasingly be dominated by clashing worldviews is not inconsistent with the analysis presented here. Huntington sees the ultimate origins of incommensurable worldviews in religion, arguing that the West derives its unique identity from its Judeo-Christian heritage. See Samuel P. Huntington, *The Clash of Civilizations and the Remaking of the World Order* (New York: Simon and Schuster, 1996), esp. chs. 2, 6. I suspect, however, that western Christianity was as important to the creation of western identity for its role in propagating the Latin language as it was for spreading a particular theology. Many of the ideas of freedom, democracy, and toleration, as well as those relating to knowledge, science, and rationality that have come to characterize the modern western worldview have their origins in the poetry and philosophy of ancient Greece. The arrival of Christianity in Europe ended the critical tradition of Greece, and these ideas were largely forgotten. Their rediscovery and propagation among the learned classes during the Renaissance was, ironically, made possible by widespread knowledge of Latin.

115. Thomas Kuhn, "Theory-Change as Structure-Change: Comments on the Sneed Formalism," *Erkenntnis* 10 (1976): 190–91, italics mine.

116. On this point, I agree with Popper. *The Myth of the Framework,* 37.

117. Kenneth N. Waltz, *Theory of International Politics* (Reading, MA: Addison-Wesley, 1979).

118. In Waltz's formulation, structure is defined by (1) ordering principle, (2) functional differentiation among the units of a system, and (3) the distribution of capabilities across the units. Because states are held to dwell in perpetual anarchy (defined as the lack of an international sovereign), each is forced to provide for the security and welfare of its citizens in more or less the same fashion. Because anarchy is held constant and states are held to be functionally similar units, changes in the distribution of capabilities are the only dynamic element in Waltz's conception of structure. See Waltz, *Theory of International Politics*, ch. 5. The argument that anarchy inevitably produces homogeneous units has been forcefully challenged. See John Gerard Ruggie, "Continuity and Transformation in the World Polity: Toward a Neorealist Synthesis," in *Neorealism and Its Critics*, ed. Robert O. Keohane (New York: Columbia University Press, 1986), 131–57; Rodney Bruce Hall and Friedrich V. Kratochwil, "Medieval Tales: Neorealist 'Science' and the Abuse of History," *International Organization* 47 (Summer 1993): 479–91; and Hendrik Spruyt, *The Sovereign State and Its Competitors: An Analysis of Systems Change* (Princeton: Princeton University Press, 1994). For a spirited defense of the Neorealist position, see Markus Fischer, "Feudal Europe, 800–1300: Communal Discourse and Conflictual Practices," *International Organization* 46 (Spring 1992): 427–66.

119. Waltz, *Theory of International Politics*, chs. 7–9.

120. Ibid., 15.

121. Ibid., 131.

122. Ibid., 165–66; Randall L. Schweller, *Deadly Imbalances: Tripolarity and Hitler's Strategy of World Conquest* (New York: Columbia University Press, 1998).

123. For an argument that an unstable and passing unipolarity characterizes the post–cold war system, see Christopher Layne, "The Unipolar Illusion: Why New Great Powers Will Rise," *International Security* 17 (Spring 1993): 5–51. The durability of unipolarity has been argued by William C. Wohlforth, "The Stability of a Unipolar World," *International Security* 24 (Summer 1999): 5–41. Multipolarity was recognized by John J. Mearsheimer in "Back to the Future: Instability in Europe After the Cold War," *International Security* 15 (Summer 1990): 5–56.

124. Robert O. Keohane, "Institutional Theory and the Realist Challenge After the Cold War," in *Neorealism and Neoliberalism: The Contemporary Debate*, ed. David A. Baldwin (New York: Columbia University Press, 1993), 284–91.

125. Robert O. Keohane, "Theory of World Politics: Structural Realism and Beyond," in *Neorealism and Its Critics*, ed. Robert O. Keohane (New York: Columbia University Press, 1986), 182–90. For Waltz's critique of disaggregating power relationships according to issue areas, see his *Theory of International Politics*, 130.

126. Ruggie, "Continuity and Transformation in the World Polity," 131–57; Ruggie, *Winning the Peace: America and World Order in the New Era* (New York: Columbia University Press, 1996), 161–65; and Wendt, *Social Theory of International Politics*, 103.

127. The same would appear to be the case in the natural sciences. For example, in their study of the controversy between Mendelian and biometrician biologists, MacKenzie and Barnes found that "although the opposed communities did have occasional, temporary problems of communication, overall the evidence suggests that they were able to understand each other remarkably well." D. MacKenzie and B. Barnes, "The Biometry-Mendelism Controversy," in *Natural Order*, ed. B. Barnes and S. Shapin (Beverly Hills, CA: Sage, 1979), 201.

128. This is the essence of Waltz's critique of early quantitative studies that sought

to test hypotheses on the effects of polarity on the frequency of war. See Waltz, *Theory of International Politics*, 14–15; and J. David Singer, Stuart Bremer, and John Stuckey, "Capability Distribution, Uncertainty, and Major Power War, 1820–1965," in *Peace, War, and Numbers*, ed. Bruce M. Russett (Beverly Hills, CA: Sage, 1972), 19–48.

129. Hull, *Science as a Process*, 494.

130. Ibid., 493.

131. King, Keohane, and Verba, *Designing Social Inquiry*, 26.

132. Hull, *Science as a Process*, 7.

133. Although the argument here is somewhat different, it is related to and in part derived from ideas found in Philip Kitcher, "Genes," *British Journal for the Philosophy of Science* 33 (1982): 337–59.

134. See D. C. F. Rentz, *The Tettigoniinae* (Australia: Commonwealth Scientific and Industrial Research Organization, 1985); and D. H. Colless, "An Appendix to *The Tettigoniinae*," vol. 1, 372–84. As cited in Hull, *Science as a Process*, 489.

135. Russett, "The Democratic Peace: 'And Yet it Moves,'" 168–69.

136. Waltz, *Theory of International Politics*, 131, emphasis mine.

137. For a similar discussion, see Hull, *Science as a Process*, 496.

FOUR: If . . . Maybe

1. Two such paradoxes—*sorites* (the heap) and *falakros* (the bald man) are generally attributed to Eubilides. One stone does not constitute a heap, nor does it become a heap through the addition of another stone. Similarly, a bald man remains bald even if he were to grow a new strand of hair. See J. A. Goguen, "The Logic of Inexact Concepts," *Synthese* 19 (1968–69): 325–73.

2. "Is It Still a Harley," *Thunder Press* 5 (July 1996): 1, 69. Cited in Geoffrey C. Bowker and Susan Leigh Star, *Sorting Things Out: Classification and Its Consequences* (Cambridge: MIT Press, 1999), 43.

3. See Madeleine Mathiot, "Noun Classes and Folk Taxonomy in Papago," *American Anthropologist* 64, no. 2 (1962): 349. The Papago are a Native American tribe found in Arizona that speaks an Uto-Aztecan language.

4. Bruce Bagley, "Colombia: National Front and Economic Development," in *Politics, Policies, and Economic Development in Latin America*, ed. Robert Wesson (Stanford: Hoover Institution Press, 1984), 124–60.

5. For this, see Roy D'Andrade, "Three Scientific World Views and the Covering Law Model," in *Metatheory in Social Science: Pluralisms and Subjectivities*, ed. Donald W. Fiske and Richard A. Schweder (Chicago: University of Chicago Press, 1986), 19–41; Wesley C. Salmon, *Scientific Explanation and the Causal Structure of the World* (Princeton: Princeton University Press, 1984). For a discussion of science and the study of international politics, see Martin Hollis and Steve Smith, *Explaining and Understanding International Relations* (Oxford: Clarendon Press, 1990).

6. Karl R. Popper, *The Logic of Scientific Discovery* (New York: Harper, 1968), 39.

7. Carl Hempel, *Aspects of Scientific Explanation and Other Essays in the Philosophy of Science* (New York: Free Press, 1965), 173. The term *postdiction* refers to the possibility of determining past data on the basis of present evidence. See Hans Reichenbach, *The Theory of Probability: An Inquiry into the Logical and Mathematical Foundations of the Calculus of Probability* (Berkeley: University of California Press, 1949), 13.

8. Popper, *The Logic of Scientific Discovery,* 49.

9. Ibid., 59.

10. Ibid., 49.

11. Jack L. Snyder, "Richness, Rigor, and Relevance in the Study of Soviet Foreign Policy," *International Security* 9 (Winter 1984/85): 92.

12. See A. F. Chalmers, *What Is This Thing Called Science?* (Indianapolis: Hackett, 1976), 1–21.

13. Ibid., 13.

14. See David Hume, *Treatise of Human Nature* (1740; repr. Oxford: Oxford University Press, 2000), bk. 1, pt. 3.

15. Chalmers, *What Is This Thing Called Science?* 15.

16. The (regrettably not so hypothetical) story is merely a variation on Bertrand Russell's well-known story of the inductivist turkey, killed on Christmas Eve.

17. Because probabilistic statements also rely on an inductive inference—e.g., that on the basis of a finite number of successes through the use of probabilistic statements, all applications of the principle will lead to conclusions that are probably true—they are subject to criticism on the same grounds as induction in general. See Chalmers, *What Is This Thing Called Science?* 17–19.

18. Popper, *The Logic of Scientific Discovery,* 40–41.

19. Ibid., 42.

20. For the logical positivist, the question of the origins of theories appears "neither to call for logical analysis nor be susceptible to it. The question of how it happens that a new idea occurs to a man . . . is irrelevant to the logical analysis of scientific knowledge." Ibid., 31. For a similar statement from an influential partisan of this position in the field of international politics, see Kenneth N. Waltz, *Theory of International Politics* (Reading, MA: Addison-Wesley, 1979), 5–9.

21. Popper, *The Logic of Scientific Discovery,* 32–33, emphasis in the original. Often overlooked is Popper's conviction that the implications of theories are tested against those of other theories and not "the world."

22. Ibid., 44 and note 1, emphasis in the original.

23. Ibid., 76.

24. Ibid., 70.

25. Ibid., 68–69.

26. Ibid., 70.

27. Ibid., 69, emphasis in the original.

28. See John Ziman, *Reliable Knowledge: An Exploration of the Grounds for Belief in Science* (Cambridge: Cambridge University Press, 1978), 70–76.

29. See Hempel, *Aspects of Scientific Explanation,* 234.

30. Ibid., 174, 234, 247–49.

31. On axiomatized systems, see Popper, *The Logic of Scientific Discovery,* 71–75; and Hempel, *Aspects of Scientific Explanation,* 111. For an example of the influence of these ideas in the field of political science, see Snyder, "Richness, Rigor, and Relevance in the Study of Soviet Foreign Policy," 92.

32. Snyder, "Richness, Rigor, and Relevance in the Study of Soviet Foreign Policy," 107.

33. My arguments here follow those of the physicist John Ziman. See his *Reliable Knowledge,* 13–21. Although for most purposes mathematics is sufficiently logical to

serve as a precise and unambiguous scientific language, studies of mathematical foundations have uncovered logical inconsistencies, paradoxes, and ambiguities that cannot be resolved through formal analysis. See, for example, E. Nagel and J. R. Newman, "Gödel's Proof," in *The World of Mathematics,* vol. 3, ed. Newman (New York: Simon and Schuster, 1956) 1668–95.

34. See Bruce Bueno de Mesquita and James D. Morrow, "Sorting Through the Wealth of Notions," *International Security* 24 (Fall 1999): 58. See also James D. Morrow, *Game Theory for Political Scientists* (Princeton: Princeton University Press, 1995), esp. 6.

35. Peter C. Ordeshook, "Introduction," in *Models of Strategic Choice in Politics,* ed. Ordeshook (Ann Arbor: University of Michigan Press, 1989), 2.

36. Robert Bates, "Letter from the President: Area Studies and the Discipline," *APSA-CP: Newsletter of the APSA Organized Section in Comparative Politics* 7 (Winter 1996): 1–2. Cited in Stephen M. Walt, "Rigor or Rigor Mortis? Rational Choice and Security Studies," *International Security* 23 (Spring 1999): 6.

37. For example, in her defense of rational choice theory, Lisa Martin stresses the ability of formal mathematical models to generate complexes of related propositions tied to an underlying set of core assumptions and thereby generate cumulative knowledge: "Social science does not consist simply of compiling lists of propositions and a tally of which are true, false, or undecided." Lisa L. Martin, "The Contributions of Rational Choice: A Defense of Pluralism," *International Security* 24 (Fall 1999): 74–83, quotation 75.

Although some of her arguments are quite persuasive, she provides no explanation for the already immense and growing gap between the generation of axiomatic propositions and empirical research. Moreover, she does not address the growing body of empirical findings that call into question the empirical validity of many assumptions central to rational choice theory.

The phenomenon is neither new nor limited to political science. For example, in 1972, the eminent economist Oskar Morgenstern argued that the field of economics was in a crisis because it had turned away from empirical questions in favor of puzzles generated by mathematical models: "There is, of course, always the possibility and temptation of proving all sorts of theorems which have no empirical relevance whatsoever. . . . One cannot help but be reminded of Hans Christian Andersen's story of the Emperor's clothes." Morgenstern, "Thirteen Critical Points in Contemporary Economic Theory," *Journal of Economic Literature* 10 (December 1972): 1164–65.

Furthermore, Terry Moe has argued that rational choice theory is built upon axioms and assumptions that are concededly unrealistic and produces models that are "not even close to descriptive accuracy." Moe, "On the Scientific Status of Rational Choice Theory," *American Journal of Political Science* 23 (1979): 215–43.

38. Ziman, *Reliable Knowledge,* 28.

39. Gerard Debreu, "The Mathematization of Economic Theory," *American Economic Review* 81 (March 1991): 4–5.

40. Paul Hirsch, Stuart Michaels, and Ray Friedman, "'Dirty Hands' versus 'Clean Models': Is Sociology in Danger of Being Seduced by Economics?" *Theory and Society* 16 (May 1987): 317–36, quotation 319.

41. Ibid., 333.

42. For a critical analysis of the behavioral revolution in political science, see John G. Gunnell, *The Descent of Political Theory: The Geneology of an American Vocation* (Chicago: University of Chicago Press, 1993), 221–50.

43. David Easton, *A Framework for Political Analysis* (Englewood Cliffs, NJ: Prentice-Hall, 1965), 17.

44. Anatol Rapoport, "Mathematical Methods in Theories of International Relations: Expectations, Caveats, and Opportunities," in *Praeger Special Studies in International Politics and Government,* ed. D. A. Zinnes and J. U. Gillespie (New York: Praeger Publishers, 1976), 11.

45. Rapoport, "Mathematical Methods in Theories of International Relations," 14.

46. Gary King, Robert O. Keohane, and Sydney Verba, *Designing Social Inquiry: Scientific Inference in Qualitative Research* (Princeton: Princeton University Press, 1994), 53–54.

47. Ibid., 1–7.

48. See Imre Lakatos, "Falsification and the Methodology of Scientific Research Programmes," in *Criticism and the Growth of Knowledge,* ed. Imre Lakatos and Alan Musgrave (Cambridge: Cambridge University Press, 1970), 118. For Lakatos, a theory's ability to anticipate new facts is seen as an important evaluative criterion. But whether a fact that fits a theory was previously known is logically beside the point; the important question is which theory from a range of competing alternatives can best account for the widest range of phenomena.

49. Ziman, *Reliable Knowledge,* 32.

50. Hempel, *Aspects of Scientific Explanation,* 231–43.

51. On positivism and sociology, see Arthur L. Stinchcombe, *Constructing Social Theories* (Chicago: University of Chicago Press, 1968). On positivism and psychology, see Paul Fraisse and Jean Piaget, eds., *Experimental Psychology: Its Scope and Method* (New York: Basic Books, 1968). On positivism and political science, see, for example, King, Keohane, and Verba, *Designing Social Inquiry;* Sidney Verba, "Some Dilemmas in Comparative Research," *World Politics* 20 (October 1967): 111–27; Snyder, "Richness, Rigor, and Relevance in the Study of Soviet Foreign Policy"; and Rapoport, "Mathematical Methods in Theories of International Relations."

52. See D'Andrade, "Three Scientific World Views and the Covering Law Model," 19–41.

53. See Gabriel A. Almond and Stephen J. Genco, "Clouds, Clocks, and the Study of Politics," *World Politics* 29 (July 1977): 513.

54. Lee Cronbach, "Beyond the Two Disciplines of Scientific Psychology," *American Psychologist* 30 (February 1975): 126.

55. See Robert W. Cox, "Social Forces, States, and World Orders: Beyond International Relations Theory," in *Neorealism and Its Critics,* ed. Robert O. Keohane (New York: Columbia University Press, 1986), 205–54, quotation 209; and Richard K. Ashley, "The Poverty of Neorealism," in *Neorealism and its Critics,* 255–300, quotation 258.

56. Ziman, *Reliable Knowledge,* 26.

57. See Imre Lakatos, "Popper on Demarcation and Induction," in *The Philosophy of Karl Popper,* ed. P. A. Schlipp (La Salle, IL: Open Court, 1974), 241–73; W. V. O. Quine, "Two Dogmas of Empiricism," in Quine, *From a Logical Point of View* (New York: Harper and Row, 1961), 20–46; and Chalmers, *What Is This Thing Called Science?* 60–64.

58. Popper, *The Logic of Scientific Discovery,* 106.

59. Ibid., 59; Hempel, *Aspects of Scientific Explanation,* 234.

60. Hempel, *Aspects of Scientific Explanation,* 235.

61. Ibid., 83.

62. In medical and psychological research, the relevant distinction is between experimental and clinical studies.

63. For a discussion of the inferential difficulties associated with quasi-experiments, see Lieberson, *Making It Count: The Improvement of Social Research and Theory* (Berkeley: University of California Press, 1985), 14–43.

64. Thomas D. Cook and Donald T. Campbell, *Quasi Experimentation: Design and Analysis Issues for Field Settings* (Chicago: Rand McNally, 1979), 6. Cited in Lieberson, *Making it Count,* 15.

65. See, for example, Paul L. Lazerfeld, "Interpretation of Statistical Relations as a Research Operation," in *The Language of Social Research: A Reader in the Methodology of Social Research,* ed. Lazerfeld and Morris Rosenberg (Glencoe: Free Press, 1955), 115; also King, Keohane, and Verba, *Designing Social Inquiry,* 124–28.

66. The claim applies to natural as well as social phenomena. Given the precepts of quantum physics, every process, reaction, or element is in some sense unique. And although experimental control might allow researchers to reproduce the results of experiments, their equivalence is a function of similarities along theoretically relevant dimensions only.

67. The question of what constitutes a "case" has generated a great deal of controversy among methodologists. I am quite content to accept the definition offered by Eckstein: "A phenomenon for which we report and interpret only a single measure on any pertinent variable." Harry Eckstein, "Case Study and Theory in Political Science," in *Handbook of Political Science,* vol. 7, *Strategies of Inquiry,* ed. Fred Greenstein and Nelson W. Polsby (Reading, MA: Addison-Wesley, 1975), 85. For a somewhat different formulation, see King, Keohane, and Verba, *Designing Social Inquiry,* 52–53.

On other aspects of experimentation, see Arend Lijphart, "Comparative Politics and the Comparative Method," *American Political Science Review* 65 (September 1971): 685; Eckstein, "Case Study and Theory in Political Inquiry," 85ff.; Alexander L. George and Timothy J. McKeown, "Case Studies and Theories of Organizational Decision-Making," *Advances in Information Processing in Organizations* 2 (1985): 24–29; Alexander L. George, "Case Studies and Theory Development: The Method of Structured, Focused Comparison," in *Diplomatic History: New Approaches,* ed. Paul G. Lauren (New York: Free Press, 1979), esp. 49–58; Ernst Nagel, *The Structure of Science* (New York: Harcourt Brace and World, 1961), 452; and Hubert M. Blalock Jr., *Causal Inferences in Nonexperimental Research* (Chapel Hill: University of North Carolina Press, 1964), 26.

68. Eckstein, "Case Study and Theory in Political Science," 118.

69. Ibid., 118–19.

70. Assertions of this sort are too numerous to list, but see Robert Dahl, *Modern Political Analysis* (Englewood Cliffs, NJ: Prentice-Hall, 1963), 8; and King, Keohane, and Verba, *Designing Social Inquiry,* esp. 6–7. For a particularly confused discussion of how to test theories, see Stephen Van Evera, *Guide to Methods for Students of Political Science* (Ithaca, NY: Cornell University Press, 1997), 27–40.

71. Helen V. Milner, *Resisting Protectionism: Global Industries and the Politics of International Trade* (Princeton: Princeton University Press, 1988).

72. Eckstein, "Case Study and Theory in Political Science," 116–20.

73. Thomas Kuhn, *The Structure of Scientific Revolutions* (Chicago: University of Chicago Press, 1962), 99.

74. For related discussions, see Lakatos, "Falsification and the Methodology of Sci-

entific Research Programmes," 154–77; and King, Keohane, and Verba, *Designing Social Inquiry,* 209–12.

75. Ziman, *Reliable Knowledge,* 27.

76. Ibid., 26–27.

77. The limitations to operational precision are limitations in principle and not merely in practice. See, for example, Stephan Körner, *Experience and Theory* (London: Routledge and Kegan Paul, 1966).

78. See Stanley Lieberson, "Einstein, Renoir, and Greeley: Some Thoughts about Evidence in Sociology," *American Sociological Review* 57 (February 1992): 1–15; and Ronald W. Clark, *Einstein: The Life and Times* (New York: World Publishing, 1971).

79. Robert Jervis regards the phenomenon to be characteristic of more general psychological processes: "Scientists maintain cognitive consistency and retain their images and beliefs in the face of discrepant information. This is done in the belief that the basic theory is correct and that information that is not compatible with it must be either invalid or susceptible of reinterpretations. The cost of this practice is that major discoveries will be missed and the paradigm will continue to be accepted even when enough discrepant information is available to discredit it." Jervis, *Perception and Misperception in International Politics* (Princeton: Princeton University Press, 1976), 156–72.

80. Quoted in Jervis, *Perception and Misperception in International Politics,* 159.

81. See Bronisław Kuchowicz, "Neutrinos from the Sun," *Reports on Progress in Physics* 39, pt. 2 (1976): 291–344.

82. V. Trimble and F. Reines, "Solar Neutrino Problem—Progress Report," *Reviews of Modern Physics* 45 (1973): 1–5. Cited in Ziman, *Reliable Knowledge,* 36.

83. The results come from the Sudbury Neutrino Observatory, a Canadian facility located two kilometers underground to avoid interference from other forms of radiation; the facility consists of 1,000 tons of heavy water surrounded by a network of approximately 10,000 photo multiplier tubes. See S. Fukuda, Y. Fukuda, M. Ishitsuka et al., "Solar B-8 and Hep Neutrino Measurements from 1258 Days of Super-Kamiokande Data," *Phsyical Review Letters* 86, no. 25 (2001): 5651–55; and Fukuda, Fukuda, Ishitsuka et al., "Constraints on Neutrino Oscillations Using 1258 Days of Super-Kamiokande Solar Neutrino Data," *Physical Review Letters* 86, no. 25 (2001): 5656–60.

84. For the most developed articulation of balance of power theory, see Kenneth N. Waltz, *Theory of International Politics* (Reading, MA: Addison-Wesley, 1979), esp. 103–28.

85. Ibid., 105, 125–26. In the field of international politics, the debate over whether states pursue absolute or relative gains (or under what conditions one or the other type of behavior prevails) has generated considerably more heat than light. For a sampling of the debate, see the David A. Baldwin, ed., *Neorealism and Neoliberalism: The Contemporary Debate* (New York: Columbia University Press, 1993), esp. Joseph M. Grieco, "Anarchy and the Limits of Cooperation: A Realist Critique of the Newest Liberal Institutionalism," 116–42; Duncan Snidal, "Relative Gains and the Pattern of International Cooperation," 170–208; Robert Powell, "Absolute and Relative Gains in International Theory," 209–33; Stephen D. Krasner, "Global Communications and National Power: Life on the Pareto Frontier," 234–49; and Michael Mastanduno, "Do Relative Gains Matter? America's Response to Japanese Industrial Policy," 250–68. See also John C. Matthews III, "Current Gains and Future Outcomes: When Cumulative Relative Gains Matter," *International Security* 21 (Summer 1986): 112–46.

86. Waltz, *Theory of International Politics,* 126.

87. Raymond Aron, *Peace and War: A Theory of International Relations,* trans. Richard Howard and Annette Baker Fox (New York: Praeger, 1967), 44.

88. In addition to the writings of Waltz and Aron, see Glenn H. Snyder, *Alliance Politics* (Ithaca, NY: Cornell University Press, 1997), 192; William H. Riker, *The Theory of Political Coalitions* (New Haven: Yale University Press, 1962), 71; Stephen Walt, *The Origins of Alliances* (Ithaca, NY: Cornell University Press, 1987), 31–32; and Arnold Wolfers, "Alliances," in D. Sills, ed., *International Encyclopedia of the Social Sciences,* vol. 1 (New York: Macmillan, 1968), 268–71.

89. Examples include Waltz, "The Emerging Structure of International Politics," *International Security* 18 (Fall 1993): 75–76; John J. Mearsheimer, "Back to the Future: Instability in Europe after the Cold War," *International Security* 15 (Summer 1990): 5–57; and Christopher Layne, "The Unipolar Illusion: Why New Great Powers Will Rise," *International Security* 17 (Spring 1993): 5–51.

90. See Josef Joffe, "Who's Afraid of Mr. Big?" *The National Interest* 64 (Summer 2001): 43–52. For a sampling of French rhetoric, see Hubert Védrine and Dominique Moïsi, *Les Cartes de la France à l'heure de la Mondialisation* (Paris: Fayard, 2000).

91. See, for example, Gunther Hellmann and Reinhard Wolf, "Neorealism, Neoliberal Institutionalism and the Future of NATO," *Security Studies* 3 (Autumn 1993): 3–43; Robert O. Keohane and Lisa L. Martin, "The Promise of Institutionalist Theory," *International Security* 20 (Summer 1995): 39–51; and Richard Ned Lebow, "The Long Peace, the End of the Cold War, and the Failure of Realism," *International Organization* 48 (Spring 1994): 249–77.

92. Josef Joffe presents an exception to the general reaction of realist scholars. In recent analyses, he has adopted arguments traditionally associated with liberal theorists, asserting that the incentives for others to balance against the United States are diminished by American self-restraint and the collective benefits provided by a web of international institutions both created and sustained by U.S. leadership. See Joffe, "Who's Afraid of Mr. Big?"

93. See Celeste A. Wallander, "Institutional Assets and Adaptability: NATO After the Cold War," *International Organization* 54 (Autumn 2000): 705–35; and Helga Haftendorn, Robert O. Keohane, and Celeste Wallander, eds., *Imperfect Unions: Security Institutions over Time and Space* (Oxford: Oxford University Press, 1999).

94. Kenneth N. Waltz, "Structural Realism after the Cold War," *International Security* 25 (Summer 2000): 19.

95. Peter D. Feaver, "Correspondence," *International Security* 25 (Summer 2000): 167.

96. Jervis, *Perception and Misperception in International Politics,* 161.

97. Lieberson, "Einstein, Renoir, and Greeley," 5.

98. See Donald W. Fiske, "Specificity of Method and Knowledge," in *Metatheory in Social Science,* ed. Fiske and Schweder, 63.

99. For a prominent example of this phenomenon in the field of international politics, see the debate over the deterrence datasets compiled by Paul Huth and Bruce Russett: Huth and Russett, "What Makes Deterrence Work? Cases from 1900 to 1980," *World Politics* 36 (July 1984): 496–526; Huth and Russett, "Testing Deterrence Theory: Rigor Makes a Difference," *World Politics* 42 (July 1990), 466–501; Richard Ned Lebow and Janice Gross Stein, "Deterrence: The Elusive Dependent Variable," *World Politics* 42 (April 1990): 336–70.

100. Lieberson, "Einstein, Renoir, and Greeley," 5.

101. Lee J. Cronbach, "Prudent Aspirations for Social Inquiry," in *The Social Sciences:*

Their Nature and Uses, ed. W. H. Kruskal (Chicago: University of Chicago Press, 1982). Cited in D'Andrade, "Three Scientific World Views and the Covering Law Model," 27–28, emphasis in the original.

102. See Ziman, *Reliable Knowledge,* 36.

103. To be fair, Popper never claimed that one could establish the empirical validity of universal statements. Rather, he maintained that such statements, insofar as they have not been falsified on the basis of the *modus tollens,* are accepted as possibly true. Because of the problems associated even with single observation statements, however, I maintain that we must treat falsifications as equally provisional.

104. "Woods Issues Open Statement on Race," *Reuters News Service,* 13 June 1995.

105. Although one might expect the two statements to be symmetrical and reflect a linear relationship—that is, the degree to which a given exemplar is similar to a prototype is the inverse of the degree to which it is different—psychologists find that this is not always the case. Because distinctive features weigh more heavily in assessments of difference than common features, and common features more heavily in judgments of similarity, assessments of the degree of membership and nonmembership in a given set are often asymmetrical. See Amos Tversky, "Features of Similarity," *Psychological Review* 84 (July 1977): 327–52.

106. Gregg C. Oden, "Integration of Fuzzy Logical Information," *Journal of Experimental Psychology: Human Perception and Performance* 3, no. 4 (1977): 573.

107. Although I am critical of some of his conclusions, Ragin offers the best available treatment of fuzzy sets, fuzzy logic, and their implications for the social sciences. See Charles C. Ragin, *Fuzzy-Set Social Science* (Chicago: University of Chicago Press, 2000), esp. ch. 6.

108. That is, the categories need not be dichotomous, only mutually exclusive.

109. This is at odds with the standard social science procedure of treating the individual properties or features of a given observation as analytically distinct and separable variables whose effects are constant across any given population of cases. See Ragin, *Fuzzy-Set Social Science,* 41.

110. For a similar argument, see Ragin, *Fuzzy-Set Social Science,* 35–42, 120–45.

111. In contemporary quantum physics, this position derives from both the recognition that randomness and indeterminism are inherent in nature and the role accorded the individual observer in depicting "reality." As Henry Pierce Stapp argues: "Since the conceptual structure of classical physics is recognized as fundamentally an invention of the mind that is useful for organizing and codifying experience, the knowledge of the observer emerges in the end, as the fundamental reality upon which the whole structure rests." See Henry Pierce Stapp, "The Copenhagen Interpretation," *American Journal of Physics* 40 (1972): 1098–1116, esp. the discussion of Bohr's ideas. See also Niehls Bohr, "Über die Erkenntnisfragen der Quantenphysik," in *Die Deutungen der Quantumtheorie,* ed. Kurt Baumann and Roman Sexl (Brauschweig: Vieweg, 1984), 156–62; and Bryce S. DeWitt, "Quantum Mechanics and Reality," *Physics Today* (September 1979): 30–35. For an argument that chance must be integrated into the explanation of many social outcomes, see Lieberson, *Making It Count,* 94–99, 225–27.

112. For a more detailed discussion of the following general points, see Ragin, *Fuzzy-Set Social Science,* 43–63.

113. Ernst Mayr, *Populations, Species, and Evolution* (Cambridge, MA: Harvard University Press, 1970), 12. See also Mayr, *Systematics and the Origins of Species* (New York:

Columbia University Press, 1942); and Mayr, *Animal Species and Evolution* (Cambridge, MA: Harvard University Press, 1963).

114. Mayr, *Animal Species and Evolution,* 136. See also Mayr, *Populations, Species, and Evolution,* 182.

115. Supporters of the biological species concept either question or deny the existence of asexual species. See W. J. Bock, "Species Concepts, Speciation, and Macroevolution," in *Modern Aspects of Species,* ed. K. Iwatsuki et al. (Tokyo: University of Tokyo Press, 1986), 31–57, esp. 33; and Michael T. Ghiselin, "Species Concepts, Individuality, and Objectivity," *Biology and Philosophy* 4 (1987): 127–43.

116. Philip Kitcher, "Some Puzzles about Species," in *What the Philosophy of Biology Is: Essays Dedicated to David Hull,* ed. Michael Ruse (Dordrecht, Holland: Kluwer, 1989), 183–208, quotation 190.

117. See ibid., 191–92.

118. The debate between Mayr and Hull concerns not only the borders of populations but also the status of organisms and species as units of analysis for theories of evolutionary biology. Whereas Mayr's approach rests on the proposition that species are classes or sets, with individual organisms as their constituent members, Hull argues that the relationship between organisms and species is that of parts to wholes. Because species are "spatio-temporally restricted entities" rather than "spatio-temporally unrestricted classes," Hull (together with Ghiselin) maintains that species are properly regarded as historical individuals. Based on the proposition that scientific laws apply to classes and not individuals, Hull rejects the claim that individual species constitute the proper unit of analysis with respect to biological laws. See David Hull, "Are Species Really Individuals?" *Systematic Zoology* 25 (1976): 174–91; Hull, "A Matter of Individuality," *Philosophy of Science* 48 (1978): 335–60; and Michael Ghiselin, "A Radical Solution to the Species Problem," *Systematic Zoology* 23 (1974): 536–44.

119. Kitcher, "Some Puzzles about Species," 193.

120. Ibid.

121. For a survey of the attempts, see Joel Cracraft, "Species as Entities of Biological Theory," in *What the Philosophy of Biology Is,* 31–52.

122. Because of these problems, paleontologists are increasingly denying the reality of species. See Joel Cracraft, "Phylogenetic Analysis, Evolutionary Analysis, and Paleontology," in *Phylogenetic Analysis and Paleontology,* ed. Cracraft and N. Eldredge (New York: Columbia University Press, 1979), 7–39; Cracraft, "Species Concepts and the Ontology of Evolution," *Biology and Philosophy* 2 (1987): 329–46; and N. Eldredge, *Unfinished Synthesis* (Oxford: Oxford University Press, 1985).

123. O. Rieppel, "Species Are Individuals: A Review and Critique of the Argument," *Evolutionary Biology* 20 (1987): 298. Cited in Cracraft, "Species as Entities of Biological Theories," 39.

124. See the discussion in Ragin, *Fuzzy-Set Social Science,* 48–49. The question of relevant population can be treated as one of establishing scope conditions, but this too challenges the common assumption that populations are given and unproblematic. See Henry Walker and Bernard Cohen, "Scope Statements: Imperatives for Evaluating Theories," *American Sociological Review* 50, no. 3 (1985): 288–301.

125. See Ragin, *Fuzzy-Set Social Science,* 64–87.

126. Again, the problem is not one of causes operating only probabilistically. Rather, it is one of a population that comprises cases of varying degrees of membership.

127. Ragin, *Fuzzy-Set Social Science,* 51.

128. See, for example, George Mivart, *On the Genesis of Species* (New York: D. Appleton, 1871), 107.

129. Stephen Jay Gould, "Not Necessarily a Wing," *Natural History* (October 1985), 12–25.

130. See Martha Finnemore, *National Interests in International Society* (Ithaca, NY: Cornell University Press, 1996), 65. See also Finnemore, "International Institutions as Teachers of Norms: The United Nations Educational, Scientific, and Cultural Organization and Science Policy," *International Organization* 47 (Fall 1993): 565–98.

131. Stephen D. Krasner, "Sovereignty: An Institutional Perspective," *Comparative Political Studies* 21 (April 1988): 66–94, quotation 78.

132. See Wallander, "Institutional Assets and Adaptability: NATO After the Cold War," 705–35; and Haftendorn, Keohane, Wallander, eds., *Imperfect Unions: Security Institutions over Time and Space.*

133. See Kathleen Thelen, "Timing and Temporality in the Analysis of Institutional Evolution and Change," *Studies in American Political Development* 14 (Spring 2000): 101–8; David Soskice, "The Institutional Infrastructure for International Competitiveness: A Comparative Analysis of the UK and Germany," in *Economics for the New Europe,* ed. Anthony B. Atkinson and Runato Brunetta (London: Macmillan, 1991), 45–66; and Kathleen Thelen and Ikuo Kume, "The Rise of Nonmarket Training Regimes: Germany and Japan Compared," *Journal of Japanese Studies* 25 (Winter 1999): 33–64.

134. For early versions of functionalist and neofunctionalist theory, see David Mitrany, *A Working Peace System: An Argument for the Functional Development of International Organization* (London: Royal Institute of International Affairs, 1943); Ernst B. Haas, *Beyond the Nation State: Functionalism and International Organization* (Stanford: Stanford University Press, 1964); Ernst B. Haas, "International Integration: The European Union and the Universal Process," in *International Political Communities: An Anthology* (Garden City, NY: Anchor Books, 1966), 93–130; and Ernst B. Haas, *The Uniting of Europe: Political, Social, and Economic Forces 1950–1957* (Stanford: Stanford University Press, 1968). When the process of European integration stalled, functionalism lost many adherents but was rediscovered in the 1990s when the pace and depth of integration appeared to accelerate. For samples of the newer literature, see Jeppe Tranholm-Mikkelson, "Neofunctionalism: Obstinate or Obsolete? A Reappraisal in the Light of the New Dynamism of the EC," *Millennium* 20 (Spring 1991): 1–22; Wayne Sandholtz, *High-Tech Europe: The Politics of International Cooperation* (Berkeley: University of California Press, 1992); and Paul Pierson, "The Path to European Union: An Historical Institutionalist Account," *Comparative Political Studies* 29 (April 1996): 123–64.

135. If the links between morphology and function are weak, highly contextual, or historically contingent, then the standard debate over whether "function follows form" or "form follows function" is largely beside the point. For a similar argument, see Thelen, "Timing and Temporality in the Analysis of Institutional Evolution and Change," esp. 107; and Kathleen Thelen and Sven Steinmo, "Historical Institutionalism in Comparative Politics," in *Structuring Politics: Historical Institutionalism in Comparative Analysis,* ed. Steinmo, Thelen, and Frank Lonstreth (New York: Cambridge University Press, 1992).

136. King, Keohane, and Verba, *Designing Social Inquiry,* 21.

137. To suggest that a population is characterized by marginal and prototypical

members is not to say that it is comprised of individuals that can be ranked according to their scores on a continuous measure. Because the features according to which judgments over degree of membership are not uniform across the set, they are not amenable to the composition requisite for the construction of a continuum.

138. See, for example, Heinrich August Winkler, "Bürgerliche Emanzipation und nationale Einigung," in *Probleme der Reichsgründungszeit, 1848–1879,* ed. H. Böhme (Berlin: Kiepenheuer and Witsch, 1968); Margaret Anderson, *Practicing Democracy: Elections and Political Culture in Imperial Germany* (Princeton: Princeton University Press, 2000); Ralph Dahrendorff, *Society and Democracy in Germany* (Garden City, NY: Doubleday, 1969); and Talcott Parsons, "Democracy and Social Structure in Pre-Nazi Germany," in Parsons, *Essays in Sociological Theory* (Glencoe, IL: Free Press, 1954).

139. Sheri E. Berman, "Modernization in Historical Perspective: The Case of Imperial Germany," *World Politics* 53 (April 2001): 431–62. For earlier critiques of the proposition that German history is inconsistent with general historical patterns of economic and political modernization, see David Blackbourn and Geoff Eley, *The Peculiarities of German History* (New York: Oxford University Press, 1984); Roger Fletcher, "Recent Developments in German Historiography," *German Studies Review* 7 (October 1984); Thomas Nipperdey, "Wehler's Kaiserreich," in Nipperdey, *Gesellschaft, Kultur und Theorie* (Göttingen, Germany: Vandenhoeck and Ruprecht, 1976); and Nipperdey, *Nachdenken über die deutsche Geschichte* (Munich: Beck, 1986).

140. Edward D. Mansfield and Jack Snyder, "Democratization and the Danger of War," *International Security* 20 (Summer 1995): 5–38. For a discussion of the problems associated with constructing a dataset of democratic states, see chapter 3.

141. I suspect that most persons would argue that Britain is more representative of the set of all democratic states than it is of the set of monarchies. By contrast, Jordan—a state that, like Britain, has both a hereditary monarch and an elected parliament—would be considered more representative of the set of monarchies and—because the monarch enjoys both *de jure* and *de facto* primacy in political affairs—at best a marginal democracy.

142. The examples are taken from Philip Kitcher, *Science, Truth, and Democracy* (Oxford: Oxford University Press, 2001), 49.

FIVE: Social Behavior and the Indeterminacy of Norms

1. The ability to distinguishing friend from foe has long been regarded as a necessary condition for the emergence of society and as central to the study of political relationships. See Carl Schmitt, *Der Begriff des Politischen: Text von 1932 mit einem Vorwort und drei Corrolarien* (Berlin: Duncker and Humblot, 1963). For an attempt to model the emergence of stable cooperative interactions on the basis of a repeated Prisoner's Dilemma game, see Robert Axelrod, *The Evolution of Cooperation* (New York: Basic Books, 1984).

2. See Friedrich V. Kratochwil, *Rules, Norms, and Decisions: On the Conditions of Practical and Legal Reasoning in International Relations and Domestic Affairs* (Cambridge: Cambridge University Press, 1989), 11.

3. Abram Chayes and Antonia Handler Chayes, *The New Sovereignty: Compliance with International Regulatory Agreements* (Cambridge: Harvard University Press, 1995), 113.

4. Kratochwil, *Rules, Norms, and Decisions,* 70.

5. For an examination of the variety of theoretical understandings of sexual violence

and their implications for understanding the role of sexual violence in war, see Inger Skelsbæk, "Sexual Violence and War: Mapping Out a Complex Relationship," *European Journal of International Relations* 7 (June 2001): 211–37.

6. In one of the most public rape trials of recent memory, lawyers representing William Kennedy Smith successfully secured his acquittal by arguing that his accuser had in fact "said yes." See Mary Jordan, "Jury Finds Smith Not Guilty of Rape," *Washington Post,* 12 December 1991, A01.

7. Although surgical castration generally is no longer practiced in advanced industrialized states, many are increasingly adopting policies similar to that of the state of California, which in 1996 amended its penal code to allow for chemical castration for repeat sexual offenders as well as for first-time offenders where the victim is under 13 years of age. See the California Board of Prison Terms at www.bpt.ca.gov.

8. Compare, for example, Morgenthau's "Six Principles of Political Realism" to chapters 11 and 13 of Hobbes's *Leviathan.* Hans Morgenthau, *Politics Among Nations: The Struggle for Power and Peace,* 3d ed. (New York: Alfred Knopf, 1966), 4–15; and Thomas Hobbes, *Leviathan* (1651; repr. New York: MacMillan, 1962), 80–86, 98–102.

9. See variously Waltz, *Theory of International Politics;* Robert Gilpin, *U.S. Power and the Multinational Corporation* (New York: Basic Books, 1975); and Gilpin, *War and Change in World Politics* (Cambridge: Cambridge University Press, 1981).

10. See Kratochwil, *Rules, Norms, and Decisions,* esp. chs. 2–4.

11. Following Locke, contemporary liberal scholars of international politics stress the role of norms in solving coordination problems in pursuit of collective rewards. For examples, see Arthur A. Stein, "Coordination and Collaboration: Regimes in an Anarchic World," in *International Regimes,* ed. Stephen D. Krasner (Ithaca, NY: Cornell University Press, 1983), 115–40; Robert O. Keohane, "The Demand for International Regimes," in *International Regimes,* 141–71; and Lisa L. Martin, "Interests, Power, and Multilateralism," *International Organization* 46 (Autumn 1992): 765–92.

12. For an extension of this argument to the field of international politics, see Hedley Bull, *The Anarchical Society* (New York: Columbia University Press, 1977).

13. It is the individual's need for self-esteem and the links between self-esteem and social approbation that make symbolic forms of positive and negative sanction possible. For example, the Mennonite and Amish practice of shunning is effective only when potential malefactors wish to remain a member of the community in good standing. When identity and self-image are linked to group membership, the liberal image of society as comprised merely of an aggregation of individuals with preexisting "preferences" breaks down. Hence, the question of compliance with norms has been argued to be part of a larger question of how individual action in a social context allows agents and structures (the "self" and society) to reproduce themselves.

14. Since Rawls's seminal article, the distinction is often cast in terms of "regulative" versus "constitutive" norms. Because, however, many constitutive norms also regulate behavior, I have chosen to present the distinction in somewhat less categorical terms. See John Rawls, "Two Concepts of Justice," *Philosophical Review* 64, no. 1 (1955): 3–33.

15. Thus, John Gerard Ruggie argues that the norms codified at Bretton Woods were operative prior to 1958. See Ruggie, *Constructing the World Polity: Essays on International Institutionalization* (New York: Routledge, 1998), 95.

16. The methodological problem is similar to that confronting analyses of power. See, for example, the discussions of the "second" and "third" faces of power in Peter

Bachrach and Morton S. Baratz, "Decisions and Nondecisions: An Analytical Framework," *American Political Science Review* 57 (1963): 632–42; and Steven Lukes, *Power: A Radical View* (New York: Macmillan, 1974).

17. For a critical analysis of the classic structure of arguments, which take the form of premise-warrant-conclusion, see Stephen Edelson Toulmin, *The Uses of Argument* (Cambridge: Cambridge University Press, 1958), esp. ch. 3.

18. See Kratochwil, *Rules, Norms, and Decisions,* 213.

19. William Twining and David Miers, *How To Do Things with Rules* (London: Weidenfeld and Nicolson, 1976), 154.

20. *M'Alister* (or *Donoghue*) *v. Stevenson,* House of Lords Privy Council Cases, *Law Reports* (1932), 562–623.

21. *Donoghue v. Stevenson,* 579.

22. See A. L. Goodhardt, "The Ratio Decidendi of a Case," *Modern Law Review* 22 (March 1959): 117–24.

23. In addition to the Charter, see "Declaration on Principles of International Law Concerning Friendly Relations and Co-operation Among States in Accordance with the Charter of the United Nations," General Assembly Resolution 2625 (XXXV 1970).

24. Louis Henkin, *How Nations Behave: Law and Foreign Policy,* 2d ed. (New York: Columbia University Press, 1979), 169–70.

25. Although the argument here is in some important respects different, it was inspired by a discussion in Twining and Miers, *How To Do Things with Rules,* 124–27.

26. See Robert Kennedy, *Thirteen Days: A Memoir of the Cuban Missile Crisis* (New York: W. W. Norton, 1971), 99; Abram Chayes, *The Cuban Missile Crisis: International Crises and the Role of Law* (New York: Oxford University Press, 1974); and Chayes and Chayes, *The New Sovereignty,* 9. But international lawyers were not of one opinion. See, for example, James S. Campbell, "The Cuban Crisis and the UN Charter: An Analysis of the United States Position," *Stanford Law Review* 16, no. 1/4 (1963): 160–76; and W. L. Standard, "The United States Quarantine of Cuba and the Role of Law," *American Bar Association Journal* 49, no. 8 (1963): 744–48.

27. Christopher Stone, "From a Language Perspective," *Yale Law Journal* 90 (1981): 1149–92, quotation 1158.

28. Psychological research has shown that whereas actors tend to accord greater weight to situational factors in explanations and appraisals of their own behavior, observers are more likely to attribute the behavior to the actor's personality or disposition. See Harold Kelley, "Attribution Theory in Social Psychology," in *Nebraska Symposium on Motivation,* vol. 15, ed. David Levine (Lincoln: University of Nebraska Press, 1967); Kelley, *Attribution in Social Interaction* (Morristown, NJ: General Learning Press, 1971); and Thomas Ruble, "Effects of Actor and Observer Roles on Attribution of Responsibility for Success and Failure," *Journal of Social Psychology* 90 (1973): 41–44.

29. Kratochwil, *Rules, Norms, and Decisions,* 63.

30. In their analysis of states' compliance with international legal obligations, Chayes and Chayes found that noncompliance often results from the fact that states lack the resources—financial, organizational, or intellectual—to meet their obligations. See Chayes and Chayes, *The New Sovereignty,* 25, 197–201.

31. For an analysis of the links between practical and legal reasoning, see Kratochwil, *Rules, Norms, and Decisions,* 227–36. See also Chayes and Chayes, *The New Sovereignty,* 1–28.

32. Charles S. Peirce, *Philosophical Writings,* ed. J. Buchler (New York: Dover, 1955), 151–52.

33. The study of framing effects has emerged as central to the constructivist project in the subfield of international politics. Scholars are not only interested in how frames are constructed and come to be adopted by a larger group, but also how they can be used strategically to promote the individual actor's interests. See Rodger A. Payne, "Persuasion, Frames, and Norm Construction," *European Journal of International Relations* 7 (March 2001): 37–61; Martha Finnemore and Kathryn Sikkink, "International Norm Dynamics and Political Change," *International Organization* 52 (Fall 1998): 887–917; John D. McCarthy, "The Globalization of Social Movement Theory," in *Transnational Social Movements and Global Politics: Solidarity Beyond the State,* ed. Jackie Smith, Charles Chatfield, and Ron Pagnicco (Syracuse: Syracuse University Press, 1997), 243–59. A related discussion, influenced by Jürgen Habermas's theory of communicative action has been conducted in the German *Zeitschrift für Internationale Beziehungen.* See Harald Müller, "Internationale Beziehungen als kommunikatives Handeln: Zur Kritik der utilitaristischen Handlungstheorien," *Zeitschrift für Internationale Beziehungen* 1 (June 1994): 15–44; Müller, "Spielen hilft nicht immer: Die Grenzen des Rational-Choice-Ansatzes und der Platz der Theorie des kommunikativen Handelns in der Analyse internationaler Beziehungen," *Zeitschrift für Internationale Beziehungen* 2 (December 1995): 371–91; Thomas Risse-Kappen, "Reden ist nicht billig: Zur Debatte um Kommunikation und Rationalität," *Zeitschrift für Internationale Beziehungen* 2 (June 1995): 171–84; Philip Genschel and Thomas Plümper, "Wenn Reden Silber und Handeln Gold ist: Kooperation und Kommunikation in der internationalen Bankenregulierung," *Zeitschrift für Internationale Beziehungen* 3 (December 1996): 225–53; and Frank Schimmelfennig, "Rhetorisches Handeln in der internationalen Politik," *Zeitschrift für Internationale Beziehungen* 4 (December 1997): 219–54.

34. Ruggie, *Constructing the World Polity,* 94.

35. See Kratochwil, *Rules, Norms, and Decisions,* 8, 13, 30, 34.

36. Robert Jervis, *The Logic of Images in International Relations* (New York: Columbia University Press, 1989), 174–75. See also Jervis, *Perception and Misperception in International Politics,* ch. 2.

37. See Zehfuss, "Sprachlosigkeit schränkt ein: Zur Bedeutung von Sprache in konstruktivistischen Theorien," *Zeitschrift für Internationale Beziehungen* 5 (June 1998): 109–37, quotation 125, my translation. See also Alexander Wendt, "Anarchy Is What States Make of It: The Social Construction of Power Politics"; and Wendt, *Social Theory of International Politics* (Cambridge: Cambridge University Press, 1999).

38. American social psychology has traditionally been rooted in the assumption that social relations are reducible to the presocial needs, desires, and drives of individuals. By contrast, the relatively new and predominantly European field of reflexive social psychology regards the individual's identity and cognitive structures and processes as in part historically constituted through social processes. See, for example, Heiner Keupp, *Psychische Störungen als abweichendes Verhalten: Zur Soziogenese psychischer Störungen* (Munich: Urban and Scharzenberg, 1972); Heiner Keupp, ed., *Zugänge zum Subjekt: Perspektiven einer Reflexiven Sozialpsychologie* (Frankfurt: Suhrkamp, 1993); and Heiner Keupp and Manfred Zaumseil, *Die gesellschaftliche Organisierung des psychischen Leidens: Zum Arbeitsfeld klinischer Psychologen* (Frankfurt: Suhrkamp, 1978). The limitations of reductionist social psychological theories have been recognized by those who have applied

them to other fields. For example, in his analysis of how individual foreign policy decision makers and organizations involved in formulating national foreign policies "learn," Jack Levy found that the relationship between individual psychological structures and processes on the one hand, and social and political context on the other, is reciprocal rather than unidirectional: "Social psychology provides some guidance on these questions, but it tends to neglect the role of social and political context within which learning by political leaders takes place." See Jack S. Levy, "Learning and Foreign Policy: Sweeping a Conceptual Minefield," *International Organization* 48 (Spring 1994): 279–312, quotation 311.

39. See Thomas Schelling, *The Strategy of Conflict* (Cambridge, MA: Harvard University Press, 1960), 53–80.

40. Aristotle, *Rhetoric,* trans. E. S. Forster (Cambridge, MA: Harvard University Press, 1966), 1357a12–13.

41. Stephen D. Krasner, "Structural Causes and Regime Consequences: Regimes as Intervening Variables," in *International Regimes,* ed. Krasner (Ithaca, NY: Cornell University Press, 1983), 1.

42. See Susan Strange, "*Cave! Hic Dragones:* A Critique of Regime Analysis," in *International Regimes,* ed. Krasner, 337–54.

43. John Gerard Ruggie, "International Regimes, Transactions, and Change: Embedded Liberalism in the Postwar Economic Order," in *International Regimes,* ed. Krasner, 196.

44. See Friedrich Kratochwil and John Gerard Ruggie, "International Organization: A State of the Art on an Art of the State," *International Organization* 40 (Autumn 1986): 763–64; also Kratochwil, *Rules, Norms, and Decisions,* 60–64.

45. The original ABM treaty permitted the deployment of two ABM sites on each side. In a protocol signed at the Moscow summit in 1974, the number of missile sites allowed for each side was reduced to one.

46. According to Article XIII of the ABM Treaty, the Standing Consultative Commission is "to consider questions concerning compliance with the obligations assumed and related situations which may be considered ambiguous." The SCC is not a judicial body but rather an institutionalized forum where the signatories can negotiate mutually acceptable interpretations of treaty language. See Antonia Handler Chayes and Abram Chayes, "From Law Enforcement to Dispute Resolution: A New Approach to Arms Control Verification and Compliance," *International Security* 14 (Spring 1990): 147–64.

47. The details of the SCC decisions remain classified. But see Patricia McFate, "Assessing Verification and Compliance" and Abram Chayes and Antonia Handler Chayes, "Living Under a Treaty Regime," in *Defending Deterrence: Managing the ABM Treaty into the 21st Century,* ed. Antonia Handler Chayes and Paul Doty (Washington, DC: Pergamon-Brassey, 1989).

48. Kratochwil, *Rules, Norms, and Decisions,* 240–41.

49. See, for example, Ralf Kleinfeld, "Was können die Deutschen vom niederländischen 'Poldermodell' lernen?" in *Wohlfahrtsstaat: Krise und Reform im Vergleich,* ed. Josef Schmid and Reiner Niketta (Marburg, Germany: Metropolis, 1998), 113–38; Petra Pinzler, "Die Niederlande haben ihren Sozialstaat erfolgreich umgebaut: Ein Vorbild auch für uns?" *Die Zeit,* 10 January 1997, 3; and Fritz Scharpf, *Crisis and Choice in European Social Democracy* (Ithaca, NY: Cornell University Press, 1991).

50. See Rolf G. Heinze, Josef Schmid, and Christoph Strünck, *Vom Wohlfahrtsstaat*

zum Wettbewerbsstaat: Arbeitsmarkt- und Sozialpolitik in den 90er Jahren (Opladen, Germany: Leske and Budrich, 1999).

51. For a more detailed explication of the research summarized here, see Robert Henry Cox, "The Social Construction of an Imperative: Why Welfare Reform Happened in Denmark and the Netherlands but Not in Germany," *World Politics* 53 (April 2001): 463–98.

52. See Jacob Torfing, "Towards a Schumpeterian Workfare Postnational Regime: Path-Shaping and Path-Dependency in Danish Welfare State Reform," *Economy and Society* 28 (August 1999), 369–402.

53. Since most statistical methods of analysis proceed from the assumption that the "cases" or "observations" used to generate data are causally independent of one another, they are usually inappropriate to the analysis of path-dependent processes. On the assumptions underlying most quantitative analysis as well as recent efforts to adapt statistical approaches to the study of path-dependent processes, see John E. Jackson, "Political Methodology: An Overview," in *New Handbook of Political Science,* ed. Robert E. Goodin and Hans-Dieter Klingemann (Oxford: Oxford University Press, 1996), 717–48.

54. For an excellent discussion of the various issues surrounding the question of sequencing and the implications of these for the development of explanations and theories in the social sciences, see Paul Pierson, "Not Just What, but *When:* Timing and Sequence in Political Processes," *Studies in American Political Development* 14 (Spring 2000): 72–92.

55. For a general treatment of path dependency and the study of politics that builds on insights taken from the economists' notion of "increasing returns," see Paul Pierson, "Increasing Returns, Path Dependence, and the Study of Politics," *American Political Science Review* 94 (June 2000): 251–67. For applications of the concept in the field of international relations, see Stephen Krasner, "Sovereignty: An Institutional Perspective," in *The Elusive State: International and Comparative Perspectives,* ed. James A. Caporaso (Newbury Park, CA: Sage, 1989), 69–96; and Hendrik Spruyt, *The Sovereign State and Its Competitors* (Princeton: Princeton University Press, 1994). North has suggested that institutional form is often best accounted for in terms of path-dependent processes, an approach that has been extended by Riker and Weimer to the analysis of the development of property rights in former socialist countries. See Douglas C. North, *Institutions, Institutional Change and Economic Performance* (Cambridge: Cambridge University Press, 1990); and William H. Riker and D. L. Weimer, "The Economic and Political Liberalization of Socialism: The Fundamental Problem of Property Rights," *Social Philosophy and Policy* 10 (Summer 1993): 79–102.

56. The term is taken from Robert Wuthnow, *Communities of Discourse: Ideology and Social Structure in the Reformation, the Enlightenment, and European Socialism* (Cambridge, MA: Harvard University Press, 1989).

57. Pierson, "Increasing Returns, Path Dependency, and the Study of Politics," 265.

58. See the discussion of unit homogeneity and constant causal effects in King, Keohane, and Verba, *Designing Social Inquiry,* 91–94. Under the assumption of unit homogeneity, the principle of random selection is held to provide a selection rule that is automatically uncorrelated with all variables and thus reduces dramatically the risk of selection bias. On the question of case selection, the principle of randomness and its limitations, see *Designing Social Inquiry,* 115–49.

59. On the incomplete nature of most rules, of which implied exceptions is but one aspect, see Twining and Miers, *How To Do Things with Rules,* 127–28.

60. Ragin, *Fuzzy-Set Social Science,* 52.

61. Beth A. Simmons, "International Law and State Behavior: Commitment and Compliance in International Monetary Affairs," *American Political Science Review* 94 (December 2000): 819–35.

62. Ibid., 830–31.

63. Ibid., 828 and note 18.

64. Ibid., note 18.

65. According to Article XVIII of the original Articles of Agreement: "Any question of interpretation of the provisions of this Agreement arising between any member and the Fund or between any members of the Fund shall be submitted to the Executive Directors for their decision." In 1969 this article was amended to provide for a special committee on interpretation.

66. Chayes and Chayes, *The New Sovereignty,* 236.

67. Ibid., 238, 241.

68. For a much more pessimistic appraisal of IMF compliance, see Jeffrey D. Sachs, "Strengthening IMF Programs in Highly Indebted Countries," in *The International Monetary Fund in a Multipolar World: Pulling Together,* ed. Catherine Gwin and Richard E. Feinberg (New Brunswick, NJ: Transaction Books, 1989), esp. 101–7.

69. Andrew Sullivan, *Virtually Normal: An Argument about Homosexuality* (New York: Knopf, 1995), 171–72.

70. See Morris Kaplan, *Sexual Justice: Democratic Citizenship and the Politics of Desire* (New York: Routledge, 1997).

71. Shane Phelan, "Queer Liberalism," *American Political Science Review* 94 (June 2000): 431–42.

72. Andrew P. Cortell and James W. Davis Jr., "How Do International Institutions Matter? The Domestic Impact of International Rules and Norms," *International Studies Quarterly* 40 (December 1996): 451–78.

73. For similar discussions, see Harald Müller, "The Internalization of Principles, Norms, and Rules by Governments: The Case of Security Regimes," in *Regime Theory and International Relations,* ed. Volker Rittberger (Oxford: Clarendon Press, 1993), 383; and Chayes and Chayes, *The New Sovereignty,* 119.

74. For a discussion of how to measure salience in a nontautological fashion, see Andrew P. Cortell and James W. Davis Jr., "Understanding the Domestic Impact of International Norms: A Research Agenda," *International Studies Review* 21 (Spring 2000): 68–73.

75. For an analysis of the effects of rhetoric in international politics, see Frank Schimmelfennig, "Rhetorisches Handeln in der internationalen Politik," *Zeitschrift für Internationale Beziehungen* 4 (December 1997): 219–54.

76. For a detailed analysis of the case, see Cortell and Davis, "How Do International Institutions Matter?" 464–71.

77. Thomas Risse, "The Socialization of International Norms into Domestic Practices: Arguing and Strategic Adaptation in the Human Rights Area," paper presented at the conference on "Ideas, Culture, and Political Analysis," Princeton University, 15–16 May 1998, Princeton, New Jersey.

78. G. John Ikenberry, "Creating Yesterday's New World Order: Keynesian 'New Thinking' and the Anglo-American Postwar Settlement," in *Ideas and Foreign Policy: Be-*

liefs, Institutions, and Political Change, ed. Judith Goldstein and Robert O. Keohane (Ithaca, NY: Cornell University Press, 1993), 78–79.

79. The formulation is Mlada Bukovansky's. See Bukovansky, "American Identity and Neutral Rights, from Independence to the War of 1812," *International Organization* 51 (Spring 1997): 232. But see also Thomas J. Biersteker, "The 'Triumph' of Neoclassical Economics in the Developing World: Policy Convergence and the Bases of Governance in the International Economic Order," in *Governance without Government: Order and Change in World Politics,* ed. James N. Rosenau and Ernst-Otto Czempiel (Cambridge: Cambridge University Press, 1997), 120; and Joseph Nye, "Nuclear Learning and U.S.-Soviet Security Regimes," *International Organization* 41 (Summer 1987): 372, 400.

80. The position is maintained even by prominent proponents of rational choice theory. See, for example, Jon Elster, *Nuts and Bolts for the Social Sciences* (Cambridge: Cambridge University Press, 1989), 113–23.

SIX: Methods for the Production of Practical Knowledge

1. Charles C. Ragin, "Introduction: Cases of 'What Is a Case?'" in *What Is a Case? Exploring the Foundations of Social Inquiry,* ed. Ragin and Howard S. Becker (Cambridge: Cambridge University Press, 1992), 1, emphasis in the original.

2. See Douglas Harper, "Small *N*'s and Community Case Studies," in *What Is a Case?* ed. Ragin and Becker, 139–58.

3. My thinking on this has been influenced by David L. Hull, *Science as a Process: An Evolutionary Account of the Social and Conceptual Development of Science* (Chicago: University of Chicago Press, 1988), esp. 496, 508–9.

4. The claim that social constructivism is relativist and/or nihilist is common enough. See, for example, John J. Mearsheimer, "The False Promise of International Institutions," *International Security* 19 (Winter 1994/95): 41ff.

5. Hull, *Science as a Process,* 512–13.

6. I do not mean to imply that investigations into the genealogy of concepts are without merit. Indeed, exploring the social/cultural origins of basic language terms and related scientific concepts can provide valuable insights into broader and/or deeper structures of meaning that shape human behavior.

7. See Jennifer Platt, "Cases of Cases . . . of Cases," in *What Is a Case?* ed. Ragin and Becker, 21–52.

8. Hull, *Science as a Process,* 516.

9. For philosophical arguments in favor of essentialism, especially when applied to "natural kinds," see Hilary Putnam, "The Meaning of 'Meaning,'" in *Minnesota Studies in the Philosophy of Science,* vol. 7, ed. Keith Gunderson (Minneapolis: University of Minnesota Press, 1975), 131–93; and Saul A. Kripke, "Naming and Necessity," in *Semantics of Natural Language,* ed. Donald Davidson and Gilbert Harman (Dordrecht, Holland: Reidel, 1972), 253–355.

10. This is a heady claim, but insofar as concepts and conceptual categories and not their "empirical referents" are the building blocks of science, it is, I maintain, correct. A weaker version of the claim would posit that although uniform populations might be found in the realm of the physical elements, they are unlikely to characterize the biological or social worlds. Again, a reference to species seems apt: "More often than not, more variation exists within species than between closely related species. Sometimes a

single set of genes exists that all, or nearly all, the organisms belonging to a particular species possesses; sometimes not. It does not matter." Hull, *Science as a Process*, 513. Indeed, without the assumption of heterogeneous sets, neither biological nor social evolution would be possible.

11. On this point, I find the position set forth by Gary King, Robert O. Keohane, and Sidney Verba quite balanced, even though I disagree with the thesis that a single logic of inference applies to qualitative and quantitative research. See King, Keohane, and Verba, *Designing Social Inquiry: Scientific Inference in Qualitative Research* (Princeton: Princeton University Press, 1994), 35–36, 43.

12. See Adam Przeworski and Henry Teune, *The Logic of Comparative Social Inquiry* (Malabar, FL: Krieger, 1982). See also David D. Laitin, "The Political Science Discipline," paper presented at the Annual Convention of the American Political Science Association, 30 August–2 September 2001, San Francisco, California.

13. For example, David Collier, "The Comparative Method: Two Decades of Change," in *Comparative Political Dynamics: Global Research Perspectives,* ed. Dankwart A. Rustow and Kenneth Paul (New York: Harper Collins, 1991), 7–31; David Collier, "The Comparative Method," in *Political Science: The State of the Discipline,* ed. Ada W. Finifter (Washington, DC: American Political Science Association, 1993), 105–19; James Mahoney, "Nominal, Ordinal, and Narrative Appraisal in Macrocausal Analysis," *American Journal of Sociology* 4 (January 1999): 1154–96; James Mahoney, "Strategies of Causal Inference in Small-N Analysis," *Sociological Methods and Research* 28 (May 2000): 387–424; Andrew Bennett, "Lost in the Translation: Big (N) Misinterpretations of Case Study Research," paper presented at the 38th Annual Convention of the International Studies Association, 18–22 May 1997, Toronto, Canada; Timothy J. McKeown, "Case Studies and the Statistical Worldview," *International Organization* 53 (Fall 1999): 161–90; and Fritz K. Ringer, "Causal Analysis in Historical Reasoning," *History and Theory* 28, no. 2 (1989): 153–72.

14. For some exceptions, see Alvin E. Roth, "Laboratory Experimentation in Economics: A Methodological Overview," *Economics Journal* 98 (December 1988): 974–1031; Thomas L. Palfrey, ed., *Laboratory Research in Political Economy* (Ann Arbor: University of Michigan Press, 1991); and Morris Fiorina and Charles R. Plott, "Committee Decisions under Majority Rule," *American Political Science Review* 72 (June 1978): 575–98.

15. For a discussion along these lines, see Arend Lijphart, "Comparative Politics and the Comparative Method," *American Political Science Review* 65 (September 1971): 682–93.

16. See, however, the critique of this position developed in chapter 4.

17. For example, even the terms *case* and *observation* are cause for dispute. For a variety of views on appropriate terminology, see Harry Eckstein, "Case Study and Theory in Political Science," in *Handbook of Political Science,* vol. 7, *Strategies of Inquiry,* ed. Fred Greenstein and Nelson Polsby (Reading, MA: Addison-Wesley, 1975), 85; King, Keohane, and Verba, *Designing Social Inquiry,* 51–53; and Bennett, "Lost in the Translation: Big (N) Misinterpretations of Case Study Research."

18. In statistical analysis one should control only for those intervening variables that are truly independent of any antecedent causes. That is, if one knows that economic development always follows rising levels of education, one should not include a measure for economic development in a regression analysis. The reason for this is that the regression analysis would incorrectly attribute part of the causal effect to economic development.

19. Statisticians refer to this as the problem of multicoliniarity.

20. Hubert M. Blalock Jr., *Social Statistics*, 2d ed. (New York: McGraw Hill, 1979), 205.

21. For a variety of perspectives on the degrees of freedom problem, see Donald T. Campbell, "'Degrees of Freedom' and the Case Study," *Comparative Political Studies* 8 (July 1975): 178–93; David Collier, "The Comparative Method"; John H. Goldthorpe, "Current Issues in Comparative Macrosociology: A Debate on Methodological Issues," *Comparative Social Research* 16 (1997): 1–26; and King, Keohane, and Verba, *Designing Social Inquiry*, 118–22.

22. John Stuart Mill, *A System of Logic: Ratiocinative and Inductive* (1843; repr. London: Longmans, 1967).

23. Ibid., 256.

24. Mill himself was skeptical of the utility of his methods for the study of social phenomena (ibid., 573–78), but many social scientists are more optimistic. For arguments in favor of applying Mill's methods to the analysis of social phenomena, see Jukka Savolainen, "The Rationality of Drawing Big Conclusions Based on Small Samples: In Defense of Mill's Methods," *Social Forces* 72 (June 1994): 1217–24; Theda Skocpol, "Emerging Agendas and Recurrent Strategies in Historical Sociology," in *Vision and Method in Historical Sociology*, ed. Theda Skocpol (Cambridge: Cambridge University Press, 1984), 356–91; Theda Skocpol, "Analyzing Causal Configurations in History: A Rejoinder to Nichols," *Comparative Social Research* 9 (1986): 187–94. For critiques of Mill's methods and their use in the social sciences, see Goldthorpe, "Current Issues in Comparative Macrosociology"; Stanley Lieberson, "Small-N's and Big Conclusions: An Examination of the Reasoning in Comparative Studies Based on a Small Number of Cases," *Social Forces* 70 (December 1991): 307–20; Stanley Lieberson, "Causal Analysis and Comparative Research: What Can We Learn from Studies Based on a Small Number of Cases?" in *Rational Choice Theory and Large-Scale Data Analysis*, ed. Hans-Peter Blossfeld and Gerald Prein (Boulder, CO: Westview, 1998), 129–45; and Elizabeth Nichols, "Skocpol on Revolution: Comparative Analysis vs. Historical Conjuncture," *Comparative Social Research* 9 (1986): 163–86.

25. Barbara Geddes, "How the Cases You Choose Affect the Answers You Get: Selection Bias in Comparative Politics," in *Political Analysis*, vol. 2, ed. James A. Stimson (Ann Arbor: University of Michigan Press, 1990), 131–50.

26. For a discussion of omitted variable bias in statistical research design, see King, Keohane, and Verba, *Designing Social Inquiry*, 168–82.

27. This was the essence of David Spiro's critique of the first published works proclaiming the existence of the "democratic peace." See Spiro, "The Insignificance of the Democratic Peace," *International Security* 19 (Fall 1994): 50–86.

28. Lijphart, "Comparative Politics and the Comparative Method," 690.

29. Paul Diesing, *How Does Social Science Work? Reflections on Practice* (Pittsburgh: University of Pittsburgh Press, 1991), 338.

30. For example, the question of whether random fluctuations in nature "wash out" over time or cumulate and ramify in complex and unpredictable ways is a central focus of chaos and complexity theorists, as well as of evolutionary biologists. See James Gleick, *Chaos: Making a New Science* (New York: Viking, 1987); Stephen Jay Gould, *Wonderful Life* (New York: W. W. Norton, 1989); Stephen H. Kellert, *In the Wake of Chaos: Unpredictable Order in Dynamical Systems* (Chicago: University of Chicago Press, 1993); and Charles Perrow, *Normal Accidents: Living with High-Risk Technologies* (New York: Basic

Books, 1984). For applications of these ideas in history and social science, see Robert Jervis, *Systems Effects: Complexity in Political and Social Life* (Princeton: Princeton University Press, 1997); G. A. Reisch, "Chaos, History, and Narrative," *History and Theory* 30, no. 1 (1991): 1–20; and Diana Richards, "Is Strategic Decision Making Chaotic?" *Behavioral Science* 35 (July 1990): 219–32. Joseph Agassi has challenged the position that replication and corroboration of experimental results produces reliable knowledge. Because the tests upon which science proceeds are based on subsidiary hypotheses regarding methods and measures, we never know whether results are true or only a product of a particular methodological protocol. Agassi provides numerous examples where hypotheses have been corroborated again and again only to be rejected by new test procedures as well as cases where accepted refutations were themselves later refuted. See Joseph Agassi, *Science in Flux* (Dordrecht, Holland: Reidel, 1975).

31. For now I am setting aside the interesting question of the ways in which hypothetical future events can influence the present, but I shall address it below.

32. The title of this section was inspired by James G. March, Lee S. Sproull, and Michal Tamuz, "Learning from Samples of One or Fewer," *Organization Science* 2 (February 1991): 1–13.

33. Carl G. Hempel, *Aspects of Scientific Explanation and Other Essays in the Philosophy of Science* (New York: Free Press, 1965), 174, 234, 247–49; Carl G. Hempel, "Explanation in Science and History," in *Frontiers of Science and Philosophy,* ed. Robert G. Colodny (Pittsburgh: University of Pittsburgh Press, 1962), 1–33; and Carl G. Hempel, "Reasons and Covering Laws in Historical Explanation," in *The Philosophy of History,* ed. Patrick Gardiner (New York: Oxford University Press, 1974), 90–91.

34. Sidney Verba, "Some Dilemmas in Comparative Research," *World Politics* 20 (October 1976): 113.

35. Alexander Rosenberg, *Sociobiology and the Preemption of Social Science* (Baltimore: Johns Hopkins University Press, 1980). See also the discussion of Rosenberg in Diesing, *How Does Social Science Work?* 91–92. For a problematic effort to apply ideas taken from sociobiology to the study of international politics, see Bradley Thayer, "Bringing in Darwin: Evolutionary Theory, Realism, and International Politics," *International Security* 25 (Fall 2000): 124–51.

36. Diesing, *How Does Social Science Work?* 91.

37. Donald Davidson, "Actions, Reasons, and Cases," in Davidson, *Essays on Actions and Events* (Oxford: Oxford University Press, 1980), 16–17.

38. Alasdair MacIntyre, "The Antecedents of Action," in MacIntyre, *Against the Self-Images of the Age: Essays on Ideology and Philosophy* (South Bend, IN: University of Notre Dame Press, 1978), 196. As cited in Ringer, "Causal Analysis in Historical Reasoning," 155.

39. Ringer, "Causal Analysis in Historical Reasoning," 157, emphasis added.

40. Ibid., 156.

41. March, Sproull, and Tamuz, "Learning from Samples of One or Fewer," 3.

42. Ringer, "Causal Analysis in Historical Reasoning," 157.

43. The same could be said with respect to the processes that gave rise to the ice patch. Because changing prevailing weather patterns would require us to rewrite more history, identifying the weather as the accident's cause is less appealing.

44. Recent years have witnessed a renewed interest among social scientists in the centrality of counterfactual reasoning to causal analysis, as well as the uses of counterfac-

tual thought experiments for purposes of theory development. See, for example, James D. Fearon, "Counterfactuals and Hypothesis Testing in Political Science," *World Politics* 43 (January 1991): 169–95; Philip E. Tetlock and Aaron Belkin, eds., *Counterfactual Thought Experiments in World Politics: Logical, Methodological, and Psychological Perspectives* (Princeton: Princeton University Press, 1996); Geoffrey Hawthorn, *Plausible Worlds: Possibility and Understanding in History and the Social Sciences* (New York: Cambridge University Press, 1991); and Neal J. Roese and James M. Olson, eds., *What Might Have Been: The Social Psychology of Counterfactual Thinking* (Mahwah, NJ: Erlbaum, 1995).

45. James D. Fearon, "Causes and Counterfactuals in Social Science: Exploring an Analogy Between Cellular Automata and Historical Processes," in *Counterfactual Thought Experiments in World Politics,* ed. Tetlock and Belkin, 41.

46. Philip E. Tetlock and Aaron Belkin, "Counterfactual Thought Experiments in World Politics," in *Counterfactual Thought Experiments in World Politics,* ed. Tetlock and Belkin, 23.

47. Versions of this argument can be found in Graham Allison, *Essence of Decision: Explaining the Cuban Missile Crisis* (Boston: Little, Brown, 1971), 230–37; and Alexander L. George and Richard Smoke, *Deterrence in American Foreign Policy: Theory and Practice* (New York: Columbia University Press, 1974), 447–93.

48. Richard Ned Lebow and Janice Gross Stein, "Back to the Past: Counterfactuals and the Cuban Missile Crisis," in *Counterfactual Thought Experiments in World Politics,* ed. Tetlock and Belkin, 119–48, quotation 129.

49. Bruce Bueno de Mesquita, "The Benefits of a Social Scientific Approach to Studying International Affairs," in *Explaining International Relations since 1945,* ed. Ngaire Woods (New York: Oxford University Press, 1966), 49–76, quotation 52.

50. Robert Bierstedt, "Toynbee and Sociology," *British Journal of Sociology* 10 (June 1959): 95–104, quotation 96–97.

51. For a similar argument, see Jack S. Levy, "Too Important to Leave to the Other: History and Political Science in the Study of International Relations," *International Security* 22 (Summer 1997): 22–33, esp. 25.

52. Thomas E. Bell and K. Esch, "The Fatal Flaw in Flight 51-L," *IEEE Spectrum* 24 (February 1987): 36–51; and R. Boisjoly, "Ethical Decisions: Morton Thiokol and the Space Shuttle Challenger Disaster," *American Society of Mechanical Engineers Journal* 87–WA/TS–4 (1987): 1–13. Both cited in March, Sproull, and Tamuz, "Learning from Samples of One or Fewer," 9. The history of the space shuttle program is not unique. See Perrow, *Normal Accidents: Living with High-Risk Technologies,* esp. the chapters on nuclear power generators and the accident at Three Mile Island.

53. Scott D. Sagan, *The Limits of Safety: Organizations, Accidents, and Nuclear Weapons* (Princeton: Princeton University Press, 1993); and Sagan, "The Commitment Trap: Why the United States Should Not Use Nuclear Threats to Deter Biological and Chemical Weapons Attacks," *International Security* 24 (Spring 2000): 85–115, esp. 107.

54. Richard Smoke and Alexander George, "Theory for Policy in International Affairs," *Policy Sciences* 4 (1973): 387–413.

55. William H. Starbuck and F. J. Milliken, "Challenger: Fine-Tuning the Odds until Something Breaks," *Journal of Management Studies* 25 (July 1988): 319–40. As cited in March, Sproull, and Tamuz, "Learning from Samples of One or Fewer," 9. For a discussion of the problems associated with overestimating the probability of past outcomes that were the products of complex and/or nonlinear processes, see Lars-Erik Cederman,

"Rerunning History: Counterfactual Simulation in World Politics," in *Counterfactual Thought Experiments in World Politics,* ed. Tetlock and Belkin, 247–67.

56. Amos Tversky and Daniel Kahneman, "Availability: A Heuristic for Judging Frequency and Probability," in *Judgement Under Uncertainty: Heuristics and Biases,* ed. Daniel Kahneman, Paul Slovic, and Amos Tversky (Cambridge: Cambridge University Press, 1982), 163–78.

57. See Paul T. B. Wong and Bernard Weiner, "When People Ask 'Why' Questions, and the Heuristics of Attributional Search," *Journal of Personality and Social Psychology* 40, no. 4 (1981): 650–63; Sam B. Sitkin, "Learning Through Failure: The Strategy of Small Losses," *Research in Organizational Behavior* 14 (1992): 231–66; Theresa K. Lant and David B. Montgomery, "Learning from Strategic Success and Failure," *Journal of Business Research* 15 (December 1987): 503–17; and Jervis, *Perception and Misperception in International Politics,* 275–79.

58. Baruch Fischoff, "Hindsight ≠ Foresight: The Effect of Outcome Knowledge on Judgement Under Uncertainty," *Journal of Experimental Psychology: Human Perception and Performance* 1, no. 3 (1975): 288–99; B. Fischoff, "For Those Condemned to Study the Past," in *Judgement Under Uncertainty,* ed. Kahneman, Slovic, and Tversky (Cambridge: Cambridge University Press, 1982), 422–44; and Daniel Kahneman and Carol A. Varey, "Propensities and Counterfactuals: The Loser Almost Won," in *Research on Judgement and Decision Making: Currents, Connections, and Controversies,* ed. William M. Goldstein and Robin M. Hogarth (Cambridge: Cambridge University Press, 1997), 321–44.

59. For a discussion of current psychological research on the role of memory in judgment and choice, see Reid Hastie and Bernadette Park, "The Relationship between Memory and Judgement Depends on Whether the Judgement Task Is Memory-Based or On-Line," in *Research on Judgement and Decision Making,* ed. Goldstein and Hogarth, 431–53; and Nancy Pennington and Reid Hastie, "Explanation-Based Decision Making: Effects of Memory Structure on Judgement," in *Research on Judgement and Decision Making,* ed. Goldstein and Hogarth, 454–81.

60. For arguments on how to discipline prediction in the absence of generally valid laws, see Janice Gross Stein, "Five Scenarios of the Israeli-Palestinian Relationship in 2002," *Security Studies* 7 (Summer 1998): 195–212; Steven Weber, "Prediction and the Middle East Peace Process," *Security Studies* 6 (Summer 1997): 167–79; and Stephen Bernstein et al., "God Gave Physics the Easy Problems: Adapting Social Science to an Unpredictable World," *European Journal of International Relations* 6 (March 2000): 43–76; and George and Smoke, "Theory for Policy in International Affairs," esp. 411–13. For a skeptical appraisal of the prospects for using hindsight to generate accurate future scenarios and effective strategy, see Richard K. Betts, "Is Strategy an Illusion?" *International Security* 25 (Fall 2000): 5–50.

61. The differences between causal and constitutive processes is a subject of much debate. For a discussion of the subject and the implications for the study of international politics, see Alexander Wendt, *Social Theory of International Politics* (Cambridge: Cambridge University Press, 1999), 25–29.

62. March, Sproull, and Tamuz, "Learning from Samples of One or Fewer," 2.

63. Donald Campbell, "Degrees of Freedom and the Case Study," in *Qualitative and Quantitative Methods in Evaluations Research,* ed. Thomas D. Cook and Charles S. Reichardt (Beverly Hills, CA: Sage, 1979), 49–67.

64. The seminal works are Alexander L. George, "The Causal Nexus between Cognitive Beliefs and Decisionmaking Behavior: The 'Operational Code' Belief System," in *Psy-*

chological Models and International Politics, ed. Lawrence S. Falkowski (Boulder, CO: Westview Press, 1979); Alexander L. George, "Case Studies and Theory Development: The Method of Structured, Focused Comparison," in *Diplomacy: New Approaches in History, Theory, and Policy,* ed. Paul G. Lauren (New York: Free Press, 1979), 43–68; Alexander L. George and Timothy J. McKeown, "Case Studies and Theories of Organizational Decision Making," *Advances in Information Processing in Organizations* 2 (1985): 21–58; The method is further developed in Alexander L. George and Andrew Bennett, *Case Studies and Theory Development* (Cambridge, MA: MIT Press, forthcoming).

65. George, "Case Studies and Theory Development," 46. Sidney Verba makes a similar argument: "The unique historical event cannot be ignored, but it must be considered as one of a class of such events, even if it happened only once." Verba, "Some Dilemmas in Comparative Research," 114.

66. Given the arguments of chapter 2 on the theory-dependence of observation, the critical reader will ask how researchers can possibly identify previously unknown causal mechanisms on the basis of observation. The answer, I believe, is twofold. Crucial is the documented capacity of the human brain to recognize (or construct) patterns in sensory data, particularly patterns associated with motion, which begins no later than birth and is highly developed by the age of two. The second step involves the extension of primitive and prototypical patterns to novel observations through which they can be reinforced or used as the basis for generating new perceptual constructs and the subsequent articulation of such patterns in culturally relevant linguistic terms. See William T. Greenough et al., "Experience and Brain Development," *Child Development* 58 (June 1987): 539–59; Charles M. Keller and Janet Dixon Keller, "Imagining in Iron, or Thought Is Not Inner Speech," in *Rethinking Linguistic Relativity,* ed. John J. Gumperz and Stephen C. Levinson (Cambridge: Cambridge University Press, 1996), 115–29; and John Ziman, *Reliable Knowledge: An Exploration of the Grounds for Belief in Science* (Cambridge: Cambridge University Press, 1978), 43–56, 95–105, 114–15.

67. George and McKeown, "Case Studies and Theories of Organizational Decision Making," 35. See also George, "Case Studies and Theory Development," 47.

68. Insofar as process tracing requires us to translate historical descriptions into theoretical terms that provide an explanation that is both internally coherent and coherent with regard to the perspectives of the actors themselves, it bears a certain resemblance to the method of interpreting texts and actions advocated by Paul Ricoeur. See Ricoeur, "The Model of the Text: Meaningful Action Considered as a Text," in *Interpretive Social Science: A Reader,* ed. Paul Rabinow and William M. Sullivan (Berkeley: University of California Press, 1979), 73–101. See also Ringer, "Causal Analysis in Historical Reasoning," 165.

69. George and McKeown, "Case Studies and Theories of Organizational Decision Making," 36.

70. Jacob B. Chassan, "Stochastic Models of the Single Case as the Basis of Clinical Research Design," *Behavioral Science* 6 (January 1961): 42–50. See also Chassan, "Statistical Inference and the Single Case in Clinical Design," *Psychiatry: Journal for the Study of Interpersonal Processes* 23 (1960): 173–84. For a similar argument applied to the field of comparative politics, see Juan J. Linz and Amando de Miguel, "Within-Nation Differences and Comparisons: The Eight Spains," in *Comparing Nations: The Use of Quantitative Data in Cross-National Research,* ed. Richard L. Merritt and Stein Rokkan (New Haven: Yale University Press, 1966), 268.

71. I am of course assuming that crucial turning points in historical processes are the

products of localized developments. The inferential value of single-case analysis declines as the number of independent or stochastic changes in the values assigned to theoretical terms and/or the number of hypothesized mechanisms consistent with the data uncovered through process tracing increases. See Olav Njolstad, "Learning from History? Case Studies and the Limits to Theory-Building," in *Arms Races: Technological and Political Dynamics,* ed. Olav Njolstad and Nils Petter Gleditsch (London: Sage, 1990), 220–46. For a general discussion of the difficulties associated with mapping complex mechanisms, see Jervis, *Systems Effects,* 73–91.

72. Process tracing can also be used to eliminate variables that remain after large- or small-N comparative case studies. For example, Skocpol was able to use process tracing to eliminate "ideologically motivated vanguard movements" as a cause for social revolutions. Although ideologically motivated vanguard movements were found in each of the cases she analyzed, they were not linked systematically to widespread revolts against landlords and agents of the state. See Theda Skocpol, *States and Social Revolutions: A Comparative Analysis of France, Russia, and China* (Cambridge: Cambridge University Press, 1979), esp. 170–71.

73. George and McKeown, "Case Studies and Organizational Decision Making," 37–38. See also Earl Hunt, Janet Marin, and Philip Stone, *Experiments in Induction* (New York: Academic Press, 1966), 140; John Steinbrunner, *The Cybernetic Theory of Decision* (Cambridge, MA: Harvard University Press, 1977), 110–12; and Robert Jervis, *Perception and Misperception in International Politics* (Princeton: Princeton University Press, 1976), 181–202, 319–42.

74. George and McKeown, "Case Studies and Theories of Organizational Decision Making," 36.

75. For a similar argument, see Paul Veyne, *Comment on écrit l'histoire* (Paris: Éditions de Seuil, 1979), 114.

76. Of course the problem might also be one of redundant causation. For thoughts on how to address the question through resort to counterfactual analysis, see Michael McDermott, "Redundant Causation," *British Journal for the Philosophy of Science* 46 (1995): 523–44. Counterfactual analysis is particularly difficult when the analyst confronts complex systems that are characterized by redundancies and multiple feedback loops. For example, even if a critical element or action had not been present, the underlying forces might have produced a similar effect. See Jervis, *Systems Effects,* 74.

77. The accomplishments of inductivist research programs in my own field of international politics are modest at best. Perhaps the most important and systematic of such undertakings is the University of Michigan's Correlates of War Project. Although over the course of four decades the project has produced volumes of valuable empirical data, it has yet to come up with anything resembling a comprehensive theory that can account for established regularities. Reports of the project's findings can be found in J. David Singer, ed., *Quantitative International Politics: Insights and Evidence* (New York: Free Press, 1968); J. David Singer, Stuart Bremer, and John Stuckey, "Capability Distribution, Uncertainty, and Major Power War," in *Peace, War, and Numbers,* ed. Bruce M. Russett (Beverly Hills, CA: Sage, 1972), 19–48; J. David Singer and Melvin Small, *National Material Capabilities Data Set,* Study 9903 (Ann Arbor, MI: Inter-University Consortium for Political and Social Research, 1993); and Singer and Small, *Correlates of War Project: International and Civil War Data, 1816–1992,* Study 9905 (Ann Arbor, MI: Inter-University Consortium for Political and Social Research, 1994). For a discussion of the project and

its relationship to theory building, see David Dessler, "Beyond Correlations: Toward a Causal Theory of War," *International Studies Quarterly* 35 (September 1991): 337–55.

78. Andrew Bennett and Alexander L. George, "Developing and Using Typological Theories in Case Study Research," paper presented at the 38th Annual Convention of the International Studies Association, 18–22 May 1997, Toronto, Canada. See also Eckstein, "Case Study and Theory in Political Science," esp. 104–8.

79. In its most general form, deterrence is the persuasion of another actor that the costs and/or risks of a given course of action he might otherwise take outweigh its benefits. Largely in response to the perceived threat posed by the Soviet Union to the United States and its allies, the search for conditions necessary and sufficient to deter a Soviet attack and the spread of communism became a primary focus of American military and academic analysis during the cold war. The classic works on deterrence include Bernard Brodie, *The Absolute Weapon: Atomic Power and World Order* (New York: Harcourt Brace, 1946); Brodie, *Strategy in the Missile Age* (Princeton: Princeton University Press, 1965); Thomas C. Schelling, *The Strategy of Conflict* (Cambridge: Harvard University Press, 1960); Schelling, *Arms and Influence* (New Haven: Yale University Press, 1966); Herman Kahn, *On Thermonuclear War* (Princeton: Princeton University Press, 1960); Kahn, *Thinking about the Unthinkable* (New York: Horizon, 1962); William W. Kaufmann, *The Requirements of Deterrence* (Princeton: Center for International Studies, 1954); and Glenn H. Snyder, *Deterrence and Defense* (Princeton: Princeton University Press, 1961).

80. Alexander L. George and Richard Smoke, *Deterrence in American Foreign Policy: Theory and Practice* (New York: Columbia University Press, 1974).

81. In the 1950s and 1960s, deterrence theory developed largely through the application of rational choice and game theoretic analysis to the problem of deterrence conceived in terms of confrontations in which a "defender" issues a "threat" to deter an attack by a "challenger" on a "commitment" or "protégé." See, for example, Paul Huth and Bruce Russett, "What Makes Deterrence Work? Cases from 1900–1980," *World Politics* 36 (July 1984): 498.

82. George and Smoke, *Deterrence and American Foreign Policy,* 534–48.

83. See, for example, Richard Ned Lebow, *Between Peace and War* (Baltimore: Johns Hopkins University Press, 1981); Janice Gross Stein, "Calculation, Miscalculation, and Conventional Deterrence I: The View from Cairo," in *Psychology and Deterrence,* ed. Robert Jervis, R. Ned Lebow, and Janice G. Stein (Baltimore: Johns Hopkins University Press, 1985); Janice Gross Stein, "Extended Deterrence in the Middle East: American Strategy Reconsidered," *World Politics* 39 (April 1987): 326–52; Janice Gross Stein, "Deterrence and Reassurance," in *Behavior, Society, and Nuclear War,* vol. 2, ed. Philip Tetlock et al. (New York: Oxford University Press, 1990), 8–72; Richard Ned Lebow and Janice Gross Stein, *We All Lost the Cold War* (Princeton: Princeton University Press, 1994); Susan Peterson, *Crisis Bargaining and the State: The Domestic Politics of International Conflict* (Ann Arbor: University of Michigan Press, 1996); Ted Hopf, *Peripheral Visions: Deterrence Theory and Soviet Foreign Policy in the Third World, 1965–1990* (Ann Arbor: University of Michigan Press, 1994); Jonathan Mercer, *Reputation and International Politics* (Ithaca, NY: Cornell University Press, 1995); and James W. Davis Jr., *Threats and Promises: The Pursuit of International Influence* (Baltimore: Johns Hopkins University Press, 2000).

The assertion that qualitative case studies have contributed to better theory is controversial. For alternative assessments, see Christopher Achen and Duncan Snidal, "Rational Deterrence Theory and Comparative Case Studies," *World Politics* 41 (January

1989): 143–69; and Paul Huth and Bruce Russett, "Testing Deterrence Theory: Rigor Makes a Difference," *World Politics* 42 (July 1990): 466–501.

Largely a result of advances in the broader field of game theoretical analysis, in particular sequential signaling games under conditions of incomplete information, deductive models of deterrence have been subject to refinements that have identified inconsistencies in earlier formulations. See, for example, James D. Fearon, "Signaling versus the Balance of Power and Interests," *Journal of Conflict Resolution* 38 (June 1994): 236–69; Fearon, "Domestic Political Audiences and the Escalation of International Disputes," *American Political Science Review* 88 (September 1994): 577–92; and Robert Powell, *Nuclear Deterrence Theory: The Search for Credibility* (Cambridge: Cambridge University Press, 1990).

As research progresses along two very different paths, the once unified community of deterrence theorists has largely split into two opposing camps, which increasingly ignore one another.

84. George and McKeown, "Case Studies and Theories of Organizational Decision Making," 40–41.

85. Michal Tamuz, *Monitoring Dangers in the Air: Studies in Ambiguity and Information,* Ph.D. dissertation, Stanford University, 1988.

86. Geoffrey C. Bowker and Susan Leigh Star, *Sorting Things Out: Classification and Its Consequences* (Cambridge, MA: MIT Press, 1999), 107–62. A straightforward example is the relatively high rate of stillbirths reported in Roman Catholic countries where abortion is illegal.

87. Lawrence J. Korb, "The Readiness Gap," *New York Times Magazine,* 26 February 1995, 40–41.

88. George, "Case Studies and Theory Development," 60; Alexander L. George, "The Role of the Congruence Method for Case Study Research," paper presented at the 38th Annual Convention of the International Studies Association, 18–22 May 1997, Toronto, Canada; and Bennett, "Lost in the Translation," 10.

89. Important contributions from the first wave include Hedley Bull, *The Anarchical Society: A Study of Order in World Politics* (New York: Columbia University Press, 1977); Robert W. Cox, "Social Forces, States, and World Orders: Beyond International Relations Theory," *Millennium: Journal of International Studies* 10 (Summer 1981): 126–155; Friedrich V. Kratochwil, *Rules, Norms, and Decisions: On the Conditions of Practical and Legal Reasoning in International Relations and Domestic Affairs* (Cambridge: Cambridge University Press, 1989); and Alexander Wendt, "Anarchy Is What States Make of It: The Social Construction of Power Politics," *International Organization* 46 (Spring 1992): 391–425. For a sampling of scholarship stressing the mediating impact of domestic politics, see Andrew P. Cortell and James W. Davis Jr., "How Do International Institutions Matter? The Domestic Impact of International Rules and Norms," *International Studies Quarterly* 40 (December 1996): 451–78; Audie Klotz, "Norms Reconstituting Interests: Global Racial Equality and U.S. Sanctions against South Africa," *International Organization* 49 (Summer 1995); Thomas J. Biersteker, "The 'Triumph' of Neoclassical Economics in the Developing World: Policy Convergence and Bases of Governance in the International Economic Order," in *Governance without Government: Order and Change in World Politics,* ed. James N. Rosenau and Ernst-Otto Czempiel (Cambridge: Cambridge University Press, 1997), 102–31; and Amy Gurowitz, "Mobilizing International Norms: Domestic Actors, Immigrants and the Japanese State," *World Politics* 51 (April 1999): 413–45.

90. For examples of how case studies have led to more nuanced propositions on the

effects of international norms, see Cortell and Davis, "How Do International Institutions Matter?"; Thomas Risse-Kappen, "Ideas Do Not Float Freely: Transnational Coalitions, Domestic Structures and the End of the Cold War," *International Organization* 48 (Spring 1994): 185–214; and Jeffrey T. Checkel, "Norms, Institutions, and National Identity in Contemporary Europe," *International Studies Quarterly* 43 (March 1999): 83–114. For a survey of efforts to identify the mechanisms lending salience to international norms in domestic political debates, see Andrew P. Cortell and James W. Davis Jr., "Understanding the Domestic Impact of International Norms: A Research Agenda," *International Studies Review* 2 (Spring 2000): 65–87.

91. Veyne, *Comment on écrit l'histoire,* 83–84.

92. King, Keohane, and Verba, *Designing Social Inquiry,* 48.

93. Douglas Chalmers, *Integrating Theories: Dealing with Diversity of Theoretical Forms in Political Science* (forthcoming), ch. 3.

94. James W. Davis Jr., *The Forgotten Variable: The Role of Promises in Deterrence,* Ph.D. dissertation, Columbia University, 1995.

95. See Bennett and George, "Developing and Using Typological Theories in Case Study Research"; Daniel Little, "Causal Explanation in the Social Sciences," *Southern Journal of Philosophy* 34 (Supplement S 1996), 31–56; and Charles Ragin, *The Comparative Method: Moving Beyond Qualitative and Quantitative Strategies* (Berkeley: University of California Press, 1987).

96. The definition of typologies is taken from Arthur Stinchcombe, *Constructing Social Theories* (Chicago: University of Chicago Press, 1968), 43–45. The definition of typological theories comes from Bennett and George, "Developing and Using Typological Theories in Case Study Research," 4–5.

97. For an example of such methodologists' claims, see Chalmers, *Integrating Theories,* ch. 3.

98. Although less controversial when applied to inductively generated typologies, the argument also applies to deductively generated typologies once we move from the realm of logic to that of empirical observation, for reasons discussed in chapter 4.

99. See Bruce Bagley, "Colombia: National Front and Economic Development," in *Politics, Policies, and Economic Development in Latin America,* ed. Robert Wesson (Stanford: Hoover Institution Press, 1984), 124–60. Most contemporary typologies of regime characteristics date to Juan J. Linz, "Totalitarian and Authoritarian Regimes," in *Handbook of Political Science: Macropolitical Theory,* ed. Fred Greenstein and Nelson Polsby (Reading, MA: Addison-Wesley, 1975), 175–412. In the field of comparative politics, the typology is most closely associated with research on "transitions," which in the wake of the cold war has undergone a revival. See Juan J. Linz and Alfred Stepan, *The Breakdown of Democratic Regimes* (Baltimore: Johns Hopkins University Press, 1986); Guillermo O'Donnell, Philippe C. Schmitter, and Lawrence Whitehead, eds., *Transitions from Authoritarian Rule: Comparative Perspectives* (Baltimore: Johns Hopkins University Press, 1986); Samuel P. Huntington, *The Third Wave: Democratization in the Late Twentieth Century* (Norman: Oklahoma University Press, 1991); Larry Diamond, Juan Linz, and Seymour Martin Lipset, *Politics in Developing Countries: Comparing Experiences with Democracy* (Boulder, CO: Lynne Rienner, 1995); Renske Doorenspleet, "Reassessing the Three Waves of Democracy," *World Politics* 52 (April 2000): 384–406.

100. Bennett and George, "Developing and Using Typological Theories in Case Study Research."

242   Notes to Pages 185–187

101. Ziman, *Reliable Knowledge,* 26–27.

102. At least since Durkheim, sociology has been influenced by a holistic understanding of social systems. See Emile Durkheim, *The Rules of Sociological Method* (Glencoe, IL: Free Press, 1938); Walter Buckley, *Sociology and Modern Systems Theory* (Englewood Cliffs, NJ: Prentice-Hall, 1967); Jonathan Turner, *A Theory of Social Interaction* (Stanford: Stanford University Press, 1988); David Knoke, *Political Networks: The Structural Perspective* (Cambridge: Cambridge University Press, 1990); and Niklas Luhmann, *Social Systems* (Stanford: Stanford University Press, 1995).

103. Jervis, *Systems Effects,* 3–28.

104. For example, the nineteenth-century mathematician Henri Poincaré demonstrated that the motion of as few as three bodies, although governed by strict physical laws, defies exact solution. See ibid., 6.

105. Even when actors pursue simple strategies, these can interact in ways that produce outcomes, which, though ordered, are neither predictable nor stable. See Joshua Epstein and Robert Axtell, *Growing Artificial Societies: Social Science from the Bottom Up* (Washington, DC: Brookings Institution, 1996); and Nigel Gilbert and Rosaria Conte, eds., *Artificial Societies: The Computer Simulation of Social Life* (London: University College London Press, 1995). For an earlier effort to theorize emergent properties in social systems, see Thomas Schelling, *Micromotives and Macrobehavior* (New York: W. W. Norton, 1978), esp. 147–55.

106. The analogy is not original to me. See Alexander L. George, "Knowledge for Statecraft: The Challenge for Political Science and History," *International Security* 22 (Summer 1997): 44–52.

107. This is especially true of conditions referred to as "syndromes." See Anthony S. Fauci et al., eds., *Harrison's Principles of Internal Medicine,* 14th ed. (New York: McGraw-Hill, 1998), esp. 3, 9.

108. Effective action in complex social systems may require more than one effort to promote or redirect a course of events. See Jervis, *Systems Effects,* 291–95.

109. George, "Knowledge for Statecraft," 50.

110. Smoke and George, "Theory for Policy in International Affairs," 411.

111. For a similar conclusion, see Friedrich Kratochwil, "Changing Relations between State, Market and Society, and the Problem of Knowledge," *Pacific Focus* 9 (Fall 1994): 43–59, esp. 47.

Bibliography

Achen, Christopher, and Duncan Snidal (1989). Rational Deterrence Theory and Comparative Case Studies. *World Politics* 41, no. 2: 143–69.

Adler, Emanuel (1997). Seizing the Middle Ground: Constructivism in World Politics. *European Journal of International Relations* 3, no. 3: 319–63.

Agassi, Joseph (1975). *Science in Flux*. Dordrecht, Holland: Reidel.

Allison, Graham (1971). *Essence of Decision: Explaining the Cuban Missile Crisis*. Boston: Little, Brown.

Almond, Gabriel A. (1956). Comparative Political Systems. *Journal of Politics* 18, no. 2: 391–409.

Almond, Gabriel A., and Stephen J. Genco (1977). Clouds, Clocks, and the Study of Politics. *World Politics* 29, no. 4: 489–522.

Almond, Gabriel A., Harald Müller, Thomas Risse, and Ido Oren (2001). Forum: Responses to Ido Oren. *European Journal of International Relations* 7, no. 3: 399–408.

Almond, Gabriel A., and Sidney Verba (1963). *The Civic Culture: Political Attitudes and Democracy in Five Nations*. Princeton: Princeton University Press.

Amsterdam, Anthony G., and Jerome Bruner (2000). *Minding the Law*. Cambridge, MA: Harvard University Press.

Anderson, Margaret (2000). *Practicing Democracy: Elections and Political Culture in Imperial Germany*. Princeton: Princeton University Press.

Archer, Ronald P. (1995). Party Strength and Weakness in Colombia's Besieged Democracy. In *Building Democratic Institutions: Party Systems in Latin America,* ed. S. Mainwaring and T. R. Scully, 164–99. Stanford: Stanford University Press.

Aristotle (1966). *Rhetoric*. Translated by E. S. Forster. Cambridge, MA: Harvard University Press.

Armstrong, Sharon Lee, Lila R. Gleitman, and Henry Gleitman (1983). What Some Concepts Might Not Be. *Cognition* 13:263–308.

Aron, Raymond (1967). *Peace and War: A Theory of International Relations*. Translated by R. Howard and A. Baker Fox. New York: Praeger.

Ashley, Richard K. (1986). The Poverty of Neorealism. In *Neorealism and Its Critics,* ed. R. O. Keohane, 255–300. New York: Columbia University Press.

——— (1987). The Geopolitics of Geopolitical Space: Toward a Critical Social Theory of International Politics. *Alternatives* 12, no. 4: 403–34.

Aslin, R. N., and D. B. Pisoni (1989). Some Developmental Processes in Speech Perception. In *Child Phonology*. Vol. 2, *Perception,* ed. G. H. Yeni-Komshian, J. F. Kavanagh, and C. A. Ferguson, 67–96. New York: Academic Press.

Assmann, Jan (1997). *Das kulturelle Gedächtnis: Schrift, Erinnerung und politische Identität in frühen Hochkulturen*. Munich: Beck.

Axelrod, Robert (1984). *The Evolution of Cooperation*. New York: Basic Books.

Azar, Edward E. *Conflict and Peace Data Bank (COPDAB), 1948–1978: Daily Events File*. Ann Arbor, MI: Inter-University Consortium for Political and Social Research (ICPSR), Study I7767.

Bachrach, Peter, and Morton S. Baratz (1963). Decisions and Nondecisions: An Analytical Framework. *American Political Science Review* 57 (September): 632–42.

Bagley, Bruce (1984). Colombia: National Front and Economic Development. In *Politics, Policies, and Economic Development in Latin America,* ed. R. Wesson, 124–60. Stanford: Hoover Institution Press.

Bahrick, Lorraine E., and Jeffrey N. Pickens (1988). Classification of Bimodal English and Spanish Language Passages by Infants. *Infant Behavior and Development* 11, no. 3: 277–296.

Baldwin, David A. (1989). *Paradoxes of Power*. New York: Basil Blackwell.

——, ed. (1993). *Neorealism and Neoliberalism: The Contemporary Debate*. New York: Columbia University Press.

—— (1997). The Concept of Security. *Review of International Studies* 23, no. 1: 5–26.

Banks, Michael (1985). The Inter-Paradigm Debate. In *International Relations: A Handbook of Current Theory,* ed. M. Light and A. J. R. Groom, 7–26. London: Pinter.

Barnett, Michael (1995). Sovereignty, Nationalism, and Regional Order in the Arab States System. *International Organization* 49, no. 3: 479–510.

—— (1998). *Dialogues in Arab Politics: Negotiations in Regional Order*. New York: Columbia University Press.

Bartleson, Jens (1995). *A Genealogy of Sovereignty*. Cambridge: Cambridge University Press.

Bassili, John N. (2001). Symposium on Social Identity. *Political Psychology* 22, no. 1: 111–98.

Bates, Robert (1996). Letter from the President: Area Studies and the Discipline. *APSA-CP: Newsletter of the APSA Organized Section in Comparative Politics* 7, no. 1: 1–2.

Bell, Thomas E., and K. Esch (1987). The Fatal Flaw in Flight 51-L. *IEEE Spectrum* 24, no. 2: 36–51.

Bennet, Andrew (1997). Lost in the Translation: Big (N) Misinterpretations of Case Study Research. Paper read at the 38th Annual Convention of the International Studies Association. 18–22 May. Toronto, Canada.

Bennet, Andrew, and Alexander L. George (1997). Developing and Using Typological Theories in Case Study Research. Paper read at the 38th Annual Convention of the International Studies Association. 18–22 May. Toronto, Canada.

—— (1999). *Condemned to Repetition? The Rise, Fall, and Reprise of Soviet-Russian Military Interventionism, 1973–1996*. Cambridge, MA: MIT Press.

Berlin, Brent, and Paul Kay (1969). *Basic Color Terms: Their Universality and Evolution*. Berkeley: University of California Press.

Berman, Sheri E. (2001). Modernization in Historical Perspective: The Case of Imperial Germany. *World Politics* 53 (April): 431–62.

Bernstein, Stephen, Richard Ned Lebow, Janice Gross Stein, and Steve Weber (2000). God Gave Physics the Easy Problems: Adapting Social Science to an Unpredictable World. *European Journal of International Relations* 6, no. 1: 43–76.

Best, C. T. (1988). Examination of Perceptual Reorganization for Nonnative Speech Contrasts: Zulu Click Discrimination by English-Speaking Adults and Infants. *Journal of Experimental Psychology: Human Perception and Performance* 14, no. 3: 345–60.

Betts, Richard K. (2000). Is Strategy an Illusion? *International Security* 25, no. 2: 5–50.

Bialystok, E., and D. R. Olson (1987). Spatial Categories: The Perception and Conceptualization of Spatial Relations. In *Categorical Perception: The Groundwork of Cognition*, ed. S. R. Harnard, 511–31. Cambridge: Cambridge University Press.

Bierstedt, Robert (1959). Toynbee and Sociology. *British Journal of Sociology* 10, no. 2: 95–104.

Biersteker, Thomas J. (1997). The "Triumph" of Neoclassical Economics in the Developing World: Policy Convergence and Bases of Governance in the International Economic Order. In *Governance without Government: Order and Change in World Politics*, ed. J. N. Rosenau and E.-O. Czempiel, 102–31. Cambridge: Cambridge University Press.

Blackbourn, David, and Geoff Eley (1984). *The Peculiarities of German History*. New York: Oxford University Press.

Blalock, Hubert M. Jr. (1964). *Causal Inferences in Nonexperimental Research*. Chapel Hill: University of North Carolina Press.

——— (1979). *Social Statistics*. 2d ed. New York: McGraw Hill.

Bloom, Lois (1973). *One Word at a Time*. The Hague: Mouton.

Blumenberg, Hans (1966). *Die Legitimität der Neuzeit*. Frankfurt: Suhrkamp.

——— (1975). *Die Genesis der kopernikanischen Welt*. Frankfurt: Suhrkamp.

Board of Prison Terms, State of California (2001). 6 December. www.bpt.ca.gov.

Bock, Walter J. (1986). Species Concepts, Speciation, and Macroevolution. In *Modern Aspects of Species*, ed. K. Iwatsuki, P. H. Raven, and W. J. Bock, 31–57. Tokyo: University of Tokyo Press.

Böckenförde, Ernst-Wolfgang (1976). Die Bedeutung der Unterscheidung von Staat und Gesellschaft im demokratischen Sozialstaat der Gegenwart. In *Staat, Gesellschaft, Freiheit: Studien zur Staatstheorie und zum Verfassungsrecht*, ed. E.-W. Böckenförde, 185–220. Frankfurt: Suhrkamp.

Bodin, Jean (1576). *The Six Bookes of a Commonweale*. Cambridge, MA: Harvard University Press, 1962.

Bohr, Niehls (1984). Über die Erkenntnisfragen der Quantenphysik. In *Die Deutungen der Quantentheorie*, ed. K. Baumann and R. Sexl, 156–52. Braunschweig: Viehweg.

Boisjoly, R. (1987). Ethical Decisions: Morton Thiokol and the Space Shuttle Challenger Disaster. *American Society of Mechanical Engineers Journal* 87-WA/TS-4:1–13.

Borgida, Eugene, and Richard Nisbett (1977). Differential Impact of Abstract versus Concrete Information in Decisions. *Journal of Applied Social Psychology* 7:258–71.

Bowerman, Melissa (1973). *Early Syntactic Development: A Cross-linguistic Study with Special Reference to Finnish*. Cambridge: Cambridge University Press.

——— (1989). Learning a Semantic System: What Role Do Cognitive Predispositions Play? In *The Teachability of Language*, ed. M. L. Rice and R. L. Schiefelbusch, 133–69. Baltimore: Paul H. Brookes.

——— (1996). The Origins of Children's Spatial Semantic Categories: Cognitive versus Linguistic Determinants. In *Rethinking Linguistic Relativity*, ed. J. J. Gumperz and S. C. Levinson, 145–76. Cambridge: Cambridge University Press.

Bowker, Geoffrey C., and Susan Leigh Star (1999). *Sorting Things Out: Classification and Its Consequences*. Cambridge, MA: MIT Press.

Braybrooke, David, and Charles Lindblom (1963). *A Strategy of Decision*. New York: Free Press.

Bridgman, Percy W. (1927). *The Logic of Modern Physics*. New York: Macmillan.

Brodie, Bernard (1946). *The Absolute Weapon: Atomic Power and World Order*. New York: Harcourt Brace.

——— (1965). *Strategy in the Missile Age*. Princeton: Princeton University Press.

Brugman, Claudia (1983). The Use of Body-Part Terms as Locatives in Chaltcatongo Mixtec. In *Report No. 4: Survey of California and Other Indian Languages,* 235–90. Berkeley: University of California.

Buckley, Walter (1967). *Sociology and Modern Systems Theory*. Englewood Cliffs, NJ: Prentice-Hall.

Bueno de Mesquita, Bruce (1966). The Benefits of a Social Scientific Approach to Studying International Affairs. In *Explaining International Relations since 1945*, ed. N. Woods, 49–76. New York: Oxford University Press.

——— (1985). Toward a Scientific Understanding of International Conflict. *International Studies Quarterly* 29 (June): 121–36.

——— (1992). *War and Reason: Domestic and International Imperatives*. New Haven: Yale University Press.

Bueno de Mesquita, Bruce, and James D. Morrow (1999). Sorting Through the Wealth of Notions. *International Security* 24, no. 2: 56–73.

Bukovansky, Mlada (1997). American Identity and Neutral Rights, from Independence to the War of 1812. *International Organization* 51, no. 2: 209–44.

Bull, Hedley (1966). International Theory: The Case for a Classical Approach. *World Politics* 18, no. 3: 361–77.

——— (1977). *The Anarchical Society: A Study of Order in World Politics*. New York: Columbia University Press.

Bush, George, and Brent Scowcroft (1988). *A World Transformed*. New York: Knopf.

Campbell, Donald T. (1975). "Degrees of Freedom" and the Case Study. *Comparative Political Studies* 8, no. 2: 178–93.

——— (1979). Degrees of Freedom and the Case Study. In *Qualitative and Quantitative Methods in Evaluations Research,* ed. T. D. Cook and C. S. Reichardt, 49–67. Beverly Hills, CA: Sage.

Campbell, James S. (1963–64). The Cuban Crisis and the UN Charter: An Analysis of the United States Position. *Stanford Law Review* 16, no. 1/4: 160–73.

Caporaso, James A. (1995). Research Design, Falsification, and the Qualitative-Quantitative Divide, *American Political Science Review* 89, no. 2: 457–60.

Carr, Edward H. (1939). *The Twenty-Years' Crisis, 1919–1939: An Introduction to the Study of International Relations*. London: Macmillan.

Cederman, Lars-Erik (1996). Rerunning History: Counterfactual Simulation in World Politics. In *Counterfactual Thought Experiments in World Politics: Logical, Methodological, and Psychological Perspectives,* ed. P. E. Tetlock and A. Belkin, 247–67. Princeton: Princeton University Press.

Chalmers, Alan F. (1982). *What Is This Thing Called Science?* Indianapolis: Hackett.

Chalmers, Douglas (forthcoming). *Integrating Theories: Dealing with Diversity of Theoretical Forms in Political Science*.

Chassan, Jacob B. (1960). Statistical Inference and the Single Case in Clinical Design. *Psychiatry: Journal for the Study of Interpersonal Processes* 23:173–84.

——— (1961). Stochastic Models of the Single Case as the Basis of Clinical Research Design. *Behavioral Science* 6, no. 1: 42–50.

Chayes, Abram (1974). *The Cuban Missile Crisis: International Crises and the Role of Law.* New York: Oxford University Press.

Chayes, Abram, and Antonia Handler Chayes (1995). *The New Sovereignty: Compliance with International Regulatory Agreements.* Cambridge, MA: Harvard University Press.

Checkel, Jeffrey T. (1999). Norms, Institutions, and National Identity in Contemporary Europe. *International Studies Quarterly* 43, no. 1: 83–114.

Chilcote, Ronald H. (1981). *Theories of Comparative Politics: The Search for a Paradigm.* Boulder, CO: Westview Press.

Choi, S., and Melissa Bowerman (1991). Learning to Express Motion Events in English and Korean: The Influence of Language-Specific Lexicalization Patterns. *Cognition* 41:83–121.

Clark, Eve V. (1973). Nonlinguistic Strategies and the Acquisition of Word Meanings. *Cognition* 2:161–82.

Clark, Herbert H. (1973). Space, Time, Semantics, and the Child. In *Cognitive Development and the Acquisition of Language,* ed. T. E. Moore, 27–63. New York: Academic Press.

Clark, Herbert H., and Eve V. Clark (1977). *Psychology and Language: An Introduction to Psycholinguists.* New York: Harcourt Brace Jovanovich.

Clark, Ronald W. (1971). *Einstein: The Life and Times.* New York: World Publishing.

Clinton, William J. (1994). Transcript of Clinton's Address. *New York Times.* 26 January, A17.

Cohn, Elizabeth (1999). U.S. Democratization Assistance. *Foreign Policy in Focus* 4, no. 20: 1–4.

Colles, Dorothy H. (1985). *An Appendix to The Tettigoniinae.* Vol. 1. Australia: Commonwealth Scientific and Industrial Research Organization.

Collier, David (1991). The Comparative Method: Two Decades of Change. In *Comparative Political Dynamics: Global Research Perspectives,* ed. D. A. Rustow and K. Paul, 7–31. New York: Harper Collins.

——— (1993). The Comparative Method. In *Political Science: The State of the Discipline,* ed. A. W. Finifter, 105–19. Washington, DC: American Political Science Association.

Collier, David, and Steven Levitsky (1997). Democracy with Adjectives: Conceptual Innovation in Comparative Research. *World Politics* 49 (April): 430–51.

Collier, David, and James E. Mahon, Jr. (1993). Conceptual "Stretching" Revisited: Adapting Categories in Comparative Analysis. *American Political Science Review* 87 (December): 845–55.

Converse, Philip (1964). The Nature of Mass Belief Systems. In *Ideology and Discontent,* ed. D. Apter, 202–61. New York: Free Press.

Cook, Thomas D., and Donald T. Campbell (1979). *Quasi Experimentation: Design and Analysis Issues for Field Settings.* Chicago: Rand McNally.

Coombs, Clyde H. (1967). *A Theory of Data.* New York: John Wiley and Sons.

Cortell, Andrew P., and James W. Davis Jr. (1996). How Do International Institutions Matter? The Domestic Impact of International Rules and Norms. *International Studies Quarterly* 40, no. 4: 451–78.

——— (2000). Understanding the Domestic Impact of International Norms: A Research Agenda. *International Studies Review* 2, no. 1: 65–87.

Cox, Robert H. (2001). The Social Construction of an Imperative: Why Welfare Reform Happened in Denmark and the Netherlands but not in Germany. *World Politics* 53, no. 3: 463–98.

Cox, Robert W. (1981). Social Forces, States, and World Orders: Beyond International Relations Theory. *Millennium: Journal of International Studies* 10, no. 2: 126–155.

———— (1986). Social Forces, States, and World Orders: Beyond International Relations Theory. In *Neorealism and Its Critics,* ed. R. O. Keohane, 205–54. New York: Columbia University Press.

Cracraft, Joel (1979). Phylogenetic Analysis, Evolutionary Analysis, and Paleontology. In *Phylogenetic Analysis and Paleontology: Proceedings of a Symposium Entitled "Phylogenetic Models," Convened at the North American Paleontological Convention II, Lawrence, Kansas, August 8, 1977,* ed. J. Cracraft and N. Eldredge, 7–39. New York: Columbia University Press.

———— (1987). Species Concepts and the Ontology of Evolution. *Biology and Philosophy* 2:329–46.

———— (1989). Species of Entities of Biological Theory. In *What the Philosophy of Biology Is: Essays Dedicated to David Hull,* ed. M. Ruse, 31–52. Dordrecht, Holland: Kluwer.

Cronbach, Lee (1975). Beyond the Two Disciplines of Scientific Psychology. *American Psychologist* 30, no. 2: 116–27.

Dahl, Robert A. (1957). The Concept of Power. *Behavioral Science* 2 (July): 201–15.

———— (1963). *Modern Political Analysis.* Englewood Cliffs, NJ: Prentice-Hall.

———— (1966). *Political Oppositions in Western Democracies.* New Haven: Yale University Press.

———— (1968). Power. In *International Encyclopedia of the Social Sciences,* ed. D. L. Sills, 404–15. New York: Free Press.

———— (1971). *Polyarchy: Participation and Opposition.* New Haven: Yale University Press.

Dahrendorff, Ralph (1969). *Society and Democracy in Germany.* Garden City, NY: Doubleday.

Damasio, Antonio (1994). *Descartes' Error: Emotion, Reason, and the Human Brain.* New York: Putnam.

D'Andrade, Roy (1986). Three Scientific World Views and the Covering Law Model. In *Metatheory in Social Science,* ed. D. W. Fiske and R. A. Schweder, 19–41. Chicago: University of Chicago Press.

Darwin, Charles (1859). *On the Origin of Species by Means of Natural Selection.* Chicago: Encyclopedia Britannica, 1955.

Davidson, Donald (1980). Actions, Reasons, and Cases. In *Essays on Actions and Events,* ed. D. Davidson, 3–19. Oxford: Oxford University Press.

Davis, James F. (1991). *Who Is Black? One Nation's Definition.* University Park: Pennsylvania State University Press.

Davis, James W., Jr. (1995). The Forgotten Variable: The Role of Promises in Deterrence. Ph.D. dissertation, Columbia University, New York.

———— (2000). *Threats and Promises: The Pursuit of International Influence.* Baltimore: Johns Hopkins University Press.

Debreu, Gerard (1991). The Mathematization of Economic Theory. *American Economic Review* 81, no. 1: 1–7.

de Bruyn, Sander M., and Johannes B. Opschoor (1997). Developments in the Throughput-Income Relationship: Theoretical and Empirical Observations. *Ecological Economics* 20, no. 3: 255–68.

Declaration on Principles of International Law Concerning Friendly Relations and Cooperation Among States in Accordance with the Charter of the United Nations, United Nations General Assembly Resolution 2625. XXXV 1970.

Der Derian, James, and Michael J. Shapiro, eds. (1989). *International/Intertextual Relations: Postmodern Readings of World Politics*. Toronto: Lexington Books.

Desch, Michael C. (1998). Culture Clash: Assessing the Importance of Ideas in Security Studies. *International Security* 23, no. 1: 141–70.

Dessler, David (1991). Beyond Correlations: Toward a Causal Theory of War. *International Studies Quarterly* 35, no. 3: 337–55.

Devine, Donald (1972). *The Political Culture of the United States*. Boston: Little, Brown.

DeWitt, Bryce S. (1970). Quantum Mechanics and Reality. *Physics Today* 23, no. 9: 30–35.

Diamond, Larry, Juan J. Linz, and Seymour Martin Lipset (1995). *Politics in Developing Countries: Comparing Experiences with Democracy*. Boulder, CO: Lynne Rienner.

Diesing, Paul (1971). *Patterns of Discovery in the Social Sciences*. New York: Aldine.

——— (1991). *How Does Social Science Work? Reflections on Practice*. Pittsburgh: University of Pittsburgh Press.

Dixon, William J. (1994). Democracy and the Peaceful Settlement of International Conflict. *American Political Science Review* 88, no. 1: 14–32.

Donald, Merlin (1991). *Origins of the Modern Mind: Three Stages in the Evolution of Culture and Cognition*. Cambridge, MA: Harvard University Press.

Doorenspleet, Renske (2000). Reassessing the Three Waves of Democracy. *World Politics* 52, no. 3: 384–406.

Dowling, Noel T., Edwin W. Patterson, and Richard R. B. Powell (1952). *Materials for Legal Method*. 2d ed. Brooklyn: Foundation Press.

Doyle, Michael (1983). Kant, Liberal Legacies, and Foreign Affairs, Part I. *Philosophy and Public Affairs* 12, no. 3: 205–35.

——— (1986). Liberalism and World Politics. *American Political Science Review* 80, no. 4: 1151–69.

——— (1994). Liberalism and the Peaceful Settlement of International Conflict. *American Political Science Review* 88, no. 1: 14–32.

——— (1997). *Ways of War and Peace: Realism, Liberalism, and Socialism*. New York: W. W. Norton.

Duffield, John S., Theo Farrell, Richard Price, and Michael C. Desch (1999). Correspondence. Isms and Schisms: Culturalism versus Realism in Security Studies. *International Security* 24, no. 1: 156–80.

Durkheim, Emile (1897). *The Rules of Sociological Method*. Glencoe, IL: Free Press, 1938.

Easton, David (1953). *The Political System*. New York: Knopf.

——— (1965a). *A Framework for Political Analysis*. Englewood Cliffs, NJ: Prentice-Hall.

——— (1965b). *A Systems Analysis of Political Life*. New York: Wiley.

Eckstein, Harry (1975). Case Study and Theory in Political Science. In *Handbook of Political Science*. Vol. 7, *Stategies of Inquiry*, ed. F. Greenstein and N. W. Polsby, 79–137. Reading, MA: Addison-Wesley.

Eimas, Peter D. (1975). Speech Perception in Early Infancy. In *Infant Perception: From Sensation to Cognition*, ed. L. B. Cohen and P. Salapatek, 193–231. New York: Academic Press.

Ekins, P. (1997). The Kuznets Curve for the Environment and Economic Growth: Examining the Evidence. *Environmental Planning* 29.

Ekman, Paul, and Richard Davidson (1994). *The Nature of Emotion: Fundamental Questions*. New York: Oxford University Press.

Eldredge, Niles (1985). *Unfinished Synthesis.* Oxford: Oxford University Press.

Elster, Jon (1989). *Nuts and Bolts for the Social Sciences.* Cambridge: Cambridge University Press.

Emmerson, Donald (1994). Region and Recalcitrance: Questioning Democracy in Southeast Asia. Paper read at the the World Congress of the International Political Science Association, at Berlin.

Epstein, Joshua, and Robert Axtell (1996). *Growing Artificial Societies: Social Science from the Bottom Up.* Washington, DC: Brookings Institution.

Evera, Steven van (1997). *Guide to Methods for Students of Political Science.* Ithaca, NY: Cornell University Press.

Fagan, Richard (1969). *The Transformation of Political Culture in Cuba.* Stanford: Stanford University Press.

Farber, Henry, and Joanne Gowa (1995). "Polities and Peace." *International Security* 20, no. 2, 123–46.

Fauci, Anthony S., Eugene Braunwald, Kurt J. Isselbacher, Jean W. Wilson, Joseph B. Martin, Dennis L. Kasper, Stephen L. Hauser, and Dan L. Longo, eds. (1998). *Harrison's Principles of Internal Medicine.* 14th ed. New York: McGraw Hill.

Fearon, James D. (1991). Counterfactuals and Hypothesis Testing in Political Science. *World Politics* 43, no. 2: 169–95.

——— (1994a). Domestic Political Audiences and the Escalation of International Disputes. *American Political Science Review* 88, no. 3: 577–92.

——— (1994b). Signaling versus the Balance of Power and Interests. *Journal of Conflict Resolution* 38 (June): 236–69.

——— (1996). Causes and Counterfactuals in Social Science: Exploring an Analogy Between Cellular Automata and Historical Processes. In *Counterfactual Thought Experiments in World Politics,* ed. P. E. Tetlock and A. Belkin, 39–67. Princeton: Princeton University Press.

Feaver, Peter D. (2000). Correspondence. *International Security* 25, no. 1: 165–69.

Feyerabend, Paul K. (1970). Philosophy of Science: A Subject with a Great Past. In *Historical and Philosophical Perspectives of Science, Minnesota Studies in Philosophy of Science,* Vol. 5, ed. R. H. Stuewer, 172–88. Minneapolis: University of Minnesota Press.

——— (1975). *Against Method.* London: Verso.

Finnemore, Martha (1993). International Institutions as Teachers of Norms: The United Nations Educational, Scientific, and Cultural Organization and Science Policy. *International Organization* 47, no. 4: 565–98.

——— (1996). *National Interests in International Society.* Ithaca, NY: Cornell University Press.

Finnemore, Martha, and Kathryn Sikkink (1998). International Norm Dynamics and Political Change. *International Organization* 52, no. 4: 887–917.

Fiorina, Morris, and Charles R. Plott (1978). Committee Decisions under Majority Rule. *American Political Science Review* 72, no. 2: 575–98.

Fischer, Markus (Spring 1992). Feudal Europe, 800–1300: Communal Discourse and Conflictual Practices. *International Organization* 46, no. 2: 427–66.

Fischoff, Baruch (1975). Hindsight ≠ Foresight: The Effect of Outcome Knowledge on Judgement under Uncertainty. *Journal of Experimental Psychology: Human Perception and Performance* 1, no. 3: 288–99.

——— (1982). For Those Condemned to Study the Past. In *Judgement under Uncertainty:*

Heuristics and Biases, ed. D. Kahneman, P. Slovic, and A. Tversky, 422–44. Cambridge: Cambridge University Press.

Fiske, Donald W. (1986). Specificity of Method and Knowledge. In *Metatheory in Social Science,* ed. D. W. Fiske and R. A. Schweder, 61–82. Chicago: University of Chicago Press.

Fletcher, Roger (1984). Recent Developments in German Historiography. *German Studies Review* 7, no. 3: 451–80.

Foucault, Michael (1973). *The Birth of the Clinic: An Archeology of Medical Perception.* New York: Pantheon.

―――― (1979). *Discipline and Punish: The Birth of the Prison.* New York: Vintage.

―――― (1980). *The History of Sexuality.* New York: Vintage.

Fraisse, Paul, and Jean Piaget, eds. (1968). *Experimental Psychology; Its Scope and Method.* New York: Basic Books.

Fukuda, S., Y. Fukuda et al. (2001a). Constraints on Neutrino Oscillations Using 1258 Days of Super-Kamiokande Solar Neutrino Data. *Physical Review Letters* 86, no. 25: 5656–60.

―――― et al. (2001b). Solar B-8 and Hep Neutrino Measurements from 1258 Days of Super-Kamiokande Data. *Physical Review Letters* 86, no. 25: 5651–55.

Gaffney, Eugene S. (1979). An Introduction to the Logic of Phylogeny Reconstruction. In *Phylogenetic Analysis and Paleontology,* ed. J. Cracraft and N. Eldredge, 79–111. New York: Columbia University Press.

Gall, Lothar (1980). *Bismarck, der weiße Revolutionär.* Frankfurt: Propyläen.

Gallie, W. B. (1956). Essentially Contested Concepts. *Proceedings of the Aristotelian Society* 56:167–98.

Garnham, David (1986). War Proneness. *Journal of Peace Research* 23, no. 3: 279–89.

Geddes, Barbara (1990). How the Cases You Choose Affect the Answers You Get: Selection Bias in Comparative Politics. In *Political Analysis,* ed. J. A. Stimson, 131–50. Ann Arbor: University of Michigan Press.

Geert, Paul van (1985–86). In, On, Under: An Essay on the Modularity of Infant Spatial Competence. *First Language* 6:7–28.

Geertz, Clifford (1973). *The Interpretation of Culture.* New York: Basic Books.

Genschel, Philip, and Thomas Plümper (1996). Wenn Reden Silber und Handeln Gold ist. Kooperation und Kommunikation in der internationalen Bankenregulierung. *Zeitschrift für Internationale Beziehungen* 3, no. 2: 225–53.

George, Alexander L. (1979a). Case Studies and Theory Development: The Method of Structured, Focused Comparison. In *Diplomacy: New Approaches in History, Theory, and Policy,* ed. P. G. Lauren, 43–68. New York: Free Press.

―――― (1979b). The Causal Nexus between Cognitive Beliefs and Decisionmaking Behavior: The "Operational Code" Belief System. In *Psychological Models and International Politics,* ed. L. S. Falkowski, 95–124. Boulder, CO: Westview.

―――― (1997a). Knowledge for Statecraft: The Challenge for Political Science and History. *International Security* 22, no. 1: 44–52.

―――― (1997b). The Role of the Congruence Method for Case Study Research. Paper read at the 38th Annual Convention of the International Studies Association. 18–22 May. Toronto, Canada.

George, Alexander L., and Andrew Bennet (forthcoming). *Case Studies and Theory Development.* Cambridge, MA: MIT Press.

George, Alexander L., and Timothy J. McKeown (1985). Case Studies and Theories of Organizational Decision Making. *Advances in Information Processing in Organizations* 2:21–58.

George, Alexander L., and Richard Smoke (1974). *Deterrence in American Foreign Policy: Theory and Practice.* New York: Columbia University Press.

Ghiselin, Michael T. (1974). A Radical Solution to the Species Problem. *Systematic Zoology* 2:536–44.

——— (1987). Species Concepts, Individuality, and Objectivity. *Biology and Philosophy* 4:127–43.

Gilbert, Nigel, and Rosaria Conte, eds. (1995). *Artificial Societies: The Computer Simulation of Social Life.* London: University College London Press.

Gilpin, Robert (1975). *U.S. Power and the Multinational Corporation.* New York: Basic Books.

——— (1981). *War and Change in World Politics.* Cambridge: Cambridge University Press.

Glaser, Charles L. (1994–95). Realists as Optimists: Cooperation as Self Help. *International Security* 19, no. 3: 50–90.

Gleick, James (1987). *Chaos: Making a New Science.* New York: Viking.

Goguen, Joseph A. (1968–69). The Logic of Inexact Concepts. *Synthese* 19:325–73.

Goldthorpe, John H. (1997). Current Issues in Comparative Macrosociology: A Debate on Methodological Issues. *Comparative Social Research* 16:1–26.

Goodhardt, Arthur L. (1959). The Ratio Decidendi of a Case. *Modern Law Review* 22, no. 2: 117–24.

Goodman, Nelson (1992). Seven Strictures on Similarity. In *How Classification Works: Nelson Goodman among the Social Sciences,* ed. M. Douglas and D. Hull, 13–23. Edinburgh: Edinburgh University Press.

Gould, Stephen Jay (1985). Not Necessarily a Wing. *Natural History* 94, no. 10: 12–25.

——— (1989). *Wonderful Life.* New York: W. W. Norton.

——— (1999). *Rocks of Ages: Science and Religion in the Fullness of Life.* New York: Ballentine.

Gowa, Joanne (1995). Democratic States and International Disputes. *International Organization* 49, no. 3: 511–22.

——— (1999). *Ballots and Bullets: The Elusive Democratic Peace.* Princeton: Princeton University Press.

Graham, George J. (1971). *Methodological Foundations for Political Analysis.* Waltham, MA: Ginn.

Greenough, William T., J. E. Black, and C. S. Wallace (1987). Experience and Brain Development. *Child Development* 58, no. 3: 539–59.

Grieco, Joseph M. (1993). Anarchy and the Limits of Cooperation: A Realist Critique of the Newest Liberal Institutionalism. In *Neorealism and Neoliberalism: The Contemporary Debate,* ed. D. A. Baldwin, 116–42. New York: Columbia University Press.

Gunnell, John G. (1993). *The Descent of Political Theory: The Geneology of an American Vocation.* Chicago: University of Chicago Press.

Gurowitz, Amy (1999). Mobilizing International Norms: Domestic Actors, Immigrants and the Japanese State. *World Politics* 51, no. 3: 413–45.

Gurr, Ted Robert (1990). *Polity II: Political Structures and Regime Change, 1800–1986.* Ann Arbor, MI: Inter-University Consortium for Political and Social Research (ICPSR), Study I9263.

Gusterson, Hugh (1996). Nuclear Weapons Testing: Scientific Experiment as Political Ritual. In *Naked Science: Anthropological Inquiry into Boundaries, Power, and Knowledge,* ed. L. Nader, 131–47. New York: Routledge.

Haas, Ernst B. (1953). The Balance of Power: Prescription, Concept, or Propaganda? *World Politics* 5, no. 4: 422–77.

―――― (1964). *Beyond the Nation State: Functionalism and International Organization.* Stanford: Stanford University Press.

―――― (1966). International Integration: The European Union and the Universal Process. In *International Political Communities: An Anthology,* 93–130. Garden City, NY: Anchor Books.

―――― (1968). *The Uniting of Europe: Political, Social, and Economic Sources, 1950–1957.* Stanford: Stanford University Press.

Haas, Peter M. (1989). Do Regimes Matter? Epistemic Communities and Mediterranean Pollution Control. *International Organization* 43, no. 3: 377–405.

―――― (1992). Introduction: Epistemic Communities and International Policy Coordination. *International Organization* 46, no. 1: 1–35.

Haass, Richard N. (1999). *Intervention: The Use of American Military Force in the Post–Cold War World.* Washington, DC: Carnegie Endowment.

Hacking, Ian (1992). World-Making by Kind-Making: Child Abuse for Example. In *How Classification Works: Nelson Goodman Among the Social Sciences,* ed. M. Douglas and D. Hull, 180–238. Edinburgh: Edinburgh University Press.

Haftendorn, Helga (1993). Das Sicherheitspuzzle: Die Suche nach einem tragfähigen Konzept Internationaler Sicherheit. In *Regionalisierung der Sicherheitspolitik,* ed. C. Daase, 13–38. Baden-Baden: Nomos.

Haftendorn, Helga, Robert O. Keohane, and Celeste A. Wallender, eds. (1999). *Imperfect Unions: Security Institutions over Time and Space.* Oxford: Oxford University Press.

Hall, Peter A., ed. (1989). *The Political Power of Economic Ideas: Keynesianism across Nations.* Princeton: Princeton University Press.

Hall, Rodney Bruce, and Friedrich V. Kratochwil (1993). Medieval Tales: Neorealist "Science" and the Abuse of History. *International Organization* 47, no. 3: 479–91.

Handler Chayes, Antonia, and Abram Chayes (1990). From Law Enforcement to Dispute Resolution: A New Approach to Arms Control Verification and Compliance. *International Security* 14, no. 4: 147–64.

Hanson, Norwood Russell (1958). *Patterns of Discovery: An Inquiry into the Conceptual Foundations of Science.* Cambridge: Cambridge University Press.

Harding, Sandra, Elvira Scheich, and Maria Osietzki (1991). "Multiple Subject": Feminist Perspectives on Postmodernism, Epistemology, and Science. Discussion paper. Hamburg: Hamburger Institut für Sozialforschung.

Harper, Douglas (1992). Small N's and Community Case Studies. In *What Is a Case? Exploring the Foundations of Social Inquiry,* ed. C. C. Ragin and H. S. Becker, 139–58. Cambridge: Cambridge University Press.

Harsanyi, John C. (1962). Measurement of Social Power, Opportunity Costs, and the Theory of Two-person Bargaining Games. *Behavioral Science* 7 (January): 67–80.

Hastie, Reid, and Bernadette Park (1997). The Relationship between Memory and Judgement Depends on Whether the Judgement Task Is Memory-Based or On-Line. In *Research on Judgement and Decision Making: Currents, Connections, and Controversies,* ed. W. M. Goldstein and R. M. Hogarth, 431–53. Cambridge: Cambridge University Press.

Hawthorn, Geoffrey (1991). *Plausible Worlds: Possibility and Understanding in Social History and the Social Sciences.* New York: Columbia University Press.

Hegel, G. W. F. (1807). *The Phenomenology of Mind.* Translated by J. B. Baille. New York: Harper, 1967.

Heine, B. (1989). Adpositions in African Languages. *Linguistique Africaine* 2:77–127.

Heinze, Rolf G., Josef Schmid, and Christoph Strünck (1999). *Vom Wohlfahrtsstaat zum Wettbewerbsstaat: Arbeitsmarkt-und Sozialpolitik in den 90er Jahren.* Opladen, Germany: Leske and Budrich.

Hellmann, Gunther, and Reinhard Wolf (1993). Neorealism, Neoliberal Institutionalism and the Future of NATO. *Security Studies* 13, no. 1: 3–43.

Helmholtz, Hermann von (1867). *Handbuch der physiologischen Optik.* Vol. 3. Leipzig: Voss.

Hempel, Carl G. (1962). Explanation in Science and History. In *Frontiers of Science and Philosophy,* ed. R. G. Colodny, 1–33. Pittsburgh: University of Pittsburgh Press.

——— (1965). *Aspects of Scientific Explanation and Other Essays in the Philosophy of Science.* New York: Free Press.

——— (1974). Reasons and Covering Laws in Historical Explanation. In *The Philosophy of History,* ed. P. Gardiner, 90–91. New York: Oxford University Press.

Henkin, Louis (1979). *How Nations Behave: Law and Foreign Policy.* 2d ed. New York: Columbia University Press.

Hennig, Willi (1950). *Grundzüge einer Theorie der Phylogenetischen Systematik.* Berlin: Deutscher Zentralverlag.

Herrera, Geoffrey L. (2002). The Politics of Bandwidth: International Political Implications of a Global Digital Information Infrastructure. *Review of International Studies* 28, no. 1: 93–122.

Herrmann, Richard (1986). The Power of Perceptions in Foreign Policy Decision-Making: Do Views of the Soviet Union Determine the Policy Choices of American Leaders. *American Journal of Political Science* 30 (November): 841–75.

Hirsch, Paul, Stuart Michaels, and Ray Friedman (1987). "'Dirty Hands' versus 'Clean Models': Is Sociology in Danger of Being Seduced by Economics?" *Theory and Society* 16 (May): 317–36

Hirsh-Pastek, Kathy, D. Kemler-Nelson, P. Jusczyk, B. Cassidy, and L. Kennedy (1987). Clauses Are Perceptual Units for Young Infants. *Cognition* 26:269–86.

Hobbes, Thomas (1651). *Leviathan.* New York: Macmillan, 1962.

Hollis, Martin, and Steve Smith (1990). *Explaining and Understanding International Relations.* Oxford: Clarendon Press.

Holsti, Kal J. (1987). *The Dividing Discipline: Hegemony and Diversity in International Theory.* Boston: Allen and Unwin.

Hopf, Ted (1994). *Peripheral Visions: Deterrence Theory and Soviet Foreign Policy in the Third World, 1965–1990.* Ann Arbor: University of Michigan Press.

Hull, David (1976). Are Species Really Individuals? *Systematic Zoology* 25:174–91.

——— (1978). A Matter of Individuality. *Philosophy of Science* 48:335–60.

——— (1988). *Science as a Process: An Evolutionary Account of the Social and Conceptual Development of Science.* Chicago: University of Chicago Press.

Humboldt, Wilhelm von (1836). *On Language: The Diversity of Human Language-Structure and Its Influence on the Mental Development of Mankind.* Translated by P. Heath. Cambridge: Cambridge University Press, 1988.

Hume, David (1740). *Treatise of Human Nature.* Edited by D. F. Norton. Oxford: Oxford University Press, 2000.

Hunt, Earl, Janet Marin, and Philip J. Stone (1966). *Experiments in Induction.* New York: Academic Press.

Huntington, Samuel P. (1989). The Modest Meaning of Democracy. In *Democracy in the Americas: Stopping the Pendulum,* ed. R. A. Pastor, 11–28. New York: Holmes and Meier.

——— (1991). *The Third Wave: Democratization in the Late Twentieth Century.* Norman: Oklahoma University Press.

——— (1996). *The Clash of Civilizations and the Remaking of the World Order.* New York: Simon and Schuster.

Huth, Paul, and Bruce M. Russett (1984). What Makes Deterrence Work? Cases from 1900 to 1980. *World Politics* 36, no. 4: 496–526.

——— (1988). Deterrence Failure and Crisis Escalation. *International Studies Quarterly* 32 (March): 29–46.

——— (1990). Testing Deterrence Theory: Rigor Makes a Difference. *World Politics* 42, no. 4: 466–501.

Ikenberry, John G. (1993). Creating Yesterday's New World Order: Keynesian "New Thinking" and the Anglo-American Postwar Settlement. In *Ideas and Foreign Policy: Beliefs, Institutions, and Political Change,* ed. J. Goldstein and R. O. Keohane, 57–86. Ithaca, NY: Cornell University Press.

Isaak, Alan (1969). *The Scope and Method of Political Science.* Homewood, IL: Dorsey.

Is It Still a Harley? *Thunder Press* 5, no. 4: 1–69.

Jackson, John E. (1996). Political Methodology: An Overview. In *New Handbook of Political Science,* ed. R. E. Goodin and H.-D. Klingemann, 717–48. Oxford: Oxford University Press.

Jackson, Robert H. (1990). *Quasi-States: Sovereignty, International Relations, and the Third World.* Cambridge: Cambridge University Press.

Jervis, Robert (1976). *Perception and Misperception in International Politics.* Princeton: Princeton University Press.

——— (1989). *The Logic of Images in International Relations.* New York: Columbia University Press.

——— (1997). *Systems Effects: Complexity in Political and Social Life.* Princeton: Princeton University Press.

——— (2001). Signaling and Perception: Drawing Inferences and Projecting Images. In *Political Psychology,* ed. K. Monroe, 293–312. Hillsdale, NJ: Lawrence Erlbaum.

Joffe, Joseph (2001). Who's Afraid of Mr. Big? *The National Interest* 64 (Summer): 43–52.

Jordan, Mary (1991). Jury Finds Smith Not Guilty of Rape. *Washington Post.* 12 December, A01.

Juszyk, P. (1981). Infant Speech Perception: A Critical Appraisal. In *Perspectives of the Study of Speech,* ed. P. D. Eimas and J. L. Miller, 113–64. Hillsdale, NJ: Lawrence Erlbaum.

Kahn, Herman (1960). *On Thermonuclear War.* Princeton: Princeton University Press.

——— (1962). *Thinking about the Unthinkable.* New York: Horizon.

Kahneman, Daniel (1994). New Challenges to the Rationality Assumption. *Journal of Institutional and Theoretical Economics* 150, no. 1: 18–36.

Kahneman, Daniel, and Amos Tversky (1972). Subjective Probability: A Judgement of Representativeness. *Cognitive Psychology* 3:430–54.

Kahneman, Daniel, and Carol A. Varey (1997). Propensities and Counterfactuals: The

Loser Almost Won. In *Research on Judgement and Decision Making: Currents, Connections, and Controversies,* ed. W. M. Goldstein and R. M. Hogarth, 321–44. Cambridge: Cambridge University Press.

Kant, Immanuel (1795). *Perpetual Peace.* Indianapolis: Liberal Arts Press, 1957.

Kaplan, Morris (1997). *Sexual Justice: Democratic Citizenship and the Politics of Desire.* New York: Routledge.

Kaplan, Morton A. (1964). *Systems and Processes in International Politics.* New York: Wiley.

——— (1966). The New Great Debate: Traditionalism vs. Science in International Relations. *World Politics* 19, no. 1: 1–20.

Kaufmann, William W. (1954). *The Requirements of Deterrence.* Princeton: Center for International Studies.

Keet, I. P. (1992). Orogenital Sex and the Transmission of HIV. *AIDS* 6 (February): 223–26.

Keller, Charles M., and Janet Dixon Keller (1996). Imagining in Iron, or Thought Is Not Inner Speech. In *Rethinking Linguistic Relativity,* ed. J. J. Gumperz and S. C. Levinson, 115–29. Cambridge: Cambridge University Press.

Kellert, Stephen H. (1993). *In the Wake of Chaos: Unpredictable Order in Dynamical Systems.* Chicago: University of Chicago Press.

Kelley, Harold (1967). Attribution Theory in Social Psychology. In *Nebraska Symposium on Motivation,* ed. D. Levine, 192–240. Lincoln: University of Nebraska Press.

——— (1971). *Attribution in Social Interaction.* Morristown, NJ: General Learning Press.

Kempton, Willett (1981). *The Folk Classification of Ceramics: A Study of Cognitive Prototypes.* New York: Academic Press.

Kennedy, Robert (1971). *Thirteen Days: A Memoir of the Cuban Missile Crisis.* New York: W. W. Norton.

Keohane, Robert O. (1983). The Demand for International Regimes. In *International Regimes,* ed. S. D. Krasner, 141–71. Ithaca, NY: Cornell University Press.

——— (1986). Theory of World Politics: Structural Realism and Beyond. In *Neorealism and Its Critics,* ed. R. O. Keohane, 182–90. New York: Columbia University Press.

——— (1993). Institutional Theory and the Realist Challenge after the Cold War. In *Neorealism and Neoliberalism: The Contemporary Debate,* ed. D. A. Baldwin, 284–91. New York: Columbia University Press.

Keohane, Robert O., and Lisa L. Martin (1995). The Promise of Institutionalist Theory. *International Security* 20, no. 1: 39–51.

Keupp, Heiner (1972). *Psychische Störungen als abweichendes Verhalten: Zur Soziogenese psychischer Störungen.* Munich: Urban and Schwarzenberg.

——— (1993). *Zugänge zum Subjekt: Perspektiven einer reflexiven Sozialpsychologie.* Frankfurt: Suhrkamp.

Keupp, Heiner, and Manfred Zaumseil (1978). *Die gesellschaftliche Organisierung des psychischen Leidens: Zum Arbeitsfeld klinischer Psychologen.* Frankfurt: Suhrkamp.

Khong, Yuen Foong (1992). *Analogies at War.* Princeton: Princeton University Press.

King, Gary, Robert O. Keohane, and Sidney Verba (1994). *Designing Social Inquiry: Scientific Inference in Qualitative Research.* Princeton: Princeton University Press.

——— (1995). The Importance of Research Design in Political Science. *American Political Science Review* 89, no. 2: 475–81.

Kissinger, Henry A. (1968). The White Revolutionary: Reflections on Bismarck. *Daedalus* 97, no. 2: 888–924.

Kitcher, Philip (1982). Genes. *British Journal for the Philosophy of Science* 33:337–59.
—— (1984). Species. *Philosophy of Science* 51:308–33.
—— (1989). Some Puzzles about Species. In *What the Philosophy of Biology Is: Essays Dedicated to David Hull,* ed. M. Ruse, 183–208. Dordrecht, Holland: Kluwer.
—— (2001). *Science, Truth, and Democracy.* Oxford: Oxford University Press.
Klein, Bradley (1994). *Strategic Studies and World Order.* Cambridge: Cambridge University Press.
Klotz, Audie (1995). Norms Reconstituting Interests: Global Racial Equality and U.S. Sanctions against South Africa. *International Organization* 49, no. 3: 451–78.
Knoke, David (1990). *Political Networks: The Structural Perspective.* Cambridge: Cambridge University Press.
Korb, Lawrence J. (1995). The Readiness Gap. *New York Times Magazine.* 26 February, 40–41.
Körner, Stephan (1966). *Experience and Theory.* London: Routledge and Kegan Paul.
Kowert, Paul (1988). Agent versus Structure in the Construction of National Identity. In *International Relations in a Constructed World,* ed. V. Kubálková, N. G. Onuf, and P. Kowert, 101–22. Armonk, NY: M. E. Sharpe.
Krasner, Stephen D. (1983). Structural Causes and Regime Consequences: Regimes as Intervening Variables. In *International Regimes,* ed. S. D. Krasner, 1–21. Ithaca, NY: Cornell University Press.
—— (1985). Toward Understanding in International Relations. *International Studies Quarterly* 29, no. 2: 137–44.
—— (1988). Sovereignty: An Institutional Perspective. *Comparative Political Studies* 21, no. 1: 66–94.
—— (1989). Sovereignty: An Institutional Perspective. In *The Elusive State: International and Comparative Perspectives,* ed. J. A. Caporaso, 69–96. Newbury Park, CA: Sage.
—— (1993). Global Communications and National Power: Life on the Pareto Frontier. In *Neorealism and Neoliberalism: The Contemporary Debate,* ed. D. A. Baldwin, 234–49. New York: Columbia University Press.
Kratochwil, Friedrich V. (1986). Of Systems, Boundaries, and Territoriality: An Inquiry into the Foundations of the State System. *World Politics* 39, no. 1: 27–52.
—— (1989). *Rules, Norms, and Decisions: On the Conditions of Practical and Legal Reasoning in International Relations and Domestic Affairs.* Cambridge: Cambridge University Press.
Kratochwil, Friedrich V., and John Gerard Ruggie (1986). International Organization: A State of the Art on an Art of the State. *International Organization* 40, no. 4: 753–65.
—— (1994). Changing Relations between State, Market and Society, and the Problem of Knowledge. *Pacific Focus* 9, no. 2: 43–59.
—— (1995). Sovereignty as Dominuim: Is There a Right to International Humanitarian Intervention? In *Beyond Westphalia? State Sovereignty and International Intervention,* ed. G. M. Lyons and M. Mastanduno, 21–42. Baltimore: Johns Hopkins University Press.
—— (2000). Constructing a New Orthodoxy? Wendt's "Social Theory of International Politics" and the Constructivist Challenge. *Millennium: Journal of International Studies* 29, no. 1: 73–101.
Kripke, Saul A. (1972). Naming and Necessity. In *Semantics of Natural Language,* ed. D. Davidson and G. Harmann, 253–355. Dordrecht, Holland: Reidel.

Kruzel, Joseph (1994). More a Chasm than a Gap, but Do Scholars Want to Bridge It? *Mershon International Studies Review* 14 (April):179–81.

Kuchowicz, Bronisław (1976). Neutrinos from the Sun. *Reports on Progress in Physics* 39, pt. 2: 291–344.

Kuhl, Patricia K. (1989). Perceptual Constancy for Speech-Sound Categories in Early Infancy. In *Child Phonology.* Vol. 2, *Perception,* ed. G. H. Yeni-Komshian, J. F. Kavanagh, and C. A. Ferguson, 41–66. New York: Academic Press.

Kuhn, Thomas S. (1957). *The Copernican Revolution: Planetary Astronomy and the Development of Western Thought.* Cambridge, MA: Harvard University Press.

——— (1970). *The Structure of Scientific Revolutions.* Chicago: University of Chicago Press.

——— (1976). Theory-Change as Structure-Change: Comments on the Sneed Formalism. *Erkenntnis* 10:179–99.

Labov, William (1973). The Boundaries of Words and Their Meanings. In *New Ways of Analyzing Variations in English,* ed. C. J. Bailey and R. W. Shuy, 340–73. Washington, DC: Georgetown University Press.

Laitin, David D. (2001). The Political Science Discipline. Paper read at the Annual Convention of the American Political Science Association. 30 August–2 September. San Francisco, California.

Lakatos, Imre (1970). Falsification and the Methodology of Scientific Research Programmes. In *Criticism and the Growth of Knowledge,* ed. I. Lakatos and A. Musgrave, 91–195. Cambridge: Cambridge University Press.

——— (1974). Popper on Demarcation and Induction. In *The Philosophy of Karl Popper,* ed. P. A. Schlipp, 241–73. La Salle, IL: Open Court.

Lake, David A. (1992). Powerful Pacifists: Democratic States and War. *American Political Science Review* 86, no. 1: 24–37.

Lakoff, George (1987). *Women, Fire, and Dangerous Things: What Categories Reveal about the Mind.* Chicago: University of Chicago Press.

Lant, Theresa K., and David B. Montgomery (1987). Learning from Strategic Success and Failure. *Journal of Business Research* 15, no. 6: 503–17.

Lapid, Yosef (1989). The Third Debate: On the Prospects of International Theory in a Post-Positivist Era. *International Studies Quarterly* 33, no. 3: 235–54.

Lapid, Yosef, and Friedrich V. Kratochwil, eds. (1996). *The Return of Culture and Identity in IR Theory.* Boulder, CO: Lynne Rienner.

Laski, Harold J. (1956). *The State in Theory and Practice.* London: Allen and Unwin.

Lasswell, Harold D., and Abraham Kaplan (1950). *Power and Society: A Framework for Political Inquiry.* New Haven: Yale University Press.

Layne, Christopher (1993). The Unipolar Illusion: Why New Great Powers Will Arise. *International Security* 17, no. 4: 5–51.

——— (1994). Kant or Cant: The Myth of the Democratic Peace. *International Security* 19, no. 2: 5–49.

——— (1997). From Preponderance to Offshore Balancing: America's Future Grand Strategy. *International Security* 22, no. 1: 86–124.

Lazarsfeld, Paul L. (1955). Interpretation of Statistical Relations as a Research Operation. In *The Language of Social Research: A Reader in the Methodology of Social Research,* ed. P. L. Lazarsfeld and M. Rosenberg, 115–25. Glencoe, IL: Free Press.

Lebow, Richard Ned (1981). *Between Peace and War.* Baltimore: Johns Hopkins University Press.

———— (1985). Generational Learning and Conflict Management. *International Journal* 40 (Autumn): 555–85.

———— (1994). The Long Peace, the End of the Cold War, and the Failure of Realism. *International Organization* 48, no. 2: 249–77.

Lebow, Richard Ned, and Thomas Risse-Kappen (1995). Introduction: International Relations Theory and the End of the Cold War. In *International Relations Theory and the End of the Cold War,* ed. R. N. Lebow and T. Risse-Kappen, 1–21. New York: Columbia University Press.

Lebow, Richard Ned, and Janice Gross Stein (1990). Deterrence: The Elusive Dependent Variable. *World Politics* 42, no. 3: 336–69.

———— (1994). *We All Lost the Cold War.* Princeton: Princeton University Press.

———— (1996). Back to the Past: Counterfactuals and the Cuban Missile Crisis. In *Counterfactual Thought Experiments in World Politics: Logical, Methodological, and Psychological Perspectives,* ed. P. E. Tetlock and A. Belkin, 119–48. Princeton: Princeton University Press.

Lepgold, Joseph (1998). Is Anyone Listening? International Relations Theory and the Problem of Policy Relevance. *Political Science Quarterly* 113, no. 1: 43–62.

Levinson, Stephen C. (1997). From Outer to Inner Space: Linguistic Categories and Non-linguistic Thinking. In *Language and Conceptualization,* ed. E. Pederson and J. Nuyts, 13–45. Cambridge: Cambridge University Press.

Levy, J. (1993). The Transmission of HIV and Factors Influencing Progression to AIDS. *American Journal of Medicine* 95, no. 1: 86–100.

Levy, Jack S. (1989). Domestic Politics and War. In *The Origin and Prevention of Major Wars,* ed. R. I. Rotberg and T. K. Rabb, 79–100. New York: Cambridge University Press.

———— (1997). Too Important to Leave to the Other: History and Political Science in the Study of International Relations. *International Security* 22, no. 1: 22–33.

Lichtenstein, Sarah, Paul Slovic, Baruch Fischhoff, Mark Layman, and Barbara Combs (1978). Judged Frequency of Lethal Events. *Journal of Experimental Psychology: Human Learning and Memory* 4:551–78.

Lieberson, Stanley (1985). *Making It Count: The Improvement of Social Research and Theory.* Berkeley: University of California Press.

———— (1991). Small-N's and Big Conclusions: An Examination of the Reasoning in Comparative Studies Based on a Small Number of Cases. *Social Forces* 70, no. 2: 307–20.

———— (1992). Einstein, Renoir, and Greeley: Some Thoughts about Evidence in Sociology. *American Sociological Review* 57, no. 1: 1–15.

———— (1998). Causal Analysis and Comparative Research: What Can We Learn from Studies Based on a Small Number of Cases? In *Rational Choice Theory and Large-Scale Data Analysis,* ed. H. P. Blossfeld and G. Prein: 129–45. Boulder, CO: Westview.

Lijphart, Arend (1971). Comparative Politics and the Comparative Method. *American Political Science Review* 65, no. 3: 682–93.

Lindblom, Charles (1959). The Science of Muddling Through. *Public Administration Review* 19 (Spring): 74–88.

———— (1965). *The Intellegence of Democracy.* New York: Free Press.

Linne, Carl von (1735). *Systema Naturae.* Nieuwkoop, Holland: B. de Graaf, 1964.

Linz, Juan J. (1975). Totalitarian and Authoritarian Regimes. In *Handbook of Political Science: Macropolitical Theory,* ed. F. Greenstein and N. W. Polsby, 175–412. Reading, MA: Addison-Wesley.

Linz, Juan J., and Amando de Miguel (1966). Within-Nation Differences and Comparisons: The Eight Spains. In *Comparing Nations: The Use of Quantitative Data in Cross-National Research,* ed. R. L. Merritt and S. Rokkan, 267–319. New Haven: Yale University Press.

Linz, Juan J., and Alfred Stepan (1986). *The Breakdown of Democratic Regimes.* Baltimore: Johns Hopkins University Press.

Little, Daniel (1996). Causal Explanation in the Social Sciences. *Southern Journal of Philosophy* 34 (Supplement S): 31–56.

Liuzzi, Guiseppina, A. Chirianni, M. Clementi, P. Bagnarelli, A. Valenza, P. T. Cataldo, and M. Piazza (1996). Analysis of HIV-1 Load in Blood, Semen and Saliva: Evidence for Different Viral Compartments in a Cross-Sectional and Longitudinal Study. *AIDS* 10 (December): F51–56.

Liverpool, New York and Philadelphia Steamship Co. v. Commissioners of Emigration, 1885.

Lounsbury, Floyd (1964). A Formal Account of the Crow- and Omaha-Type Kinship Terminologies. In *Explorations in Cultural Anthropology,* ed. W. H. Goodenough, 351–94. New York: McGraw Hill.

Luckmann, Thomas (1963). *Das Problem der Religion in der modernen Gesellschaft.* Freiburg im Breisgau: Rombach.

Luhmann, Niklas (1995). *Social Systems.* Stanford: Stanford University Press.

Lukes, Steven (1974). *Power: A Radical View.* New York: Macmillan.

Machlup, Fritz (1963). *Essays on Economic Semantics.* Englewood Cliffs, NJ: Prentice-Hall.

MacIntyre, Alasdair (1978). *Against the Self-Images of the Age: Essays on Ideology and Philosophy.* South Bend, IN: University of Notre Dame Press.

MacKenzie, Donald (1990). *Inventing Accuracy: An Historical Sociology of Nuclear Missile Guidance.* Cambridge, MA: MIT Press.

MacKenzie, Donald, and Barry Barnes (1979). The Biometry-Mendelism Controversy. In *Natural Order: Historical Studies of Scientific Culture,* ed. B. Barnes and S. Shapin, 191–210. Beverly Hills, CA: Sage.

MacLaury, Robert E. (1989). Zapotec Body-Part Locatives: Prototypes and Metaphoric Extensions. *International Journal of American Linguistics* 55:119–54.

——— (1997). *Color Cognition in Mesoamerica: Constructing Categories as Vantages.* Austin: University of Texas Press.

Mahoney, James (1999). Nominal, Ordinal, and Narrative Appraisal in Macrocausal Analysis. *American Journal of Sociology* 4 (January): 1154–96.

——— (2000). Strategies of Causal Inference in Small-N Analysis. *Sociological Methods and Research* 28, no. 4: 387–424.

Malinowski, Bronislaw (1925). *Magic, Science and Religion and Other Essays.* Garden City, NY: Doubleday Anchor, 1948.

M'Alister (or Donoghue) v. Stevenson (1932). House of Lords Privy Council Cases. *Law Reports:* 562–623.

Malthus, Thomas Robert (1827). *Definitions in Political Economy, preceded by An Inquiry into the Rules Which Ought to Guide Political Economists in the Definition and Use of their Terms; with Remarks on the Deviations from these Rules in their Writings.* London: J. Murray.

Mansfield, Edward D. (1988). The Distribution of Wars over Time. *World Politics* 41, no. 1: 21–51.

Mansfield, Edward D., and Jack Snyder (1995). Democratization and the Danger of War. *International Security* 20, no. 1: 5–38.

Maoz, Zeev, and Nasrin Abdulali (1989). Regime Types and International Conflict, 1815–1876. *Journal of Conflict Resolution* 33, no. 1: 3–35.

Maoz, Zeev, and Bruce M. Russett (1993). Normative and Structural Causes of Democratic Peace, 1946–1986. *American Political Science Review* 87, no. 3: 624–38.

March, James G. (1978). Bounded Rationality, Ambiguity, and the Engineering of Choice. *Bell Journal of Economics* 9, no. 2: 587–608.

March, James G., and Herbert Simon (1958). *Organizations.* New York: Wiley.

March, James G., Lee S. Sproull, and Michal Tamuz (1991). Learning from Samples of One or Fewer. *Organization Science* 2, no. 1: 1–13.

Marshall, Monty G., and Keith Jaggers (2000a). *Polity IV Project: Dataset Users Manual.* College Park, MD: Integrated Network for Societal Conflict Research (INSCR) Program.

——— (2000b). *Polity IV Project: Political Regime Characteristics and Transitions, 1800–1999.* College Park, MD: Integrated Network for Societal Conflict Research (INSCR) Program.

Martin, Lisa L. (1992). Interests, Power, and Multilateralism. *International Organization* 46, no. 4: 765–92.

——— (1999). The Contributions of Rational Choice: A Defense of Pluralism. *International Security* 24, no. 2: 74–83.

Marx, Anthony W. (1998). *Making Race and Nation: A Comparison of South Africa, the United States, and Brazil.* Cambridge: Cambridge University Press.

Mastanduno, Michael (1993). Do Relative Gains Matter? America's Response to Japanese Industrial Policy. In *Neorealism and Neoliberalism: The Contemporary Debate,* ed. D. A. Baldwin, 250–68. New York: Columbia University Press.

Mathiot, Madeleine (1962). Noun Classes and Folk Taxonomy in Papago. *American Anthropologist* 64, no. 2: 340–50.

Matthews, John C. III (1986). Current Games and Future Outcomes: When Cumulative Relative Gains Matter. *International Security* 21, no. 1: 112–46.

May, Ernest R. (1973). *Lessons of the Past.* New York: Oxford University Press.

Mayr, Ernst (1942). *Systematics and the Origin of Species.* New York: Columbia University Press.

——— (1963). *Animal Species and Evolution.* Cambridge, MA: Harvard University Press.

——— (1970). *Populations, Species, and Evolution.* Cambridge, MA: Harvard University Press.

McCarthy, John D. (1997). The Globalization of Social Movement Theory. In *Transnational Social Movements and Global Politics: Solidarity Beyond the State,* ed. J. Smith, C. Chatfield, and R. Pagnicco, 243–59. Syracuse: Syracuse University Press.

McClelland, J., D. Rumelhart, and the PDP Research Group, eds. (1986a). *Parallel Distributed Processing,* Vol. 1. Cambridge, MA: MIT Press.

———, eds. (1986b). *Parallel Distributed Processing.* Vol. 2. Cambridge, MA: MIT Press.

McCune-Nicolich, Lorraine (1981). The Cognitive Bases of Relational Words in the Single Word Period. *Journal of Child Language* 8 (February).

McDermott, Michael (1995). Redundant Causation. *British Journal for the Philosophy of Science* 46:523–44.

McKeown, Timothy J. (1999). Case Studies and the Statistical Worldview. *International Organization* 53, no. 4: 161–90.

Mearsheimer, John J. (1990). Back to the Future: Instability in Europe After the Cold War. *International Security* 15, no. 1: 5–56.

——— (1994–95). The False Promise of International Institutions. *International Security* 19, no. 3: 5–49.

Mehler, Jacques, and J. Bertoncini (1979). Infants' Perception of Speech and Other Acoustic Stimuli. In *Psycholinguistics 2: Structures and Processes,* ed. J. Morton and J. C. Marshall, 67–105. Cambridge, MA: MIT Press.

Mehler, Jacques, and Emmanuel Dupoux (1994). *What Infants Know.* Cambridge: Blackwell.

Mercer, Jonathan (1995). *Reputation and International Politics.* Ithaca, NY: Cornell University Press.

Mill, John Stuart (1843). *A System of Logic: Ratiocinative and Inductive.* London: Longmans, 1967.

Miller, Joanne L., and Peter D. Eimas (1983). Studies on the Categorization of Speech by Infants. *Cognition* 13, no. 1: 135–65.

Milner, Helen V. (1988). *Resisting Protectionism: Global Industries and the Politics of International Trade.* Princeton: Princeton University Press.

Mintz, Alex, and Nehmia Geva (1992). Why Don't Democracies Fight Each Other? An Experimental Assessment of the "Political Incentive" Explanation. *Journal of Conflict Resolution* 37, no. 3: 484–503.

Mitchell, William C. (1968). Political Systems. In *International Encyclopedia of the Social Sciences,* ed. D. L. Sills, 473–79. New York: Macmillan and Free Press.

Mitrany, David (1943). *A Working Peace System: An Argument for the Functional Development of International Organization.* London: Royal Institute of International Affairs.

Mivart, George (1871). *On the Genesis of Species.* New York: D. Appleton.

Moe, Terry (1979). On the Scientific Status of Rational Choice Theory. *American Journal of Political Science* 23, no. 1: 215–43.

Morgan, T. Clifton, and Sally Howard Campbell (1991). Domestic Structure, Decisional Constraints and War: So Why Kant Democracies Fight? *Journal of Conflict Resolution* 35, no. 2: 187–211.

Morgenstern, Oskar (1972). Thirteen Critical Points in Contemporary Economic Theory. *Journal of Economic Literature* 10, no. 4: 1163–89.

Morgenthau, Hans (1966). *Politics Among Nations: The Struggle for Power and Peace.* 3d ed. New York: Alfred Knopf.

Morris, William, ed. (1969). *The American Heritage Dictionary of the English Language.* Boston: Houghton Mifflin.

Morrow, James D. (1995). *Game Theory for Political Scientists.* Princeton: Princeton University Press.

Motyl, Alexander J. (1999). *Revolutions, Nations, Empires: Conceptual Limits and Theoretical Possibilities.* New York: Columbia University Press.

Müller, Ferdinand, and Manfred Schmidt (1979). *Empirische Politikwissenschaft.* Stuttgart: Kohlhammer.

Müller, Harald (1993). The Internalization of Principles, Norms, and Rules by Governments: The Case of Security Regimes. In *Regime Theory and International Relations,* ed. V. Rittberger, 361–88. Oxford: Clarendon Press.

——— (1994). Internationale Beziehungen als kommunikatives Handeln. Zur Kritik der utilitaristischen Handlungstheorien. *Zeitschrift für Internationale Beziehungen* 1, no. 1: 15–44.

―――― (1995). Spielen hilft nicht immer. Die Grenzen des Rational-Choice-Ansatzes und der Platz der Theorie des kommunikativen Handelns in der Analyse internationaler Beziehungen. *Zeitschrift für Internationale Beziehungen* 2, no. 2: 371–91.

Nadelmann, Ethan (1990). Global Prohibition Regimes: The Evolution of Norms in International Society. *International Organization* 44, no. 4: 479–526.

Nagel, Ernest, and James R. Newman (1956). Gödel's Proof. In *The World of Mathematics,* ed. J. R. Newman, 1668–95. New York: Simon and Schuster.

―――― (1961). *The Structure of Science.* New York: Harcourt Brace and World.

Nelson, Katherine (1996). *Language in Cognitive Development: Emergence of the Mediated Mind.* Cambridge: Cambridge University Press.

Neufeld, Mark (1995). *The Restructuring of International Relations Theory.* Cambridge: Cambridge University Press.

Newsom, David D. (1995–96). Foreign Policy and Academia. *Foreign Policy* 101 (Winter):52–67.

Nichols, Elizabeth (1986). Skocpol on Revolution: Comparative Analysis vs. Historical Conjuncture. *Comparative Social Research* 9:163–86.

Nipperdey, Thomas (1976). Wehlers "Kaiserreich": Eine kritische Auseinandersetzung. In *Gesellschaft, Kultur, Theorie. Gesammelte Aufsätze zur neueren Geschichte,* ed. T. Nipperdey, 360–89. Göttingen: Vandenhoeck and Ruprecht.

―――― (1986). *Nachdenken über die deutsche Geschichte.* Munich: Beck.

Njolstad, Olav (1990). Learning from History? Case Studies and the Limits to Theory-Building. In *Arms Races: Technological and Political Dynamics,* ed. O. Njolstad and N. P. Gleditsch, 220–46. London: Sage.

North, Douglas C. (1990). *Institutions, Institutional Change and Economic Performance.* Cambridge: Cambridge University Press.

Nuyts, Jan (1990). Linguistic Representation and Conceptual Knowledge Representation. In *Layers and Levels of Representation in Language Theory,* ed. J. Nuyts, A. M. Bolkenstein, and C. Vet, 263–93. Amsterdam: Benjamins.

Nye, Joseph (1987). Nuclear Learning and U.S.-Soviet Security Regimes. *International Organization* 41, no. 3: 371–402.

Ó Tuatzail, Gearóid (1996). *Critical Geopolitics: The Politics of Writing Global Space.* Minneapolis: University of Minnesota Press.

Oden, Gregg C. (1977). Integration of Fuzzy Logical Information. *Journal of Experimental Psychology: Human Perception and Performance* 3, no. 4: 565–75.

O'Donnell, Guillermo, and Philippe C. Schmitter (1986). *Transitions from Authoritarian Rule: Tentative Conclusions about Uncertain Democracies.* Baltimore: Johns Hopkins University Press.

O'Donnell, Guillermo, Philippe C. Schmitter, and Laurence Whitehead, eds. (1986). *Transitions from Authoritarian Rule: Comparative Perspectives.* Baltimore: Johns Hopkins University Press.

Olson, D. R., and E. Bialystok (1983). *Spatial Cognition: The Structure and Development of the Mental Representation of Spatial Relations.* Hillsdale, NJ: Lawrence Erlbaum.

Onuf, Nicholas G. (1989). *World of Our Making: Rules and Rule in Social Theory and International Relations.* Columbia: University of South Carolina Press.

Ordeshook, Peter C. (1989). Introduction. In *Models of Strategic Choice in Politics*, ed. P. C. Ordeshook, 1–3. Ann Arbor: University of Michigan Press.

Oren, Ido (1995). The Subjectivity of the "Democratic" Peace: Changing U.S. Perceptions of Imperial Germany. *International Security* 20, no. 2: 147–84.

——— (2000). Is Culture Independent of National Security? How America's National Security Concerns Shaped "Political Culture" Research. *European Journal of International Relations* 6, no. 4: 543–73.

Ostrow, David G., V. J. DiFranceisco, J. S. Chmiel, D. A. Wagstaff, and J. Wesch (1995). A Case Control Study of Human Immunodeficiency Virus Type 1 Seroconversion and Risk Related Behaviors in the Chicago MACS/CCS Cohort, 1984–1992. *American Journal of Epidemiology* 142, no. 8: 875–83.

Owen, John M. (1994). How Liberalism Produces Democratic Peace. *International Security* 19, no. 2: 87–125.

Palfrey, Thomas L. (1991). *Laboratory Research in Political Economy*. Ann Arbor: University of Michigan Press.

Parsons, Talcott (1963). On the Concept of Political Power. *Proceedings of the American Philosophical Society* 107 (June): 232–62.

——— (1964). Democracy and Social Structure in Pre-Nazi Germany. In *Essays in Sociological Theory*, ed. T. Parsons, 104–23. New York: Free Press.

Payne, Rodger A. (2001). Persuasions, Frames, and Norm Construction. *European Journal of International Relations* 7, no. 1: 37–61.

Pearson, Karl (1892). *The Grammar of Science*. London: J. M. Dent and Sons.

Pederson, Eric, and Jan Nuyts (1997). Overview: On the Relationship between Language and Conceptualization. In *Language and Conceptualization*, ed. E. Pederson and J. Nuyts, 1–2. Cambridge: Cambridge University Press.

Peirce, Charles S. (1955). *Philosophical Writings*. Edited by J. Buchler. New York: Dover.

Pennington, Nancy, and Reid Hastie (1997). Explanation-Based Decision Making: Effects of Memory Structure on Judgement. In *Research on Judgement and Decision Making: Currents, Connections, and Controversies*, ed. W. M. Goldstein and R. M. Hogarth, 454–81. Cambridge: Cambridge University Press.

Pennisi, E. (2001). Taxonomy—Linnaeus's Last Stand? *Science* 291 (23 March): 2304–7.

Perrow, Charles (1984). *Normal Accidents: Living with High-Risk Technologies*. New York: Basic Books.

Peterson, Susan (1996). *Crisis Bargaining and the State: The Domestic Politics of International Conflict*. Ann Arbor: University of Michigan Press.

Phelan, Shane (2000). Queer Liberalism. *American Political Science Review* 94, no. 2: 431–42.

Pierson, Paul (1996). The Path to European Union: An Historical Institutionalist Account. *Comparative Political Studies* 29 (April): 123–64.

——— (2000a). Increasing Returns, Path Dependence, and the Study of Politics. *American Political Science Review* 94, no. 2: 251–67.

——— (2000b). Not Just What, But When: Timing and Sequence in Political Process. *Studies in American Political Development* 14 (Spring): 72–92.

Platt, Jennifer (1992). Cases of Cases . . . of Cases. In *What Is a Case? Exploring the Foundations of Social Inquiry*, ed. C. C. Ragin and H. S. Becker, 21–52. Cambridge: Cambridge University Press.

Popper, Karl R. (1968). *The Logic of Scientific Discovery*. New York: Harper.

———— (1994). *The Myth of the Framework: In Defence of Science and Rationality.* London: Routledge.

Powell, Colin, and Joseph E. Perisco (1995). *My American Journey.* New York: Ballantine.

Powell, Robert (1990). *Nuclear Deterrence Theory: The Search for Credibility.* Cambridge: Cambridge University Press.

———— (1993). Absolute and Relative Gains in International Theory. In *Neorealism and Neoliberalism: The Contemporary Debate,* ed. D. A. Baldwin, 209–33. New York: Columbia University Press.

Price, Richard (1997). *The Chemical Weapons Taboo.* Ithaca, NY: Cornell University Press.

Przeworski, Adam, and Henry Teune (1982). *The Logic of Comparative Social Inquiry.* Malabar, FL: Krieger.

Putnam, Hilary (1975). The Meaning of "Meaning." In *Minnesota Studies in the Philosophy of Science,* ed. K. Gunderson, 131–93. Minneapolis: University of Minnesota Press.

Pye, Lucian W., and Sidney Verba (1966). *Political Culture and Political Development.* Princeton: Princeton University Press.

———— (1991). Political Culture Revisited. *Political Psychology* 12, no. 3: 487–508.

Queiroz, Kevin de, and Jacques Gauthier (1990). Phylogeny as a Central Principle in Taxonomy: Phylogenetic Definitions of Taxon Names. *Systematic Zoology* 39:307–22.

———— (1992). Phylogenetic Taxonomy. *Annual Review of Ecology and Systematics* 23:449–80.

———— (1994). Toward a Phylogenetic System of Biological Nomenclature. *Trends in Ecology and Evolution* 9:27–31.

Quine, Willard V. O. (1961). Two Dogmas of Empiricism. In *From a Logical Point of View,* ed. W. V. O. Quine, 20–46. New York: Harper and Row.

Rabkin, Rhoda (1992–93). The Aylwin Government and "Tutelary" Democracy: A Concept in Search of a Case? *Journal of Interamerican Studies and World Affairs* 34 (Winter): 119–94.

Ragin, Charles C. (1987). *The Comparative Method: Moving Beyond Qualitative and Quantitative Strategies.* Berkeley: University of California Press.

———— (1992). Introduction: Cases of "What Is a Case?" In *What Is a Case? Exploring the Foundations of Social Inquiry,* ed. C. C. Ragin and H. S. Becker, 1–17. Cambridge: Cambridge University Press.

———— (2000). *Fuzzy-Set Social Science.* Chicago: University of Chicago Press.

Rapoport, Anatol (1976). Mathematical Methods in Theories of International Relations: Expectations, Caveats, and Opportunities. In *Praeger Special Studies in International Politics and Government,* ed. D. A. Zinnes and J. V. Gillespie, 10–35. New York: Praeger Publishers.

Rawls, John (1955). Two Concepts of Justice. *Philosophical Review* 64, no. 1: 3–33.

Ray, James Lee (1988). Wars between Democracies: Rare or Nonexistent? *International Interactions* 18, no. 3: 251–76.

Reichenbach, Hans (1949). *The Theory of Probability: An Inquiry into the Logic and Mathematical Foundations of the Calculus of Probability.* Berkeley: University of California Press.

Reisch, G. A. (1991). Chaos, History, and Narrative. *History and Theory* 30, no. 1: 1–20.

Rentz, David C. F. (1985). *The Tettigoniiae.* Australia: Commonwealth Scientific and Industrial Research Organization.

Repp, Bruno H., and Alvin M. Libermann (1987). Phonetic Category Boundaries Are Flexible. In *Categorical Perception: The Groundwork of Cognition,* ed. S. R. Harnard, 89–112. Cambridge: Cambridge University Press.

Richards, Diana (1990). Is Strategic Decision-Making Chaotic? *Behavioral Science* 35, no. 3: 219–32.

Ricoeur, Paul (1979). The Model of the Text: Meaningful Action Considered as a Text. In *Interpretive Social Science: A Reader,* ed. P. Rabinow and W. M. Sullivan, 73–101. Berkeley: University of California Press.

Rieppel, Olivier (1987). Species Are Individuals: A Review and Critique of the Argument. *Evolutionary Biology* 20:283–317.

Riker, William H. (1962). *The Theory of Political Coalitions.* New Haven: Yale University Press.

Riker, William H., and David L. Weimer (1993). The Economic and Political Liberalization of Socialism: The Fundamental Problem of Property Rights. *Social Philosophy and Policy* 10 (Summer): 79–102.

Ringer, Fritz K. (1989). Causal Analysis in Historical Reasoning. *History and Theory* 28, no. 2: 153–72.

Rips, Lance J. (1975). Inductive Judgements about Natural Categories. *Journal of Verbal Learning and Verbal Behavior* 14, no. 6: 665–81.

Risse, Thomas (1994). Ideas Do Not Float Freely: Transnational Coalitions, Domestic Structures and the End of the Cold War. *International Organization* 48, no. 2: 185–214.

———— (1998). The Socialization of International Norms into Domestic Practices: Arguing and Strategic Adaption in the Human Rights Area. Paper read at the conference on "Ideas, Culture, and Political Analysis." 15–16 May. Princeton University, Princeton, New Jersey.

Risse-Kappen, Thomas (1995). Reden ist nicht billig. Zur Debatte um Kommunikation und Rationalität. *Zeitschrift für Internationale Beziehungen* 2, no. 1: 171–84.

Roese, Neal J., and James M. Olson, eds. (1995). *What Might Have Been: The Social Psychology of Counterfactual Thinking.* Mahwah, NJ: Erlbaum.

Rorty, Richard (1980). *Philosophy and the Mirror of Nature.* Princeton: Princeton University Press.

Rosch, Eleanor (1973). Natural Categories. *Cognitive Psychology* 4, no. 3: 328–50.

———— (1975). Cognitive Reference Points. *Cognitive Psychology* 7, no. 4: 532–47.

———— (1983). Prototype Classification and Logical Classification: The Two Systems. In *New Trends in Conceptual Representation: Challenges to Piaget's Theory,* ed. E. K. Scholnick, 73–86. Hillsdale, NJ: Erlbaum.

———— (1988). Coherences and Categorization: A Historical View. In *Essays in Honor of Roger Brown,* ed. F. Kessel, 379–92. Hillsdale, NJ: Erlbaum.

Rosenberg, Alexander (1980). *Sociobiology and the Preemption of Social Science.* Baltimore: Johns Hopkins University Press.

Roskin, Michael (1974). From Pearl Harbor to Vietnam: Shifting Generational Paradigms. *Political Science Quarterly* 89 (Fall): 563–88.

Roth, Alvin E. (1988). Laboratory Experimentation in Economics: A Methodological Overview. *Economics Journal* 98 (December): 974–1031.

Rothmann, Dale S., and Sander M. de Bruyn (1998). Probing into the Environmental Kuznets Curve Hypothesis. *Ecological Economics* 25, no. 2: 143–45.

Rousseau, Jean Jacques (1762). *The Social Contract.* London: Dent, 1961.

Ruble, Thomas (1973). Effects of Actor and Observer Roles on Attribution of Responsibility for Success and Failure. *Journal of Social Psychology* 90 (June): 41–44.

Ruggie, John Gerard (1983). International Regimes, Transactions, and Change: Embedded Liberalism in the Postwar Economic Order. In *International Regimes,* ed. S. D. Krasner, 195–231. Ithaca, NY: Cornell University Press.

——— (1986). Continuity and Transformation in the World Polity: Toward a Neorealist Synthesis. In *Neorealism and Its Critics,* ed. R. O. Keohane, 131–57. New York: Columbia University Press.

——— (1996). *Winning the Peace: America and World Order in the New Era.* New York: Columbia University Press.

——— (1998a). *Constructing the World Polity: Essays on International Institutionalization.* New York: Routledge.

——— (1998b). What Makes the World Hang Together? Neo-utilitarianism and the Social Constructivist Challenge. *International Organization* 52, no. 4: 855–85.

Russett, Bruce M. (1969). Young Science of International Politics. *World Politics* 22, no. 1: 87–94.

——— (1990). *Controlling the Sword: The Democratic Governance of National Security.* Cambridge, MA: Harvard University Press.

——— (1993). *Grasping the Democratic Peace: Principles for a Post–Cold War World.* Princeton: Princeton University Press.

——— (1995). The Democratic Peace: "And Yet It Moves." *International Security* 19, no. 4: 164–75.

Russett, Bruce M., and John R. O'Neal (2001). *Triangulating Peace: Democracy, Interdependence, and International Organization.* New York: W. W. Norton.

Sachs, Jeffrey D. (1989). Strengthening IMF Programs in Highly Indebted Countries. In *The International Monetary Fund in a Multipolar World: Pulling Together,* ed. C. Gwin and R. E. Feinberg, 101–22. New Brunswick, NJ: Transaction Books.

Sagan, Scott D. (1993). *The Limits of Safety: Organizations, Accidents, and Nuclear Weapons.* Princeton: Princeton University Press.

——— (2000). The Commitment Trap: Why the United States Should Not Use Nuclear Threats to Deter Biological and Chemical Weapons Attacks. *International Security* 24, no. 4: 85–115.

Salmon, Wesley C. (1963). *Logic.* Englewood Cliffs, NJ: Prentice Hall.

——— (1984). *Scientific Explanation and the Causal Structure of the World.* Princeton: Princeton University Press.

Sandholtz, Wayne (1992). *High-Tech Europe: The Politics of International Cooperation.* Berkeley, CA: University of California Press.

Sartori, Giovanni (1970). Concept Misinformation in Comparative Politics. *American Political Science Review* 64, no. 4: 1033–53.

——— (1991). Comparing and Miscomparing. *Journal of Theoretical Politics* 3, no. 3: 243–57.

Sarup, Madan (1993). *An Introductionary Guide to Post-Structuralism and Postmodernism.* New York: Harvester Wheatsheaf.

Savolainen, Jukka (1994). The Rationality of Drawing Big Conclusions Based on Small Samples: In Defense of Mill's Methods. *Social Forces* 72, no. 4: 1217–24.

Schelling, Thomas (1960). *The Strategy of Conflict.* Cambridge, MA: Harvard University Press.

——— (1966). *Arms and Influence.* New Haven: Yale University Press.

——— (1978). *Micromotives and Macrobehavior.* New York: W. W. Norton.

Scherer, Klaus R. (1994). Toward a Concept of "Modal Emotions." In *The Nature of Emotion: Fundamental Questions,* ed. P. Ekman and R. Davidson, 25–31. New York: Oxford University Press.

Schimmelfennig, Frank (1997). Rhetorisches Handeln in der internationalen Politik. *Zeitschrift für Internationale Beziehungen* 4, no. 2: 219–54.

Schluchter, Wolfgang (1989). *Rationalism, Religion, and Domination: A Weberian Perspective.* Berkeley: University of California Press.

Schmitt, Carl (1922). *Politische Theorie. Vier Kapitel zur Lehre von der Souveränität.* Munich: Duncker and Humblot, 1934.

——— (1932). *Der Begriff des Politischen.* Berlin: Duncker and Humblot, 1963.

Schneider, David N. (1969). American Kin Terms and Terms for Kinsmen: A Critique of Goodenough's Componential Analysis of Yankee Kinship Terminology. In *Cognitive Anthropology,* ed. S. Tylor, 288–311. New York: Holt, Rinehart and Winston.

Schweller, Randall L. (1992). Domestic Structure and Preventive War: Are Democracies More Pacific? *World Politics* 44, no. 2: 207–13.

——— (1998). *Deadly Imbalances: Tripolarity and Hitler's Strategy of World Conquest.* New York: Columbia University Press.

Sikkink, Kathryn (1993). Human Rights, Principled Issue-Networks, and Sovereignty in Latin America. *International Organization* 47, no. 3: 411–41.

Simmons, Beth A. (2000). International Law and State Behavior: Commitment and Compliance in International Monetary Affairs. *American Political Science Review* 94, no. 4: 819–35.

Simon, Herbert (1965). *Administrative Behavior.* 2d ed. New York: Free Press.

Singer, J. David, ed. (1968). *Quantitative International Politics: Insights and Evidence.* New York: Free Press.

Singer, J. David, Stuart Bremer, and John Stuckey (1972). Capability Distribution, Uncertainty, and Major Power War, 1820–1965. In *Peace, War, and Numbers,* ed. B. M. Russett, 19–48. Beverly Hills: Sage.

Singer, J. David, and Melvin Small (1984). *Wages of War, 1816–1980: Augmented with Disputes and Civil War Data.* Ann Arbor, MI: Inter-University Consortium for Political and Social Research (ICPSR), Study I9044.

——— (1993). *National Material Capabilities Data Set.* Ann Arbor, MI: Inter-University Consortium for Political and Social Research (ICPSR), Study 9903.

——— (1994). *Correlates of War Project: International and Civil War Data.* Ann Arbor, MI: Inter-University Consortium for Political and Social Research (ICPSR), Study 9905.

Sitkin, Sam B. (1992). Learning Through Failure: The Strategy of Small Losses. *Research in Organizational Behavior* 14:231–66.

Skelsbaek, Inger (2001). Sexual Violence and War: Mapping Out a Complex Relationship. *European Journal of International Relations* 7, no. 2: 211–37.

Skocpol, Theda (1979). *States and Social Revolutions: A Comparative Analysis of France, Russia, and China.* Cambridge: Cambridge University Press.

——— (1984). Emerging Agendas and Recurrent Strategies in Historical Sociology. In *Vision and Method in Historical Sociology,* ed. T. Skocpol, 356–91. Cambridge: Cambridge University Press.

——— (1986). Analyzing Causal Configurations in History: A Rejoinder to Nichols. *Comparative Social Research* 9:187–94.

Slaughter, Anne-Marie (1995). International War in a World of Liberal States. *European Journal of International Law* 6:503–38.

Slaughter Burley, Anne-Marie (1992). Law among Liberal States: Liberal Institutionalism and the Act of State Doctrine. *Columbia Law Review* 92, no. 8: 1907–46.

Slobin, Dan I. (1996). From "Thought and Language" to "Thinking for Speaking." In *Rethinking Linguistic Relativity,* ed. J. J. Gumperz and S. C. Levinson, 70–96. Cambridge: Cambridge University Press.

Small, Melvin, and J. Davis Singer (1976). The War-proneness of Democratic Regimes. *Jerusalem Journal of International Relations* 1, no. 4: 50–69.

———— (1982). *Resort to Arms: International and Civil Wars, 1816–1980.* Beverly Hills: Sage.

Smoke, Richard, and Alexander L. George (1973). Theory for Policy in International Affairs. *Policy Sciences* 4:387–413.

Snidal, Duncan (1993). Relative Gains and the Pattern of International Cooperation. In *Neorealism and Neoliberalism: The Contemporary Debate,* ed. D. A. Baldwin, 170–208. New York: Columbia University Press.

Snyder, Glenn H. (1961). *Deterrence and Defense.* Princeton: Princeton University Press.

———— (1997). *Alliance Politics.* Ithaca, NY: Cornell University Press.

Snyder, Jack (1985). Richness, Rigor, and Relevance in the Study of Soviet Foreign Policy. *International Security* 9, no. 3: 89–108.

Sorensen, Georg (1993). *Democracy and Democratization: Process and Prospects in a Changing World.* Boulder, CO: Westview Press.

Soskice, David (1991). The Institutional Infrastructure for International Competitiveness: A Comparative Analysis of the UK and Germany. In *Economics for the New Europe,* ed. A. B. Atkinson and R. Brunetta, 45–66. London: Macmillan.

Spence, Melanie J., and Anthony J. DeCasper (1987). Prenatal Experience with Low-frequency Maternal-voice Sounds Influences Neonatal Perception of Maternal Voice Samples. *Infant Behavior and Development* 10, no. 2: 133–42.

Spiro, David (1994). The Insignificance of the Liberal Peace. *International Security* 19, no. 2: 50–86.

Spruyt, Hendrik (1994). *The Sovereign State and Its Competitors: An Analysis of Systems Change.* Princeton: Princeton University Press.

Stallmann, Martin (1960). *Was ist Säkularisierung?* Tübingen: Mohr.

Standard, William L. (1963). The United States Quarantine of Cuba and the Role of Law. *American Bar Association Journal* 49, no. 8: 744–48.

Stapp, Henry Pierce (1972). The Copenhagen Interpretation. *American Journal of Physics* 40:1098–1116.

Starbuck, William H., and F. J. Milliken (1988). Challenger: Fine-Tuning the Odds until Something Breaks. *Journal of Management Studies* 25, no. 4: 319–40.

Starr, Harvey (1992). Why Don't Democracies Fight One Another? Evaluating the Theory-Findings Feedback Loop. *Jerusalem Journal of International Relations* 14, no. 4: 41–59.

Stein, Arthur A. (1983). Coordination and Collaboration: Regimes in an Anarchic World. In *International Regimes,* ed. S. D. Krasner, 115–40. Ithaca, NY: Cornell University Press.

Stein, Janice Gross (1985). Calculation, Miscalculation, and Conventional Deterrence I: The View from Cairo. In *Psychology and Deterrence,* ed. R. Jervis, R. N. Lebow, and J. G. Stein, 34–59. Baltimore: Johns Hopkins University Press.

——— (1987). Extended Deterrence in the Middle East: American Strategy Reconsidered. *World Politics* 39, no. 3: 326–52.

——— (1990). Deterrence and Reassurance. In *Behavior, Society, and Nuclear War,* ed. Philip E. Tetlock, Jo L. Husbands, Robert L. Jervis, Paul C. Stern, and Charles Tilly, 8–72. New York: Oxford University Press.

——— (1998). Five Scenarios of the Israeli-Palestinian Relationship in 2002. *Security Studies* 7, no. 4: 195–212.

Steinbrunner, John (1977). *The Cybernetic Theory of Decision.* Cambridge: Harvard University Press.

Stinchcombe, Arthur L. (1968). *Constructing Social Theories.* Chicago: Chicago University Press.

Stone, Christopher (1981). From a Language Perspective. *Yale Law Journal* 90, no. 5: 1149–92.

Strange, Susan (1983). *Cave! Hic Dragones:* A Critique of Regime Analysis. In *International Regimes,* ed. S. D. Krasner, 337–54. Ithaca, NY: Cornell University Press.

Sullivan, Andrew (1995). *Virtually Normal: An Argument about Homosexuality.* New York: Knopf.

Tajfel, Henry (1981). *Human Groups and Social Categories: Studies in Social Psychology.* Cambridge: Cambridge University Press.

Tajfel, Henry, and John C. Turner (1979). An Integrative Theory of Intergroup Conflict. In *The Social Psychology of Intergroup Relations,* ed. W. Austin and S. Worchel, 33–47. Monterey, CA: Brooks/Cole.

Tamuz, Michal (1988). Monitoring Dangers in the Air: Studies in Ambiguity and Information. Ph.D. dissertation, Stanford University, Stanford.

Tannenwald, Nina (1999). The Nuclear Taboo: The United States and the Normative Basis of Nuclear Non-Use. *International Organization* 53, no. 3: 433–68.

Tetlock, Philip E., and Aaron Belkin (1996a). Counterfactual Thought Experiments in World Politics. In *Counterfactual Thought Experiments in World Politics,* ed. P. E. Tetlock and A. Belkin, 3–38. Princeton: Princeton University Press.

———, eds. (1996b). *Counterfactual Thought Experiments in World Politics: Logical, Methodological, and Psychological Perspectives.* Princeton: Princeton University Press.

Thatcher, Margaret (1993). *The Downing Street Years.* London: Harper Collins.

Thayer, Bradley (2000). Bringing in Darwin: Evolutionary Theory, Realism, and International Politics. *International Security* 25, no. 2: 124–51.

Thelen, Kathleen (2000). Timing and Temporality in the Analysis of Institutional Evolution and Change. *Studies in American Political Development* 14 (Spring): 101–8.

Thelen, Kathleen, and Ikuo Kume (1999). The Rise of Nonmarket Training Regimes: Germany and Japan Compared. *Journal of Japanese Studies* 25 (Winter): 33–64.

Thelen, Kathleen, and Sven Steinmo (1992). Historical Institutionalism in Comparative Politics. In *Structuring Politics: Historical Institutionalism in Comparative Politics,* ed. S. Steinmo, K. Thelen, and F. Lonstreth, 1–32. New York: Cambridge University Press.

Tickner, J. Ann (1995). Re-visioning Security. In *International Relations Theory Today,* ed. K. Booth and S. Smith, 175–97. Oxford: Oxford University Press.

Torfing, Jacob (1999). Towards a Schumpeterian Workfare Postnational Regime: Path-Shaping and Path-Dependency in Danish Welfare State Reform. *Economy and Society* 28, no. 3: 369–402.

Toulmin, Stephen Edelston (1958). *The Uses of Argument.* Cambridge: Cambridge University Press.

Tranholm-Mikkelson, Jeppe (1991). Neofunctionalism: Obstinate or Obsolete? A Reappraisal in the Light of the New Dynamism of the EC. *Millennium: Journal of International Studies* 20 (Spring): 1–22.

Trimble, V., and F. Reines (1973). Solar Neutrino Problem-Progress Report. *Reviews of Modern Physics* 45, no. 1: 1–5.

Turner, Jonathan (1988). *A Theory of Social Interaction.* Stanford: Stanford University Press.

Tversky, Amos (1972). Elimination by Aspects: A Theory of Choice. *Psychological Review* 79, no. 4: 281–99.

——— (1977). Features of Similarity. *Psychological Review* 84, no. 4: 327–52.

Tversky, Amos, and I. Gati (1978). Studies of Similarity. In *Cognition and Categorization,* ed. E. Rosch and B. B. Lloyd, 79–98. Hillsdale, NJ: Erlbaum.

Tversky, Amos, and Daniel Kahneman (1973). Availability: A Heuristic for Judging Frequency and Probability. *Cognitive Psychology* 5:207–32.

——— (1981). Judgement Under Uncertainty: Heuristics and Biases. *Science* 185:453–58.

——— (1982). Availability: A Heuristic for Judging Frequency and Probability. In *Judgement under Uncertainty: Heuristics and Biases,* ed. D. Kahneman, P. Slovic, and A. Tversky, 163–78. Cambridge: Cambridge University Press.

Twining, William, and David Miers (1976). *How To Do Things with Rules.* London: Weidenfeld and Nicolson.

Valenzuela, J. Samuel (1992). Democratic Consolidation in Post-Transitional Settings: Notion, Process, and Facilitating Conditions. In *Issues in Democratic Consolidation: The New South American Democracies in Comparative Perspective,* ed. S. Mainwaring, G. O'Donnell, and J. S. Valenzuela, 57–104. Notre Dame: University of Notre Dame Press.

Vanhanen, Tatu (1990). *The Process of Democratization: A Comparative Study of 147 States.* New York: Crane Russak.

Vedriné, Hubert, and Dominique Moisi (2000). *Les Cartes de la France à l'heure de la Mondalisation.* Paris: Fayard.

Verba, Sidney (1967). Some Dilemmas in Comparative Research. *World Politics* 20, no. 1: 111–27.

Veyne, Paul (1979). *Comment on écrit l'histoire.* Paris: Éditions de Seuil.

Wæver, Ole (1995). Securization and Desecurization. In *On Security,* ed. R. D. Lipschutz, 46–86. New York: Columbia University Press.

Walker, Henry, and Bernard Cohen (1985). Scope Statements: Imperatives for Evaluating Theories. *American Sociological Review* 50, no. 3: 288–301.

Wallander, Celeste A. (2000). Institutional Assets and Adaptability: NATO After the Cold War. *International Organization* 54, no. 4: 705–35.

Walt, Stephen M. (1987). *The Origins of Alliances.* Ithaca, NY: Cornell University Press.

——— (1999). Rigor or Rigor Mortis? Rational Choice and Security Studies. *International Security* 23, no. 4: 5–48.

Waltz, Kenneth N. (1979). *Theory of International Politics.* Reading, MA: Addison-Wesley.

——— (1993). The Emerging Structure of International Politics. *International Security* 18, no. 2: 44–79.

——— (2000). Structural Realism after the Cold War. *International Security* 25, no. 1: 5–41.

Weber, Max (1949). *The Methodology of the Social Sciences.* Translated and edited by E. A. Schils and H. A. Finch. Glencoe, IL: Free Press.

——— (1976). *Wirtschaft und Gesellschaft: Grundriss der verstehenden Soziologie.* 5th rev. ed. Tübingen: Mohr.

Weber, Steven (1997). Prediction and the Middle East Peace Process. *Security Studies* 6, no. 4: 167–79.

Weizsäcker, Carl F. von (1964). *Tragweite der Wissenschaft. 1. Schöpfung und Weltentstehung. Die Geschichte zweier Begriffe.* Stuttgart: Hirzel.

Wendt, Alexander (1992). Anarchy Is What States Make of It: The Social Construction of Power Politics. *International Organization* 46, no. 2: 391–425.

——— (1999). *Social Theory of International Politics.* Cambridge: Cambridge University Press.

Wight, Martin (1966). The Balance of Power. In *Diplomatic Investigations: Essays in the Theory of International Politics,* ed. H. Butterfield and M. Wight, 132–48. London: Allen and Unwin.

Winkelstein, Warren, Jr., D. M. Lyman, N. Padian, R. Grant, M. Samuel, J. A. Wiley, R. E. Anderson, W. Lang, J. Riggs, and J. A. Levy (1987). Sexual Practices and Risk of Infection by the Human Immunodeficiency Virus. *Journal of the American Medical Association* 257, no. 3: 321–25.

Winkler, Heinrich A. (1968). Bürgerliche Emanzipation und nationale Einigung. Zur Entstehung des Nationalliberalismus in Preußen. In *Probleme der Reichsgründungszeit, 1848–1879,* ed. by H. Böhme, 226–42. Berlin: Kiepenheuer and Witsch.

Wittgenstein, Ludwig (1953). *Philosophical Investigations.* New York: Macmillan.

Wohlforth, William C. (1999). The Stability of a Unipolar World. *International Security* 24, no. 1: 5–41.

Wolfers, Arnold (1962). National Security as Ambiguous Symbol. In *Discord and Collaboration: Essays on International Politics,* ed. A. Wolfers, 147–66. Baltimore: Johns Hopkins University Press.

——— (1968). Alliances. In *International Encyclopedia of the Social Sciences,* ed. D. L. Sills, 268–71. New York: Macmillan.

Wong, Paul T. B., and Bernard Weiner (1981). When People Ask "Why" Questions, and the Heuristics of Attributional Search. *Journal of Personality and Social Psychology* 40, no. 4: 650–63.

Woods Issues Open Statement on Race. *Reuters News Service,* 13 June 1995.

Woodward, Bob (1991). *The Commanders.* New York: Simon and Schuster.

Wråkberg, Urban (2002). The Politics of Naming: Contested Observations and the Shaping of Geographical Knowledge. In *Narrating the Arctic: A Cultural History of Nordic Scientific Practice,* ed. Michael Bravo and Sverker Sörlin, 155–97. Canton, MA: Watson Pub. International.

Wuthnow, Robert (1989). *Communities of Discourse: Ideology and Social Structure in the Reformation, the Enlightenment, and European Socialism.* Cambridge, MA: Harvard University Press.

Young, Oran (1969). Professor Russett: Industrious Tailor to a Naked Emperor. *World Politics* 21, no. 3: 486–511.

Zehfuss, Maja (1998). Sprachlosigkeit schränkt ein: Zur Bedeutung von Sprache in konstruktivistischen Theorien. *Zeitschrift für Internationale Beziehungen* 5, no. 1: 109–37.

Ziman, John (1978). *Reliable Knowledge: An Exploration of the Grounds for Belief in Science.* Cambridge: Cambridge University Press.

Zinnes, Diana A. (1976). *Contemporary Research in International Relations: A Respective and a Critical Appraisal.* New York: Free Press.

Index